I would like for little sister to have that and what
on the books in back pay, if anything should happen.
certainly do miss all you folks and would surely
seeing you, each and everyone. I'll bet that that
year old little sister of mine has grown up
recognition since I last saw her. I certainly
that she had a nice birthday. I wish that I
get my pictures in the mail that I know you all
sent me _____ that I received from you
and _____ Tiko.

There is little more to write about and so I guess
shall close.

Devotedly yours,
Bill

C HARRIS
MCWHORTER / GAGE   CINGPAC ADV
CONNORS   MARCORPS

020343   NCR 2899

COM 3RD FLEET SENDS ACTION COMINCH AND CNO. INFO
CINGPAC ADV. PASS TO MAR CORPS HEADQUARTERS.

YOUR 312107.

LIEUT HARRIS IN THE PINK AND WITNESSED SURRENDER ON
MISSOURI. HE IS STARTING FOR GUAM TOMORROW. COM
3RD FLEET AND STAFF REJOICE WITH MAJ GEN HARRIS.

COMINCH AND CNO......ACT

MARCORPS...........

CONFIDENTIAL

020343

N.Y. Times
Dec 11, 1945

14   L

ENSIGN J. GLENNON
OF WAVES TO WED

Kin of Navy and Marine Corps
Officers Engaged to Capt.
William F. Harris, USMC

Capt. James Blair Glennon, USN
(retired), and Mrs. Glennon of Indian Head, Md., have made known
here the engagement of their
daughter, Ensign Jeanne Lejeune
Glennon of the Waves, to Capt.
William Frederick Harris, USMC,
son of Maj. Gen. Field Harris, director of Marine Corps aviation,
and Mrs. Harris of Washington.
The wedding will take place in the
spring.

The prospective bride, an alumna
of Gunston Hall in Washington,
D. C., attended Sweet Briar College and was graduated in 1944
from George Washington University. She is stationed at the Navy
Department in Washington. Ensign Glennon is a granddaughter
of the late Lieut. Gen. John Archer
Lejeune, USMC, and Mrs. Lejeune
of Norfolk, Va., and the late Rear
Admiral James Henry Glennon,
USN, and Mrs. Glennon of Washington. She is a sister of Lieut.
Col. James Blair Glennon Jr.,
USMC, whose engagement to Ensign Margaret Ellen Wyatte of the
Waves was announced in September.

Captain Harris, who was graduated from the United States Naval
Academy in 1939, served with the
Fourth Marines on Corregidor and
returned from Japan in September
after being liberated from a prisoner-of-war camp in Tokyo. He is
stationed in Quantico, Va. The
bridegroom-elect is a grandson of
Mrs. Naomi Chinn of Washington
and the late Mr. and Mrs. Andrew
Walter Harris of Lexington, Ky.

We have lost our boy; Col
Latsenburg, his regimental commander,
came in today, and told me. He said
it happened about five o'clock in
the morning on their march from
Hagoroo-ne to Katoie. The date was
probably Dec 7th, and was about
36 hours after I saw him.

Bill's pitiful little battalion,
which was not much bigger than
a company, was the rear guard
of the battered regiment on their
march out. One of his little companies
was attached. He went over to
see what he could do, and
was seen no more. I feel
sure he is not a prisoner.
Latsenburg told me what
wonderful job that he had done with
his battalion.

I am numb over the shock, and can't
think very clearly. You will
have to work out something for
Jeanne & the children. Don't
rush it, but you can do this.

VALOR

ALSO BY DAN HAMPTON

Operation Vengeance:
The Astonishing Aerial Ambush That Changed World War II

Chasing the Demon:
A Secret History of the Quest for the Sound Barrier,
and the Band of American Aces Who Conquered It

The Flight:
Charles Lindbergh's Daring and Immortal 1927
Transatlantic Crossing

The Hunter Killers:
The Extraordinary Story of the First Wild Weasels,
the Band of Maverick Aviators Who Flew the Most Dangerous
Missions of the Vietnam War

Lords of the Sky:
Fighter Pilots and Air Combat, from the Red Baron to the F-16

Viper Pilot:
A Memoir of Air Combat

VALOR

THE ASTONISHING WORLD WAR II SAGA OF ONE MAN'S DEFIANCE AND INDOMITABLE SPIRIT

DAN HAMPTON

St. Martin's Press
New York

First published in the United States by St. Martin's Press, an imprint of St. Martin's Publishing Group

VALOR. Copyright © 2022 by Ascalon, LLC. All rights reserved. Printed in the United States of America. For information, address St. Martin's Publishing Group, 120 Broadway, New York, NY 10271.

www.stmartins.com

Map: U.S. Army Map Service
Endpapers: Author's collection, courtesy of Katey Harris-Meares
Designed by Meryl Sussman Levavi

Library of Congress Cataloging-in-Publication Data

Names: Hampton, Dan, author.
Title: Valor : the astonishing World War II saga of one man's defiance and
    indomitable spirit / Dan Hampton.
Other titles: Astonishing World War II saga of one man's defiance and
    indomitable spirit
Description: First edition. | New York : St. Martin's Press, 2022. | Includes
    bibliographical references. |
Identifiers: LCCN 2021061801 | ISBN 9781250275851 (hardcover) |
    ISBN 9781250275868 (ebook)
Subjects: LCSH: Harris, William Frederick, 1918–1950 (?) | United States. Marine
    Corps. Marine Regiment, 4th — Biography. | World War, 1939–1945 — Prisoners
    and prisons, Japanese. | Prisoners of war — United States — Biography. |
    Prisoners of war — Philippines — Biography. | Prisoners of war — Japan —
    Biography. | Ofuna Naval Interrogation Center (Japan)
Classification: LCC D805.J3 H274 2022 | DDC 940.54/7252092 [B] — dc23
LC record available at https://lccn.loc.gov/2021061801

Our books may be purchased in bulk for promotional, educational, or business use. Please contact your local bookseller or the Macmillan Corporate and Premium Sales Department at 1-800-221-7945, extension 5442, or by email at MacmillanSpecialMarkets@macmillan.com.

First Edition: 2022

10 9 8 7 6 5 4 3 2 1

CONTENTS

AUTHOR'S NOTE

Dear Reader,

Much of the historical content contains derogatory ethnic or racial terms that reflect common sentiments expressed by those fighting the Second World War. These have been left as originally written in this text to present the historical documents as completely as possible, and are not the opinion of the author.

—Dan Hampton

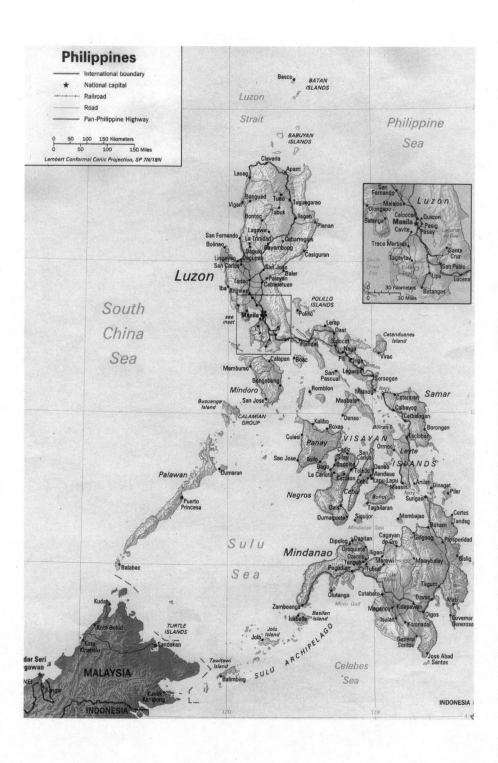

In valor there is hope.

— Tacitus

PROLOGUE

Nuns cheered, pointing excitedly at the sky, and a few waved.

One of them, her long black veil bobbing wildly, even danced a little jig. Silence was a normal rule in the convent's walled garden, but this morning, as sunlight glinted from the planes wheeling overhead, no one cared. Big, twin-engined bombers cut wide silver streaks through the blue morning sky above the Philippine island of Luzon, and everyone below was overjoyed to see them. Perched on a wooded hilltop, the Dominican Maryknoll convent overlooked Baguio, a resort town and summer capital of the Philippine Commonwealth.

Sister Miriam Louise, an impish young woman born Louise Kroeger in Jefferson City, Missouri, stopped dancing and squinted against the sun at the planes. She felt particularly relieved—relieved and proud. Her countrymen were here in force to protect these islands, and what could ease the building tension in the Pacific faster than American warplanes arriving in the Philippines? She had heard the Dominican fathers discussing the powerful new aircraft; B-17s, called a Flying Fortress, and knew they had recently arrived at Clark Field, eighty miles south of Baguio toward Manila. Surely these were those planes out early for training flights on this bright Monday morning.

They were not.

Two miles overhead, Captain Ryosuke Motomura of the Imperial Japanese Army Air Force (JAAF) stared past the nose of his Ki-21 "Sally" bomber at Luzon's lush countryside, then glanced at the map on his leg. Baguio. No mistake. A veteran of China, the pilot was accustomed to finding targets he'd never seen before and identifying them from the air—just like this one. Motomura had lifted off in the foggy, predawn darkness from his base at Choshu just over three hours ago. Leading eighteen bombers of the 14th Army Air Regiment to the far tip of Formosa, he'd turned the formation south across the Bashi Channel, and headed 231 miles across open water for Cape Bojador on Luzon's northeastern coast. From here it was a 140-mile flight down the coast to the port of San Fernando on Lingayen Gulf, a forty-five-degree left turn, and the final twenty-five miles to Baguio.

The town was easy to see. It was really the only thing out here, and for once there were accurate maps, courtesy of a Japanese officer who lived here during the past year. Loakan Airport was his main reference; a straight gray line cut into the saddle of the mountains south of town. Working back along the ridgeline, Motomura found a pronounced hill sticking out like a bumpy green tongue, and this was the site of an American base named Camp John Hay. Flying the planned course on time, at 13,000 feet and 250 miles per hour, the captain had done his part, and when the town passed beneath the right wing his bombardier began counting down over the intercom.

As 2,200 pounds of bombs tumbled from its belly, the aircraft abruptly jolted upward. Far below, smiles froze and cheering voices tapered off in confusion as little dark flecks fell from the aircraft. What could those be? Today, December 8, marked the Feast of the Immaculate Conception, one of the holiest days of the Catholic year. It was Monday in the Philippines, but east of the International Date Line today was still Sunday, December 7, 1941. Maybe the Army Air

Force was dropping food or candy for the children. But as the wobbling black specks nosed over and suddenly gathered speed, the nuns stopped cheering altogether. These were not Flying Fortresses, nor were they American planes, and they were not dropping candy.

In fact, the black flecks were 220-pound bombs; ten per aircraft, so over eighteen tons of high explosives were plummeting down toward the idyllic hill station. As the bombs disappeared into the trees, orange-and-black explosions shattered the morning calm, while two miles east of the convent the entire U.S. Army installation vanished beneath rolling dark clouds of mangled trees and earth. Clusters of shacks and small buildings in the barrio beneath the hilltop simply ceased to exist.

This was war.

Long anticipated, it was now actually here. Strikes by Imperial Japanese forces would continue throughout the day, not just in the Philippines but also on Singapore, Wake Island, Guam, and Hong Kong. Unknown to the Americans, Admiral Isoroku Yamamoto's Operation Z had actually commenced with complete secrecy thirteen days earlier with Operations Order 5:

> The task force, keeping its movements strictly secret and maintaining close guard against submarines and aircraft, shall advance into Hawaiian waters, and upon the very opening of hostilities shall attack the main force of the United States fleet in Hawaii and deal it a mortal blow.

Vice-Admiral Chuichi Nagumo, commanding a strike fleet carefully concealed by a bleak, horn-shaped inlet in the northern Kuril Islands, weighed anchor at 0600 the following morning. On November 26, 1941, thirty-two warships of the Imperial Navy cleared the snow-covered, volcanic shoreline of Hitokappu Bay and, cloaked in ice fog and blowing sleet, came around toward their target three thousand miles away to the southeast: the Hawaiian island of Oahu, and the home port of the U.S. Pacific Fleet.

By dawn on December 7, after crossing the North Pacific Ocean undetected, Nagumo's six big carriers swung into the trade winds and surged ahead at thirty knots. A Zero fighter piloted by Lieutenant Commander Shigeru Itaya wobbled into the air off the *Akagi*, followed by 182 other aircraft. At 0753 in Hawaii, the leader of the Pearl Harbor strike, Commander Mitsuo Fuchida, had his radioman tap out "Tora, Tora, Tora" back to Nagumo's flagship, the aircraft carrier *Akagi*.* This code phrase, translated into English as "Tiger, Tiger, Tiger," indicated that complete surprise over the American fleet had been achieved, and the attack was proceeding as planned. Less than two hours later, eighteen American warships were destroyed, and 2,403 lay dead in Pearl Harbor.

Within forty-five minutes, news of the attack traveled 4,800 miles east to the War Department in Washington, D.C., and into the office of Henry Lewis Stimson, the U.S. secretary of war. Stimson immediately dispatched cablegram number 736 some 8,500 miles west to the commander of United States Army Forces in the Far East headquarters in Manila: General Douglas MacArthur.

HOSTILITIES BETWEEN JAPAN AND THE UNITED STATES COMMA BRITISH COMMONWEALTH COMMA AND DUTCH HAVE COMMENCED STOP JAPANESE MADE AIR RAID ON PEARL HARBOR THIS MORNING DECEMBER SEVENTH STOP CARRY OUT TASKS ASSIGNED IN RAIN-BOW FIVE

By 0330 local time, all Japanese airmen waiting to fly from Formosa knew of the successful attack on Hawaii. Now overhead Baguio

---

* Time measurement during this era was confusing. Some time zones were, and still are, displaced in thirty-minute increments. Hawaiian Standard Time was ten hours, thirty minutes behind Greenwich Mean Time, while Japan was nine hours ahead of GMT. Japan (and the Philippines) was also separated from Pearl Harbor by the International Date Line, so 0753 on Sunday, December 7, 1941 was 0323, Monday, December 8, 1941, in Tokyo and Manila.

five hours later, Captain Motomura was satisfied to have struck his first blow in this war, but was well aware the Americans were alert now for an attack on the Philippines. Banking up to the right over Baguio, he caught glimpses of the dark peaks and rugged valleys of Luzon, while to the west he could see the blue shimmer of Lingayen Gulf. Across the Cordillera Central, Motomura knew that twenty-five army Ki-48 light bombers from Kato, also on Formosa, were hitting the enemy airfield at Tuguegarao, while the Imperial Navy was striking at Clark and Iba Fields.

But this was not his problem.

He had hit his target and now fully expected to fight his way out back up the coast, then across the sea to Formosa, so perhaps the navy would distract the Americans long enough for him to get away. Like most of the Japanese military, Motomura was surprised by the lack of opposition since the Philippines constituted the bulk of regional American power. The islands were headquarters for the formidable Far East Air Force (FEAF) and the U.S. Asiatic Fleet.

"The United States," Zero pilot Matasake Okumiya later recalled, "was an enemy whom we expected to offer bitter resistance." Of primary concern to the attackers, this meant the 24th Pursuit Group and its 115-odd fighters, mostly P-40 Warhawks. According to intelligence reports, the 3rd Pursuit Squadron was at Iba, while the 17th and 21st were at Nichols Field in Manila. Both were targets for the eighty-one Imperial Navy land-based bombers, called Bettys by the Allies, of the Takeo Air Group. The big prize, Clark Field, was to be hit by twenty-seven Type 96 bombers, or Nells, from the Tainan Air Group. All attacks were coordinated and planned to occur simultaneously with the JAAF strikes in northern Luzon.

It didn't happen that way.

Delayed by fog on Formosa, the Tainan and Takeo groups were actually just getting airborne as Tuguegarao and Camp John Hay were bombed. In fact, the only Japanese strike occurring as planned came from the light aircraft carrier *Ryūjō* against Davao, Mindanao, in the southern Philippines. One hundred forty miles off the eastern coast, she turned into the wind at 0400 with Chief Flight Petty Officer Mutsuo Sagara leading three Type 96 Claude fighters off her deck toward the west.

Lieutenant Takahide Aioi, commander of the little carrier's twelve-plane fighter group, followed with six additional planes as escort for thirteen *kankō*, or carrier attack aircraft, which the Americans called a Kate.* The Japanese found an empty airfield that they bombed and strafed anyway, then Aioi destroyed a pair of moored PBY-4 flying boats in nearby Malalag Bay. The raid accomplished little except to add greater chaos to a morning that, due largely to one man, already had a surplus of confusion.

In his opulent, fifth-floor penthouse atop the Manila Hotel, General Douglas MacArthur had been awakened by an 0330 call from his chief of staff, Brigadier General Richard Sutherland, confirming the Pearl Harbor news. In an inexplicably leisurely manner, the general took nearly ninety minutes to dress and walk across Burgos Avenue and past the golf course to his headquarters at 1 Calle Victoria. Inside the Walled City, MacArthur dithered for the next three hours, apparently shocked that the Japanese had not done what was expected of them, until at 0755 when he received a call from Brigadier General Leonard Gerow on behalf of General George C. Marshall. Marshall, the U.S. Army chief of staff, and everyone else in Washington, wanted to know what was happening in Manila. Had MacArthur received the War Department cablegrams warning about imminent hostilities and then the assault against Hawaii? Had the Philippines been attacked?

"No attack at all," the general informed Gerow, but this was not a satisfactory reply. MacArthur had ignored the warnings and failed to respond to the cablegrams, and Marshall wanted answers. Yet by now

---

* Abbreviated from *kanjo kōgeki-ki*, the Nakajima B5N2, Type 97 attack aircraft could either drop Long Lance torpedoes or carry a single 534-pound bomb. Kates sank five battleships at Pearl Harbor, including the USS *Arizona*.

Davao had been bombed, and Major General Lewis H. Brereton, commander of the FEAF, had been trying for hours to obtain Mac-Arthur's permission to attack Formosa with his B-17 heavy bombers. Hearing Pearl Harbor's fate at 0430, Brereton immediately ordered his units to prepare for an attack, which he expected at dawn. Lieutenant Boyd D. "Buzz" Wagner's 17th Pursuit Squadron taxied all eighteen of its fully armed P-40Es to the south end of Nichols Field at 0600 and waited for the takeoff order. The 3rd Pursuit Squadron, eighty-five miles northwest of Manila on the coast, was also ready with twenty-four fighters.

For the next two hours, with no command guidance from Mac-Arthur, units largely reacted, or did not react, individually. Brereton did his best, but was caught in a very bad spot; on the one hand he *knew* what had to be done, but on the other he had a direct order *not* to fight unless attacked. At 0745 a report came into Nichols about inbound Japanese aircraft, and Buzz Wagner thundered down the runway with his squadron to intercept them. They did locate bombers, but it was a flight of 19th Bomb Group B-17s scrambled out of Clark on the initiative of Major Dave Gibbs, the acting commander. He'd launched all his heavy bombers to get them off the ground, but the situation was so chaotic there was no coordination with anyone.

As Baguio was bombed, MacArthur seemed finally aware that a state of war had existed for several hours, yet would not authorize an attack on Formosa. It has been postulated that he risked American lives due to pressure from Philippine president Manuel Quezon, who wished to declare the islands neutral in hopes the Japanese would spare them. This could not happen if the United States launched air strikes against Formosa. In any event, MacArthur did nothing. "The General says no," Sutherland relayed to Brereton when the latter pressed for permission to counterattack. "Don't make the first overt act."

Disbelieving and sputtering with rage, Brereton reminded Sutherland that Pearl Harbor had already been attacked, then angrily stomped out, heading for his own headquarters across town at Nielson

Field. American forces throughout the Philippines were in various states of disbelief or denial, and this allowed the Japanese to prosecute their attacks despite the weather issues.

Just after 1000 in Manila the big problem was that the fighters scrambled earlier were running out of fuel and returning to land. The expected enemy attack had not come, and as the adrenaline wore off, so did the intense edge of combat. Had the Japanese not been delayed by fog and attacked as planned, they would have had a much different reception over Luzon. As it was, the American fighter pilots were tired, hungry, and wondering if the whole thing wasn't an enormous mistake. Adding to the overall confusion, at 1014 General MacArthur finally contacted Brereton directly for the first time, and told him that "the decision on offensive action was his to make."

Nearly seven hours had passed since MacArthur was informed about Pearl Harbor, hours that could have made a decisive difference if the B-17s had been ordered to hit Formosa, or if a coordinated combat air patrol among the fighter units had been initiated. Nonetheless, Brereton was planning an attack on Formosa about the same time the airborne fighters landed at Clark to refuel. Having passed the responsibility to an officer who would get things moving, MacArthur was now fortunately out of the tactical picture—but it was too late.

Private Tom Lloyd was the SCR-270B radar operator on duty at Iba Field at 1120, when he picked up a big "echo" on his oscilloscope 129 miles out to sea. A few minutes later another group appeared some fifteen miles behind the first. Echoes of that size could only be large formations of aircraft. Now there were two approaching the Philippine coast. This was duly reported to the Air Warning Service Operations center at Nielson Field, plotted diligently on the big glass board, then relayed via teletype to the 24th Pursuit Group operations center at Clark. By 1145 the 3rd Pursuit Squadron was off the ground, as was the 21st from Nichols Field.

Amid conflicting reports and contradictory radio calls, the fighters were not given accurate information, and the situation, already tense, worsened considerably. Flights split up or lost sight of each other; some who did join up decided to test their six .50-caliber guns, which had never been fired before, and this added to the chaos. One group of twelve P-40s led by Lieutenant Ed Dyess of the 21st Pursuit Squadron was ordered to Clark but then redirected south to Manila Bay.

Apparently, a formation of enemy planes was inbound, so Dyess was to orbit over Corregidor and protect the Cavite Naval Yard. Leveling off at 15,000 feet, his Warhawks wheeled around at about 1210 and raced south at three hundred miles per hour toward the mouth of the bay. Eight minutes later, directly over the dark, tadpole-shaped island of Corregidor, Dyess brought his twelve fighters around in a sweeping left turn back toward Cavite. Two miles beneath him air raid klaxons on the island began wailing, followed shortly by those at the navy base in Mariveles Bay. To the nervous Americans manning the anti-aircraft guns, every aircraft was an enemy, and they all knew the Japanese were coming.

In fact, they had arrived.

As Dyess and his Warhawks orbited over Corregidor, the Imperial Navy's 11th Air Fleet appeared at Clark Field. From 22,400 feet over Luzon, future ace Saburo Sakai stared down incredulously at Clark Field. "Instead of encountering a swarm of American fighters diving at us in attack, we looked down and saw some sixty enemy bombers and fighters nearly parked along the airfield runways. They squatted there like sitting ducks. Pearl Harbor had been hit more than five hours before," he wrote. "Surely they had received word of that attack and expected one against these critical fields!"

One army sergeant frantically called his headquarters to report enemy aircraft overhead, and the duty officer asked how he knew there were Japanese planes. "We don't have so many goddamn many!" he yelled back.

The Tainan Air Group's bombers did their work. "Long strings of bombs tumbled from the bays . . . the attack was perfect. The entire base seemed to be rising into the air with the explosions. Pieces of airplanes, hangars . . . great fires erupted and smoke boiled upwards. The American base was a shambles." Based on the number of bombers, it was later estimated that 636 bombs impacted the airfield in thirty seconds.

On the dock at Mariveles, fifty-three miles south of Clark on the tip of Bataan, a twenty-three-year-old Marine lieutenant instinctively looked up when he heard the sirens. Seeing specks flashing in the sun high above, he yelled, "Clear the dock! First platoon off to the left of the building here." Men raced down across an open loading area through some trees and hid along the muddy banks of the Riptrap River. Gratified to see his well-trained platoon jump on command, Lieutenant William Frederick Harris wasn't surprised. Standing two inches over six feet and carrying 185 muscular pounds, he was accustomed to obedience. Besides, these were Marines—the best there were.

Tugs carrying the 1st Battalion, 4th Marines had departed Subic Bay at 0602 that very morning heading for Mariveles, but Bill Harris and the other officers had already been awake for three hours. Sirens at the U.S. Naval Base, Subic Bay, saw to that, and during the din a breathless messenger arrived informing them that Pearl Harbor was attacked. America was now at war. Like the others, Bill was incensed. "My poor country!" he later wrote. "To be struck below the belt like this! Well, I know one thing. These little bastards'll find they've stirred up a real hornet's nest."

Though most believed war inevitable, it hadn't seemed real till right now. A professional considered it, planned for it, and listened to others' experiences, but until it actually happened the thought of war was an intellectual exercise. Not now. Crouching here in a ditch at the tip of the Bataan Peninsula made it very real indeed.

"I can hardly believe it," Bill recorded later. "I've heard stories of old veterans ever since I was a small kid, but I never really thought I'd ever be in actual combat myself. I wonder how I'll react. One thing, I know I'll do my best for the old States. She's sure worth it if any country is. Besides, I'll be fighting for Mama and Dad, too." Well, for his mother Katharine, at any rate. Bill knew his father, Brigadier General Field Harris, was a decorated Marine aviator and could take care of himself.

Bill Harris and the other officers had raptly listened on the tug's radio to Don Bell's early morning broadcast from KZRH in Manila. As the ship cleared Subic Bay heading south down the Bataan coast, Bell's calm voice announced, "A most distressing incident has occurred. News just now flashed from Hawaii says Pearl Harbor has just been bombed. As yet we have no details about this, but indications are that the news is true. It seems that early this morning a large number of strange planes suddenly attacked Pearl Harbor . . . reliable sources think they came from Japan."

Every half hour the tug's captain let the Marine officers troop into his cabin to listen to radio updates. On bright, glittering water under clear blue skies it seemed surreal to imagine what was happening beyond Bataan's dark green hills. As Deek Watson's soft tenor voice crooned "I don't want to set the world on fire," the music was interrupted at 0830 by another flash from Don Bell. "We have just had word from Baguio that they are under a bombing attack up there. Before we could get any of the details our source of communication quit on us."

By noon the Marines had pulled past the protective nets strung across Mariveles Harbor, and Bill stared at the low silhouettes of ten moored American submarines. Smart. It was smart to disperse the boats like that. He knew the other subs attached to the Asiatic Fleet lay just across Manila Bay, and it seemed ironic that here he was in a ditch, barely thirty miles from his childhood home at Cavite. Bill had Naval Academy classmates on those boats, just as he had here with the 4th Marines, and that was a comforting thought, though they were all a long, long way from Annapolis at the moment.

Departing from China on the very day Nagumo secretly sailed from Japan, the 4th Marines Regiment had arrived in the Philippines a week earlier. Apparently, navy leadership doubted the army's ability to protect the vital bases at Olongapo and Mariveles, and from what Bill had seen he thought they were correct. The Far East Air Force had enough planes, and the army pilots he'd met seemed like top-notch fellows, but the infantry was something else. It made sound tactical sense to put the Marines, the best combat troops in the Philippines, here at Mariveles.

As long as Manila Bay was in American hands, then the islands were useless to the Japanese, and it would remain secure as long as Corregidor, nicknamed the Rock, held. Control of the bay meant reinforcements, ammunition, and all the necessary commodities of war could be brought in by sea. With minefields across the channels and Marines holding Mariveles, the Japanese would find it an impossible nut to crack.

He certainly hoped so.

As the all clear sounded, Lieutenant Bill Harris was first to stand with his hard, blue eyes sweeping the horizon, but there was no sign of aircraft. Yet in less than an hour, fully half of the Far East Air Force had been wiped out. The 19th Bomb Group, America's only asset capable of immediate offensive action against the Japanese, lost twelve of fifteen heavy bombers destroyed on the ground. The only operational radar site in the Philippines was also destroyed, leaving the American defenders blind to subsequent raids. Only four of the 20th Pursuit Squadron's twenty fighters got airborne from Clark, and Iba's 3rd Pursuit Squadron was all but destroyed. Of five available fighter squadrons, two effectively ceased to exist, and one of those remaining flew aircraft unfit for combat against the Japanese Zero.

The Philippines were now open for invasion—and, in fact, it had already begun. Nearly five hundred men of the Yokohama Special Naval Landing Force (SNLF) splashed ashore on Batan Island, 140 miles north of Cape Bojador—and more were coming. The entire Japanese 14th Army, backed by its own 5th Air Group and the Imperial Navy's 11th Air Fleet—541 aircraft in all—were embarking from Formosa and would arrive within days.

Bill Harris had no way of knowing all this at the moment, though he would find out soon enough. For now, it was enough to know the Japanese had attacked and that he was where he needed to be: right in the middle of it. From atop the little embankment, he could see across North Channel into the bay, and the dark outline of Corregidor. Bristling with gun emplacements, it was a symbol of American military might in the Philippines, and the young officer, now at war so far from home, felt determined and proud.

"The United States Fleet'll be in Singapore in a month," he would later write to his mother. "Reinforcements for us ought to be right behind. We'll be sitting pretty then, with our fleet and planes working over the Japs."

He couldn't have been more mistaken.

Within days the young Kentuckian would be abandoned along with thousands of others and caught in a desperate battle with only two possible outcomes: capture or death.

PART I

DECEMBER 1941–JUNE 1942

Those who beat their swords into plowshares usually end up plowing for those who kept their swords.

—Benjamin Franklin

✻

ONE

DETERMINATION

My dear Mama,

We're so cut off the States that it seems useless to write, but I think I shall anyhow just in case something turns up to take a letter back . . . no messages from my battalion got through before the Japanese cut our radio communication.

UNDER WASHINGTON'S WEAK AFTERNOON SUN SOME 8,590 MILES EAST of Luzon, Katharine Chinn-Harris put the letter down gently and thought of Bill. A picture flashed in her mind from a morning long ago. She'd come outside during a rainstorm and found an umbrella on the ground over a pair of skinny, protruding legs; he'd found an ant pile and was keeping the insects dry so he could watch them. Then once in Haiti he very seriously told his pesky little sister Nancy that if she didn't leave him alone, her pet turtle would end up in a voodoo bag. He was mischievous and clever, and quite able to charm others with his striking blue eyes and glossy black hair. She smiled at the memories. He'd been a good little boy.

But he was no longer a boy.

Billy was now Bill, a Marine officer and a grown man, and thank God for it. She knew he could look out for himself, but he was still her son. The only one she would ever have, and so far, far away from 1882 Columbia Road Northwest here in Washington, D.C. So far from her. She could picture where he was now, though, unlike so many mothers across the United States, because she'd lived in the Philippines. As a twenty-year-old bride it had been exciting and exotic, though the post in Cavite was a world away from her home in Harrodsburg, Kentucky.

Her husband, dashing First Lieutenant Thomas Field Harris, had been a ramrod-straight Marine sporting a pencil-thin mustache that matched his dark hair. Utterly fearless, he was also polished, calm, and soft-spoken, attributes befitting a man descended from one of the oldest families in Kentucky. They'd been introduced at a cotillion in Lexington in 1916 when she was sixteen, and though four years older, Field corresponded regularly during his final semesters in the Naval Academy. Joining the Great War in 1917, the United States found itself critically short of officers, so both Annapolis and West Point commissioned their senior classes during April. Faced with a long separation, Katie decided they should elope before he was sent to war. His cousin, Willis Field, drove the young couple across the Ohio River to New Albany, Indiana, because a minor could marry there without parental consent. Her mother cried later, but even at seventeen Katharine Chinn knew who and what she wanted: Field Harris.

Posted aboard the battleship *Nevada*, Harris was in the Caribbean when his son Billy arrived at Good Samaritan Hospital in Lexington on March 6, 1918.* They then spent five months in New London, Connecticut, when Captain Harris received orders for the U.S. Naval Station in Cavite. She'd packed up several big Hartmann wardrobes and leather steamer trunks, and they were off.

Traveling to the Philippines with twenty-month-old Billy had been daunting, but Field made the journey with her, and it was quite an

---

* Born Frederick Forsythe Harris, he'd been called "Billy" since birth, though no one seems to know why. His name was later legally changed to William Frederick Harris.

adventure for a young woman. Six days by rail across the country took the couple from Washington's Union Station to Chicago, where they stayed overnight at the Palmer House. From there, they traveled past Denver through the Rocky Mountains to Salt Lake City, ending at the Oakland Mole on San Francisco Bay. There was no Golden Gate Bridge in those days, so they'd taken the Eureka ferry and stayed in the marvelously opulent Palace Hotel. Departing from Pier 26 for Manila on the SS *Admiral Farragut*, the Harrises arrived in the Philippines in November 1919.

Twenty-two years ago, she shook her head and stared from the window.

That was hard to believe. She was now forty-two years old, and little Billy was Lieutenant William Frederick Harris, leading men into combat on the other side of the world. Katie stared out the window at Kalorama Park. The Triangle, as it was known, was a quiet corner in northwest Washington quite close to Rock Creek. Three presidents had lived in the area, along with her fellow Kentuckian, Supreme Court Justice Louis Brandeis. This beaux arts building, whitewashed with stone lintels and black iron railings, stood a half mile north of Dupont Circle and was quite convenient to the downtown area around the Capitol should she ever wish to descend into that frenzied madhouse.

The suite of rooms here belonged to her mother, Naoma Forsythe Chinn, who was happy for the company while her daughter was in town and asked few questions. Field was at Marine Corps headquarters every day helping to plan the Pacific War, but Katie preferred to remain away from most of it. Oh, she'd been well educated and raised to be presentable in any social setting, so none of that bothered her when necessary, yet the green hills of Virginia, just across the Potomac, were ideal for solitude when Washington became oppressive.

But Katie was lonely. Her daughter Nancy was away at school, and Field, as expected from a Marine general, was quite busy at the moment. He'd become an aviator in April 1929, and though she'd enjoyed Pensacola, his new fascination with aircraft frightened her. She vividly recalled his interest in the First Transcontinental Air Race as they'd traveled west to California in 1919. It was going on over their heads and he knew, he just *knew*, that aircraft represented the future of warfare. He had a point. While it took them six days to cross the country, a young army lieutenant named Belvin Maynard had done it in only three days.*

In November 1941, about the time Bill was leaving China, his father returned from Egypt, where he'd served as a military attaché observing Britain's Eighth Army in the Western Desert. Field was certain, as were most competent military professionals, that war with Japan was imminent, and he was temporarily posted to Marine Headquarters in Washington. On Sunday, December 7, they went riding in the morning on the Virginia side of the Potomac and were driving back into the city early that afternoon.

Despite the December chill, the situation was quite pleasant. Christmas was just weeks away, they were both together again, and their daughter would be home for the holidays. On the AM car radio, they were listening to the Redskins playing the Philadelphia Eagles when, after lunch, the broadcast was interrupted:

"The Japanese have attacked Pearl Harbor from the air . . ."

She'd been surprised, but not shocked, since her husband had often discussed it. For his part, Field Harris was nonplussed. The only surprise for him was that Pearl had been hit, not the Philippines, where the hammer had been expected to fall first. Tuning through the stations, the next broadcast they caught was from New York:

"Japanese bombs have fallen on Hawaii and the Philippine Islands . . . keep tuned to this station for further details."

She thought of Cavite, and genteel Manila as she and Field had

---

* Lieutenant Maynard landed in San Francisco after three days, six hours, and forty-seven minutes in a De Havilland DH-4 named *Hello Frisco*.

known it: the Army-Navy Club near Rizal Park overlooking the bay, her first real home as a married woman in Malate, and the polo grounds where she'd taken baby Billy to watch his father play on warm, relaxed Sunday afternoons. What, she wondered, would remain of that world?

Many Americans simply did not *know* what to do, even the few who knew where Pearl Harbor actually was. By late afternoon on December 7, crowds gathered outside the White House and War Department, hoping to learn something from groups of tight-lipped officers passing by. Less than a mile from her place at Kalorama, a small angry mob appeared around the picturesque Japanese Embassy on Massachusetts Avenue, and by nightfall units of the 3rd Cavalry Regiment from nearby Fort Myer appeared. With gas masks and fixed bayonets, the soldiers were posted to crucial bridges and facilities around the Capitol, and their presence, though necessary, added to the day's unreality.

Inconsistent, impulsive, but understandable, reactions swept the country. In New York, Mayor Fiorello La Guardia ordered all 2,500 Japanese in the city confined to their homes, while Mayor Edward Joseph Kelly immediately closed every Japanese restaurant in Chicago. Responses seemed more extreme as the news traveled west toward the Pacific, perhaps because over forty thousand Japanese nationals resided in California, about half of the eighty thousand nisei in the United States. Or perhaps because the West Coast was two thousand miles closer to the Japanese and would bear the brunt of invasion, if one came.

Field Harris, like most military officers, was quite skeptical of this fear. Japan didn't have the capability or industrial capacity to fight America in a long-term war, much less invade a nation twenty-five times larger in terms of sheer landmass. With nearly twice the population, the United States possessed eighty times the automotive manufacturing capacity and produced five tons of steel for every Japanese ton. Prescient Imperial officers like Isoroku Yamamoto, commander of the Combined Fleet, were well aware of these disparities and had no intention of giving Washington time to mobilize. A series of deep, hard strikes within the Pacific would, it was hoped, force America to the negotiating table before its tremendous industrial power could be brought to bear.

Japanese militarists such as Hideki Tojo dismissed the United States as weak and effeminate, and they were quick to point out American high unemployment, financial contractions from the Great Depression, and general disinterest in warfare. These factors, they claimed, could not withstand Japan's martial culture, spiritual superiority, and burgeoning economy. At their peril, they ignored their nation's introduction to Americans in 1853, when Commodore Matthew Perry steamed his "Black Ships" into Edo Bay and forced the Tokugawa Shogunate to meet his demands over the muzzles of his cannons.

Japan's economy, like much of its vaunted capabilities, was quite fragile. It was growing only because 28 percent of national income derived from unsustainable military spending. This was highly significant because even during the throes of the Great Depression, the United States generated *seventeen times* the national income of Japan, and this with an underachieving, underperforming economy. If something occurred to awaken American nationalism, to unify the country with a single, clear purpose, the result would be an overwhelming combination of economic power merged with military might. All that was needed was a spark to light the fire, a spark provided by the Imperial Navy on December 7, 1941.

As night fell on Washington that Sunday, panic spread throughout California, and Katie Harris, who lived there when Field was assigned to the Naval Air Station, San Diego, heard the news from friends there. Despite pledges of loyalty from large numbers of nisei, the government was unconvinced, or felt it could not take chances at such a critical time. Military and police units blocked roads, placed anti-aircraft guns atop buildings, and closed the ports of Monterey and Los Angeles. The FBI rounded up scores of Japanese nationals for questioning and even arrest, including an entire baseball team, the L.A. Nippons, who were playing a Paramount team in Hollywood.*

A radio appeal was broadcast asking for volunteers to form a civilian defense council, and bands of heavily armed men showed up to fight off the perceived imminence of Japanese invasion. Caught up in the moment, Americans wanted to *do* something—anything. Fortunately, despite false rumors of enemy submarines spotted off the coast and the imagined threat of paratroopers dropping into Hollywood, saner heads generally prevailed. People were told to go home, unload their weapons, and wait for some real news. That evening, the Harrises, along with millions of their fellow Americans, listened to Eleanor Roosevelt's well-modulated, motherly voice on the radio:

> Good evening, ladies and gentlemen, I am speaking to you tonight at a very serious moment in our history. The Cabinet is convening and the leaders in Congress are meeting with the President. The State Department and Army and Navy officials have been with the President all afternoon. In fact, the Japanese ambassador was talking to the President at the very time that Japan's airships were bombing our citizens in Hawaii and the Philippines and sinking one of our transports loaded with lumber on its way to Hawaii.
>
> I should like to say just a word to the women in the country tonight. I have a boy at sea on a destroyer, for all I know he may be on his way to the Pacific. Two of my children are in coast cities on the Pacific. Many of you all over the country have boys in the services who will now be called upon to go into action. You have friends and families in what has suddenly become a danger

---

* The FBI did wait till the game was over. Paramount won 6–3.

zone. You cannot escape anxiety. You cannot escape a clutch of fear at your heart and yet I hope that the certainty of what we have to meet will make you rise above these fears.

We must go about our daily business more determined than ever to do the ordinary things as well as we can and when we find a way to do anything more in our communities to help others, to build morale, to give a feeling of security, we must do it. Whatever is asked of us I am sure we can accomplish it. We are the free and unconquerable people of the United States of America.

I have faith in you. I feel as though I was standing upon a rock and that rock is my faith in my fellow citizens.

Brave words, encouraging words—and just what the country needed to hear. Yet with the fear only a parent can know, Katie constantly thought of her son. Field was often away, so she and Bill had always been close. To the rest of the world she was Katharine Chinn-Harris, descendant of the noble Norman-French DeCheyne family, which possessed large estates in Scotland and eventually sired Raleigh Chinn. Chinn's wife was Mary Ball, half sister to George Washington's mother, and the couple made the Atlantic crossing to Lancaster Country, Virginia, in 1713. Also related to the Boones of Kentucky, the Chinns produced landowners, judges, explorers, and military officers, but to her only son Katharine was always just "dearest Mama."

The day following Pearl Harbor's mauling, Franklin Delano Roosevelt left the White House just past noon in a black limousine. Accompanied by his son, Major James Roosevelt, a Groton and Harvard graduate who had just been accepted to the Marine Raiders, the president made his way to Capitol Hill. Beginning at 1230 he spoke for less than ten minutes, and several memorable phrases resonated with Katie Harris.

Yesterday, December 7, 1941—a date which will live in infamy— the United States of America was suddenly and deliberately attacked by naval and air forces of the Empire of Japan. The United States was at peace with that nation, and, at the solicitation of Japan, was still in conversation with its government and its Emperor looking toward the maintenance of peace in the Pacific.

No matter how long it may take us to overcome this premeditated invasion, the American people, in their righteous might, will win through to absolute victory.

Hostilities exist. There is no blinking at the fact that our people, our territory and our interests are in grave danger. With confidence in our armed forces, with the unbounding determination of our people, we will gain the inevitable triumph, so help us God.

Immediately put before the Seventy-Seventh U.S. Congress, Roosevelt's request for a declaration of war passed unanimously in the Senate within minutes. The House vote concluded 388–1 in favor at 1310, and America was once again at war.* The president was inspirational, to be sure, but the hard truth was that the United States was woefully ill prepared for war and on extremely shaky footing. Only the logistical limitations of its enemies and the vastness of the oceans on both coasts prevented invasion. While the American president was declaring war, the Japanese invaded northern Luzon, French Indochina, Thailand, and the Malay Peninsula. For America, the immediate situation was quite grim.

Two days following Roosevelt's speech, the British battleship *Prince of Wales* and battle cruiser *Repulse* sortied from Singapore to repel an inbound Japanese invasion fleet. Sighted by a submarine, the big warships were attacked from the air and sunk off Malaysia near Kuantan. Fortunately, Nazi Germany and Fascist Italy were preoccupied with Russia and North Africa, respectively, though they rapidly declared war on the United States. Within a week, Japanese forces landed in

---

* The single dissenting vote came from Jeannette Rankin, a pacifist Republican from Montana.

Hong Kong, and three days before Christmas the Imperial 14th Army invaded central Luzon near Lingayen Bay. Japanese forces in northern Luzon occupied Baguio, including the Maryknoll convent.

Katie knew the city well, having spent several hot Philippine summers there. During those dark, confusing weeks she listened and waited, in vain, for some news of Bill, but even with his connections Field Harris could discover nothing. The Philippines were in turmoil, and it was apparent that all the money, effort, and materiel expended for its defense could not halt the Japanese. The elder Harris was aware that no effort would be made to save the cutoff American defenders, and Bill's fate was largely in his own hands. Field had raised his son to be independent, to think. He clung to that knowledge, and was suddenly glad that Bill had been raised on military posts all over the world. He was a tough, resilient officer, and that would have to sustain him because no relief from America would come to the Philippines. Wisely, he said nothing of it to his wife, as she would only worry more.

On December 23, word reached Washington that despite a futile and one-sided battle, the Marine garrison on Wake Island had been overwhelmed. At the same time, three thousand miles to the west, General MacArthur declared Manila an open city, then fled to Corregidor with his family, staff, and personal Chinese cook. Forty-eight hours later, as Winston Churchill and Franklin Roosevelt celebrated a muted Christmas in the White House, Major General Christopher Maltby surrendered Hong Kong to the Japanese.

Field Harris also discovered that Admiral Thomas C. Hart, commander in chief of the U.S. Asiatic Fleet, had transferred operational control of the 4th Marines to General MacArthur. There really was no choice since evacuation was impossible, and they were the best fighters in the Philippines, yet Harris was dismayed. Marines being led by an army general, especially MacArthur, was less than optimum. He was aware of MacArthur's real reputation, despite the efforts of the general's personal public relations consultant, and knowing this man now commanded his son was not at all good news.*

Remaining outwardly calm and self-possessed, Katie was aware of more than her husband realized. He was speaking of potential American actions in the Pacific later in 1942, and if there was a plan to intervene on Bataan he would certainly have mentioned it. That he mentioned nothing about the Philippines told her everything, and Katie fought to overcome the grim foreboding she felt every day. Yet, she was a product of a strong generation raised during tumultuous times, and had been an officer's wife too long to fall into hysterics.

And there were hysterics.

On the southern shores of Lake Michigan, the 3,700-acre "Gary Works" steel factory was screened from potential enemy bombers by a massive, man-made smokescreen. Overzealous army officers convinced Carnegie Illinois Steel of the danger, and twenty locomotives burning oil-soaked coal raced along the mill-yard tracks while steel furnaces belched specially mixed oil and tar. Within a half hour an immense black toxic cloud covered the plant, but it blew away in minutes to envelop a neighboring town. The army conceded it may have overreacted.

Across America armed groups of jittery, angry, and armed citizens appeared with vague, self-made mandates to round up "suspicious" people. A duck hunter was killed on Lake Michigan by a National Reserve Armory sentry when he unfortunately pulled alongside a Coast Guard training ship. One of the more bizarre efforts was led by Princess Silver Star, aka Mrs. Charles Matteson, who created a rifle brigade composed of forty heavily armed Chippewa women. Her plan was to personally fight off German or Japanese paratroopers who

---

* Aware of "Dugout Doug," a disdainful nickname given to MacArthur largely because he remained safe in Corregidor's Malinta Tunnel Complex while his men fought and died on Bataan. Even his supporters were hard-pressed to defend the general after he fled to Australia, leaving the defenders of Bataan and Corregidor to their fates.

were, of course, targeting Pontiac, Michigan. According to *The New York Times*, Mrs. Matteson stated, "We have rifles, we have some ammunition, and we know how to shoot."

R. F. Sedgely, Inc., a Philadelphia gunsmith, advertised "Immediate Delivery" for Springfield Model 1903 rifles, complete with bayonet and optional tear gas pistols. Merchants everywhere adapted their products to fit the new reality, as they saw it. "Air raid suits" and "blackout dinner costumes" were marketed; door-to-door salesmen sold bags of sand specially treated, they insisted, to extinguish all manner of enemy incendiary fires caused by aerial bombs; a line of padded women's hats also appeared to protect the wearer from any falling objects. Aircraft silhouettes began appearing in print to aid American civilians in identifying the hordes of enemy bombers that were no doubt poised and waiting to raid the United States. Helpful advice was plentiful: "If you can see the full underside silhouette a bomb may hit near you in the next split second," suggested *Life*'s December 22 issue.

Enterprising construction companies all over the country were advertising bomb shelters, or offering to convert existing buildings into havens safe from enemy aircraft. Armored doors and reinforced concrete could be added to homes for as little as two hundred dollars, although luxury models with a bathroom and air-conditioning cost upward of four thousand dollars. Rubber immediately became an unattainable commodity, and new tires vanished overnight. Golf balls were deemed nonessential, and on a single December morning Manhattan's Abercrombie & Fitch sold twenty-four thousand of them before lunch. The aura of unreality was exacerbated by officials such as J. W. Farley, director of the Massachusetts Committee on Public Safety, who confidently stated, "The Germans can easily reach our shores with bombers, and it is highly probable that they may try to slip an airplane carrier close enough to our shores to launch an attack."*

---

* The German *Kriegsmarine* launched a single aircraft carrier, the *Graf Zeppelin*, in 1938. It was never completed and never operational.

Field Harris was well aware that Nazi Germany did not have the capability, or the will, to attack the United States directly, especially with its Russian offensive stalled for the winter. As for Japan, her priorities remained acquiring the resource-rich Dutch East Indies and eliminating all Allied resistance in the Pacific before America could intervene effectively. What America needed now was time, time to convert peacetime industries to the production of ships, planes, and the thousands of other components from underwear to ammunition required to fight a global war. Time to put two million men into military service during the next year, to organize, train, and deploy units to Europe and the Pacific. To begin, President Roosevelt requested a budget increase of an astounding 56 *billion* dollars, and Congress expanded the draft to all men between twenty and forty-four years.*

It was a good start, but Americans wanted more. They demanded revenge, and this was an aspect of the United States most Japanese underestimated or discounted altogether—rage. A white-hot national anger that unified America with a single-minded purpose: destroy Japan. Germany was now an enemy also, but pure contempt and loathing was focused on all things Japanese. Katie Harris saw and heard evidence of this on the streets, the radio, and in print.

A barbershop sign proclaimed "Free Shaves for Japs—Not Responsible for Accidents"; performances of Gilbert and Sullivan's *The Mikado* and Puccini's *Madama Butterfly* vanished overnight; products made in Japan were burned, including Santa Claus figurines and artificial Christmas trees, which were rumored to be time bombs. Songs aired within days, sometimes within hours, after Pearl Harbor: "When the Little Yellow Bellies Meet the Cohens and the Kelleys"; the popular Charlie Tobias and Cliff Friend ditty, "We Did It Before and We Can Do It Again!"; or "Taps for Japs." America was enraged, and it was evident everywhere.

Effective fearmongering was often centered on women and their

---

* Over 1 trillion dollars in 2020.

potential treatment at the hands of the Japanese. Much of this was true, based on hard facts emerging from China or former British colonies, where women were systematically gang-raped. Some of it was not true, as General Masaharu Homma permitted no such actions in the Philippines, whether the women were Filipina or American. In the Maryknoll convent above Baguio, Sister Miriam Louise and the others were protected by a Japanese officer, who told his soldiers the nuns "were holy women and must not be treated like other women."

While the politics careened hard right and the economy lurched into high gear, a more visible sign of America's resolve took shape. Within a month of Pearl Harbor, navy Captain Francis Stuart Low, an academy upperclassman of Field Harris, was in Norfolk, Virginia, inspecting the new aircraft carrier *Hornet*, which had just returned from sea trials. While waiting to return to Washington, he noticed the runway was painted to replicate a carrier deck from the air so pilots could practice landings on land before attempting them at sea. As he watched, a big army bomber approached and landed directly on the end of the simulated "deck."

Low had an epiphany.

A strike against Japan by carrier planes had already been discussed and dismissed as too risky, and the navy's aircraft were wrong. Both the Douglas Devastator and Dauntless were designed for attacking ships, so their payloads were too small, and both lacked the capability to fly long distances. This is what the army specialized in doing, but their bigger bombers could not fly off a carrier deck—or could they? Watching the planes land at Norfolk made Low think about it. For the operation he had in mind, the bombers just needed to take off, so there was no question of their needing to perfect the exacting art of landing on an aircraft carrier. It could be done, he decided, with the right type of plane and the right man commanding the mission.

Returning to Washington, Low worked out the details and put forth an audacious plan to Admiral Ernest J. King, chief of naval operations:

bomb Japan. Low argued that this would show Americans that their military was capable of fighting back and reveal to Japan that their sacred Home Islands were not invulnerable. Such an affront to their national pride might also sow some seeds of doubt in their military leaders. If successful, this would also provide a much-needed morale boost for the American public while upsetting Japanese plans. Most important, a raid against the Home Islands would be offensive, and this was vital in warfare. A defensive mindset was dangerous, especially against an enemy who moves fast and hits hard.

In fact, Field Harris was already involved in planning America's first offensive campaign against Japan, but this was months away. In the light of the ongoing Philippine fiasco something—anything—was needed to break Japan's momentum. Low's plan surfaced at this time and rapidly gathered support, especially since Roosevelt himself had asked that Japan be bombed as soon as possible. It would take some time to work out the operational details, but the "Tokyo Raid" would shortly become a reality. In the meantime, those at home like Katie Harris faced every single day one at a time, hoping for the best, or at least hoping for news of those they loved.

Unfortunately, all the news from the Philippines had been bad so far. She was aware that the 4th Marine Regiment—and Bill, she prayed—had been moved to Corregidor to hold that island, block Manila Bay, and anchor the Allied fighting retreat. No one was talking much about what would happen when the army fell back to the end of the Bataan Peninsula with nowhere else to go. Finally, in late January 1942 Katie received a bit of news . . . and hope. Bill was alive! She had a letter from him dated earlier in the month and though vague due to censorship, and not especially optimistic, her son had survived the initial Japanese onslaught. "My outfit has been bombed a good bit," he wrote, "a little terrifying at first; but after I got used to them, they bothered me hardly at all."

As of New Year's Day, he was also a first lieutenant and was pleased with the pay raise. It would help him, he thought, replace what he lost during the invasion, which was everything he owned. "If I get through the war O.K., I won't mind losing a little property," he told his mother, and she knew it was his understated way of relating how dire the situation was there. "There isn't much to write about that I can mention," Bill added at the end, and Katie understood from that that her boy was in the thick of it and could not divulge any details.

Still, as of a few weeks ago he was alive. This, she realized with a sharp pang, was very likely the new reality. Retroactive knowledge. He was alive . . . then. There was no way to know about the present, and the future, at the moment, was an impenetrable, dark cloud hanging over the free world. It was no good thinking about this, or planning for it.

Katie touched the letter again.

"Devotedly yours," he had signed it, and this was both reassuring and quite sad. The last human fingers on the page belonged to her son. Fingers she had held when he was a baby, and fingers that had twined in her hair, or squeezed hers when he'd been hurt. Her throat tightened, and Katharine Chinn-Harris fought back a wave of despair that left her hollow and threatened unwelcome tears. This also was not something to think about. Not now. Pushing down the sadness, she knew that optimism and determination would have to see her, and millions of other mothers, sisters, and wives, through this, however much more of "this" remained. Staring out the window, she blinked and thought how awful it would be to have already received a Western Union telegram: a few terse, impersonal lines from the War Department telling her that Bill would never return. At least that had not happened. Not yet.

Despite her best efforts, Katie's eyes were moist, and she wiped them with the back of one hand. Over twenty years as a Marine wife and mother taught her to look problems squarely in the eye and meet disaster head-on. President Roosevelt was right; unbounded determination was what would eventually see them all through to the other side. In the end, besides submission, there was no choice. No choice at all.

Two

A LITTLE PIECE OF HELL

RED AND GREEN FLARES SLICED THROUGH THE DARKNESS NORTH OF Corregidor, illuminating lines of Japanese invasion barges bobbing on the waves. "God, how many of 'em do you reckon there are?" A Marine on the island's eastern ridgeline tail hissed. Just then, a beach-defense searchlight cut a bright white swath through the darkness and waved over the landing craft. It was just before midnight on May 5, 1942, and the Marines were manning a pair of .30-caliber machine guns on the scrubby low hills between East Point and Kindley Field. The men were covering a low, flat area where the Japanese were believed to be coming ashore, and they were definitely in the right spot.

"A lot more than there are of us . . . but there'll be a whole lot less of 'em pretty soon," Private First Class Hayes replied grimly, then opened fire as the first of eight barges grated onto the beach. From higher ground on both sides of them the staccato barking of emplaced .50-caliber guns drowned out his own weapon. It didn't matter. Even after the searchlight was shot out, the machine gunners fired by moonlight and poured lethal streams of lead into the Japanese.

Nearly a mile west up the coastline, Lieutenant Bill Harris had his own problems. Major Lang's "Able" Company had been understrength in Shanghai, and nearly six months of combat hadn't improved the situation. Lang himself had been killed yesterday, and Captain Lewis Pickup was now in command of the company. Only 100 men remained from the 180 who left China in December, and Bill was the only surviving commissioned officer from the original company. He had less than thirty fit for duty in his 1st Platoon, and they had to cover a half-mile beachfront between Infantry and Calvary Points.

Walking the perimeter earlier that night, he talked quietly with his men and tightened up a few gaps in the line. Noting the lack of barbed wire, particularly the double-apron configuration, he wished they'd scrounged more but there was nothing to be done about it now. By 10:45 P.M., Harris was standing on a rise near the narrow coast road behind Battery Kysor's 155mm guns, staring across the North Channel, when the south tip of Bataan suddenly lit up. This was followed by the "shattering roar of gun discharges," all apparently pointed directly at him.

Sprinting for the nearest hole, an empty ammunition storage locker some fifty yards away on the bluff, Bill knew he'd never make it. Shells screamed overhead, more terrifying than usual because it was night, and he dove through a hole in the brush. Throwing himself flat with his hands pressed over his ears, Harris squeezed his eyes shut as explosions burst all around him. Treetops exploded into clouds of nasty splinters, and the concussions bounced him off the ground, floating with soil and debris, before dropping him like a rag doll. Tasting blood when his teeth cracked together through his tongue, Bill remembered an Annapolis instructor who had served in the Great War warning the midshipmen to keep their mouths open during an artillery bombardment. It was humorous in a lecture hall, but absolutely not funny here.

Wide-eyed and heart pounding, Bill staggered to his feet and lurched through the torn brush toward the foxhole. Flashes suddenly pierced the darkness, like thousands of light bulbs going off, and he knew another salvo from Bataan was incoming. Disoriented, ears ringing, and temporarily blinded, he stumbled forward a few feet then dropped. Pushing his face into the dirt, Bill choked on the dust as the Japanese artillery fire thudded into Corregidor's northern coastline. A "stunning, shocking roar sprang up in every direction," he would recall, and the awesome concussion from all the high explosives slammed his body deeper into the dirt.* For a moment he lay there, stunned, then scrambled to his feet and in a lopsided, crouching run Bill made it to the bluff as the next salvo shrieked down.

There!

The hole was just ahead, and he dove in like a swimmer, arms out-stretched, as exploding shells threw up huge chunks of earth and brush. Rolling into a corner, he crouched, teeth chattering, frightened beyond any point he'd ever imagined. Artillery fire was so random and imper-sonal. There was no way to fight like one would a man, and in an instant everything you were, or could be, might be obliterated. Bill shivered and hugged his knees. *How in hell did I ever make it here? Oh Jesus . . . it sounds as if there's a shell hitting every square foot up there. God, I'm scared!*

For twenty minutes he huddled and trembled against the concrete wall. It was hard, but also something solid between his skin and mil-lions of red-hot metallic shards whistling though the air. Then the barrage stopped, abruptly and completely. Relief washed over him like warm water, and Bill felt weak. He had survived, though the sud-den silence was nearly as shocking as the shelling had been. Blinking through the hanging dust, he realized that the thunder in his ears had subsided and knew that he should get out of the hole. He didn't want to. He wanted to stay right here, but he had to get out and check on his platoon. They were his men and his responsibility.

Then he heard it.

A distant sound . . . almost like airplane engines. Frowning, Bill slowly rose and winced as blood flowed painfully into his cramped

---

* Wainwright's staff estimated a dozen shells impacted every minute. Over the course of the periodic sustained bombardments, this added up to nearly two million pounds of high explosives.

muscles. It couldn't be aircraft—not in the middle of the night. Clambering up from the hole, he stood a moment and inhaled deeply, smelling sea air mixed with cordite and the heavy stink of shredded vegetation. There . . . again. Engines. Looking out over the black water, Harris realized the noise came from north and east of Bataan near Lamao. That was supposedly the Japanese assembly point, where their landing barges were moored, and it was less than ten miles away across the bay. Bill's mouth went dry and his breathing quickened when he realized what the sound had to be.

Invasion. The Japanese were landing.

Flares suddenly arced up over the water off to his right, near Corregidor's eastern tail. The lieutenant broke into a trot toward his platoon's beach positions, but when he came through the brush, he saw they were empty. The men were still in their foxholes expecting to be shelled again.

"Damn it, you guys!" he growled loudly. "Do you want to be caught here with your pants down? Now's our goddamn chance to hit back. Don't fuck it up!" Tracers zipped through the air around Calvary Point a half mile to the east, followed by the staccato popping of multiple machine guns. Dark shapes emerged from darker holes beneath the trees and moved out into the firing positions. Staying on the bluff, Bill watched the fireworks with his men for an hour. Then it stopped and the moon rose, so he decided to walk up to the 2nd Platoon positions near Calvary Point and get some news, if possible. Combat officers are expected to make life-or-death decisions based on imperfect information, but he had no information at all, which made him uneasy.

He wasn't the only one.

The Japanese were having significant problems also, and had the defenders known it the battle would have certainly progressed much differently. Those barges around Cavalry Point held Colonel Gempachi Sato's 1st Battalion, 61st Imperial Infantry, and comprised the first assault wave. The beach between Infantry and Cavalry Points was the intended landing zone, and this was exactly why Bill Harris's

1st platoon had dug in there. Both the 1st and 2nd Battalions from the 61st Regiment were supposed to land there together, some two thousand men and veterans of China, then overcome the Americans and fight inland. Half the attackers were to cut the main road and capture Kindley Field, which would isolate the Americans on Corregidor's tail and provide an airfield for resupply. The other half was to advance west toward Malinta Hill and the dock areas.

As Harris approached Cavalry Point, the Japanese had made it ashore and established a beachhead—but it was the wrong beach. The assault was planned for high tide to bring the barges in over any obstacles, and also because the east-to-west current in Manila Bay would push the barges ashore. Fortunately for the Americans, the Japanese did not know the North Channel current flowed west to east, *against* the barges, and this deposited the 1st Battalion one thousand yards farther east than intended. Even without beach-defense searchlights, the moonlight was bright enough for shooting, and the Marines opened up with everything they had: rifles, pistols, grenades, machine guns, and even Air Corps twenty-five-pound bombs that they slid down chutes from the cliffs onto the Japanese.

"American high-powered machine guns poured a stream of bullets on us from all directions," a Japanese lieutenant remembered. "Rifle fire added to the hail of death. Our men who were huddled in the center of the boat were all either killed or wounded. Those who clung to the sides were hit by shells that pierced the steel plating. Desperately I gave the signal and led the charge against the shore defenses. In that mad dash for shore many were drowned as they dropped into the water mortally wounded. Many were killed outright . . . if it had not been for the fact that it was the dark hour before the dawn, pitch black, I doubt if any of us would be alive today to tell the story."

Even anti-aircraft guns from Kindley Field joined in when possible. Nonetheless, by 2330 much of Sato's battalion was ashore at North Point with a beachhead, and was now moving inland through a ravine near North Point. From his headquarters in Malinta Hill, Wainwright

sent a message to General Marshall in Washington that he knew signaled the beginning of the end.

LANDING ATTACK ON CORREGIDOR IN PROGRESS.
ENEMY LANDED NORTH POINT. FURTHER DETAILS AS
SITUATION DEVELOPS

As the general sent his dispatch, along the North Point ravine
Gunnery Sergeant "Tex" Haynes emptied a five-round clip into
the Japanese, then drew a pair of .45-caliber pistols. When these
were empty, the Marine yanked a .30-caliber machine gun from
its mount, draped two ammunition belts across his shoulder, and
headed down into the ravine, firing as he went. Unable to match his
ferocity, the Japanese finally killed Haynes with a grenade. Surging
up onto the high ground north of Kindley Field, Sato's men then
pushed the survivors of Gunnery Sergeant John Mercurio's 2nd Platoon back west along the shoreline.

Making his way east, Lieutenant Harris ran into these men, realized a successful enemy landing had been accomplished, and correctly
concluded the Japanese had cut the tail of Corregidor by crossing
south near Kindley Field. Bringing all the Marines he could find back
to the 1st Platoon positions near Infantry Point, Bill deployed his remaining men in an "all-around" defense centered on his command
post. Harris intended to anchor the American left flank against whatever came, but by 0200 there were only these two platoons between the
advancing Japanese battalion and Malinta Hill. Tracers arced all over
eastern Corregidor, and Harris wondered if he'd guessed wrong about
the Japanese plan.

He had not.

Sato's 2nd Battalion, also intended for Bill Harris's beach between
Cavalry and Infantry Points, was pushed by the east-flowing current
onto Corregidor's tail into the waiting guns of the 3rd Platoon and Captain Noel Castle's Mobile Weapons Company at Kindley Field. Out

of two thousand Japanese assault troops in the first wave, fewer than eight hundred reached the shore alive. "I truly believe we killed every Jap on the beach," Roy Hays recalled. As the sky lightened slightly in the east, Hayes said that "we saw eight landing barges bobbing in the surf, and there was no sign of life on any of them."

But there were definite signs of the enemy inland.

Sato's mangled battalion had pushed west around Kindley Field and advanced the half mile to its immediate objective, Battery Denver. Situated on a low rise overlooking Corregidor's tail, Denver consisted of four three-inch anti-aircraft guns, plus six machine guns. Bombarded from 1900 till 2230 when Captain Paul R. Cornwall of the 60th Coast Artillery (Anti-Aircraft) and his men emerged, there wasn't much left. All communications equipment was destroyed, and the sound of Japanese Nambu light machine guns came from the north side of Kindley Field.*

"During the night our own troops began to withdraw toward Malinta Tunnel," Cornwall later wrote. "There seemed to be no coordination of units in the area at all and no reinforcements nor support from the rear." Denver was abandoned, and the advancing Japanese were delighted to make use of its redoubtable fortifications to effectively cut Corregidor in half. Captain Lewis Pickup, commanding Company A since Major Lang's death, considered using Harris's men to attack from the north. Unfortunately, more barges had been sighted, and the risk of leaving the thinly defended beach was too great, so Bill's platoon remained sandwiched between the Japanese at Denver and those coming ashore now.

With Denver taken, Colonel Howard decided the existing threat was more serious than a potential landing on the Rock's west coast, so he committed Major Max Schaeffer's regimental reserve. Formed from the 4th Regiment's Service and Headquarters personnel, it was augmented by marines who escaped Bataan and a handful of Filipino

---

* A Type 96 machine gun. Unofficially named for its designer, Kijirō Nambu.

flying cadets. But the reserve was predominantly marine, with Captain Bob Chambers leading Company O, and Company P commanded by Bill Harris's classmate, Lieutenant William Hogaboom. Unfortunately, the 750 yards between Malinta Hill and Denver was a saddle in the hills and a completely exposed area. The timing was bad as well, since the Japanese commenced a periodic barrage that caught the Marines in the open. Additionally, Sato had placed machine guns on the hilltop covering the saddle, and these repeatedly raked the attacking Americans. Three counterattacks by Schaeffer failed to dislodge the Japanese.

Between 0200 and 0400 Sato made no major advances past Denver, though he continued strengthening his positions with reinforcements straggling ashore and probed forward with platoon-sized units. This was an old Japanese trick to gather information, create confusion, and sometimes panic an enemy into retreating. Any soldier who could speak English was used, and in one case a Japanese infantryman ran down a hill screaming in a perfect American accent, "the Japs are right behind me!"

By 0430 Howard committed his last available force to retaking Denver. This was the regiment's 4th Battalion (Provisional), commanded by Major Francis H. "Joe" Williams, which moved east from Malinta in four columns. Only Williams and five sergeants were Marines. The four companies were commanded by army or navy officers, and the men were primarily beached sailors hastily trained by Williams. These men were generally older and had years of service, but they knew nothing of infantry tactics or close combat. One of the company commanders, army captain Harold E. Dalness, later recalled the battalion was "a group of 500 sailors with 500 rifles—nothing more."

Bill Harris, on the north edge of the faltering American defensive line, heard the noise from Schaeffer's assaults and decided to take a squad toward Denver. Perhaps his 1st Platoon could help, or at least he might find out what in the hell was happening. Bill was heading south toward the island's center at 0600, just as Williams's battalion prepared to attack, when "about seventy-five yards to the east down the road a large group of men, perhaps a full platoon, emerged on the run from the dark vegetation." His men immediately opened fire with rifles and a BAR.*

Screaming as they were hit, the Japanese scattered into the trees and ditches, then returned fire. A vicious firefight developed, and dark objects plopped to the ground near the Marines, with one landing at Bill's feet. *Grenade!* Instantly scooping up the little Type 97 "pineapple," he hurled it back and ducked when it exploded. A fierce, hoarse cry rang out; twenty enemy soldiers sprang from the shadows thirty yards ahead and charged. The BAR barked again; then everyone else began firing. In the moonlight, Harris plainly saw the Japanese bayonets gleaming and swept the slide back on his big .45-caliber pistol. One soldier leapt directly at him, shouting insanely, and the lieutenant fired point-blank into the man's chest.

"The muzzle flash momentarily lit up a savage, toothy face," he noted, "and the man stopped abruptly as though he had run into a tree. He staggered, dropped his rifle, and grabbed his breast with both hands." Breathing hard, Bill "stepped in and kicked him in the testicles. He screamed and went down." Kicking him again in the face, the Marine shoved his pistol into its holster, snatched up the dying man's Arisaka rifle, and wheeled to face the others. Two of the closest Japanese were fighting with a Marine, and a third was tugging his bayonet from a body on the ground.

Bill twisted his wrist to keep his captured bayonet horizontal, then lunged forward and drove the sixteen-inch blade between the man's ribs into his kidney. The soldier "grunted loudly and staggered, then dropped his rifle, and started running down the road." The other Japanese spun around to face Harris, but the Marine he was fighting thrust forward at the same time. As the soldier parried that attack, Bill stuck

---

* Browning Automatic Rifle (BAR) M1918. A 1942 U.S. Marine rifle squad of nine men usually had one of these, which served as a highly portable light machine gun.

him through the throat. Shocked, the man froze and was quickly impaled by the other Marine. The third soldier was still trying to free his bayonet when Harris sprang toward him. Leaving his rifle in the dead American, the man screamed, turned, and tried to escape down the road. Bounding after him, Bill jabbed the bayonet through the man's back into his lungs, and the soldier went down shrieking.

Wrenching the blade free, he saw at least eight Japanese yelling wildly and charging toward the remaining Americans. Another BAR fired from behind him, and a few attackers dropped; then another squad of Marines joined in from somewhere. The next few minutes were a blur of hand-to-hand combat. Bill bayonetted another enemy soldier straight through the heart, but then found himself fighting for his life against a fresh opponent. "With every quick thrust, the Jap shrieked in savage triumph," Harris wrote. "It was truly all [I] could do to hold the little bastard off."

In desperation, the lieutenant threw the rifle like a spear at the man's face, then turned and bolted up the side of the draw. Drawing his pistol from the holster, Bill spun around and fired twice into the soldier's chest. "The Jap was stopped, then knocked down," he recalled. "Two hits! Thank God!"

More Marines appeared, and suddenly the Japanese soldiers were gone. It was dawn now, so Harris led the survivors back to the CP on the high ground; from two nine-man squads only four men, including the lieutenant, were still on their feet. Three more Americans were alive, but wounded so badly they would die within the hour. While Bill organized his remaining men, Major Williams and the 4th Battalion commenced their frontal assault on Denver near Water Tank Hill. Without artillery or heavy weapons support, the attack bogged down, and by 0800 Colonel Howard sent in the last troops available: sixty men from the 59th Coast Artillery under Captain Herman H. Hauck.

The Japanese were having issues as well. Though he held the high ground, Colonel Sato was more or less stuck there. He was running short of ammunition since most of it was thrown overboard by sailors manning the assault barges in their haste to escape the American guns. Under the current conditions, there was only enough to last through the morning. Colonel Motohiko Yoshida, General Homma's chief of staff, wrote, "When I recall all this I cannot but break into a cold sweat."

According to the Japanese plan, Colonel Sato was to have captured Malinta Hill by dawn, but he could not now advance from his position atop Denver without replacements and ammunition. This was complicated by the fact that only twenty-one of fifty-two available landing craft had survived the initial assault, so reinforcement was slow. Fearing his attack had failed, General Homma ordered the 7th Tank Regiment to provide armor support, and at 0830 three tanks were landed at the North Point beachhead. Spotted by the Americans, these turned out to be a pair of Type 97 medium tanks and, surprisingly, a U.S. Army M3 Stuart light tank.

Captured from either the 192nd or 194th Tank Battalion on Bataan, the Stuart was lighter than the Japanese tanks, but with powerful twin Cadillac engines it towed the heavier Type 97s up the bluffs onto the flat ground north of Kindley Field. By 0900 the latest American counterattack had stalled, losing fifteen officers and over 150 enlisted men against the Japanese emplacements. Two white flares arced up from Denver, and another mind-numbing, bone-cracking 240mm barrage crashed down from Bataan. Then, while the Marines regrouped, the tanks suddenly appeared. There were no antitank weapons on Corregidor, and few things terrify infantrymen more than armored vehicles. When Colonel Howard learned of their presence, he ordered the 4th Battalion back to the road junction near the Malinta Tunnel entrance.

Runners were also sent to the Marine positions on the north end of the line with orders to withdraw back to Malinta Hill, but Bill Harris had already reached that conclusion. His scouts came back reporting Japanese reinforcements pouring ashore with tanks, so the lieutenant rounded up twenty-seven survivors from Company A, organized them into three squads, and fell back. Heading down the road through the draw where his wild bayonet fight occurred, Harris turned west at the road junction and got his men into the trench area on the east face of Malinta. This had been turned into the last line of defense, with railroad ties and pilings blocking both roads around the hill.

Major Williams, though wounded, was in overall command of the survivors from both the 1st and 4th Battalions, about one hundred men, and he deployed them here as a last defense. Williams briefed him on the situation, assigned him to what remained of Captain Robert Chamber's Company O, then said, "Now get the dope across to your men that no matter what happens we're going to fight it out on this line to the end. We retreat no farther. Do you understand?"

"Yes sir."

"I'm having a load of Molotov cocktails sent from the rear, so we'll soon be set for those tanks."

Bill wasn't optimistic about that, but did as he was told. One bright spot was discovering his classmate Bill Hogaboom had lived through the night and was here on the slope. Both Marine officers caught up a bit and, knowing they might very well die in the next few hours, remembered a few highlights from their years at Annapolis. "We were a long, long way from the Chesapeake," Harris remembered thinking. "All I could do was die, but I'd do it like one of the Spartans at Thermopylae. I promised myself that."

Two hundred yards away, deep in the Malinta complex, General Wainwright was also thinking of death. At least eight hundred of his men were dead this morning, and over a thousand lay wounded in the hospital lateral annex. To the west, artillery from Bataan was pounding Cheney and James Ravines, just as it had blanketed his north shore last night. Clearly, the Japanese were planning another landing, probably tonight, on western Corregidor.

He could not hold out. Wainwright long understood that there would be no reinforcements and no relief. Washington had made the agonizing decision that America's few resources in the Pacific must go to defending the Hawaiian Islands and U.S. West Coast, not the Philippines. As a soldier, he could appreciate that strategy, but as the general in command here, it was a bitter reality. He held the lives of the remaining men and women in his hands, and that weighed heaviest on his mind. While there was even a faint hope of holding out, Wainwright was prepared to fight, but when Bataan fell in April, he knew the Corregidor defenders were on borrowed time.

Now, at 1000 on this hot morning of May 6, 1942, he faced his own agonizing reality. All communications had been knocked out, and the only electrical power came from emergency generators. There was food, but ammunition was running low. Fifty-six of his 75mm beach-defense guns were gone, along with most of his other seventy-two batteries. Now the enemy had landed tanks, and there were no antitank weapons on the island; no one had foreseen the need since no enemy could get past Corregidor's guns and land. Tanks were a game changer. The psychological impact was greater than the physical damage thus far, but if they got to the mouth of Malinta Tunnel and opened fire down the 836 feet of its long, perfectly straight length—the thought was horrific.

"But it was the terror that is vested in a tank that was the deciding factor," Wainwright recalled years later. "I thought of the havoc that even one of these could wreak if it nosed into the tunnel, where lay our helpless wounded and their brave nurses."

In the end, there was no real choice other than death, and had there only been able-bodied men remaining, the general might have chosen differently. Many of the fighting men outside the tunnel preferred fighting to the death, Bill Harris among them, but Wainwright could not condemn the wounded to be butchered in their beds. And then there were the nurses . . . seventy-seven of them. The British garrison at Singapore had surrendered at night, and in the ensuing confusion rape and murder were widespread.

"We can't hold out very much longer," Wainwright told Brigadier General Lewis Beebe, his chief of staff. "Maybe we could last throughout the day, but the end certainly must come tonight. It would be better to clear the situation up now, in daylight." With reluctance and dread, the general passed word that he would surrender Corregidor at noon. It was an impossible situation, unless everyone on the island was to be sacrificed. In fact, at the same time Colonel Sato was preparing a coordinated attack on the tunnel face with his tank support. Wainwright was also correct about another imminent assault: Major General Kureo Taniguchi was scheduled to land on western Corregidor that very night with the 37th Infantry Regiment, one battalion of the 8th Infantry, and additional tanks.

Outside on Malinta's east face, Bill Harris and the other Marines sweated in the heat and awaited the word. Japanese fighters strafed their positions, but did no damage, and Bill wanted to get back to fighting. He hoped to use Molotov cocktails to destroy the tanks, and thought he knew how to do it. As the planes flew off north, Captain Chambers emerged from the tunnel mouth, scrambling up the rocky slope to join Harris and Hogaboom.

"Major Williams just got word from the Fourth Marine Headquarters that General Wainwright is going to surrender. Have your men destroy their weapons and report back to the tunnel."

Stunned, neither lieutenant moved. Harris's first reaction was shame. "Shame that the forces of the United States, of which he was a member, had been vanquished. Shame that the flag of the United States would fall where I had fought to keep it flying." Inside Malinta, Colonel Sam Howard felt the same. Bitterness, desperation, and, lastly, shame. "My God . . . I had to be the first Marine officer ever to surrender a regiment." He burned the regimental colors and prepared for the worst.

No one defending the island could be blamed for those feelings, but strategically the battle could be viewed as a calamitous Japanese defeat. Momentum in war is important, and they were now five months late. Five months, from December 1941 to April 1942, with a sizable American force behind their lines; five months without the use of Manila Bay; and five months without the 14th Army. This was also time gained for the United States to mobilize, organize, and begin deploying—months that were used to strengthen Australia, train pilots and Marines, and build up a domestic industrial base.

Nonetheless, the surrender contingency, called Pontiac, was put into effect immediately. All codebooks and classified papers were incinerated and encryption equipment was destroyed, as were all weapons except .45-caliber pistols. Corregidor's Voice of Freedom shortwave radio began broadcasting the surrender message on 9645 kHz at 1030, May 6, 1942. At 1100 and 1145 it was repeated in Japanese.

Lieutenant Bill Harris delivered his own message to his men. "I want you to know that you're the finest group of men I've ever known. There's not a man here of whom I can't honestly say I'm proud. It was an honor to have commanded you." The young officer had been awake for thirty-one hours, and the combined strain of combat command during the shelling, invasion, and hand-to-hand fighting suddenly hit him as the adrenaline leaked away. He was utterly exhausted and desperately thirsty. Slowly getting to his feet, Bill staggered down the incline to the tunnel entrance and stepped inside. The contrast was startling, and he stopped, blinking, in the cool shade. When his eyes focused, Harris noticed an army sergeant standing against the wall.

"Say, where's the water in here?" he asked the man.

"Back there where it's always been." The sergeant was rude and abrupt, with beady eyes and a sly look that Harris immediately disliked. Boiling over, Bill snapped, "You dirty little son of bitch!" and, still clutching the rifle, stepped forward and drew his pistol. "You've been hiding your stinking ass in here for five months, and you can't even give a courteous answer to someone who's been out fighting. For two cents, I'd kill you. In fact"—he glared at the man and raised his pistol—"I'd do it for nothing." This soldier had comfortably sat out the siege while Bill and his men fought and died.

Wide-eyed, the sergeant backed up and instinctively raised his arms. Nothing this man had seen on Corregidor prepared him for a confrontation with an angry Marine officer fresh from combat. They stared at each other for a moment, the lieutenant deadly serious and the rear-echelon sergeant plainly terrified. Slowly, Bill relaxed and let the pistol drop against his leg. With a final hard look at the man, Harris continued down the tunnel and turned left into the first lateral. This led around to the quartermaster area and into the navy complex. Carefully making his way past rows of desks and typists, he wondered what the hell they could be typing. What kind of paperwork possibly mattered now?

Within the navy tunnel the officers' mess was a fairly large, cool cave dug from the rock. Inside, as Bill remembered, were several big water coolers on a table in front of a mirror. Stepping up, he caught a glimpse of himself and was startled. Dirty. He was dirty and gaunt. His khakis were torn, stained with dark mud and sweat. The web belt sagged on his right hip from the holster, and with his knife and rifle Bill looked as menacing as he felt. It was like looking at a stranger, he thought, rubbing his cheeks and chin with a free hand. He'd never seen himself with a beard, and the ten-day growth was matted, dark, and thick. His hand, Bill noticed absently, was the same muddy-brown color as his shirt.

The first cooler was empty so he smacked it and reached for the next, which seemed full. There were real glasses on the table . . . incredible. Quickly filling one with cold, clear water, Bill closed his eyes, letting the water cut through the dust in his mouth and trickle down his dry throat. Better than the best martini he'd ever had. Better than fresh juice in Shanghai. Better than—

"Hey you!" A high-pitched, nasal voice behind him made Bill jump. "You can't be in here. This is for officers only."

Turning very slowly and deliberately, Harris found himself facing a pasty-faced young navy lieutenant. The man was unbelievably immaculate. Pressed khakis, clean-shaven, and, as Bill looked down with open astonishment, he saw that the little prick was wearing shined shoes. *What kind of world has this asshole been living in for the last month?* he thought, shaking his head. Seeing his face, the naval officer backed away a step and swallowed hard. The man opened his mouth to speak, but nothing came out, and after seeing his own reflection Bill nearly pitied him. Nearly—until he remembered the Marine lying dead with a Jap bayonet in his chest, the sound of bullets zipping past his head, or the terror of the continuous artillery bombardments. Pity vanished. Like the army sergeant, this guy had been nowhere near any action, risked nothing, and slept safely every night. Eyes hard, he slammed the glass down and it shattered. Screw him.

Bill didn't actually say a thing. There was no need. All the frustration, loss, and rage must have shown in his expression. Then the man's large, round eyes fell to Harris's collar and, seeing the lieutenant's bar with the Marine Corps globe and anchor, he stammered an apology. Backing up hastily, the naval officer collided with the wall, yelped, then turned and ran out. Taking a deep breath, Bill filled his canteen from the cooler and walked out into the tunnel. Making his way toward the east entrance, he passed a gaggle of men in the quartermaster area and discovered everyone who wanted fresh clothing could get it. Minutes later, holding new shoes, underwear, socks, and khakis, Harris bumped into Colonel Sam Howard.

At fifty-one, his regimental commander looked a decade older at the moment, but he smiled nonetheless and extended his hand. "Hello, Bill. I'm certainly glad to see you. I had heard you were killed."

Harris grinned back at that, his dark face lighting up. "Not quite yet, sir."

"Just a moment before you go." Howard jerked his head sideways. "I have a treat for us. I don't think any more of this is likely to show up soon, and we can't delay much."

This said, the colonel pulled a fifth of Scotch from a haversack he was carrying.

"Damn," Bill muttered, smiling even wider. "Where'd this come from, Colonel?"

"The back part of this lateral is home to the senior members of the general's staff. They had a big final party last night, and I liberated this from their private stock." Everyone nearby had a swallow, then wolfed down a quick meal of corned beef hash with apples. Bill slumped on the concrete, and as his second wind evaporated, the combination of a meal, Scotch, and fatigue put him under.

Meanwhile, the final bits of Plan Pontiac were put into effect. Before the communications equipment was destroyed, Corporal Irving Strobing, manning the Army Signal Corps set, sent this message out to Hawaii:

My name is Irving Strobing. Get this to my mother, Mrs. Minnie Strobing, 605 Barbey Street, Brooklyn, N.Y. They are to get along O.K. Get in touch with them as soon as possible. Message, my love to Pa, Joe, Sue, Mac, Harry, Joy and Paul. Also, to all family and friends. God bless 'em all. Hope they be there when I come home. Tell Joe, wherever he is, go give 'em hell for us. My love to you all. God bless you and keep you. Love. Sign my name and tell my mother how you heard from me.

The final act was to lower the American flag on the hill and run up a white bedsheet in its place. At 1200 exactly, Captain Paul D. Bunker lowered the Stars and Stripes from the Old Spanish flagpole near the topside parade ground. Val Gavito, who was present for this, wrote: "The flag was slowly lowered while we all stood at a salute, taken off the rope without it touching the ground and placed in a small bonfire started for this purpose. When the flag was completely burned, a white sheet was raised in its place."

Just before the flag was lowered, the navy communications officer, Commander Melvyn McCoy, handed a scrap of paper to his radioman and told him to send it, unencoded, to the Pacific Fleet Headquarters in Honolulu. At 1155 on May 6, 1942, Corregidor broadcast its final message:

"Going off the air now. Goodbye, and good luck."

The girl was beautiful.

Long, wavy brown hair tumbled over her suntanned shoulders as she turned and smiled—and what a smile. Even, white teeth gleamed against her tanned skin and perfectly matched narrow spaghetti straps holding up a thin sundress. It was pressed against her body in the sea breeze, showing her curves and taking his breath away. She motioned with one hand so he stepped forward, heart beating, and the girl put a small hand on his shoulder. He reached for it . . .

Bill Harris woke with a start, his hand gripping a wrist that was shaking his shoulder. It was Bill Hogaboom, his academy classmate, and he was saying something.

"Jesus! You're hard to wake up . . . the Nips are coming."

No beach and no girl. Just a hard, concrete reality. Sighing heavily, Bill sat up awkwardly and stifled a groan. Everything hurt. Standing, he slowly tried to stretch the kinks out and winced. Suddenly, those ahead in the tunnel parted and "a moment later, in came a short, slight Japanese soldier, clad in yellowish tan, with roll leggings and a baseball-type cloth hat from whence hung flaps to his shoulders," Bill recounted. "With a helmet strapped on his back, this Jap was carrying a ready, bayonetted rifle. He seemed to look straight at me, and I froze in position, staring back at the shiny bayonet. Another Jap appeared, and then another, and another. Soon at least a platoon had arrived."

Six Japanese officers appeared, all carrying swords, and walked through the tunnel. They noticed a few of the young army nurses and Bill tensed, but they did nothing. More enemy soldiers appeared, and there was a good deal of milling about. Harris got the sense that they didn't really know what to do with the prisoners. Japanese did not surrender, and apparently had not given much thought about how to handle this.

Then something happened that he would never forget. One American stepped forward from the crowd and bowed obsequiously. He was wearing a ridiculous rose-colored kimono over khaki uniform pants, and when he straightened up Bill recognized the pinched face. It was the same shitty army sergeant from the front of the tunnel. *That son of a bitch!* Harris thought. *He's even lower than I thought. Wish I'd at least punched his face in. Damn! I wouldn't guide these bastards to a full urinal.*

Speaking rapid Japanese, the sergeant was plainly offering to guide the Japanese, and they appeared somewhat surprised. After a few minutes, soldiers gestured for everyone to stand back against the walls, and the army sergeant began pointing out the American officers. Like everyone else, Bill knew the stories from Singapore and China and wondered if they were all about to be bayonetted or shot. *If he sees me, I'll be first*, Harris thought. *But I'll kill him, at least, before they get me.* Yet the sergeant seemed to be concentrating on the army officers, and was pointing derisively at one captain, in particular. As the officers stepped forward, the Japanese gabbled at the wristwatches and rings, then had the Americans turn out their pockets. It wasn't to be murder, not yet anyway, just looting.

A short, stocky soldier looked up at Bill. His eyes were dark brown, nearly black, and he had a fat face. Arrogant, pushy, and loud, he pointed at Bill's wrist and shouted, "Watchu!"

"No watchu."

Harris stared down, unable to conceal his contempt, and the soldier noticed. His face stiffened. "Ny kah?" He shouted again, and Bill noticed the man had a gold tooth.

"No. Watch. For. You."

Motioning for the American to raise his hands, which he did very slowly, the soldier searched Bill's pockets. Discovering a wallet, watch, and his Naval Academy class ring, the Japanese grinned, grunted, then thrust them into his shirt pocket. "Watchu mine." he roared, enraged. "Watchu mine. Liar!"

Lying was apparently regarded as defiance, and the soldier was furious. Holding his rifle in his left hand, the man struck Harris ten times across the face as hard as he could. However, the Japanese was so short he could only reach the underside of the lieutenant's left jaw. Clenching his teeth, Bill kept his jaw low and absorbed the blows. Still, the man was hitting with all his strength and, though his vision blurred, he never looked away. Glaring down at the soldier with all the hate he felt at the moment, which was considerable, he thought, *For two cents, I'd grab your goddamn neck and wring it until the blood squirts out of your eyes.*

The other Japanese began moving on down the tunnel and, with a reluctant, hate-filled glance over his shoulder, the soldier who'd slapped Bill did the same. The situation in Malinta settled down somewhat after that, with the Marine officers continuing to talk and speculate among themselves. No one had any experience with surrender, and they wondered if they'd all be kept on Corregidor or taken to the mainland. Or, worst of all, to Japan.

Bill Harris, in considering his situation, had no intention of suffering either fate. He might have been forced, under orders, to surrender for the good of the wounded and the nurses, but no one could order him not to escape. With that in mind, he lay down on the hard concrete to sleep for the night and felt better. The unreality of the day had passed, and he knew this was the new reality. New, that is, until he could create something better for himself and anyone else willing to continue fighting back.

As it turned out, surrendering Corregidor was just as confusing as the battle had been. The Japanese were in no hurry to accept and, since they viewed this act as a disgrace, did not consider surrender a priority. Any force on the verge of surrender was defeated anyway, so why bother? Saving lives was not important. In the case of Corregidor, Lieutenant General Homma would agree to accept surrender only if it included *all* American forces on the fortified islands in Manila Bay and the rest of the Philippines. General Wainwright, though given command after MacArthur fled to Australia, resisted the Japanese demand in hopes that U.S. forces, particularly those on Mindanao, would continue fighting.

Masaharu Homma was having none of it.

He understood completely that Wainwright was attempting to negotiate a local surrender only, leaving the rest of the Philippines free to fight. Having lived a decade in the United Kingdom, Homma spoke fluent English and had earned the British Military Cross while serving with the East Lancashire Regiment on the Western Front in 1918. Unlike most Japanese generals, he was aware that a different culture was not necessarily a weaker one. Homma publicly ordered that prisoners of war were to be treated fairly, and that the Filipinos were to be considered brothers, not enemies. He knew the Western code of conduct and was certain that any violation of it on his part would cause more trouble than it was worth.* The Japanese general had less experience with the Americans, but did not intend to spend the war hunting down guerillas. Homma meant for Corregidor's surrender to be the end of it.

Again, Major General Wainwright found himself in a corner with no choice. He tried to confine the surrender to the fortified islands in the bay—Fort Mills (Corregidor), Fort Hughes, Fort Frank, and Fort Drum—but the Japanese refused. There was also a considerable delay in meeting with General Homma, and in the meantime sporadic fighting, including aerial attacks, continued on Corregidor. By late afternoon, the Type 97 tanks were within yards of Malinta's entrance with their 47mm guns aimed down the tunnel. An eight-

---

* Homma stated in his postwar trial that the conquest of Corregidor forced him to delegate responsibility for the Bataan prisoners to Major General Yoshitake Kawane, who orchestrated the infamous Death March to Camp O'Donnell. The trial became a case study for the limit of a commander's control over their subordinates. Many felt Homma was wrongfully held accountable, while others fiercely advocated his punishment. Found guilty, Masaharu Homma was executed by an American firing squad in Manila on April 3, 1946. Kawane was hanged.

man flamethrower squad also appeared, nozzles pointed inside, and the message was obvious: accept the Japanese terms, or those in the tunnel will die. Wainwright later wrote, "That was it. The last hope vanished from my mind."

As Bill Harris dreamed of freedom, an escape was actually made from nearby Fort Hughes on Caballo Island. Lieutenant Commander John H. Morrill, captain of the minesweeper *Quail*, had scuttled his ship the day before, and when word arrived of the impending surrender, he set out for Australia on May 6 in a thirty-six-foot motor launch with seventeen of his men. Thirty days later, the ragged group had crossed 1,900 miles of enemy territory and limped into Darwin. Bill would hear of this magnificent feat later, and it provided much-needed inspiration. At the moment, however, he had other issues.

Awaking in Malinta, his gut was burning, his muscles were tight, and cramps shot through him once in a while. Bad food would do that, and he hoped that's all it was. There was no organization today. The Americans milled around inside, and the Japanese didn't seem to care. Soldiers walked down the main tunnel and there were sentries at either end, but they also seemed tired and a bit careless. These were combat troops, and very likely needed a rest as well.

A night's sleep certainly made a difference to Bill, and he began thinking again. He'd been really beaten down yesterday with no fight left at all after the surrender, but he had to get away. There was no other way for him, and Harris regretted being so exhausted yesterday. Still, what chance was there of getting off the Rock unless he swam for it? Three miles or so across the North Channel back to Bataan wasn't so bad, but then he remembered seeing all the sharks beyond Officers' Beach and was less excited about that option. Maybe that's why the Japanese were so casual about guarding the prisoners.

Eventually, the Americans got word that everyone below the rank of colonel was to move to Malinta's west entrance and wait, which they did. The Japanese then marched the line of men out onto the Bottomside area of the island and turned left toward the South Dock. There had been much speculation during the night that the Japanese were taking them by boat to the mainland, so maybe this was it.

It was not.

Continuing south, they turned east along the coast road back toward yesterday's battlefield. As a car approached, the prisoners were made to move back so it could pass, and Bill swore. It was a new 1942 Buick; in fact, it was Major Williams's car. He'd bought it in Shanghai and shipped it to Olongapo with the regiment. There were two Japanese officers in the back now, with a chauffeur up front. Bill stared harder as it passed, then swore again. The chauffeur was the same worthless army sergeant who'd shown up in a kimono and collaborated with the enemy.*

"He's a miserable bastard," Harris wrote later. "Absolutely without self-respect. And the hell of it is that a guy like that will probably operate enough to get sufficiently good treatment to live through it, while better men will die. I bet that guy would stop at nothing to get ahead with the Nips. He makes you ashamed. I thank God that at least he's not a Marine."

Continuing east, the column passed by the final Marine defensive positions and out onto the no-man's-land, where the reserves and Williams's 4th Battalion had been chewed to pieces. Marching up the rise toward Water Tank Hill, Bill walked straight into a thick, cloying stench that folded over everyone. Sickeningly sweet, it penetrated everything, and some around him began to gag. Putrid and rotting, the smell made his eyes water and got into his mouth. Bill felt bile surge up to the back of his throat, and fought back the vomit. Dead bodies lay everywhere, and they seemed to be moving. Flies . . . flies and rats. He tried not to look, but couldn't help staring at the nearest corpse. Either American or Filipino, "It was purplish black in hue and extraordinarily swollen," he remembered. "The head indeed looked

---

* This wretched person was Sergeant John David Provoo, later known as the Traitor of Corregidor.

almost double sized, and the flies swarmed over it in great buzzing hordes."

Retching and spitting, the men made it up the low hill, then turned down toward the coast. The air cleared immediately, and two miles across the blue water of Caballo Bay, Bill could see the dark silhouette of Fort Drum. As the road sloped downward now, they came around a corner, and out of the trees a low valley opened up. Fronted by the bay, there were hills on three sides and two huge buildings on the east side off the beach. He knew this place. This was the storage facility for the 92nd Coast Artillery, called the Garage, and the buildings were old seaplane hangars. Funneling into the area, each officer had a large O followed by a number painted on his shirt; Bill was O37. The Garage was now the holding area for all the American and Filipino prisoners taken on Corregidor, though the two groups were segregated by the Japanese. Tents made from blankets or anything that would provide a bit of shade from the burning sun sprang up all over the hillsides. The biggest immediate concern was water.

"I was so thirsty I couldn't tell how hungry I probably was," Bill recalled. Water details were sent up the next day to the tunnel entrance on the south side of Malinta Hill. There were three water spigots there, and the men kept busy for hours filling canteens. Food details were also sent inside Malinta to the food-storage lateral, and barracks bags were packed with supplies. "Apparently," Harris wrote, "the Japanese had no use for corned beef, navy beans, and Vienna sausages.

But the Americans did. Now, with food, water, and the initial shock of surrender behind them, there was time to consider options—namely, escape. The Imperial Army 4th Division was moved out to recover from the mauling it had received, and garrison troops from Fort Hughes were brought in to guard the prisoners. Most troops were disinterested or bored, and since Japan controlled everything nearby, where could the Americans escape to?

Nevertheless, Bill was back to his old plan of swimming the North Channel and getting over to Bataan. It was crawling with enemy soldiers, but anything—*anything*—was better than being here. The flies "swept through the camp like prairie fires," he remembered. "No one was unscathed, and the prisoners began to look worse than lepers." A few of his fellow Marine officers were up for trying to escape, and so was a young Army Air Forces lieutenant he'd befriended named Ed Whitcomb.* A navigator with the 19th Bombardment Group, Whitcomb's B-17 was destroyed at Clark Field, and he'd joined the ad hoc infantry during their fighting retreat down the Bataan Peninsula. Escaping to Corregidor on April 9, Whitcomb had commanded a 75mm beach-defense gun on Monkey Point.

"It would be a long haul across there." Ed pointed toward the Cavite shore. "They say it's about eight miles to the shore across the South Channel." Harris agreed. Both men were miserable and, like every other prisoner, covered with sores from the flies, with "little pus-filled blisters which burned like acid."

The filthy things lived in the open-air latrines, and there was no escape from them. Some eleven thousand men were crammed into an area roughly the length of three football fields, and perhaps half again as wide. The latrine pits were fifteen feet long, seven wide, and maybe five feet deep. Spanned by boards every three feet, they were a festering, maggoty breeding ground for disease. "Every individual at defecation seemed to be clothed in a living outer garment, fabricated of dirty, sickening flies," Harris recalled disgustedly. "And they could not be kept off the food. They were maddening, the way they destroyed all peace." Dysentery ran rampant, and the men "were always at the latrines, were always defiling their clothes and beds."

And men died.

Harris never knew how many, but at least twenty-five a day were hauled away and buried. Bill himself was struck down with dysentery, and knew he was now too weak to attempt a swim. *Oh God*, he re-

---

* Whitcomb would survive the war to eventually become the forty-third governor of Indiana.

called thinking one day, if I ever get over this, I'll never complain again. Too weak even to bathe, he could barely drag himself to a pit when his bowels ran. Even that was dangerous. One man fell in, and died an unimaginable death drowning in rotting excrement before he could be dragged out. But corpsmen passed around antimicrobial sulfa drugs that eased the dysentery somewhat, and the men were given little bottles of permanganate solution for the sores, which kills germs through oxidation. It was also an astringent, so quite useful in drying blisters or oozing wounds. Permanganate was purple, so the entire camp was now full of spotted, purple men, which would have been amusing under other circumstances, but no one laughed here.

In a week, Bill had recovered enough to walk again, and he volunteered for anything that got him away from camp: trash collecting and disposal; burial detail; and, most gratifying, wood gathering. This last detail was under extremely loose supervision, and parties were sent north of camp to the center of the island. Harris knew this part of the island intimately since it had been the 1st Battalion's area of responsibility. Bill told himself this was it, and when the moon was right, he'd swim for it. He'd also have to find his uncle Squire, a navy commander and his father's younger brother, and persuade him to come along.

The next day he'd decided. Rumors circulated that the Japanese were shipping them to the mainland soon, so Bill planned on escaping that very night. Heading out again with the wood detail, the lieutenant ambled back to camp a little farther north than usual to reconnoiter. From the coast road he could see what remained of Battery Kysor with Officers' Beach just below it, and beyond that lay Bataan. Just three miles away! There were no enemy boats or patrols, and they hadn't had time to mine the coast. Harris was excited. He was getting out of this little piece of hell tonight. Walking back down the road toward the 92nd Garage area, Bill passed a parked army truck near the guard hut when a Japanese corporal suddenly appeared. The man had a crank in one hand and he pointed at the truck, then at Bill.

Yeah . . . I'll do no work for you, you little bastard, Harris wrote of the incident. Shaking his head, he pointed at the O preceding the number on his back, turned, and continued down the road. For perhaps ten seconds, nothing happened. Then he heard running feet and was spun around hard by his right arm. The corporal was livid and "screaming at the top of his lungs, his face flushed and distorted with wrath." The big Marine stared coldly back. He'd been yelled at by better men than this at Annapolis and Quantico, though this one had a weapon. This particular Japanese didn't look like the others he'd seen. "There was something about him that reminded me of a sewer rat," Bill remembered. "His eyes especially, but his face generally was the epitome of depravity."

The soldier hit him on the jaw with the crank several times, and Harris glared down at the man without flinching. Infuriated, the Japanese snarled, spat, and hit the American officer again. Through the pain, Bill mentally swore. *Someday the shoe will be on the other foot . . . and I'll be killing bastards like you then.* The man suddenly stopped, breathing hard, and looked down the road toward the hut. Three other Japanese suddenly appeared and formed a semicircle around Bill, "One of whom was a senior non-commissioned officer wearing a conventional, two-handed Nip sword. This man was truly gigantic for a Japanese, being in fact no more than two inches shorter than me, with a thick, stout torso, and a harsh, brutal face. He spoke for some seconds now with my tormentor, the two of them jabbering back and forth in quick, loud tones. Then he turned and walked up to me, fist clenched, his black eyes hard and cruel."

For the first time since his bayonet fight, Bill was frightened. He had no weapon and was weak from dysentery; one-on-one wouldn't be so bad, but there were now four of them. The man struck like a snake, and Bill's head snapped back like it was hinged. A half-dozen powerful blows drove him fifteen or twenty feet down the road, with the Japanese cursing and snarling. "*Kono yarou*," he snarled. "*Busu!*" Piece of shit. Woman.

Bill's vision blurred, and spots shot out under his eyelids. Staggering, he managed to remain on his feet. Unclenching his jaw, the Marine bared his teeth slightly and glared, bright-eyed and full of hate, at the Japanese soldier. *Son of a bitch . . . I'd like to cut off his tiny balls and shove them down his dirty throat*, Harris recalled thinking. The blows kept coming, but Bill refused to reveal pain, fall to his knees, or show any weakness. In the end, he wasn't sure if he was on his feet or not, but when his mind cleared a bit, Bill realized he was still standing. Rage, frustration, and hate welled up, and with his eyes swollen shut, the Marine in him didn't care anymore. "Fucking yellow monkeys! I'm gonna fry your little nuts and make you choke on 'em . . . fuck you!"

He was aware that the punching suddenly stopped. Swallowing painfully, he opened both eyes, squinted at the soldiers, and tried to think of something else, anything else, but it wouldn't come. They did not understand his words, but they understood him perfectly and were at once shocked, then enraged. Holding out a hand, the big sergeant took a club from one of the others. Roughly spinning Harris around, a soldier kicked his legs apart and motioned for him to raise his arms.

The first blow across his buttocks took Bill's breath away. Eyes wide and gasping, he was trying to suck in air when the next came, and the next. Finally sagging to his knees, Bill vomited. With phlegm hanging from his mouth, Harris was hauled upright, and the beating continued. Hammer blows struck his legs and lower back, and the lieutenant staggered sideways, numb with pain. His vision narrowed, then blurred, and Bill felt his legs give way.

Dust. He tasted dust and realized his face was in the road. Cursing . . . there was more cursing, and each time the Japanese sergeant shook him, Bill's head hit the road. It took all three of the other soldiers to get the big American on his feet, but they did; and the beating resumed. His jaw popped, and this time he tasted blood as his teeth cut the tongue. Bill tried to clench his jaw but couldn't feel it. Raising his arms feebly, he felt them struck aside—hard.

Up . . . stay up! his mind screamed, and he willed his knees to lock so he wouldn't fall again. Somewhere in the back of his mind he realized they were beating him to death. No. No! It will not happen. *I won't die here.* The Marine officer swayed sideways, letting his head fall back on his shoulders. Cracking open a swollen eye, he caught a glimpse of the sun and a bit of blue sky before fists thudded into him again. Just under the jaw this time. Waves of nausea washed out the pain and his eyes clouded over. There was nothing now. No Marine Corps; no mother, father, or little sister. He felt nothing. Another blow sent stars shooting across his eyelids and, surprisingly, the girl's face from his dream. *I know her . . .* Then, and as everything in his mind went from gray to black, Lieutenant Bill Harris collapsed, his head in a puddle of blood and vomit.

I won't die here.

✵

THREE

TWILIGHT PASSING

EVERYTHING ON HIM HURT.

Bill's lids scraped drily over his eyeballs, and that hurt as well. Light leaked in, burning a bit, as if he hadn't opened his eyes in a long, long time. This also hurt, so he squeezed them shut again. Wriggling a few fingers, the lieutenant gingerly lifted an arm, and that wasn't so bad. Letting his fingers slowly explore his face, he felt swollen, broken lips and a bruised chin. Opening his mouth, Bill yawned, and pain shot through his jaw so badly that light flashed and his eyes flew open. Blinking and turning his head, this was so painful, he groaned and shut his eyes. I won't do that again, he thought miserably. What in the hell happened to me?

"Shit . . . I'm sure glad to see you come to." The voice sounded familiar, yet a long way off, like from a deep hole. *Where in the hell am I?* Cracking an eye again, he got a blast of light, and realized how badly his head was throbbing. What does work? Toes . . . they were all right. He ran a tongue over his teeth and didn't feel anything chipped or broken.

"You've been out almost twenty-four hours."

Out? Squeezing his eyes shut again, Bill slowly raised a hand and ignored the pain. Shifting slightly, he felt the muscles in his back spasm and instantly stopped moving. *My back . . .* Harris groaned, then remembered. The beating by the gate. The ugly soldier with the crank, and that fucking animal of a sergeant. *I'll get strong again*, he promised himself with a deep, slow breath. *Strong enough to kill that piece of shit with my bare hands. I'll shove that silly sword up his ass and laugh while he bleeds to death.*

"Honestly, I was afraid they'd killed you." He recognized the voice now. Ed Whitcomb.

"Maybe they did." He tried to focus on the other man's dim shape.

The army officer chuckled, and Bill heard him get up. "How about some chow?" There was some clinking as he gathered up the mess tins, then disappeared along the camp's perimeter, because no one cut through the middle if it could be helped. Harris grunted and very slowly sat up. He was half inside his own makeshift tent, and someone had covered him with blankets. Bill did remember being very, very cold at some point. As for now, he didn't feel like eating, but if he'd really been unconscious for a day, he needed food.

Staring from beneath the sagging blanket flap at the miserable, teeming Garage area, Bill felt nauseated. It was hot, and the whole place stank of urine and open-air latrines baking in the sun. Mixed with nearly twelve thousand unwashed bodies, a foul funk hung over the little space like a heavy blanket. Flies buzzed everywhere and, combined with the sounds from thousands of men, filled the air with a low, irritating murmur that never ceased. Relief came only at night or when the wind shifted, which was another reason his little group was on the camp's western edge near the beach.

From here, Bill surveyed the whole hellish scene. Drab olive blankets or even filthy bedsheets were strung over old poles or bits of wood and covered the flat area between the hangars and the trees. Men moved slowly about to other tents or down to the rocky little beach. Many just sat there for hours staring at the water. Life, as they'd all known it, was over. For others, men like Bill Harris, this was a temporary setback. These men stood a bit straighter, walked with some purpose, and their eyes were clear. Others, and it was shocking to see, had already given up. Bill knew he'd never understand that. He'd been taught, and truly believed, that as long as one lived, there was hope. He was alive and intended to remain so.

Ed reappeared, stepping awkwardly over the rocks and between the men on the beach while balancing the mess tins. Plopping down beside his friend, Whitcomb handed over a battered cup with some rice and corned beef on the bottom. The rice was cold, and the meat was probably left over from 1918, but Bill suddenly felt ravenous. Wolfing it down, he took the proffered canteen of sweet lukewarm coffee and drank. Better. His head ached less, and he noticed his vision sharpening. Both men sat in silence watching the Garage area, and Harris wished they'd gotten here first so they could be inside one of the two enormous hangars. How cool it must be, and no sand.

"Ed," he swallowed and slowly asked. "Exactly what happened?"

"You really want to hear?"

"Yes."

"Well, I didn't get there until it was half over, but that dirty Japanese son of a bitch beat you with that club, and his fist, and kicked you until I didn't see how you could possibly live through it. It was the most awful thing to watch. When he finally finished, they all looked at you and laughed and walked away. I picked you up quick then, and brought you back here. Then I went for a doctor. He said all we could do was to cover you up and wait, so that's what we did."

Bitter burning anger . . . it rose up as Ed told his story. Anger at not being able to fight back, and knowing full well he was a match for any of these men without their clubs and guns. He was angry at the nitwits in Washington who were supposed to see this coming and did nothing or, worse, disregarded the situation. Everyone out here certainly knew the Japanese were going to attack. Hell, anyone with a brain west of the Potomac River could see it happening, but he expected nothing better from politicians or generals. Most of them, anyway. There were exceptions, like his father or Jonathan Wainwright, but Bill, and many of those now trapped as prisoners of war, knew Douglas "Dugout Doug" MacArthur was certainly not such an exception.

"First," he wrote years later, "MacArthur went and lost all our planes without their ever doing a Goddamned thing. Next, he moved all the troops into the Bataan-Corregidor trap, just to make it easy for the Japs to knock us under. Then by God, just before the trap closed, he ran away and got a medal of honor.* If he had moved us to the hills, we would have been fighting the Japs yet and would have been occupying plenty of their troops doing so, too. Instead of that, he had to go move us into that Goddamned Bataan trap. You'd think even a child would know better than to do that."

While Bill Harris and tens of thousands like him were stuck here, the self-styled Hero of the Pacific was safely and comfortably ensconced in the finest suite of Melbourne's Menzies Hotel, well clear of any personal danger. It was a moot point now. Harris, and anyone who would join him, had to get out now, before the Japanese relocated or executed them. Throughout the morning, other officers drifted in to check on him, and they all talked. Today was May 19, and everyone agreed that the Japanese would move them across the bay to the mainland very soon, which was why Corregidor's North and South Docks had been repaired. If the enemy intended to butcher them, surely it would have been done ten days ago to spare the effort of containing prisoners. A few men clung to the rumor that they would be held in a resort near Tagaytay, while others, rather implausibly, believed they would be repatriated to the United States through Vladivostok. Why the Japanese would return captured men during a war was not discussed; hope, even false hope, was a welcome distraction.

On one thing, most agreed: escape would be easier once they were

---

* As with much of MacArthur's "heroism," it was carefully staged, and in this case our nation's highest award for valor was bestowed for political reasons. As General George Marshall himself stated, "there is no specific act of General MacArthur's to justify the award of the Medal of Honor under a literal interpretation of the statutes." MacArthur, of course, did not object and saw nothing wrong with adding this sacred award to his collection.

on the mainland. Squire Harris, who had dropped in to check on Bill, agreed. The older man doubted he could make the swim and planned to make his escape once back on the mainland. There were more choices, to be sure, and Filipinos there who would be fighting the Japanese. There was some merit to this point of view, but Bill's gut instincts rejected it. Right now, the prisoners were in a gray area created by the confusion of battle, but Japanese disorganization faded each day. The more time they had to consider and address the problem, the harder it would be to escape. Also, and this was a priceless advantage, the Americans had a geographic advantage here, such as it was. Bill had been over every inch of Corregidor during his months here: trails, beaches, hiding places—he knew them all. On the mainland, there would be none of this. "A man who stays here could be in Japan then, or another world," he wrote of his conversation with Hogaboom. "How long do you think you could survive this camp?"

As his friends chatted quietly, Bill drifted off to sleep thinking of the girl's face again. Who was she? Awakening with late morning's sticky heat, he felt vastly better with no headache. Though incredibly stiff, he could sit up without groaning, and noticed a few recent changes in the Garage area. In addition to segregating the Americans and Filipinos, the Japanese organized officers and enlisted men into separate groups, which could be preparatory to movement. Food was also strictly rationed, so the Japanese were running out of it and simply using up what remained. More signs of impending change.

Bill watched all day from beneath the blanket, napping and gathering his strength. He noted the guards seemed more indifferent than ever—and, best of all, organized work parties left camp periodically to empty trash, bring water, or collect firewood. This last detail interested him the most, and he fell asleep thinking of it. By the time he awoke the next morning, Bill Harris was ready to resume his plan. Walking to the beach, he swam a few yards and lay back, the sun on his face, floating in the tepid water, and evaluated his condition. Ed Whitcomb and Bill Hogaboom kept his sores covered with permanganate, so they were drying and healing, and the dysentery had abated for the time being. His backside was blackened from the base of the spine to his knees, yet he could move well enough, and his stamina seemed fine.

Bill was certain he could do it; besides, there was no real choice. That evening, in low tones, he spoke to his friends about it. "I've got a proposition for you guys," he now told them. "I'm fed up with this place, and I'm going to take off. How about you two coming along?"

They were interested and intent. Whitcomb had decided on escaping and simply said, "Hell, I've had that idea myself, but I was going to wait until I thought you were okay again before putting it to you."

"What's your scheme?" Hogaboom asked.

"We'll sneak out of here at night going out behind that back latrine up there. It'll be a snap, as you know. We'll head up over the hill to my old defense sector; and when we get there, we'll get one of those short two-by-twelve timbers which you used, Ed, for top cover support for your machine-gun emplacements. We'll strap our gear to that and tie the damned thing to me. Then we'll swim to Bataan. I'll pull, and you two push."

"What will we do when we get there? And how will we eat?" Whitcomb wanted to know.

"We'll live off the country. The Filipinos will help us plenty, for one thing."

"I don't know. Everyone in camp seems to think they've turned against us."

"Japanese propaganda. They fought damned well—as well as the Americans did. You can't dispute that. The ones in my platoon I'd trust to the limit; and they were just typical average Filipinos. I think they're just about all that way, but suppose they have changed over. We could still steal from them and kill wild pigs and monitor lizards. In the long run, we'll eat better than we will here."

"How about sharks? That's three or four miles we'll have to swim, and you know as well as I do that these waters are infested with them. Do you remember that big one we saw in January?"

"Yeah, but he's the only one I've seen. I say it'll be damned bad luck to be at the same place with a shark at the same time. Anyhow, I'll take my chances with sharks any day, and will let other people take theirs with the Japs."

Harris and Whitcomb volunteered that afternoon for the wood detail, and noted there was no head count or real organization. They were marched out to the crossroads below Water Tank Hill and ordered to gather wood, then return in one hour. The two officers headed directly over the little hill toward Bill's former command post four hundred yards away. It felt strange, like "walking in a ghost-land," he observed, and the landscape was ghostly. Surreal. Memories flooded back: images of a few better times, and the faces of his men as he'd last seen them. There were no bodies now, but Bill clearly remembered the area as it had been. Like a photograph. American and Filipino corpses had gone into a mass grave, but the Japanese bodies were taken to Kindley Field, where a hand was severed from each one and returned to their families; then the remains were burned.

He and Ed quickly scoured the place. They found some rope and tossed it into an undamaged dugout behind one of the 37mm gun positions. Dry and concealed, this would serve very well as a hiding place tomorrow once they were clear of the work detail and awaiting darkness. Walking farther around the road bend behind Kysor, they came into the draw where Bill's wild bayonet fight occurred. He found both .30-caliber machine-gun emplacements and a four-foot plank they could use to float their gear in the channel. Carrying this back to the first dugout, Harris also discovered his old cache of C-rations, so the men added four cans of meat and beans to their small hoard. Gathering some firewood, they headed back to the rendezvous and then into camp. No one counted heads, and no one seemed to care. In fact, many men straggled back to camp alone or in small groups.

This was all good.

The next morning the men met and decided today was the day. Groups of Japanese officers had appeared on the camp's fringes that morning and appeared to be counting the prisoners. Repairs on the docks had finished, so Harris concluded they were about to be moved, or executed. Either way, it was time to go. Hogaboom, to his surprise, decided against the attempt. "I tell you, Bill, I just don't think there's a chance your way. A guy has to be sensible in weighing his chances. I don't want the freedom of death. You'll be shark meat almost certainly, so I've made up my mind to stick it out here."

Bill was disappointed. He and Hogaboom had been friends since Annapolis, but in the end every man has to call it the way he sees it. In any event, nothing was going to stop him from getting out, and Whitcomb was equally committed. Both men packed a web belt, canteen, and change of clothing into their hip haversacks, figuring that if they stayed in the middle of the group no one would notice the gear. They ate lunch at noon, then settled down in the heat, with the flies, to wait for afternoon work call.

On the way out to gather wood, a guard eyed Harris's haversack but said nothing, and once the formation split, both men made it safely to the dugout within ten minutes and settled down to wait. "I found several bottles about half-full of quinine tablets," Ed Whitcomb recalled. "Into another bottle I squeezed thirty paper dollars and sixty pesos, which I had managed to keep from the Japanese, and [I] put them in the hip pocket of my trousers with my silver wings and dog tags."

For five hours the men waited, tense and alert for every sound. Once they heard a faint Japanese voice, and later a siren sounded. Had their absence been discovered? Bill didn't see how that was possible, but one never knew. Maybe the guard had made a head count. Maybe someone, to curry favor with the enemy, had informed against them. He didn't want to believe that, but people you thought you knew could behave very differently under adverse circumstances. He tried not to think about the loathsome, kimono-wearing army sergeant at Malinta, because if there was one like him, there were likely others. Bill knew men who talked the talk during peacetime, yet when the iron began flying, they failed miserably. Others who never seemed to have their act together became calm, cool, and collected.

But no one came after them.

As the heat faded, so did the light. Bright white, to ocher, and finally the horizon became a deep orange smudge as darkness spread, and the moon rose. Quiet. It was so quiet that both officers were uneasy. It seemed incongruous that "at that time, one of the most important and probably the most dangerous in our lives, everything should have been so peaceful and quiet," Whitcomb wrote. "Both of us would have been more at ease if there had been bombing and shelling." Too keyed up to speak much, the men did manage to each eat a C-ration, knowing they'd need the energy before dawn.

At about 2030, all was dark and still, so they crept cautiously from the dugout, pausing in the trees above the draw. Listening a few minutes, they heard nothing, not even birds, and Harris idly recalled he hadn't even seen a bird since the invasion. Slowly walking down to the road in the draw, they remained in the shadows and walked north toward Infantry Point. Where the road bent right toward Kysor, they stopped again and listened. Nothing. Nothing but the rhythmic slap of waves on rocks. Carrying the board between them, Bill led the way left over the bluff and down through the scrubby trees onto the rocky beach.

Narrow and pale in the faint moonlight, it ran about seventy-five yards north, then disappeared beneath the steep cliff that formed Infantry Point. Stepping awkwardly over the rocks, they stopped some fifty yards up the shoreline where the water was still calm and lashed their packs to the board. "We both tore our trouser legs off high above the knees," Ed Whitcomb remembered, "thus converting them from army khakis to swimming shorts."

Bill pulled his canvas pistol belt from the haversack, flipped it around his waist, then fastened the buckle. Looping the excess rope from the board through the belt, he paused a moment, staring across at Bataan's black outline. It looked much farther than during the day, and he tried not to think of the sharks, especially the one here just a few weeks earlier. Would he feel the teeth ripping into him, or would it mercifully send him into shock? The thought of being attacked from beneath in the dark made him shudder. The Marine took a deep breath and pushed the thoughts out of his mind. It didn't matter. They were committed and nothing—nothing—would get him back onto Corregidor.

A single light glowed from Cochinos Point on Bataan, which Bill remembered well from that long-ago December day when the 3rd Battalion steamed into Mariveles Bay. Facing north as he was, the light was to his left, and a steady breeze directly hit his right cheekbone. If he could keep these references and swim straight, they could cross the three-mile-wide North Channel in about four hours. If the current held steady; if the weather didn't change; and if nothing went wrong. Lots of ifs; still, there wasn't a choice, and that made this easier. Enough. "Let's get going and stop this dammed thinking," Bill remembered whispering to Ed Whitcomb. A half hour later, outlined with silver-blue phosphorescence, Bill Harris sank into the warm water off Corregidor's Infantry Point and, with Ed pushing the plank from behind, began a slow breaststroke through the darkness of Manila Bay toward the looming outline of Bataan.

It was slow going from the beginning. The waterlogged plank and lashed haversacks were difficult to pull, so for thirty minutes the men didn't say anything. They became accustomed to the rhythm, the water, and unseen dangers all around. Imagination, even for the most disciplined of men, can be either a tremendous asset or debilitating liability. Both officers knew this and forced the idea of sharks circling beneath their feet or Japanese patrol boats from their minds. As real as those threats were, there were visible threats to worry about, like the black mass swelling over the bay's eastern shore as the stars over Manila disappeared. Big, violent thunderstorms were commonplace this time of year, particularly after dark when the land cooled, and this one was coming fast. Glancing back, Bill couldn't see any details of Corregidor, just an indistinct smudge behind them to the left. It was the same up ahead. The darkness of Bataan was lost in the surrounding water and sky. That meant they were probably midway through the channel, which was good news, but he had no visual references for navigation. There was only the wind, so Bill kept it on his right cheekbone and grimly swam on.

Drizzle began, followed by cold, heavy drops plunking into the water and onto their heads. Curtains of rain swept in across the bay, and under a hard, driving downpour, they found themselves closed in by "walls of black water and a visibility only in feet," Bill recalled. Waves built into rollers that pulled at the plank as they slid by, forcing the men to swim harder. All they could do was swim, and hope the storm wasn't driving them back toward Corregidor.

"As I swam along, I cupped my hand to my lips to catch a few drops of fresh water . . . I managed to get a few drops before a big wave swept over me and choked me." Letting go of the plank, Whitcomb spluttered and gagged, treading water and trying to breathe. Blinking away the burning salt spray, he suddenly realized he was alone, bobbing like a bottle on the waves. "Bill!" he screamed. "Hey Bill! Where are you?!" The thought of being alone in the North Channel, at night with the sharks, was terrifying. Maybe those planning on escaping from the mainland had been right after all. This was foolish and ridiculous. Heart pounding, Ed shouted again. "Bill, for Christ's sake, where are you?"

"Ed!" Muffled by rain and roaring wind, the voice sounded faint and far away, but then Harris was there: a big, solid presence, and Whitcomb felt relief flow through him like a warm drink. "We'd better check with each other and talk to each other more. Wonder where we are . . . haven't seen the light for some time."

They'd been in the water for over three hours now, and both men felt the Bataan coast was nearby—at least it should be. But everything was black: the water, the sky . . . even the air seemed dark. No light— none at all. Swimming with no reference would be futile and danger- ous, so they decided to tread water and wait for the storm to subside a bit. Thirty minutes passed; then the wind dropped to a light breeze and the waves subsided. Overhead, the storm swept west out to sea, and diamond pinprick stars suddenly appeared through torn clouds. Though the sky cleared out above, mist had formed on the channel sur- face, and visibility was murky. Nonetheless, it was somewhat clearer now, and suddenly Bill raised a dripping arm. "There it is!"

A light, fuzzy through the mist and not so far away. Relieved and en- ergized, they began swimming again. Minutes passed and as the visibility improved, Harris realized there was a row of lights below a brighter one off to the left. A ship . . . it was a ship moored offshore; a single light glowed on the masthead, and the row beneath were running lights. Voices floated out over the water, and both men froze, treading water. "It's a ship," Bill whispered tensely. "Let's get the hell outa here before they see us."

Angling to the right a few hundred yards, they tried not to splash, and a coastline suddenly appeared from the mist. Both men stopped, surprised, and stared at an undulating shoreline with groupings of lights at each high spot. "Jesus Christ!" Bill was shocked and immediately angry when he realized where they were. "That's Middleside . . . and Topside up there. The damned wind must have shifted! Looks like the North Mine Dock to me."

They were back off Corregidor, maybe eight hundred yards from the dock, and the ship had to be a cargo vessel. That meant . . . that meant they were a mile down the coast from Infantry Point. Nearly four hours, and they were back here! Ed Whitcomb swore, and both men turned back out into the bay. Tired, cold, and discouraged, they began paddling again. By now the moon had risen, and with no storm Bill could clearly see the tip of Bataan. Still, it was well past midnight and sunrise was about 0530, and by then they needed to be ashore and out of sight.

There wasn't enough time.

Grimly, both officers settled into a mechanical routine; pull, kick, pull, kick . . . a pause, then again. After two hours Bill realized the sky was somewhat lighter so he could see better, and that made his heart beat faster. Being caught in the channel by a patrol boat after all this, and then returned to Corregidor. He was under no illusions as to their fate if *that* happened, and another beating was too awful to contemplate. Filling his lungs with heavy salt air, Bill dug deeper into the water with each stroke. There was no choice—they just had to make it.

Suddenly, Ed began thrashing. Swearing in a high-pitched, fear-filled voice, he pulled hard on the plank and tried to throw a leg over one end. *Shark*. It had to be a shark . . . Bill thought as he spun around, let go of the plank, and tensed his legs to kick.

"What is it?!"

Whitcomb felt the thing pass by again, then realized it wasn't just one fish, but many. Hundreds of them. "Nothing," he managed to gasp, treading water and breathing hard.

"Knock that shit off," Harris replied sharply. "I've heard that splashing attracts barracudas." But he felt the clammy little things too, and fought back the revulsion. With night passing, the bay was alive with little fish: terapons and threadfish that nibbled on toes and fingers. It seemed, he remembered later, as if "the very water was alive." Anything was better than sharks, though he knew full well that schools of little fish would attract the bigger killers. Pushing that thought aside again, they continued across the channel.

Bill could feel little at this point. His muscles moved automatically, and the meager effects of the last meal had long since worn off. Drained and out of fuel, he was very, very cold. Teeth chattering, he stroked on through the water and thought of the Garage. The heat, the flies . . . and the complete loss of freedom. They *had* to go on. They had to make it. *This world is for the strong, not the weak,* he wrote afterward, and he was strong. He would survive, no matter what happened. That helped, and Harris raised his head a bit. At least for this sunrise he was a free man again, and his life was in his own hands.

Ninety minutes passed, and by then Bill was no longer sure of anything. His ribs were raw and chafed from the canvas belt and his feet felt like blocks of wood. There was no controlling his chattering teeth now, and he'd given up trying. Eyes stinging from the salt water, Harris squinted over the waves then abruptly stopped. Kicking awkwardly, he was staring ahead when the plank thudded into his shoulder blades. Ed was swimming sidestroke and didn't know he'd stopped until they collided. A very faint glow spread up along the eastern sky, and there, a hundred yards before them, was a line of big seagoing barges. Rocking on the waves, they appeared empty.

"What do you think," Bill gasped between his chattering teeth, "about crawling on one of these barges . . . and hiding for the day?" His tongue felt thick and furry.

"Hell . . . no." Whitcomb was also shaking badly. "I'd rather take a chance . . . and go on . . . and get this . . . over with."

Paddling forward between the widest gap, by the time they made it through the barges the sky was light blue, and Bill could make out trees along a low shoreline. "Ed! Look!" He was excited now, and waved an arm ahead. "There it is! No more than four hundred yards either!"

It was true. Dawn arrived suddenly in the Philippines, and with it came a clarity they'd missed for nine hours. There was nothing quite like a bright sunrise following a dark, dangerous night to give a man hope, and they had it now. "We were landing in the center of a cove in the shape of a roughly ninety-degree circular arc," Bill recorded. "The gray-blue [sky] continued to brighten. Off to the right was a rock boat jetty from which a road led inland."

There was also a substantial stone bungalow about thirty yards back from the water. It was certainly occupied, and with that line of barges just offshore, it seemed logical that whoever was inside was Japanese — or worked for them. Neither man was in the mood to take more chances, and they decided to get ashore fast, then make it into the trees. Bill felt his feet touch solid ground for the first time since the previous night, and his spirits soared. *We did it . . . we actually did it!*

Straightening his legs, Harris winced as pain stabbed through the cramped, cold muscles, and he tried not to fall. Gasping, Bill kept going, pulling Ed and the plank over the rocks, "Like two sea monsters emerging from the water." Whitcomb would never forget that moment. "We struggled our way onto the shore." Harris recalled, "Our muscles evidently still thought they were swimming . . . and [we] awkwardly and clumsily tripped and nearly fell time and again, our progress almost like the flopping of a pair of seals."

Dragging the plank, both men stumbled a hundred yards down the beach past the bungalow to the stone jetty. Breathing hard, they got across the road and into the trees on the far side, then stopped, hands on their knees and sucking in air. They were free! No more camp or filth or Japanese bastards. Untying the haversacks, they left the plank and pushed farther inland away from the road. Mount Mariveles loomed green and large off to the north, but the foothills were at least three miles distant and neither man was up for that today. A few hundred yards into the trees, Bill and Ed halted in a small clearing and collapsed. Ravenously hungry, they tore into the last C-rations and wolfed down a quick meal. Feeling better, both officers stripped off their wet clothes and hung them on the bushes to dry. Mentally and physically spent, as the morning warmth soaked into their tight, cold muscles and exhausted bodies, they stretched out naked beneath the rising sun and fell fast asleep, free men again.

Late afternoon had deepened the shadows, and Bill Harris slowly rose, stiff and still cold. Cold. Who would have believed that yesterday, he thought, and pulled on his dry, torn clothes. He woke Ed Whitcomb, and both men stared across the choppy North Channel at Corregidor's dark outline. It was hard to believe the pounding that little island had taken; millions of pounds of high explosives, and thousands of bombs from aircraft. All those dead men. Even those who didn't know they were dead yet. Yet, despite being surrounded by the enemy, with no food or weapons, both officers were certain they'd done the right thing. Hogaboom, Uncle Squire, and others like Squire, might believe there was a better chance of escape from a mainland prisoner of war camp, but Harris knew opportunities had to be seized whenever they appeared — especially in war.

I don't think you can ever appreciate freedom until you lose it, he remembered thinking, gazing at the Rock. To me, it was always just a word. I knew people had fought and died for it, but I didn't really and truly realize why. I sure do now. There's hardly anything so important as just to be able to say to yourself, "Well, I think I'll go there and do this" and then to be able to go right ahead and do it. I never fully understood before just what the old States really has to offer. It must be hell to live in a country where you're not free. He knew then and there he would never forget.

"Come on." Bill jerked his head toward the northeast. "Let's get a move on and take advantage of this daylight enough to get inland a ways."

"Okay." Ed pulled on his shoes, then looked up. "You know," he casually remarked, "I've gone into this thing blindly long enough. Now I want to find out where we're going and how. What're your ideas?"

"To get the hell out of southern Bataan — fast — and to get away from these Japs. What I think we ought to do is to head for some sparsely inhabited place not too far off where there aren't many Japs and are plenty of friendly natives."

"I haven't the slightest idea of where we are, except that I feel certain we are somewhere west of Cabcaben Field. If we can find the field, I'm sure we can find some Filipinos who will give us food."

It was a reasonable plan, and Whitcomb had spent January through April 1942 at Cabcaben, so he knew the area. Foothills leading directly up Mount Mariveles were about three miles to the northwest, and that was the quickest way inland, but it was also the most exposed. All roads on southern Bataan came together below the mountain, and the Japanese would be thick in the area, so they needed to avoid lines of communication. About four miles due west, directly behind them, was Mariveles Harbor, so the only way out was northeast to the ridgeline overlooking Cabcaben Field, then up along its spine to the mountain. Once there, they could skirt the peak and come down on Bataan's west coast.

Emerging from the bushes, Harris picked a peak across Manila Bay for a reference and began walking. A breeze coming in from the North Channel kept the bugs away, and the terrain here was mostly flat with scattered groves of coconuts or mangos for cover if needed. By the sun, Bill figured the time at around 1700, which gave them about three hours of light. The ridgeline was two miles away, and even with caution they should have no problem in getting to it before night fell. Cautiously angling across the open fields, they came across piles of discarded clothing, boots, and weapons: the detritus of war, but no Japanese.

Whitcomb vividly recalled the first few days of April 1942, only six weeks earlier, which were the last days of the Allied defense of Bataan. Back in December 1941, General Homma, commanding the 14th Imperial Japanese Army, had been given two weeks to conquer the Philippines, but by April was still hung up by the stubborn Allied defense of Bataan. Without control of the peninsula, there could be no conquest of Corregidor, and Manila Bay would remain useless to the Japanese. The Philippines were vital to southern Imperial expansion into the resource-rich Dutch East Indies and Malaya, so time was precious. Under immense political and military pressure to end the fighting, Homma's 4th Division and 65th Brigade managed to breach the last Allied defensive positions about thirteen miles up the peninsula between Orion and Bagac. Blowing a gap through Brigadier General George Parker's II Corps sector in eastern Bataan, the Japanese headed south around Mount Samat and Mount Mariveles. As Allied forces in the east crumbled, the right flank of I Corps, deployed west of the mountains, was now exposed, and Brigadier General Albert Monmouth Jones was forced to fall back. Tens of thousands of American and Filipino soldiers were now in full retreat toward the only way off Bataan: the port of Mariveles.

Arriving at Cabcaben back in January 1942, Ed Whitcomb was part of a communications section made up of men like him who lost their aircraft during the Japanese attacks on Clark Field. In charge of setting up the radio transmitter and receiver, he also patched together a telephone exchange linking Cabcaben and Bataan Fields to their headquarters up the road near Little Baguio, northeast of Mariveles. Meant as an auxiliary strip, Cabcaben was just a field "scraped off the rice paddies . . . at the point nearest to the bay," and by early April they were down to just a few P-40 fighters and the men were slowly starving to death on one-quarter rations. Jim Dey, another stranded officer, came in one day with honest-to-God *meat*, and Whit remembered being thrilled. "What's this?" he asked. "Petrified squirrel?"

"No boy," Dey replied with a grin. "That's the real stuff. Monkey."

"Monkey? Where did you capture him?"

"Didn't capture him. He turned himself in. Said the other monkeys had accused him of looking like a Jap."

Monkey meat, iguana stew, and mangoes. Whit nearly smiled at the memory. Nearly. He'd kill for a bit of that now. Up ahead was the ridge above Cabcaben he knew so well. It was there that two National Guard anti-aircraft outfits, the 200th and 515th Coast Artillery had dug in to cover I Corps' straggling retreat. Called the New Mexico Brigade, they arrived in the Philippines during the fall of 1941 and were considered invaluable since most of the men spoke fluent Spanish.* They waited up there while fragments of the 14th Engineers, 26th Cavalry, 31st U.S. Infantry, and 57th Philippine Scouts staggered by and collapsed here in improvised bivouacs, this same area was used as

---

* In the chaotic battlefield reorganization during the Battle of Bataan, this unit was also called the Provisional Coast Artillery Brigade.

a refugee camp for thousands of civilians streaming south ahead of the Japanese and as a staging ground for part of the infamous Bataan Death March. It was here Bill and Ed passed through on their way east to the ridge.

"We were able to find shoes, long trousers, and khaki shirts which fit each of us fairly well," Whitcomb later wrote. But there was no food except onions, which both men peeled and ate immediately. Harris was particularly pleased. He'd found a workable rifle, several bandoliers of ammunition, and, the biggest prize of all: an officer's abandoned lensatic compass.* A dirt road led inland, and they decided to chance it rather than walking cross-country. After all, Bataan had fallen six weeks ago, and much of the Japanese 14th Army was busy elsewhere. With Cabcaben off their right shoulders and Mariveles Harbor to the left, the mountain loomed ahead, its eastern slopes already dark while the western face was gilded red from the sunset. It appeared closer than it was, and Bill knew the foothills were at least two miles away, and the high ground he wanted to cross were another four miles distant.

They'd never make it tonight, and sleeping anywhere near the East Road, the main artery connecting Cabcaben and Mariveles, would be ridiculously stupid. Cresting a small rise, Harris suddenly froze and stuck out an arm to stop Whitcomb. There, about a quarter mile ahead, a Japanese soldier stood in the middle of the road. Fortunately, the man was also staring at the sunset and had his back to them. Off to one side was a small booth, obviously a checkpoint or an entrance to a bivouac. Either way, they'd gone as far as possible here and ducked off the road into the brush.

Angling away with the rise between them and the sentry, they ducked into a line of trees and, after ten minutes, emerged near the

---

* A compact, tough instrument, designed for land navigation, the folding cover contains a sighting wire used with a lens on the opposite side. Accurate bearings can be taken by sighting through the lens and wire at a landmark, then following a bearing displayed on the inner compass.

East Road, roughly halfway between Cabcaben and Little Baguio. Scampering across the hard-packed dirt surface, they dropped, panting, into the bushes on the other side. Remaining in the tree line, they abruptly came to an open area on a plateau, and Ed suddenly recognized the place. The tents, cots, and mosquito netting were all gone, but there was no mistaking the site of the 12th Medical Battalion's Army General Hospital Number Two. He'd spent some happy, decent hours here with off-duty nurses like Evelyn Whitlow, Harriet Lee, and Alice Hahn, but a gloomy air still hung over the place. At its height, before the surrender, there were over seven thousand casualties packed into open-air wards scattered among the trees. Unlike Hospital Number One up the road at Little Baguio, malaria was a real problem here at the Real River, and many weakened men succumbed to the disease.

On the morning of April 7, he and Jim Dey had hitched a ride with the nurses on a convoy of garbage trucks headed into Mariveles. The women had been ordered to Corregidor, and Whitcomb had seen them several times over the following months, but he had no idea what happened to them after the Rock fell. Ed tried not to think about it. Brutality, at least by civilized standards, was normal for many Imperial soldiers. One such atrocity occurred right here in Hospital Two when a Japanese major named Hishashi Sekiguchi found a young American refugee convalescing with her two-month-old baby, and he encouraged his men to gang-rape her.

Ed and Bill made it to the rise overlooking the river when rain began to fall, and within minutes they were both drenched, cold, and stumbling down the bank into the valley. Crossing the Real, Harris led them up the opposite side onto an east-west ridgeline between Cabcaben and Mount Mariveles. As visibility dropped to a few feet, Bill took a quick sighting through the compass, and they headed up a ridgeline into the mountain. It was slow going, and now completely dark. Both men knew they should stop, but the memories from Corregidor were too stark, and the realization that they could be recaptured anytime and returned to that hellhole kept them moving. But even guts, fear, and willpower could only take them so far. They'd swam the channel last night, and set out on this three-hour uphill hike with little rest. Even men in top condition would have found the last twenty-four hours a challenge.

"I just had no energy at all," Harris remembered. "Each step required a definite effort. I wasn't thinking about anything, really . . . wasn't taking in the surroundings. I was just walking ahead step by step like a hypnotic."

Stumbling along the ridge, they finally could go no farther, physically or geographically. "We found ourselves entangled in a thicket so dense that, regardless of which way we attempted to go, we found ourselves unable to move." Collapsing beside a log, their bodies simply quit. Wet, cold, and surrounded by their enemies, both men were so exhausted after the last twenty-four hours that nothing mattered but sleep.

Sunday, May 24, dawned bright and hot with no memory of the cold, drenching downpour from the previous night. Stiff and hungry, both officers realized they'd come down off the ridge toward the Real River, which accounted for the thick vegetation. Making their way back up the slope, they found a trail leading to a little meadow, and there "I saw a sight that caused me to break away from Bill and run," Whitcomb recalled.

Cashew trees.

Narrow trunks, about the thickness of man's leg, branched out a yard above the ground into a fifteen-foot-wide spreading canopy. Clumps of fist-sized red and orange bulbs hung everywhere, and from each one protruded a single nut. Grabbing them by the bunch, Bill and Ed sat down and feasted on cashews in the sun. "We . . . were delighted with our first breakfast on Bataan," Whitcomb remembered fondly. "The sun was shining, the atmosphere was cool and pleasant, and we were on our way."

Indeed they were, but it was seventeen-odd miles across rough mountain terrain, through Japanese territory, to the west coast. Bill had decided to try for Subic Bay since he knew the land and surrounding area from his time there in December. It was the best place to find a boat, and from there they could set off for China, about six hundred miles north, or French Indochina to the west. The Japanese already had these areas under control, so they would be far less alert. Either objective seemed more attainable than attempting a two-thousand-mile trek south to Australia, especially with the Imperial Navy roaming at will through the Dutch East Indies, Malaya, and around New Guinea.

Stuffing their pockets with cashews, the men set out along the ridgeline. Keeping in the trees whenever possible, they skirted a bare spot north of the meadow and steadily continued up the climbing terrain. This ridge paralleled the Real River and, from where they stood, seemed as if it would take them about halfway up Mount Mariveles. Trudging slowly upward all morning, sometimes Harris could follow the trail, but often it just vanished. Still, by staying near the crest and correcting toward the mountain peak when possible, the men covered over two miles and ascended one thousand feet before gratefully halting on the edge of another meadow. To the west, the Real had all but vanished into the thick, dark trees of a very steep valley, and to the east the vegetation thinned out as the foothills flattened toward the coast of Manila Bay. Up ahead the terrain was clearly discouraging, and Bill could see the actual hike was now just beginning. Enjoying the midmorning sun, both officers tugged off their shoes and hung their socks up to dry. They plopped down against a pair of rocks. Neither moved, and the burning in their tired muscles lessened somewhat.

The view was spectacular.

Southeast of the meadow on the coast, Ed Whitcomb could just make out the bend in the coastline where Cabcaben Field lay, and his mind again wandered back to Bataan's final hours six weeks ago. So much had occurred and changed since then, but he had no problem remembering the details as the Japanese closed in. Ed had watched Captain Joe Moore, commander of the 20th Pursuit Squadron, lift off on April 8 in the only remaining P-40 fighter on the peninsula. Disappearing into the twilight, Moore threaded his way through the islands some 350 miles south to Cebu. This left Cabcaben with one flyable aircraft; a beat-up, single-engine amphibian biplane called a Duck.* Made by Grumman, this particular plane was the sole survivor of Patrol Squadron 10, formerly based in Mariveles Bay. Lieutenant Roland John Barnick, one of Moore's fighter pilots, managed to get the Grumman's engine working with a cylinder head salvaged from another Duck sunk in the bay.

"It was the funniest looking plane I had ever seen," recalled Colonel Carlos Romulo. "It looked like something salvaged from the city dump." The voice behind Corregidor's Voice of Freedom broadcasts to the Filipino people, Romulo was a marked man by the Japanese and had been ordered to safety once Bataan's fall became imminent, which meant Barnick's Duck. Six men crammed themselves into a plane meant to hold four, and Whitcomb watched Barnick, who was a fighter pilot and had never flown the Duck, try to get it off the ground. At eighteen minutes past midnight on April 9, after dumping extra luggage and gear, the Grumman struggled a few feet into the air on its third attempt. Barnick screamed at his passengers to "quit shaking the plane!" But they were not. At that precise moment, a severe earthquake struck, and Whitcomb remembered thinking it was a massive bombing. The shocks were so bad that the captain of an American submarine operating off the Philippine coast thought he'd run aground.

From his position on Corregidor, Bill never saw the Duck's hair-raising takeoff, but he did witness the anti-aircraft batteries on the Rock open up at the low-flying aircraft, and he did feel the earthquake. These were nothing compared to an earsplitting explosion and blinding flash that lit up southern Bataan that same morning. From

---

* Officially a J2F-4.

the meadow now, he could plainly see Cemetery Ridge, a blasted, barren hill once utilized as the II Corps' ammunition depot—the largest ordnance dump in the Philippines. Ordered destroyed, it was blown at 0200 on April 9, along with the nearby motor pool and army engineer depot. To the right of this area was another bare spot: a brown scar against the green skin of the jungle, which was all that remained of General Hospital Number One.

It was a preposterous location for the peninsula's main medical facility, but when established in late December 1941, no one believed Bataan could fall. Little Baguio was so named due to its breezy, mosquito-free climate, just like Baguio up in northern Luzon. Ten open-air wards were created from old motor-pool garages, and supplies were relatively plentiful for a few months. However, as the Japanese closed in during late March and readied their final assault, the hospital, despite prominently displayed red crosses, was hit by air strikes during the siege of Bataan.

Captain Alvin Poweleit, a doctor serving at Hospital One, described a March 27 attack as "legs, arms, heads, and bodies strewn all over the area," with miscellaneous body parts "suspended from a nearby tree." The stench of charred flesh hung over the area, and "we knew we were on borrowed time," another surgeon remembered. Whitcomb, stationed just down the road, recalled that the hospital's time ran out just after 1000 on April 7 when large-scale air strikes hit the entire area, and at least ten bombs hit the compound. "Ward 5 took a direct hit, killing 45 to 75 patients and wounding about 100 more," Poweleit recalled. Despite the carnage, the doctors and nurses operated straight through for the next twenty-four hours until word filtered down that Bataan was to be surrendered.

Staring to his left toward Manila Bay, Bill could just see over the next ridgeline to the jungles of eastern Bataan. After a four-month delay, it was here, on April 3, where the Japanese 4th Division smashed through the Orion-Bagac Line east of Mount Samat and drove the shattered II Philippine Corps south to the peninsula's tip. After a four-month delay, General Homma, pressured by Tokyo, *had* to complete the conquest of the Philippines by crushing the remaining defenders on Bataan. Only then could Corregidor be subdued and Manila Bay opened for the Imperial Army's thrust into the Dutch East Indies. In a combined assault of aircraft, armor, and over 190 artillery pieces, the Japanese punched through the line and scattered the Philippine II Corps. Out of hope, and resigned to the reality that no reinforcements were coming, the Americans and Filipinos fell back to the open area near Cabcaben.

MacArthur, now perfectly safe in Australia, continued his attempts to direct the fighting on Bataan from Melbourne and ordered a counterattack the following day. Major General Clifford Bluemel, 3,950 miles closer to the enemy than MacArthur, openly derided the order as blatantly "ridiculous" since there was no food, and wounds and sickness had reduced the number of effective fighters to less than 15 percent. A week earlier, II Corps numbered 28,000 men, but now fewer than eight hundred limped past Cabcaben.

Major General Edward Postell King, commander of the Philippine-American forces on Bataan, knew there was no choice but surrender or annihilation. Dispatching emissaries to the Japanese on the morning of April 9, 1942, King waited for an answer while everyone who could, Ed Whitcomb included, found a way across the North Channel to Corregidor. He hadn't seen the surrender, but knew the area and could see it now from the meadow. About a mile and a half up the coast atop a plateau above the Lucanin River lay Bataan Airfield, the peninsula's main fighter strip, and two miles farther was the little port of Lamao. It was there, at an experimental farm station on the south bank of the Lamao River, where King surrendered the Bataan Philippine-American forces on April 9, 1942.

Bill Harris, from Corregidor's north shore, had watched the circling warplanes, heard the distant thumps from artillery, and saw clouds of dust rise as thousands of refugees clogged the East Road into Mariveles. He knew that on April 9 Ed and another pilot named Jim Dey jumped aboard the last motor launch out of the harbor and sped across the channel toward Corregidor, eating pineapples they'd bought on the dock.

Pineapples. A delicious thought he put out of his mind entirely as they slowly rose to their feet. About three miles away to the northwest was a great scar near the mountain's summit, probably from some ancient avalanche, and Bill took a quick bearing. He had often seen it from Corregidor, but never imagined one day hiking to the place. Weaving upward along the ridge, the Marine noted the terrain was becoming steeper and more difficult. The crevasses were pronounced, and the trees much taller and thicker. Gathering small, pungent wild onions as they walked, occasionally the men spotted a wild pig darting away, and weird birdcalls floated down from the treetops. Spotting two big monkeys, probably macaques, calmly watching them from the lower branches, they paused and stared back.

"The way they're staring at you, they must think you're their long-lost brother," Ed joked and pointed. "As a matter of fact, now that I think about it, maybe you are."

"What do you mean, staring at me? What's got them figuring is what you're doing on the ground . . . and where's your tail."

That remark elicited a chuckle, but the levity wore off as they continued slogging upward. Every step sent burning cramps into their calf muscles, and hunger became a deep, hollow pit in his stomach that Bill never thought he'd fill again. He "drank water as constantly as I could to answer my stomach's continual, unsatisfied craving . . . to fill up that dully agonizing, abdominal void." Whitcomb drained his canteen as well, and both men were soon out of water. Every time Bill swallowed, he felt the skin at the back of his throat stick together, and the sensation brought back ugly memories of Corregidor. This was worse now as they could hear a rushing stream far below in one of the canyons, but neither man had the strength to climb down and then back up. Harris was certain that by following the contours they would eventually find the headwaters.

After three hours, they'd hiked over two miles and ascended at least another thousand feet by Bill's reckoning. Weak-kneed and gasping, both men simply crumpled on the lip of a hill where the trees thinned out. The bad news was that the avalanche area was only a mile distant as a crow flies, but they weren't crows. At least two steep crevasses were in the way, and the scar was a thousand feet higher. Yet the good news was water. Bill could hear it rippling over rocks at the bottom of the first crevasse, and this was enough to get them moving again.

Rocky and steep, the slope dropped five hundred feet in two hundred yards, but they managed to zigzag and stumble to the bottom. Throwing themselves flat in the mud, both officers gulped down mouthfuls of clear, cool water and then pushed back and sagged into the riverbank. There were no mosquitoes, and a wonderful, slight breeze found its way through the trees. "The water was delightfully cold," Harris wrote. "And I noticed at once the very palpable relief felt in my stomach . . . I drank and drank to push it out as much as possible."

Filling their canteens, Bill and Ed paused frequently as they groped back up the hill to the ridgeline. Crossing over the second crevasse and up onto the knobby hill, Harris could plainly see the scabby mark on the hillside and was gratified it was so much closer. No more than a half mile, he reckoned, and nudged Ed's bony shoulder. Nodding, the army officer followed as they clawed their way up the slope. By midafternoon, just as Bill was thinking of collapsing for the day, the slope suddenly fell away, and the trees parted to reveal a plateau. Sucking in fresh air, he straightened painfully, laced his hands behind his head, and realized they were near the bottom of the scar. The rest of it was plain to see, slashing up along the mountain's eastern face before vanishing into the trees below the summit. It was "covered with huge boulders and there were very few trees," Whitcomb recalled.

Utterly played out, they sank down again against a flat-faced rock and closed their eyes. It was delicious to not move, not think, and, this high up, not worry about the Japanese. "For a long time [we] looked out across the bay to Manila to the east and to Corregidor to the south of us," Ed wrote. "We sat in this quiet and peaceful spot, which seemed far closer to heaven than to the hell we had experienced over the past months." Harris agreed. Fascinated by the sight of Corregidor, where he'd passed the last five months of his life and endured so much pain, Bill recalled that from atop the mountain the island appeared "like a half-submerged, westward-swimming sea monster with a massive, long, joined head and body and an equally long, low tail."

Lost in their own thoughts and bone-tired, both fell asleep there in the warmth below Mariveles's summit. When they awoke, the sun had dipped far to the west, and everything east of them was darkening. Neither man was excited to continue climbing, and Bill estimated the peak to be a half mile away laterally, but at least another fifteen hundred feet vertically from the scar. "Did you ever hear the story of the great whore?" Ed asked, staring toward the summit.

"No, I don't think so. Why?"

"She said that her objective was to go to heaven. Well, ours isn't. Let's stop this damned climbing and start skirting the mountain on the west side. We're plenty high enough."

Bill agreed wholeheartedly. He knew Mariveles was an ancient volcano, and there was no definite peak up there past the lip—just an immense jungle-filled bowl. There was, he recalled, a river running down from the north edge, but after today's trek he had no interest in cutting his way through such a tangled mess. They agreed to follow the contours around the mountain's south slopes over to its western side, and once there make a choice: continue to the coast or cut across country north to Subic Bay. That would depend on the Japanese, but now, tonight, progress depended on how far they could go without passing out.

A thousand feet lower in the next valley they found another stream and topped off their canteens. By the time Bill and Ed scrambled up the next ridgeline, the summit was smothered with dark, heavy clouds sweeping in from the east. Angling across the next saddle, they stood atop the next ridge, gasping in a surprisingly cold wind. It cut through the thin summer khakis, and with no meat on their bones, both men began shivering uncontrollably. Then the rain came; cold sheets of it driving down from the cloud bellies. Soaked and hungry, they could go no farther.

Ed saw it first.

A slab of rock protruding from the leeward side of the hill away from the rain. Jabbing his friend, he pointed. Bill wiped his face and squinted through the gray downpour. It would have to do, and they stumbled to it arm in arm. Miserably, both men huddled together as far back as possible. It wasn't dry, but it was less wet, and still cold. Bill felt Ed move closer, and the warmth was good. Wailing eerily through the rocks, he felt the wind was carrying lost souls from the tens of thousands of men who died violently nearby—men who died young, before their time. To his weary mind, it seemed they were now coming for him.

Shaking his head, Bill struggled to master his own imagination, well aware that there were enough real demons on this mountain without adding more. Surrounded by his enemies, he was at least five hundred miles from the few American soldiers on Mindanao, if there were any, and over eight thousand miles from home. These were all good reasons for despair, but Bill wouldn't permit it. He'd gotten this far by not surrendering, physically or mentally, and he reminded himself that through the driving rain and across the narrow channel to the south were eleven thousand men who would go no farther.

But he would.

Harris had survived months of starvation, siege, and brutal combat during which others had died, but not him. He had been *ordered* to surrender; he had *not* capitulated. Refusing to submit, Bill had been nearly beaten to death, but still swam eight hours across shark-filled waters to freedom, and was now free again. That, he knew after losing it briefly, meant everything. Just forty-eight hours earlier, he had been at the nonexistent mercy of his enemies, but everything was different now.

No matter what lay ahead, the lieutenant intended to survive, and that gave him a boost, despite freezing and once again starving. His eyes cleared, and suddenly the rain slackened. Like gray shrouds, the cloud decks rolled back, retreating out to sea beneath the silver light of a full moon. Bill could make out nearby trees between wet hanging tendrils, then the next valley, and as he watched, the wet veil lifted to reveal the sawtooth coast of southwestern Bataan.

Inhaling the fresh, rain-scrubbed air, the young officer felt some strength return. Not physical strength—that would take a few hot meals and lots of sleep—but the strength of renewed hope. Twilight had passed into night with the storm, and the geography of Bataan and Corregidor that dictated his life these past months had vanished with it. Bill could see neither of them now that this very long day finally faded into night, and the metaphor was not lost on him. Here and now, atop Mount Mariveles on this wet, miserable Sunday in May 1942, he stared down the western slopes, and instead of impossible, enemy-occupied terrain, the young officer saw an opportunity. A chance to get all the way off Bataan, out of the Philippines, and back into the war. A war that had been thrust on him as it had been on millions of others; a war he did not want to fight, but must now fight.

Not because he wished to be thrown back into combat—no sane man would—but because he was trained for this and had taken an oath. Words perhaps, but words with iron, commitment, and a meaning that separated the best of men and women from the worst. Words he would honor. Winning the war, absolutely and irrevocably, was the shortest way home now, and Lieutenant Bill Harris, USMC, would do everything possible to that end.

Twilight had passed indeed.

PART II

July 1942–December 1942

Adversity introduces a man to himself.

—Albert Einstein

✳

FOUR

RED SUMMER

SHE WAS A MONSTER.

Eight hundred sixty-two feet from bow to stern, nearly three football fields in length, the enormous battleship carried 2,800 men within her heavily armored hull. Seventy feet longer than the German battleship *Bismarck*, she displaced twice the tonnage of the USS *North Carolina* and mounted nine massive 18.1-inch guns. Each turret alone weighed the same as a US *Fletcher*–class destroyer and contained three sixty-nine-foot-long Type 94 barrels capable of throwing a shell the weight of a 1942 Chevy twenty-five miles away. To her designers and builders, she was the *Great Harmony*, the world's largest battleship.

In 1942, the Americans knew her as *Yamato*.

Holding 6,300 tons of fuel oil, she could steam nonstop from Tokyo Bay to Darwin then back again and, if required, twelve Kanpon boilers generated enough power to move her bulk through the water at twenty-seven knots. Yet, by early summer 1942, *Yamato* had never fired a shot in anger: she hadn't needed to. Japan's successful war strategy stemmed from two premises: a surprise attack on the U.S. Pacific Fleet at Pearl Harbor, and the completion of its two-pronged southern operation. One prong launched from Formosa into the

Philippines to clear out the Americans and secure Manila Bay, while the second prong swept through French Indochina to Malaya, where both converged on Japan's ultimate prize: the Dutch East Indies.

On the last day of December 1941, a desperate Allied unified command was established in the Southwest Pacific to stop the Japanese advance. ABDACOM (American, British, Dutch, Australian Command) had no real chance of holding Java or Malaya, but it was hoped the combined effort would buy some time and protect the sea-lanes into Australia. In fact, bitter resistance on Bataan and Corregidor *did* significantly delay the northern prong, but in the end Corregidor capitulated two months after Lieutenant General Hein ter Poorten surrendered Java.

Field Harris, returning from North Africa in November 1941 as a newly promoted brigadier general, knew all this. By late May over a million American men had been inducted into the American military and even the Marine Corps, smallest of the service branches, was expanding madly. Like other progressive officers, Field knew any Pacific war would be a naval, marine, and air war; it had to be, despite the fervent desires of conventional big-army generals like Douglas MacArthur. The Pacific was different; only by sea and air could such vast spaces be crossed for men to fight on obscure bits of land. Flyspecks on a map, to be sure, but flyspecks controlled by the Japanese, and the tremendous distances involved were appalling. It was four thousand miles from Washington, D.C., to Berlin, but over twice that to Tokyo. To get to Manila, American materiel and men then had to travel seven thousand miles farther west past San Francisco. The long supply line from the United States would be a problem, especially since the Philippines were less than 1,500 sea miles from the Japanese Home Islands.

Now, in May 1942, the Japanese controlled the Pacific from the Gilberts west to Sumatra, and from the Chinese coast south to New Britain. Wake Island had been attacked on December 11, but the tiny Marine garrison of 27 officers and 422 men commanded by Major

James Patrick Devereux beat back the initial invasion with their six five-inch guns. This shocked the Japanese, who lost most of their 450-man Special Naval Landing Force, along with the destroyers *Hayate* and *Kisaragi*. It should have been a vivid warning that the Americans were definitely not easily defeated like the Chinese or colonial troops, and were vicious fighters once provoked. However, cut off and abandoned, Commander Winfield Scott Cunningham's fate was sealed if the Japanese returned, which they did in force on December 23, 1941, and Wake was surrendered that afternoon.*

On Christmas Day 1941, on Hong Kong's Queens Pier, Major General Christopher Maltby, commanding British troops in China, surrendered to the Imperial Army. January was worse, with the Japanese assaulting Bataan, invading Borneo and the Dutch East Indies, and capturing the port of Rabaul in New Britain. Singapore, Britain's great colonial bastion in the Far East, fell on February 15, 1942, and four days later Japanese aircraft bombed Australia's Northern Territory. Vice Admiral Chuichi Nagumo, who led the attack on Pearl Harbor, brought the big fleet carriers *Akagi, Hiryu, Kaga,* and *Soryu* out of the Moluccas to launch his first wave, and before noon 188 Japanese aircraft attacked Darwin Harbor, sinking eleven ships, including an American destroyer.† A second wave of bombers from the newly acquired Dutch East Indies struck again and, all told, at least 236 Australians and Americans lost their lives.

Three days later, the USS *Langley,* America's first aircraft carrier now serving as a seaplane tender, sortied from Fremantle with thirty-two P-40 fighters of the 13th Pursuit Squadron. She was bound for India by way of Ceylon when Vice Admiral Helfrich, the Dutch officer commanding Allied naval units in Java, ordered her to Tjilatjap. Desperate for air support, Helfrich wanted her planes and pilots.

---

* Commander Cunningham and Major Devereux survived over 1,300 days in captivity and returned to active duty. Cunningham became a rear admiral, while Devereux retired a brigadier general and served four terms in Congress.
† USS *Peary* (DD-226).

Unfortunately, a Japanese reconnaissance plane spotted her south of Java in the Indian Ocean, and on February 27, thirty-one 11th Air Fleet aircraft flew from Bali's Denpasar airfield and put five bombs into the old flattop.* She was burning, listing, and without functional steering; Captain Robert P. McConnell ordered her abandoned at 1332 and scuttled. In the middle of all this, on February 23, the I-17, a Japanese Type B cruiser submarine, slid up the California coast, surfaced off Coal Oil Point, and shelled the Elwood Oil Field near Santa Barbara. Proof enough, many said, that Japanese civilians and nisei in California were a fifth column acting on behalf of the emperor, or how else would such a vulnerable area be pinpointed?[†]

Just sixty-nine days after Pearl Harbor, this event sent a nervous West Coast into a frenzy of overreactions. Blackouts were ordered and, astonishingly, with the world at war and America backed against the wall with a Japanese knife at her throat, rioters and looters smashed windows, broke into stores, and stole merchandise. Frightened people with jittery nerves saw the bogeyman everywhere: saboteurs, snipers around defense plants, and armed bands of Japanese crossing the California-Mexico border near Baja were all "seen" and reported. Nor were these phenomena confined to California; Chicago's mayor Edward Joseph Kelly, a grammar school dropout and career sewer contractor, ridiculously stated, "Don't let anyone tell you that you are too far away from the battle for aerial attack. If the Japanese can go four thousand miles to strike by air at Hawaii, it is also possible for them to strike at Chicago . . ."

In Washington, D.C., Katie Harris read that the capital was expected to be bombed and that people were going to "die by the thousands here on these streets." Through her husband she knew enough about

---

* After *Langley*'s conversion from the collier *Jupiter*, Lieutenant Commander Godfrey de Courcelles Chevalier, USN, made the first landing on her deck on October 22, 1922, in an Aeromarine seaplane.

† In fact, her commander, Kozo Nishino, had captained a prewar merchant vessel and had actually picked up oil from the Elwood pier.

enemy aircraft to wonder how, exactly, Axis bombers would get so close to the American coast, while Field openly scoffed at such nonsense. Still, most Americans couldn't tell an Army P-40 Warhawk from a Japanese Zero, so the hysteria was not surprising. Other things did surprise her though, as life in Washington continued to change. Rationing began in January, at least for gasoline, rubber, and food. "Never announce to the American public an impending shortage," *The New Yorker* warned, but that was exactly what occurred. Katie recalled the same thing during the Great War, and wasn't shocked when beef, fruit, and canned vegetables began vanishing, though much of the shortage was due to hoarding.

Sugar was first. During 1941 the average American consumed 114 pounds of it; it was a national resource and, according to many, absolutely essential. Restaurants, cafeterias, diners, and hotels quickly put away their bowls and cubes, and housewives purchased as much as possible, often several months' worth. Panic shifted to flour, then bounced over to anything in a can. Freezers became popular items, and were packed with meat if one could find it. Butchers could be "tipped" to provide extra, and one in Queens, New York, received some five hundred bottles of booze for Christmas from his grateful customers.

If not, there was always the black market, which was thriving in 1942. At least 25 percent, and eventually as much as 50 percent, of American business was estimated to be through illegal means as the government tightened the nation's collective belt. Most Americans seemed skeptical that nearly everything had to be rationed for the war effort. Metals, rubber, and gasoline they could shrug off and justify, but jam, dried fruit, biscuits, and firewood seemed excessive. Wristwatches were among the highest valued items, with some marked up fifty dollars over normal prices. Whiskey was another question mark, as the government decreed that 30 percent of its production was necessary for the war effort, which elevated rum to the bestselling spirit in America. Fortunately, there was no shortage of rye or gin, and satirist

H. L. Mencken happily decreed that "despite all the wars and rumors of wars the supply of sound liquor in this great republic remains almost infinite."

Nevertheless, as rationing went into effect the majority of Americans tried to comply, whether from genuine patriotism, shaming, or fear of the consequences. Civilian losses of gasoline were transformational, and hit closer to home than bobby pins or zippers, as life fundamentally changed. Men in suits on bicycles became commonplace, and use of public transportation soared. Gasoline stocks on the East Coast plummeted after the first German Type IX U-boats reached North American shores on January 13, 1942, with the submarines sending 156,939 tons of shipping to the bottom during their first three weeks. Eventually, over four hundred U.S. merchant ships would go down in 1942 alone. This was greatly aided by American disdain for blackouts, and a collective failing to realize that bright shorelines from Atlantic City to Miami perfectly silhouetted merchant vessels for enemy subs prowling offshore.

Like everyone, Katie Harris was skeptical when the government instituted a thirty-five-mile-per-hour national speed limit in hopes of curtailing the fuel drain, which was even less effective than pleading with the public to voluntarily stop drinking coffee. At the end of April, fuel deliveries to eastern stations were half of their prewar levels, and emergency gasoline rationing was instituted the following month by the Office of Price Administration (OPA). This required the Government Printing Office to print 700 million booklets, a print run that, according to historian William Klingaman, was large enough "to form a tower of paper fifteen miles high."

Katie duly applied for and received the common black A card, which permitted the holder three gallons per week and was deemed adequate for those with no direct connection to the war effort. Factory workers could get a green B card allowing eight gallons weekly, while defense workers, police, doctors, and fourteen other vital professions

could obtain a bright red C card.* The coveted X card permitted un-
limited gasoline usage for those vitally important to the war effort and
national security, so 250 congressmen immediately applied for this,
as they considered themselves both vital and irreplaceable. Not only
themselves, but also family members and secretaries. This occurred as
First Lady Eleanor Roosevelt and Donald Nelson, head of the Office
of Production Management, both used A cards. Katie was embarrassed when the Democratic Senate majority leader Alben W. Barkley
(Kentucky) brazenly stated, "I am going to take whatever I am entitled
to without apology." Politicians, who generally deserved the disdain,
never seemed to accurately gauge the nation's mood, or to quite grasp
the magnitude of public loathing.

To wit, in late January a law, PL 77–411, was quietly passed amid
the confusion of the war's first month while Americans were fighting
for their lives on Bataan. Utilizing the Civil Service Retirement Act of
1920, the law provided lucrative pensions for lawmakers over and above
their existing benefits. Katie was aware that a congressman sitting at a
desk several miles south of her made about $800 per month, excluding
perks, while draftees being sent to combat were paid $50 per month, and
an average American family survived on $1,885 *per year*. Even her son,
as an officer with three years' service, was paid only $175 per month.
Katie Harris, and over 80 percent of the voting public, thought it dis-
graceful for well-fed, warm, dry, and utterly safe legislators to earn more
than the captain of an aircraft carrier. Reaction was so vehement it bordered on humorous; people sent boxes of old clothes, used sundries,
and other tokens of disgust to their congressmen, while the press had a
field day. "Unless it is erased from the statute books . . . all future pleas
for economy and sound government [are] a mockery." It was, according
to one voter in Michigan, an example of "pure bone-headedness."

---

* The C card actually had the professions listed on the sticker, and the holder was
required to check the box that applied.

Nevertheless, by late spring 1942, despite a small percentage of cheaters, cowards, draft dodgers, and profiteers, an overwhelming majority of Americans accepted war as the "new normal" and resolutely did their best. "This war is a new kind of war," President Roosevelt gravely stated during a fireside chat. "It is different from all other wars of the past." Citizens, who would send their sons to combat and toil away in factories to produce the sixty thousand aircraft, hundreds of ships, and tens of thousands of tanks required, wholeheartedly agreed. The president's budget of $58 billion was quickly approved by the Seventy-Seventh Congress, with an astounding 89 percent allocated toward defense spending, and an April revision increased this to $68 billion—an unimaginable sum for most citizens.

Yet this would not come cheap, and for the first time many Americans were now paying income taxes to help finance the war effort. The poorest Americans contributed 1.7 percent, while a middle-class family earning $2,379 per year paid 8.9 percent. This was not a new idea. The Revenue Act of 1861 was enacted to fund the Union forces fighting the Civil War, and Katie well remembered her father's anger over a similar law in 1913. With such precedents, and facing a global life-and-death struggle, President Roosevelt encountered little opposition. A "victory" premium of five cents per dollar was also levied against the eighteen million Americans who were not subject to income tax, yet made at least twelve dollars weekly.

Roosevelt also hit corporations with a 40 percent tax and introduced a whopping 90 percent rate against excess profits. Surcharges were added for telephones, telegraph messages, and gifts. With so many now paying who never previously bothered, payroll withholding and quarterly tax payments were created to eliminate bookkeeping and delays, which now guaranteed a steady stream of money into the treasury. This was not generally resented since everyone's burgeoning prosperity was due to the war effort.

A myriad of changes, both cultural and physical, were occurring because of this, and Katie followed the home front developments

keenly. It was now fashionable for women to work professionally outside the home in ways unheard of just a few years earlier. Many men
working in plants resented that women were capable of doing "their"
work, and unions, always motivated by their own best interests, resisted female encroachment, but it wouldn't last. It could not. Over
500,000 women, some 10 percent of the available total, were already
employed in war production jobs, and the demand was forecasted to
increase by another five million as greater numbers of men left for war.*

Interestingly, with orders pouring in, defense contractors were finding many advantages to hiring women. They were punctual, did not
generally damage tools or equipment, and had fewer accidents than
men. With smaller hands, females could often get to difficult areas in
aircraft fuselages and easily handle intricate fuses, parts, and electron-
ics. Amusingly, many of the remaining men began dressing better and
shaving more often. At the Douglas Aircraft plant in Santa Monica,
which Warner Bros. set designers made disappear beneath five million square feet of chicken wire, bomb shelters were shut down to
prevent amorous lunchtime coupling.

Prevented by her age from working, Katie Harris nonetheless ap-
plauded the results. Such a sea change, in her opinion, was long
overdue, though tragic in that it took a world war to shatter outdated
paradigms and usher in a new era. Nonetheless, in early summer of
1942, there were still some Americans who questioned the conflict's
necessity. Quakers, Mennonites, Seventh-day Adventists, and other
groups, to varying degrees, sought exemption from combat on religious grounds. Some twenty-five thousand of these men would
bravely serve in noncombatant roles, and another twenty thousand
were classified for "alternative service" in the United States to fight fires
or to undertake various essential construction projects. Yet some six
thousand men, mostly Jehovah's Witnesses, refused not only to register
for the draft but also to serve their country in *any* capacity, and were

---

* By the end of 1942, over twelve million women would enter the workforce.

promptly jailed for the duration. Katie, with a husband, brother-in-law, and a son in harm's way, was unsympathetic toward those who wanted the safety and advantages of American life but were unwilling to fight for those rights.

Deep in the Virginia countryside, 150 miles from Katie's apartment, nineteen-year-old Jeanne Glennon would have wholeheartedly agreed. Under the shadow of the Blue Ridge Mountains, exclusive Sweetbriar College lay nestled in the trees along Rutledge Creek just south of Amherst. Founded in 1901, its purpose was "to impart to its students such education in sound learning, and such physical, moral and religious training as shall, in the judgment of the directors, best fit them to be useful members of society." Graduating from the Gunston Hall school for young women in Washington, D.C., two years earlier, there was never any doubt Jeanne would be a proper, "useful" young lady. Her paternal grandfather, James Glennon, retired as a rear admiral and her father, navy Captain James Blair Glennon, married Ellie Murdaugh Lejeune, daughter of Marine Lieutenant General John Archer Lejeune, the "Greatest of All Leathernecks."*

This distinguished lineage was much to live up to, yet Jeanne had always felt equal to the task; it was expected, and she was completely at ease within her rarefied social circle. Quite striking, with wavy, shoulder-length brown hair and warm, intelligent eyes, she had always looked straight at life without blinking, confident and calm, ready for anything. That is, until December 7, 1941. Her father was a naval officer, and her brother James, a Marine lieutenant, graduated from Annapolis in 1939. Jeanne had been raised in the world of military officers and knew something of the risks that went with the privileges, yet that day suddenly made it all very, very personal.

"Japanese warplanes set fire to the U.S. battleship *Oklahoma* Sun-

---

* "Leatherneck" is derived from a heavy leather collar formerly attached to U.S. Marines' uniforms to protect from sword cuts or to improve military bearing, depending on the source.

day in a sudden raid on Pearl Harbor and Honolulu," read the head-line that made her sick with worry. "The White House announced Sunday that heavy damage had been inflicted . . . and that there prob-ably had been heavy loss of life." For the first time in her life, Jeanne Lejeune Glennon experienced the new and unwelcome grip of fear, one that millions of American families would feel over the next sev-eral years. She worried about her brother, of course, but there was another reason: the *Oklahoma*. She'd never seen it, of course, but she knew all about it. Second of the *Nevada* class, the battleship was six years older than Jeanne, mounted ten fourteen-inch guns along her 583-foot length, and held a crew of 1,353 men, consisting of a comple-ment of seventy-seven Marines, a fifteen-man aviation detachment, and 1,179 seamen. *Oklahoma* also carried eighty-two naval officers on her muster role, including Ensign Marshall Eugene Darby, a class of 1940 Annapolis graduate and collegiate swimmer.

He was also Jeanne's boyfriend.

Sick with worry, she, and thousands of other American families, waited for some kind of news, any news, amid the chaos of this new and sudden war. Hours stretched into days, and rumors flew; one minute all the battleships were sunk and the next Hawaii was being invaded; Japanese were crossing from the Mexican border, and Impe-rial soldiers were invincible. Jeanne had been in a military family too long to fall prey to hysteria, but very quickly she discovered the only certainty in her world immediately following Pearl Harbor was that no one knew anything for certain.

Until the Thursday after Pearl Harbor, December 11, when the ini-tial casualty lists were released. At first, Ensign Darby was posted as missing, and though this was bad, at least she had some hope. Perhaps Marshall had made it to shore but was injured; or maybe he was lying unconscious in a hospital and no one knew his identity. But three days later an expanded list, along with official notification, confirmed the *Oklahoma* had taken nine torpedoes from Japanese Nakajima 97 Kates that roared in low over the Southeast Loch, and the warship capsized in the shallow water along Ford Island's Battleship Row. As a junior engineering officer, Marshall's battle station was deep below-decks, which put him at great risk during a torpedo attack. As of December 14, Ensign Darby had not been found and was now listed as MISSING—PRESUMED DEAD.*

Strong as she was, this was a horrible blow for a nineteen-year-old girl in love, so she left Sweetbriar and returned to Washington, D.C., to be with her parents. Their Dexter Street house was nestled in a beautiful wooded enclave west of Georgetown Heights bordering Glover Park, and it was a quiet place to heal. However, the rest of the capital was nearly unrecognizable; designed for a population of a half million, it was bulging with at least 800,000 people, and increasing by 5,000 per month. There was simply no place to put them. Tent cities, shanties, and railroad boxcars were all used by those flocking to Washington for work. People were even sleeping in Union Station just to have a roof over their heads and a toilet. Congress was calling for $500 million to build new facilities, while President Roosevelt was "urging construction on the Mall for the housing of war workers," which entailed tearing up the mile-long park between the Capitol and the Washington Monument.

By late May, over 10 percent of American males aged twenty-one to thirty-five had been inducted into the military; the army alone put three hundred thousand men into uniform every month, yet this hadn't slowed social life much. On the contrary, much of the nation seemed desperate to pack as much living as possible into the days ahead. Nightclubs were jammed, and in establishments like the Jefferson Gold Room a couple could dance until closing for less than two dollars. Some of this, at least for those going to combat zones, was due to the very real chance of never returning, but also a very human

---

* As of 2020, Ensign Marshall E. Darby's remains have yet to be identified. Originally, only 35 of 429 casualties were accounted for, but through the efforts of the Defense POW/MIA Accounting Agency, this number has risen to 100 positive identifications as of December 2017.

inclination to use the crisis, *any* crisis, to get away with as much as possible.

Now that there was a war to blame, contempt and loathing for an Asian culture long viewed as barbaric rose to the surface, which fueled American resolve to win the war in a way never inspired by Germany or Italy. "I wouldn't dare send a tablecloth out to a laundry after my family finishes spilling eggs on it," ran a cartoon caption. "They might mistake it for a Japanese flag!" Kansas governor Payne Ratner ordered his police to ban Japanese from traveling on state highways, and Governor Chase Clark of Idaho stated, "Japs live like rats, breed like rats, and act like rats." Journalist E. V. Durling opined in April 1942 that "perhaps we are libeling the rodents when we refer to the Japs as rats."

Jeanne had never given Japan much thought before, though her father and brother had long been convinced the island nation would be America's next enemy. Her attitude, like those of so many others, changed after Pearl Harbor, and following Marshall's death she wanted to serve in the military. There were two problems with this: first, she was a woman and, aside from nursing, there was little opportunity—yet—but this was changing. Her father, Captain James Blair Glennon Sr., was a naval weapons expert who had served in cruisers and skippered a destroyer. Since 1938 he had commanded the Naval Ordnance Laboratory in White Oak, north of Washington, and knew the navy was close to establishing the WAVES (Women Accepted for Volunteer Service). The idea was to assign females to shore billets, thus freeing up more men for combat overseas.

This was Jeanne's second problem. To gain a commission and enter the service as an officer, she needed a college degree or two years of college, which she did have, and two years of related experience, which she did not have. Not wishing to discourage an admirable impulse, yet knowing the military, her father proposed that his daughter finish school and then serve in the WAVES as an officer. Reluctantly seeing the wisdom in this, she agreed, but only if she could complete her studies in Washington, not in the Virginia backwaters separated from her family.

Accepted for the fall semester at George Washington University, she was slowly getting excited. It was time to put the agony of Marshall's death behind her, to the extent that was possible, and move on. There was too much to be done now to win the war, and she knew that thousands of other girls were living through the same pain and loss. There was no other choice but to give up or lose hope, and this was something she would never do.

Anyway, there was enough to worry over these days. Her brother Jimmy, a marine officer, survived Pearl Harbor but would undoubtedly be in combat once America went on the offensive. There were all the other fine young men she'd met when visiting the academy who now faced lonely deaths at sea or in aircraft cockpits or who were already missing in action. Her brother's good friend Bill Harris was one of the latter, and she found herself remembering the very tall, very polite young man who came home with Jimmy several times. First was in the summer of 1936, when they embarked on their first midshipman summer cruise aboard, ironically, the USS *Oklahoma*. The last time she'd seen Bill was during the summer of 1938, before he and Jimmy left aboard the USS *Texas*. She had been only mildly interested in their adventures as there were other things for a fifteen-year-old girl to be concerned with, and Bill was soon forgotten. But now Jimmy had written that nine of his classmates, Harris among them, were dead or missing in the Philippines, and Jeanne Glennon found herself remembering his gentle smile and calm blue eyes and wondering if he too, was gone forever.

Three miles away at Marine Headquarters in the Main Navy Building on the Mall, Brigadier General Field Harris fought down that same thought every day. So, he did the only thing possible; he went about his duties and kept faith that his boy had survived. In his position with the Aviation Division, Headquarters Marine Corps, Field worked for

Brigadier General Harry Schmidt, assistant to the commandant, who essentially functioned as the chief of staff. Under pressure to correct years of peacetime neglect and expand the Marine Corps, Schmidt and Commandant Thomas Holcomb maintained a frenetic pace. Additionally, Field was working out the details of the first American offensive in the Pacific, which, due to its geography, dictated an amphibious operation. The Pacific theater would be predominantly a naval and Marine war, so there was a great deal to accomplish in a short time.

The grim strategic reality throughout the winter and spring of 1942 only exacerbated the situation and intensified the shared sense of urgency. Field knew the February 27 action near Java was catastrophic to the Allied situation in the Pacific, and later that same day the USS *Langley*, America's first aircraft carrier, was scuttled. Dutch Rear Admiral Karel Willem Doorman led the remnants of the ABDA Combined Force (ABDACOM) from Surabaya Harbor out into the Java Sea. Searching for a Japanese invasion convoy transiting the Makassar Strait, Doorman's five cruisers and nine destroyers were intercepted by an eighteen-ship escort fleet under Rear Admiral Takeo Takagi. The ensuing battle, which continued sporadically for three days, cost the Allies ten ships destroyed and the lives of some 2,300 sailors, including Admiral Doorman. The Japanese suffered damage but lost no ships, and ABDACOM was effectively stripped of naval assets. The Dutch East Indies, with its vast rubber plantations and oil fields, was lost to the Allies and open for conquest by Count Terauchi Hisaichi's Japanese Southern Expeditionary Army Group.

March was even worse.

The British evacuated Rangoon, which closed the eight-hundred-mile Burma Road and cut off overland supply to China. This was a vital, and underreported, theater of operations as Chiang Kai-shek's Nationalists were tying down a million Japanese soldiers who could otherwise make a decisive difference during the upcoming Solomon Islands campaign. Equally threatening, with the Imperial 15th Army advancing north through Burma toward India, Britain's crown jewel of wealth and resources was in grave peril. The situation was exacerbated by Gandhi, who, though an admirable man in many ways, showed appalling naïveté by encouraging his four hundred million countrymen to protest against the British and offer no active resistance to the Japanese, should they invade.

In a controversial and much-debated move, on March 1, President Roosevelt ordered Douglas MacArthur out of the Philippines. Personally, he disliked the bombastic general, but fighting back with some success MacArthur had implausibly become a symbol of the American war effort. Ironic, because MacArthur had been commanding the fight for Bataan from *inside* the Malinta Tunnel on Corregidor, and was definitely not a symbol of courage to the fighting men on the peninsula. Field Harris was appalled. He'd been dismayed when the 4th Marines were assigned to MacArthur, and he had no confidence in this particular army general's ability. Dreadfully worried about Bill, when word filtered down that MacArthur was fleeing to Australia Field was incensed. The notion of a commanding officer running to safety while leaving his men behind to face the enemy was as unforgivable as it was repugnant. MacArthur's supporters maintained that the general could not defy a presidential order, but Harris knew better. Douglas MacArthur obeyed no one but himself, and would not have hesitated to remain in the Philippines had it been to his advantage.

On the evening of March 11, Lieutenant John Bulkeley idled PT-41 clear of Corregidor's South Dock and eased through the minefield toward the turning buoy at the entrance of Manila Bay. He was carrying the general, his wife Jean, and four-year-old Arthur along with Ah Cheu, the family cook, and Major Charles Morhouse, MacArthur's personal physician. Beneath a moonless sky, Bulkeley rendezvoused with PT boats 32, 34, and 35, then headed south through a 580-mile gauntlet of Japanese ships and planes. On the morning of March 13, seasick and miserable, MacArthur was safely delivered to the Cagayan dock on Mindanao.

Taken overland to the army airfield on the Del Monte pineapple plantation, the general was expecting to meet three 19th Bomb Group B-17s from Australia that would take him the rest of the way. Only one made it through: a patched, raggedy Flying Fortress that, despite having flown 1,500 miles through enemy airspace, received no praise from an angry MacArthur, who evinced no concern over one B-17 that crashed en route. It was beneath him to travel in such a beat-up aircraft, nor did he care for the pilot, Lieutenant Harl Pease, who appeared entirely too young to be entrusted with such valuable passengers.*

Even with Bataan besieged and Australia threatened by the advancing Japanese, for two days MacArthur "heated up the radio waves with demands for new and better airplanes." A pair of B-17s eventually arrived, which also angered the general as his party was forced to leave most of their baggage behind. Airsick for most of the ten-hour flight to Australia, MacArthur finally landed at Bachelor Field south of Darwin on 17 March, 1942. "You've taken me out of the jaws of death," he had told Bulkeley on Mindanao. "And I won't forget it." Perhaps not, but to Field Harris and many others, MacArthur had already forgotten the thousands of soldiers and Marines abandoned on Bataan and Corregidor. The end of that battle was never really in doubt; nevertheless, the news of General King's April 9 surrender at Mariveles shook the U.S. military to its core.

Field Harris read Bill's last letter home, dated March 30, over and over again. "My situation out here has changed very little," his son wrote in typically understated fashion. "One thing that happened lately that really tickled me was that I saw a Japanese bomber get shot down by anti-aircraft fire." Field was proud of his son's courage. Bill was abandoned, cut off, and facing 75,000 Imperial troops of the 14th Army across a few miles of shark-infested water, and he only mentioned

---

* In fact, Pease was an accomplished pilot who would be posthumously awarded the Medal of Honor. Bailing out over New Guinea in August 1942, the twenty-five-year-old Pease was forced to dig his own grave and was then beheaded.

laughing at a downed bomber. Part of this was to get the letter past the censors, but also to spare Katie the details. It was a professional combat officer's realization that there was nothing anyone could do, so why worry about situations beyond one's control? Bill also passed along some very welcome news about Field's younger brother, Andrew Earl "Squire" Harris, a navy commander also trapped on Corregidor. "I have seen Uncle Squire quite frequently lately . . . he is always doing the nicest and most thoughtful things for me." It was good to hear. Squire was five years younger than Field and had graduated from the Naval Academy in 1925, though he took a naval commission. With the dark Harris good looks and soft voice, Squire was a calm, fun-loving, and popular officer. The 1925 Lucky Bag, the Naval Academy's yearbook, summed him perfectly: "When it comes to women, he's the snake boys, hips and all!"

Bill also wrote not to worry about any of his personal effects, as they'd been "blown up in Olongapo" and asked Katie to assign his $10,000 life insurance policy, and any back pay, to his little sister Nancy "if anything should happen." This was the last solid, real news Field had about his son, and after Corregidor's May 6 fall, he tried every possible method to get some word—any word—about Bill, but to no avail.

Yet by the middle of the month there was some good news. On the morning of April 18, the USS *Hornet* turned northwest into the wind 650 miles east of Japan, and eight minutes later began launching the army medium bombers lined up on her deck.* Captain Marc Andrew Mitscher planned steaming in to four hundred miles before commencing this operation, but at 0738 the deck watch "sighted strange ship . . . apparently enemy Gunboat of about 300 tons bearing 216 true distant 15000 yards."

---

* Commander Stephen Jurika, *Hornet*'s air intelligence officer, previously served as naval air attaché in Tokyo, and gave Captain Mitscher several of his Japanese medals for Doolittle to return. The army pilot had the decorations wired to several bombs and, in fact, did return them to Japan.

In fact, it was the *Nitto Maru*, a seventy-ton patrol craft, one of hundreds of early-warning picket boats the Japanese used in lieu of radar, and it was now radioing its discovery of American warships off the Japanese coast. Mitscher and Lieutenant Colonel Jimmy Doolittle, leader of the sixteen U.S. Army B-25s, decided to launch immediately now that the element of surprise was gone. Admiral William "Bull" Halsey, commanding Task Force 16 from the nearby USS *Enterprise*, concurred. This was a crucial decision that an aviator like Field Harris, reading the mission report, could thoroughly appreciate. It meant the chance of detection and interception was much greater now and, more crucial, fuel required to hit Tokyo would be critical, if not impossible.

Doolittle, a famous prewar racer, had earned a doctorate in aeronautics from MIT and was the father of modern American test pilots. Not given to whims, he knew the risks. But the colonel was fearless to a fault, and as a methodical, consummate professional, he knew launching ten hours and 170 miles ahead of schedule threw his meticulous plan into a shredder. Conceived in the days following Pearl Harbor by Captain Francis Low, a submariner by trade, the plan was handed to Doolittle for operational execution. For three months he had trained carefully selected crews, modified his aircraft, and worked out every conceivable detail, but now there was nothing to do but launch.

The light cruiser *Nashville* opened fire on the picket and left formation to sink her while the eighty army crewmen rushed to their planes. With *Hornet* surging ahead through heavy, gray seas at twenty-two knots, Doolittle released the brakes at 0821, and with his nose wheel lifted and flaps extended, he wobbled into the air with room to spare. Circling overhead just below the cloud deck, bombers named *Bat Out of Hell*, *Whiskey Pete*, *Ruptured Duck*, and twelve others all gathered together, then Doolittle turned west toward Japan.

But *Nitto Maru* managed a transmission before she was sunk, and twenty-nine land-based navy Type 1 Betty bombers, with a fighter escort, took off from Kisarazu on the Chiba side of Tokyo Bay to destroy the impudent Americans. Elements of the First Air Fleet, including the carriers *Akagi*, *Sōryū*, and *Hiryū*, were also diverted to aid the hunt. However, using long-range army bombers off a carrier was not something the Imperial Navy considered possible, so the search was conducted only a few hundred miles off the Japanese coast, and by this time Task Force 16 had vanished. Doolittle's Raiders, as they became known, hit targets in Kobe, Nagoya, Yokohama, and Tokyo and damaged the light carrier *Ryūhō*. After thirteen hours of flying, out of fuel and with night falling, fifteen B-25s crash-landed in China, while one made it across the Sea of Japan to the Soviet port of Vladivostok. As a young captain, Field Harris had visited that city, and he wondered if those who made it to occupied China weren't better off.

Materially, the damage from the raid was insignificant, but its psychological and strategic ramifications were enormous, and it could be argued that this single attack changed the course of the Pacific war. Tokyo overreacted on an immense scale, deploying most of the Combined Fleet to catch and kill the upstart Americans with scores of warships, which generated voluminous amounts of encoded radio communications. These were intercepted by fleet radio units in the Pacific and relayed to the navy's top cryptanalysts atop the Main Navy Building in Washington. Field Harris, who appreciated innovation and technology, was aware of Commander Lawrence Frye Safford's progress here with complex cryptology. As an attaché attached to the U.S. embassy in Cairo and intimately involved with practical intelligence gathering, Field knew very well that superior knowledge decided battles as surely as courage and firepower.

The current Japanese operational code was designated JN-25 and, since its introduction in 1939, was believed unbreakable by its creators. A two-layer cipher, it was not mechanically encrypted as were most diplomatic codes but, rather, based on traditional codebooks. First was a "dictionary" consisting of 45,000 random five-digit groups. Each sequence equated to a word or phrase in *kana*, a phonetic version of Japanese ideograms, and was subsequently assigned another five-digit group at transmission. Each message was preceded by a key that detailed the appropriate page/column/line in a second book that would decipher the message.

Station HYPO, officially the navy's Combat Intelligence Unit in Hawaii, was led by Commander Joe Rochefort, and had the lead in deciphering enemy signals. During the Combined Fleet's pell-mell pursuit of Doolittle, some 150 messages were read each day and Rochefort's team deciphered call signs for warships and air groups, base locations, and operational requirements such as fueling or personnel requests. This was a gold mine of information, though only about 15 percent of it could be deciphered within the 14th Naval District's basement in Honolulu.

But this was enough for now, and it was just in time.

With the capitulation of the Philippines and Java, the Japanese felt their First Operational Phase was complete and could now begin their deep southwest thrust into the Bismarck Archipelago and New Guinea, which would permit the conquest of Port Moresby. From here, Imperial forces would be four hundred miles across the Coral Sea and within easy striking distance of Australia's Cape York Peninsula. Operation MO, the invasion of Port Moresby, was approved as a result of the Doolittle raid, and forces gathered in Rabaul and Truk for that offensive. With the seizure of Port Moresby, the Japanese intended to invade the Solomon Islands and establish a base on Tulagi. Vital for their strategic plan was construction of an airfield on the chain's largest island, which local Melanesians called Isatabu. The Americans would come to know it well by its Spanish name: Guadalcanal.*

Controlling this island and its airstrip, the Japanese could dominate the Coral Sea, then stab southwest again to New Caledonia and the Fijis. This would sever the vital sea-lanes from California and isolate Australia from the United States. If this transpired, the only way to

---

* Pedro de Ortega Valencia, a member of Álvaro de Mendaña's 1568 expedition, named it for his own village of Guadalcanal, near Seville, in Spanish Andalusia.

reinforce Australia would be through the South Atlantic, around Africa, and across the Indian Ocean: over fourteen thousand miles and twice the present distance from the American West Coast. This was insupportable, and would very likely cause the loss of the Southwest Pacific to the Japanese.

Field Harris was aware of the danger, and by late April the sense of urgency in Washington spiked. He and other Marine officers were already drawing up plans for the first U.S. offensive in the Pacific, and Field knew Admiral King, commander in chief of the U.S. fleet (COMINCH) and chief of naval operations, traveled to San Francisco to discuss this with Admiral Nimitz.* Though not privy to the details, Harris knew the meeting dealt with countering Japan's next move and slowing the enemy momentum. Facing the admirals was the issue of aircraft carriers; with *Wasp* and *Ranger* in the Atlantic, only *Yorktown*, *Enterprise*, *Hornet*, and *Lexington* remained in the Pacific. *Saratoga* had been hit by a torpedo in January 1942 and was laid up in Bremerton, Washington, undergoing modernization and repairs. Though keels had been laid for three of the new *Essex*-class carriers, they weren't due for commissioning until late 1942 or 1943, so the existing warships and their flight crews were irreplaceable commodities.

Nimitz was bold, and with King's concurrence he ordered *Enterprise* and *Yorktown* from Pearl Harbor to link up with *Lexington* in the Coral Sea. On April 30, 1942, they sortied for "Point Buttercup," a rendezvous 250 miles west of the New Hebrides, while on that same day, 3,500 miles west of Hawaii, a small Japanese task force, including the carriers *Shokaku* and *Zuikaku*, was approaching the island of Tulagi in the Solomons. On May 4, eleven Japanese transports carrying the Imperial Army's South Seas Detachment and the 3rd Kure Spe-

---

* King's original title was Commander in Chief, U.S. (CINCUS) Fleet, but for obvious reasons he didn't care for the abbreviation, since it was pronounced "sink us."

cial Naval Landing Force steamed from Rabaul headed for the Coral Sea. Escorted by seven cruisers and the light carrier *Shoho*, this force turned south for Port Moresby by way of Louisiades Archipelago and Jomard Passage.

By May 6, as Bill Harris was captured on Corregidor, *Yorktown* and *Lexington* joined up 3,500 miles southeast of the Philippines to form Task Force 17 and, in the company of Australian rear admiral Jack Crace's heavy cruisers, steamed west into the Coral Sea. Thanks in large part to Doolittle's raid, U.S. intelligence knew enough of the JN-25 code to predict the invasion fleet's course, and Fletcher was ordered to the Jomard Passage. Sighting reports from Australian coast watchers were instrumental in confirming Japanese movements, so by May 6 the Americans had a reasonable tactical picture. The invasion fleet was south of New Britain steaming for the Louisiades, while *Shokaku* and *Zuikaku* skirted the Solomons north of U.S. carriers and were now heading into the Coral Sea.

Less than one hundred miles separated the two opposing forces during the night, yet somehow they missed. The Japanese carriers were searching south for the Americans, while Fletcher concentrated westward looking for the invasion fleet. By noon on May 7, *Lexington* and *Yorktown's* air groups discovered *Shoho* north of the Jomard Passage and reduced her to a flaming wreck, but the following morning the big carriers finally found each other. South of the Solomons and east of the Louisiades, both fleets launched strikes through the bad weather, and by early afternoon *Shokaku* had been hit by three bombs that destroyed her flight deck. Out of action, she was retiring north under escort, while *Lexington* and *Yorktown* were both damaged. Fortunately, the U.S. Navy excelled at damage control, and the carriers were still able to maneuver and recover their aircraft.

But at 1247 sparks from an electric motor ignited pent-up gasoline vapor inside *Lexington* and a series of explosions blew her guts out. By 1538 the fires were uncontrollable, and Captain Frederick Sherman gave the order to abandon ship. Later that evening as the *Yorktown*, listing and damaged, steamed southwest to safety, the destroyer *Phelps* put five torpedoes into the burning *Lexington*, and at 1952 she sank under 14,400 feet of water in the middle of the Coral Sea. In addition to the carrier, the U.S. Navy lost a destroyer, an oiler, sixty-six aircraft, and 543 killed in action. *Yorktown* was steaming back to Pearl Harbor, but preliminary damage estimates had her out of service for ninety days, which only left *Enterprise* and *Hornet* in the entire Pacific.

The Imperial Navy lost the *Shoho*, seventy-seven aircraft, and 1,074 killed in action, which gave them a tactical victory, but strategically the battle of the Coral Sea was a decisive Japanese defeat. Because of American presence in the area at midnight on May 8, the Port Moresby invasion fleet was recalled to Rabaul and took with it the opportunity to conquer New Guinea and threaten Australia. Admiral Yamamoto was furious, but his order to continue Operation MO was not followed in the confusion, nor did Vice Admiral Takeo Takagi, commander of Carrier Division 5, attempt to track the *Yorktown* and finish her off. As it stood, *Shokaku* barely made it back to Kure, and *Zuikaku* had suffered at least a 40 percent loss of aircraft and crews. For the Imperial Navy, this was a more severe setback than it appeared; no plan existed to replace large numbers of fliers because the Japanese never considered that they would lose such men. Their past experiences against Russian, Chinese, and colonial adversaries had borne this out, but this was the first time they'd faced the Americans on anything like even terms—and it should have been a warning.

Despite the losses and very grim tactical position, Field Harris knew that there were several positive aspects of the battle, at least from the American point of view. First was Port Moresby, and though no one was certain the Japanese would not try again, they failed this time. With *Shoho*'s loss they had also lost their first capital ship, and *Shokaku*, a powerful new fleet carrier, was badly mauled. These were all psychological setbacks for the Imperial Navy as well as badly needed morale boosts for the Allies, and, more than this, such defeats graphically illustrated that Japanese invincibility was a myth. They *could* be beaten; they could bleed; and they did make mistakes.

One such error was the Japanese underestimation of American capabilities, and this was evident in their somewhat cavalier attitude toward Operation MO; it was supposed to be a "safe" operation, and they simply did not grasp that the U.S. Navy was capable of suddenly appearing where not expected, ready to fight. The Doolittle raid should have illuminated this, but the Imperial High Command failed to view it that way. Field Harris could also plainly see the superiority of U.S. intelligence and the fruits of its code-breaking efforts, though this was certainly no panacea, and on the best of days only 50 to 60 percent of enemy transmissions were intercepted, with fewer than half of these successfully analyzed.

However, American intelligence was particularly adept at using all means at its disposal and corroborating these into the best possible estimate of enemy intentions. Traffic analysis between ports and ships, direction finding, and coast-watcher reports were all utilized to back up cryptanalysis. As the United States fully mobilized for war, this might just be enough to give the Allies an edge until a military foothold could be gained in the Pacific. Such a foothold, for Field and his fellow Marines, was crucial. While the Japanese had been blunted in the Coral Sea, they had successfully invaded the Solomons, and this was a tremendously dangerous situation. Without withdrawing significant troops from China, which it would not do, the Imperial Army could not invade Australia, but they could secure Guadalcanal, construct an airfield, and advance southwest to interdict the sea-lanes.

Nevertheless, until the U.S. carriers were destroyed, Japan would have no security in its new empire. Admiral Yamamoto, commander of the Combined Fleet, was quite aware of the peril, and the American performance at Coral Sea was unsettling. Having lived and traveled extensively in America, the admiral knew he had a finite amount of time to secure a defensive perimeter in the Pacific, and this was leaking from the glass more quickly than expected. Harris and others were aware that Japan's grand naval strategy advocated one great, decisive sea battle, so when the volume of encoded signals and radio traffic increased throughout May, this indicated another probable enemy thrust. Imperial Navy squadrons were permanently assigned to a specific ship, unlike their American counterparts, and when training in home waters Japanese pilots used the same radio frequencies time and again, which provided valuable intelligence on carrier locations. This was crucial since secure phone lines were passed to anchored warships via mooring buoys, and they rarely utilized radio communications while in port.

This was especially true of the magnificent anchorages within Japan's Inland Sea, the beating heart of the Imperial Navy and symbol of her might. Etajima Island was home to the Imperial Japanese Naval Academy, while the great naval dockyard and arsenal at Kure was equivalent in importance to Hampton Roads in Virginia. As dawn broke over Mount Ishizuchi on May 27, 1942, dozens of warships in Hiroshima Bay prepared to get under way, including the aircraft carrier *Akagi*, who began her long life at Kure barely twenty miles to the north. Exactly 857 feet in length, she was larger than either of the navy's new *Shokaku*-class carriers, and even longer than the giant battleship *Yamato*, which lay in the same anchorage off Hashirajima Island flying Yamamoto's flag.

At 0600 a signal from *Akagi* broke to "Commence sortie as scheduled," and clusters of idling warships fell in line behind the light cruiser *Nagara* as she led the fleet out. This Wednesday morning in 1942 was historic for two reasons: it was the anniversary of Admiral Togo's 1905 victory over the Russians in Tsushima Strait, just 150 miles to the west, and it was the day that the Mobile Striking Force steaming from Hiroshima Bay intended to finish what began at Pearl Harbor five months earlier, which only the senior officers knew. The plan was to trap, engage, and destroy the U.S. Pacific Fleet in a decisive sea battle just as Togo had done to the Russians thirty-seven years earlier. Slipping through the Iyo Nada waterway, *Nagara* passed the Cape Sada Lighthouse, entered the Bungo Channel at noon, and then turned the fleet southeast and disappeared into the open waters of the vast Pacific.

All through May the cryptanalysts in Hawaii detected an increase in enemy message and radio traffic, some quite detailed, and much of it centered on the Inland Sea and *Akagi*. Yet American intelligence efforts were confounded the day following the sailing, when the Imperial Navy abruptly switched codes from the JN-25b to the JN-25c variant, so now, at the worst possible moment, most of the previous cryptanalysis gains vanished and the slim Allied edge appeared lost. During the final days of May, many senior American officers believed Oahu might be the next Japanese target, as it should have been in December 1941, when the United States was powerless to prevent an invasion. If Hawaii and Pearl Harbor were lost, nothing remained between the West Coast and Japan except the tiny atoll of Midway.

Field Harris was among those who believed Hawaii was the likely target, but he was busy planning for something else. On May 27, a Japanese captain named Shigetoshi Miyazaki crossed the Indispensable Strait between Florida Island and Guadalcanal to conduct a survey. Commanding the Yokohama Air Group's seaplane detachment on Tulagi, Miyazaki was well qualified to suggest that the large island's central plain was suitable for an airstrip. From here, Imperial Navy land-based bombers could reach south to Brisbane and east to the Fijis; New Caledonia and all the vital sea-lanes would be untenable. This, from the American standpoint, could not be allowed to happen, and Field was crafting a U.S. response appropriately titled Task 1, later code-named Pestilence.

Planned for August, barely two months away, time was limited and the Marines lacked everything—except guts. Field was relieved, and proud, that America was mounting a substantial counterattack within eight months of Pearl Harbor, and he realized delay in the Philippines cost the Japanese dearly. The elder Harris objectively understood the reasons for writing off American and Filipino forces there, but as an officer, and especially as the father of a young fighting man, it was impossible to accept it subjectively. The headlines during the first week in May did nothing to ease the tension and pain.

"PHILIPPINES LOST" ran the May 7 *New York Times* headline. "WAINWRIGHT A PRISONER WITH END OF ORGANIZED RESISTANCE ON ISLES. ONLY GUERRILLAS REMAIN."

During lingering early-summer evenings on his Washington porch, Field desperately but quietly worried about his son and clung to a recurring pair of thoughts. First was that his boy's sacrifices helped make the delay possible and second, most fervently, was that Bill was still alive. The May 9 headline "QUEZON ARRIVES AT SAN FRANCISCO; MAKES TRIP 'UNDER SEA, ON SEA AND IN AIR' TO ESTABLISH A GOVERNMENT IN WASHINGTON. PROUD OF BRAVE FILIPINOS" embittered the general. Washington could get a puppet politician and his family and servants out of the Philippines but did nothing to aid the soldiers, pilots, and Marines trapped there. Why was Quezon's government in exile more important than the life of his son?

Springing from a generation that kept emotions private, Field always found it difficult to show affection—especially for a boy who would someday shoulder the burdens of manhood. But he *did* feel it, and was immensely proud of his son whether it was overtly demonstrated or not. In the end, there was nothing he could do for his boy now, so he just had to trust in Bill's strength, resiliency, and instincts. It was another reason the general was glad his son was surrounded by men as physically strong and mentally tough as he was. Marines were not drafted, and as an all-volunteer, amphibious warfare force they only took the best applicants as recruits.* In any event, there was enough for Field to focus on now anyway. News from the Coral Sea earlier in May had been vague, and he inherently distrusted military

---

* This would change on December 5, 1942, with Executive Order 9279. The Selective Service System was transferred into the War Manpower Commission, and every draftee went into a general pool from which the service branches then extracted the men they needed; including, much to their dismay, the Marine Corps.

press releases that, for sound reasons, exaggerated enemy casualties and understated American losses.

Meanwhile, as Nagumo steamed from the Inland Sea and Miyazaki made his fateful survey on Guadalcanal, a battle-stained, scarred American warship slowly slid into Oahu's Pearl Harbor from Mamala Bay. Horns honked and sirens shrieked from Diamond Head to Ford Island as the USS *Yorktown* proudly limped through the channel past Fort Kamehameha. Rounding Hospital Point, she took on 1,400 shipfitters, machinists, patternmakers, engineers, and dozens of other specialists. The next day, tugs would ease her into Dry Dock Number 1, where a ninety-day refit would be crammed into a forty-eight-hour emergency repair job.

On this last day of May 1942, Field Harris was aware the strategic situation in the Pacific was extremely fluid and that the impending Japanese assault would likely be decisive for both sides. Japan had momentum, and so far had reaped the attacker's inestimable benefit derived from offensive action. The Allies had been forced to react, which is a poor way to fight, and this had to change if America held hopes of victory. Delay in the Philippines had given the enemy pause, and the battle of the Coral Sea was a figurative slap in the face. The United States was at last awake, angry, and aggressive, and of one thing Field Harris was now certain—America had taken its last backward step in the Pacific.

✳

FIVE

BOOMERANG

ON MAY 27, AS THE CRUISER *NAGARA* LED ADMIRAL NAGUMO'S FLEET past Cape Sada into the open sea, Bill Harris and Ed Whitcomb lay panting among the bushes of Mount Mariveles's rocky western foot-hills. A Japanese patrol was combing the area, their split-toed shoes crunching dry leaves as they searched for the escaping Americans. Bill had no idea how they knew where to look, but they were here. Per-haps he and Ed had been seen coming off the mountain, or maybe a Filipino turned them in to curry favor with the Japanese. Either way, it was too dangerous to move, and they'd spent the entire night and most of today silently sipping warm water and swatting insects. Japs were patient, he knew, waiting for hours to ambush an enemy, and Bill had no intention of being a prisoner again, or a dead Marine.

Three nights earlier, wet and cold beneath the boulder atop Mariveles, they'd decided to work their way downslope rather than skirting the summit. Just descending made a huge difference to their morale, and they'd come down over two thousand feet the first day before crossing the Biaan River to camp on the edge of a banana field on the upper foothills. Green bananas. Small and very hard. "About the size of a piece of chalk and tasted about as good," Whitcomb recalled. Harris ate three of them, then suggested they sleep the night under cover nearby. In the morning maybe they could find ripe bananas and the Mariveles-Bagac road, which ran west of the mountain along the coast.

With a bright dawn on May 25, they found the road and began paralleling it through the banana fields along the northeast side. The trees closest to the road had been picked bare of fruit, but the men did find several abandoned American military camps strewn with discarded weapons and clothing. Harris, ever the Marine, found an M-1 Garand rifle that suited him and several bandoliers of .30–06 ammunition. "If any Japs try to capture us, I'm going to account for two or three of them before they get me," Whitcomb recalled his friend grimly stating as he handed over some extra bandoliers. Trudging northwest through the brush, they'd come across enemy campsites littered with beer and sake bottles, but no food. By now, exhaustion and hunger were taking their toll, and both officers were staggering and short of breath. *We're going to do it,* Bill kept reciting to himself. This world belongs to the strong . . . *to the strong.*

But at this point he was far from certain—until they found the horse. It was old, skinny, and had survived two armies, but did not survive Bill, who promptly shot him through the head. Quickly sawing off both front shoulders, they moved away from the road up into a steep little river valley to light a fire and enjoy their meal. Beside the little stream they tried to get a fire going, but even powder from several cartridges failed to ignite a kerosene-soaked rag. A drill and bow made from shoestrings coaxed a bit of smoke, and roasted horse steaks seemed imminent when shots suddenly rang out from down the hill.

Startled and scared, Bill and Ed dropped the bow and steaks, then clawed their way up the streambed into the rocky foothills. Leaves rustled below, and the muted sound of voices drifted up as a Japanese patrol fanned out through the trees. It must have been the rifle shot, or the horse carcass, or both. Bill knew they should have pulled the horse into the bushes, but they just didn't have the strength. He later wrote, "a lightly-framed Japanese soldier in yellow-brown khaki, wearing a soft baseball type cap, and carrying a rifle at an alert port looking sharply into the draw. Another soldier came in sight, and another, but they all passed by." In short, whispered sentences the Americans decided to stay put till dawn the next day, then continue northwest toward Bagac and the coast.

Utterly exhausted, both men slept hard until midday.

"Hey," Bill softly called. "Are you awake, too?"

"Yeah. You know what? I'm learning things. This is the first time I ever realized the true relative importance of women."

"What the hell are you talking about?"

"Well, which would you rather have right now, a ham sandwich or Sugarpuss Glamorpants?"

Despite the grim circumstances, Harris grinned. Ed, like himself, was one of those men who made jokes in dire situations, and he knew how hungry he truly was to want a ham sandwich rather than a woman. During the long hot afternoon, they waited, listened, and watched while Japanese patrols moved across the hills. "I've got a confession to make," Bill whispered. "I've been eating ants. They're a little bitter . . . but I think I feel a little stronger since I ate them."

In the heavy, quiet twilight, they slowly and stiffly crawled from the brush and made their way north across the rolling, rocky ground. Limping along the foothills toward a hairpin turn a mile away, both men were so weak they paused every few hundred yards to rest. Still, it was a relief to be walking mostly downhill, and to be off the mountain. Topping the last ridgeline, in the fading light Bill could see along the pike for a half mile in either direction, and nothing moved. Off to the left were twin inlets, and he knew Bagac lay beyond the northern one. Only three miles, if they were birds and could go direct, but along the road . . . maybe twice that distance. The thought of a night hike over broken ground didn't thrill either man, so they decided to carefully walk along the road, despite the risk. Dangerous, to be sure, but easier traveling. Quicker too, and less chance of an injury, which they could not afford.

Either way, they had hours of hiking ahead of them. It was a "battle scarred, spooky country," and for several hours they painfully shuffled along the twisting pike, marking progress by the stone kilometer markers. "We spoke never a word," Harris recalled. "We walked. Had one stopped to sit down, the other likely would not have known it." But they listened. Always. After midnight, just past a "3 Km to Bagac" marker, the trees gave way to open, undulating ground and the slopes were "strewn with innumerable, wrecked, American-type passenger automobiles and trucks." Under silver moonlight, the descending road took a hard ninety-degree left toward the coast. Relieved, Bill and Ed plopped down in the trees away from the pike and rested, certain a few minutes wouldn't slow them down too much.

It was the rumbling of a heavy vehicle that woke them at noon. Scrambling farther back under cover, they peered from the branches in time to see a U.S. Army Chevy truck barreling along with five American prisoners in the back, guarded by a Japanese soldier "who rested his back against the cab in a carelessly arrogant posture, and nonchalantly held his bayonetted rifle by the muzzle." More trucks followed, so the men cut off across country to avoid the road. Deserted camps were everywhere, and in one these Bill found another functional rifle.

Remaining under cover as much as possible, the starving Americans kept to the rough country southwest of the road. Rain fell: a cold, driving, depressing rain that ran into their ears and soaked into their pores. Bill's hunger gnawed so deeply it felt like claws scratching the inside of his belly. Just ahead, they knew, was Bagac, a tiny barrio on the China Sea, but there would be people there who could feed them. Just the thought of hot rice and pork gave them strength, and they slipped on through the mud. Topping a small rise, Bill's spirit's lifted when he saw nipa huts outlined against the moonlit sea—they made it!* Breaking into a clumsy trot, both officers came down through the trees looking for lit windows and the smell of cooking fires.

---

* Lightly constructed, the huts are built on stilts and thatched with nipa, a palm tree with large, creeping roots.

There were none.

Approaching the huts and houses, Bill could now see they were hollow shells, burned and missing walls. But there had to be *someone* here, so the men worked around through the village from the south, to the west, then ended up on the north edge. No one. Wet and cold, the disappointment was nearly crushing. "The whole village had been burned to the ground," Ed Whitcomb recalled. "How much farther could we go, and how much more disappointment could we take?" Utterly exhausted, they collapsed in a battered hut and waited for dawn. Scrounging around in daylight might yield something, and neither man could go farther now. A steady breeze off the nearby sea chilled them to the bone, but Bill found an old, rough cotton sheet and both men huddled under it to stay warm. Sometime during that miserable night, he dropped off to sleep.

This time it was the sunlight that awakened him. Confused and disoriented, he sat up, looked, and listened. Then he remembered. They were in a native hut in occupied Bataan in broad daylight! "Wake up," he hissed, punching Ed on the shoulder. "We've got to vamoose—fast." Taking off across country northeast of Bagac, they hobbled a half mile before staggering into a little cashew grove just south of the Morong road. Weak with relief and hunger, Bill and Ed stuffed themselves with nuts and enjoyed their first food, besides ants, since Sunday. The area had plainly been a field aid station, as medical supplies, wrappers, and discarded equipment lay beneath the trees . . . and a mummified corpse on a stretcher. Too tired to care, they lay down and slept again for a few hours.

Late that afternoon Bill and Ed were hiking northeast on a rough trail when their luck improved again. A young Filipino boy, perhaps fourteen or fifteen, invited them to his family home for dinner, and they gratefully accepted. He led them over the Bagac-Morong road to a tiny village and brought them to the largest of a dozen nipa huts. His parents were a "white-haired, wrinkled couple, with pleasant, dark mahogany faces" who sat them down before a stone hearth and began to cook. Bill questioned them about the Japanese, and the boy's face hardened.

"They are very bad people. They slap us, and they make us bow. Only two weeks ago some Hahpone [Japanese] soldiers go to a barrio only over there," he pointed east, "and they rape a young woman."

This wasn't surprising. The original Bataan defensive line had run from Abucay, on the east coast, through Mount Natib to Morong. General Parker's II Corps held the line east of the mountain, while General Wainwright was here in the west where they now stood. Bill remembered hearing that an actual horse-cavalry charge hit a Japanese unit approaching Morong, but he hadn't believed it.* Now, gorging themselves on rice, fresh fish, and grated coconut heaped on banana leaves, they discovered there were no Japanese in the little town. Apparently, the retreating Americans destroyed the Batalan River bridge, which made the road impassable for trucks.

This was indeed good news, if true.

Bill felt the best he had in months when they left Bagac on Friday night. It was truly amazing what a full belly, a good night's sleep, and a bath in a warm river could do for one's spirits. They knew the Morong road could not be traveled at night, so the pair decided to go at least halfway, then enter the town the following day. Stopping near the "5 Km to Morong" marker, they moved off into the brush and slept till two hours past sunrise. "What a beautiful, beautiful day it was!" Bill Harris remembered. "Truly only the Philippines could have one like that. The color of the sky was so intensely bright . . . the cloudlets, so white and fluffy."

Emerging from the hills onto a low coastal plain, the men followed a gradually curving road to the shore. Passing dikes, Bill could see farmers with crude wooden plows hitched to muddy carabao bulls tilling

---

* First Lieutenant Edwin Price Ramsey, commanding the twenty-seven-man G Troop, 26th Regiment (Philippine Scouts), did, in fact, make the last American horse-cavalry charge on January 16, 1942. His outnumbered men surprised and scattered a tank-supported Japanese army unit and held the ground for five hours.

the rice paddies. They looked at the Americans but never stopped the plodding, patient work they'd still be doing when all the wars were over. A half mile from town, Bill veered into a patch of trees so they could approach Morong without being seen. Everyone said there were no Japanese, but the men had come too far to be careless and blunder into an enemy outpost.

Peering from the trees they saw an open, common area clustered with Filipinos, no Japanese, so after watching a bit, Ed and Bill strolled out into the sun and joined them. The villagers were surprised but welcoming and plied them with questions about Corregidor. Here they met a man named Bartolome Baptista, who insisted they be guests at his country home outside Morong. For two days the officers relaxed in safety, slept under a roof, and ate. And ate. "We were literally in paradise the remainder of that day," Bill recorded. "Eating bananas, rice, camoties, duhats, bocos, and many others.* After months on Corregidor and the six days of starvation on Bataan, this eating of delicious food to absolute capacity was an ecstasy."

Harris also had a surprise reunion with one of his Filipino soldiers who had escaped Corregidor on a homemade raft, then hiked home. Ed and Bill were tempted to remain in Morong, and Baptista encouraged them to do so. It was the wrong time of year to cross the China Sea—many storms. Besides, he said, all the boats here that were big enough for such a voyage had been confiscated by the Japanese. It was also decided to move the Americans from Morong, as there might be, Baptista admitted, some among the villagers here who sought favor with the Japanese. On Sunday they left with his cousin, Salvador Savaras, and traveled three hours north to "the base of a deep, horseshoe-shaped cove opening out to the west" called Mabayo, at the mouth of Subic Bay.†

Bill stared down the cove past a wooded point to the bay. For a few

---

* Camoties are native sweet potatoes, duhats are purple berries that taste like blackberries, and bocos are immature coconuts with sweet juice and refreshing meat.
† The "cove" is actually Port Binanga, and the "wooded point of land" is Binanga Point.

long moments, he was back aboard the *President Madison*, steaming slowly into Subic on "an early December morning a long, long time before, when the First Battalion, Fourth Marines departed the ship and proceeded ashore onto the Philippines." So much had happened: the shock of war, the retreat down Bataan, and the battle of Corregidor. Not to mention his near-death experiences and the harrowing escape that brought him back here. Full circle.

Well, maybe not yet, but soon.

Savaras took them to the biggest house in Mabayo and introduced his wife. She was a mestizo with "keen, intelligent eyes" who greeted them warmly in surprisingly colloquial American English. "[Corregidor] was where I was born and raised," she explained. "We were a family of nine girls, and the American soldiers used to show us such a wonderful time." A meal was quickly served, and soon they were feasting on chicken stewed in coconut milk, boiled eggs, bananas, eggplant fried in coconut oil, rice, and, to Bill's delight, real coffee with sugar. "The kindness and generosity of the people touched us deeply," Whitcomb remembered fondly. "We felt a warm affection for them."

After several days of discussion with some fishermen, Bill and Ed decided to trust their judgment and not attempt the trip to China, which was disappointing. China was only seven hundred miles away to the north and tantalizingly close, while Australia was a daunting two thousand miles south. A compromise seemed best; American and Filipino guerillas were rumored to be on Mindanao, which was only five hundred miles south of Subic Bay, so Salvador insisted on giving them his *banca*, with which they could hopefully get as far as Balayan Bay, on the tip of Luzon. Once there, the Americans could join the guerillas or get a larger boat for Australia.

Fully equipped with "rice, dried fish, bananas, coffee, sugar, matches, and water in a three-gallon metal container," Bill and Ed set off from Port Binanga on the night of June 3, 1942. Beneath dawn's thin light, they angled north across the cove, then turned south, lowered the sail, and paddled. The little twenty-foot *banca* had a shallow draft, and the outriggers kept it stable, but Bill felt the bottom scrape coral as they hugged the shoreline. Moving farther offshore wasn't really an option, nor was raising the sail, as there were Japanese on nearby Grande Island. Both men got out several times to push the boat over the rocks, and several hours past midnight on Thursday, June 4, they rounded Binanga Point and were paddling south along the Bataan shoreline.

At the same time that Bill and Ed cleared the coral reefs, 3,300 miles to the east, Nagumo's carriers emerged from a nasty weather front and swung into the southeast-prevailing winds. Maintenance crewmen had been up since 0200 loading ammunition and warming up engines. The aircrews were up by 0245 eating a breakfast of rice, pickled plums, and dried fish during their flight briefings. At 0400, with flags flying and blinker lights flashing, the 41,000-ton *Akagi* went to general quarters and surged forward at twenty-two knots. Trailing behind her in a box formation, the *Kaga, Hiryū,* and *Sōryū* followed suit. Twenty-six minutes later, Lieutenant Shirane Ayao firewalled his fourteen-cylinder Nakajima Sakae engine, lifted his Zero fighter clear of *Akagi's* wooden flight deck, and began a climbing left turn overhead.

The other carriers launched 108 aircraft in nineteen minutes and then, at 0445, the airborne formation wheeled around southeast toward a tiny atoll 240 miles over the horizon. Barely two square miles of volcanic lava surrounded by coral, it was protected by twenty-eight Marine fighter planes, a coastal-defense battalion, and two companies from the 2nd Marine Raider Battalion. A former coaling station, transpacific cable junction, and Pan-American clipper-refueling stop, the kidney-shaped atoll had been uninhabited for most of its existence. Unknown to most, it was now a surprisingly critical piece of real estate due to its runway and twenty-five Catalina flying boats that could scout seven hundred miles in all directions. Essential for the Japanese to occupy, and for the Americans to defend, the obscure map speck was named for its location roughly halfway between Asia and North America.

Midway.

Oh God . . . Bill took a deep, long breath of fresh sea air. *It just seems too wonderful to be true.* Gripping the steering paddle in the stern while Ed crouched forward, he felt a surge of wild confidence as the *banca* cleared the coral and coasted into open water. For the moment they were free of land, hunger, and mind-numbing cross-country hikes. Though the moon was dim, the stars were magnificently bright, and both men watched for Japanese patrol boats. Passing Panibatujan Point near Morong, Bill calculated they'd come six miles from Port Binanga. Deciding to push their luck, the men paralleled the south-west coastline for another few hours, then waded ashore near a pair of jutting points to wait out the day.[*]

The following night was miserable.

Cold, driving rain soaked into everything and chilled them to the bone. From a few dim coastal lights and white wave tops crashing ashore, Bill navigated the little boat seven or eight miles across a small bay pocked with serrated inlets. Blown into a little cove just south of a deserted beach, they huddled together and shivered through dawn until the sun arose. With no map and no way to accurately measure distance, Bill's navigation was strictly intuitive. Fortunately, Annapolis required a great deal of practical sailing, and these skills were now paying off in a way he'd never imagined. Based on his sense of the geography and the looming silhouette of Mount Mariveles off to the southwest, Bill reckoned they were halfway back down Bataan near Bagac.[†]

During the night of June 7–8, the pair made it another eight miles

---

[*] Eman and Napot Points.
[†] In fact, they had come ashore on Saysain Point, just south of Bagac.

south across Bagac Bay, and, as they skimmed past the Redondo Peninsula, the shoreline suddenly faded and open water yawned ahead. Putting into a little cove, the men found a peaceful, sheltered beach with good cover, and when the sun rose over the peaks, they dried their clothes, ate a good meal, and rested. This had to be Luzon Point, or very close to it, as Mount Mariveles was due east of their little anchorage. Bill could see the spot near the summit where they'd spent that dreary wet night beneath the rock overhang. Sixteen days. America had gone to war in less time back in December, but now they were free men, not helpless prisoners at the mercy of the Japanese: strong, determined, and healthy, with their destiny in their own hands.

Free.

Bill Harris would never—*never*—take that word for granted again. Nonetheless, he knew they'd need all their strength for what was coming next: an eighteen-mile dash across Manila Bay, past Corregidor, then south to the Batangas coast. "Just before dark on June 8, 1942, we pulled the little boat down from her hiding place and shoved off," Whitcomb recalled. "There was a good breeze from the north that carried us along at a very pleasant rate for the first few hours." Enormous dark clouds swept in but blew out just as swiftly, and there was no rain. Scooting across the North Channel, Bill stared at Corregidor's low hump and recalled the dangerous eight-hour swim to safety. Yet here they were back again, like a boomerang. Would he never be rid of the Rock? Looking down at the black water now, Harris hated to think what lived in there that they'd avoided and was profoundly grateful for the leaky *banca*.

A patrol boat appeared but passed well behind them heading into the channel, and no searchlights flashed across the water from Corregidor. For a few hours all seemed well, and the little boat skimmed well over the waves as "the Great Bear and the Southern Cross set, but Cassiopeia showed," Bill wrote. He figured the time at 0300, which was cutting it close as the Cavite shore was still a few miles distant and sunrise would come about 0530. There was also an ominous change in the water and wind, with the waves deepening as the breeze stiffened, so Bill angled in toward the shoreline between Hamilo and Limit Points. It was dangerous—clutching fingers of rocks and coral reached out from the Panay Pany foothills, and the currents were treacherous—but there was no choice.

Black scudding clouds blew in off the sea as a sudden, violent squall hit them and washed water over the gunwales faster than Ed could bail. "The shore appeared to be a solid rock wall," as Bill hastily lowered the sail, Ed remembered. "There were cliffs everywhere and if we'd tried to take our boat in it would surely have been bashed to pieces." Scrambling into warm, waist-deep water about fifty feet from the shore, Whitcomb rubbed against a big fish that "was surely as large as the boat." Visions of sharks filled his mind, and he hit "the thing," then thrashed and churned the water till it swam off. Panting and frightened, they swam the boat parallel to the rocks until Bill spotted a cove. Rounding a towering rock corner, they felt the wind die abruptly and floundered up onto a small beach.*

Collapsing in a clump of bushes, they shivered till a weak dawn broke over Mount Gariliao. For two days rain lashed their faces, and wind whipped the sea to froth just beyond the cove. "It was miserable waiting," Ed wrote. "Our matches, rice, cigarettes, and everything else were soaked with salt water." Three wretched, wet days later, the wind abated, and the men tried to sail from the cove. Between the currents and winds, they lost control of the *banca* and were unable to avoid an enormous wave that tossed them back onto the beach, snapping one outrigger completely off. Without the boat or provisions, there was no choice but to head inland, which they did, and fortunately found shelter with a Filipino family nearby. According to Bill Harris, "we stayed here among the natives for about two weeks, and then we walked generally southward."

Agreeing that continuing to Balayan Bay was their best alternative,

---

* Very close to the Canyon Cove area near Nasugbu.

on June 26 both men bade farewell to their hosts, then headed south
into the Batangas Province. Following railroad tracks along the coast,
the next morning Bill and Ed found themselves on a riverbank south
of a good-sized village.* A Filipino family took them in, provided a
"delicious breakfast of rice and fish," and let them sleep through the
day on their kitchen floor. At twilight, following another meal, the pair
set off again down a narrow, flat valley between the coastal mountains
and rocky hills a few miles east. Sunday morning, June 28, dawned
comfortably cool, with a friendly farmer taking them to a grass shack up
in the eastern hills where they could rest during the day. The shack was
cool and secluded, the dry bamboo floor was comfortable enough, and
the view was magnificent. From here, on the only high ground between
the coast and Mount Batulao, "we could see the shore to the west and a
big sugar factory in the green valley below."† Ramping gently southward,
the valley's greens and browns melted into the enormous blue curve of
Balayan Bay and, after sleeping through the afternoon, both men rose at
dusk to walk down the little mountain toward the coast.‡

It was here their fortunes finally improved. Balayan, a small fishing
hamlet, lay directly on the bay, and Bill was certain they could find a
boat there to carry them farther south. Cutting four miles cross-country
but parallel to a relatively substantial dirt path, the pair found themselves on the outskirts just as the sun dipped below Mount Nasugbu
due west of the little town. Friendly Filipinos were everywhere on
the main road into town, so much so that both men were suspicious.§
Invited into a ramshackle dwelling, they nonetheless shared a wonderful fried egg and pork dinner while a neighbor left to find the mayor.
Later that night it was decided that the Americans would hide in a hut
north of town while a boat was located.

Bill and Ed spent the next few days in "hiding," though there wasn't

---

* The Lian River south of Nasugbu.
† Balayan Sugar Central Mill, now owned by the Universal Robina Corporation.
‡ Mount Miyuan.
§ The Balayan-Balibago road.

much secret about it, at least for the villagers. Nearly a hundred locals dropped by, and they all brought food: bananas, mangos, coconuts and spiced pork. "We did nothing but eat and visit with the people," Ed remembered. It seemed the villagers were all related and all hated the Japanese, so Bill finally relaxed a bit. One man brought a pair of scissors, and together with a Filipino folding knife, he trimmed their hair and gave them both a shave.* "Without any lather, it hurt like being skinned alive," but with an audience neither man allowed any visible reaction. Enduring the overwhelming hospitality and endless food for several more days, Bill finally told their host that they were leaving the following morning for Mindoro Island, about thirty miles south. "We've been away from Corregidor almost a month and we haven't covered more than fifty miles." Harris was adamant, until the host revealed their benefactor was none other than Don López, the prominent Filipino statesman who also happened to be the area's principal landowner.

Sixto Castelo López was thirty-four years old during February 1898, when the U.S. battleship *Maine* blew up and sank in Havana Harbor. Two officers and 251 sailors died, and whether the incident was intentional or accidental, it was used as a pretext for war with Spain. Filipino revolutionaries, López among them, sided with the United States in the belief they would be granted independence once America defeated Spain. On the last day of April, Admiral George Dewey's Asiatic Squadron steamed into Manila Bay and decisively defeated the Spanish colonial fleet under Admiral Patricio Montojo y Pasarón.[†] The 1898 Treaty of Paris ended the war and Spain ceded Cuba, Puerto Rico, and Guam to the United States—and her possessions in the Philippines. Those Filipinos who fought against the Spanish expected recognition

---

* A *balisong*, known in the West as a "butterfly" knife.

† Spain lost seven cruisers and four gunboats, and 348 men were killed or wounded. Dewey suffered nine men wounded and one dead, apparently from a heart attack, with no ships lost. Dewey began the battle with the now immortal order to his captain, "You may fire when you are ready, Gridley."

of their new Philippine Republic, but Washington demurred, and hostilities soon broke out between U.S. occupation forces and Filipino revolutionaries.

A *sangley* from a wealthy family, Sixto López was a schoolmate of the legendary Jose Rizal, a revolutionary whom the Spanish executed in 1902.* A natural choice to present the fledgling Philippine Republic's entreaties to Washington, López was in the United States when the 1899 Philippine-American war erupted. Returning to Manila, he voluntarily surrendered to General Arthur MacArthur and was allowed to live in Boston for the remainder of the short conflict. While there, he pled the case for his nation, stating, "Who will help me in the cause of peace? Could any cause be worthier of the genius of the statesmen of a great nation?" Joined by his sister, Clemencia, who had studied at Wellesley College, he continued his efforts until the last Filipino resistance ended in April 1902. A commission was appointed, and eventually a bicameral legislature, free public schools, and autonomous provincial governments were established with the intention of eventually granting full independence. Moderate, but Filipino to the core, Senator López saw the futility of fighting the United States and saw the much-touted Japanese Co-Prosperity Sphere, which sought to create a self-sufficient bloc of Asian countries, for what it was: a hollow promise and a lie that simply replaced European colonialism with Imperial colonialism

Willing to help those who would aid his country, the senator offered Harris and Whitcomb shelter on his hacienda seven miles northeast of Balayan, which they gladly accepted. The officers were also informed there were two other Marines hiding there, so on the first day of July, Ed and Bill set off with a guide toward the foothills of Mount Batulao. Walking through the night, by sunrise they were hiking past little huts, and the guide, clearly impressed with his role in the matter, ex-

---

* A *sangley*, or *sang lei*, is a Filipino-Chinese mestizo known as a "mixed race person of business."

plained the situation to everyone he met. "You do not need to worry." He laughed at Bill's concern. "Everyone knows about you now . . . the people of Balayan are your friends."

There was little choice but to go along with it if they wanted a boat. Finally arriving at a more substantial house, they were relieved and happy to see a pair of big Americans, one dark-haired and one blond, waiting for them. These were the first countrymen they'd seen since Corregidor, and Ed trotted the last few yards excitedly. Bill did not; he walked slowly and thoughtfully appraised both Marines. The blond was stockier, with a square powerful jaw and regular features. His blue eyes were friendly, and he was smiling widely. The other man, like Bill, hung back a bit and watched the newcomers from under heavy dark eyebrows that matched his hair. His hooded brown eyes weren't unfriendly, just wary, and he reminded Bill of a trained guard dog waiting for a command to attack. Both men appeared well-fed and moved easily like the Marines they were.

Sitting there in the shade, everyone's stories came out. The friendly blond was Private First Class Tramble Oresta Armstrong, from Brewton, Alabama. He'd joined the corps in 1939 and went to sea with the Marine detachment aboard the battleship New Mexico. Reassigned to the Philippines in 1940, Armstrong was posted to the Cavite Naval Yard until the 4th Marine Regiment arrived in December 1941. Corporal Reid Carlos Chamberlain was also a prewar leatherneck, and he enlisted during June 1938 from his home in El Cajon, California. Granted a dependency discharge the following year to care for his elderly mother, Carlos worked as an aircraft welder for Consolidated Aircraft before being recalled in June 1941. Requesting the Pacific, he arrived in the Philippines during August 1941 and was assigned to Company C of the 1st Separate Marine Brigade. Wounded at Cavite on December 10, Chamberlain was one of the few Marines participating in the fighting retreat down the Bataan peninsula.

Leading an ambush on February 25, he was nominated for a Silver Star for single-handedly eliminating a Japanese machine-gun position.

Promoted to corporal, Carlos was shuttled over to Corregidor and absorbed into the 3rd Battalion with all the other stragglers.* It was here he met Tramble Armstrong, and both men remained on the Topside sector near the James Ravine during the fighting. When the Rock fell on May 6, they vowed never to be captured and escaped that same night from Breakwater Point. Their platoon sergeant, Harry Pinto, reported that he saw them "get into a small cabin launch along with two Navy men in uniform and several Filipinos in civilian clothes, and head toward Cavite shore." According to Chamberlain, there were actually three army soldiers, another Marine, and ten Filipinos.

Expecting to be fired upon at any time, they motored eight miles across Manila Bay into Limbones Cove on the Cavite shore. Everyone hopped into the cold water, then swung the boat around and shoved it back out to sea with the throttle open. By the time Chamberlain and Armstrong reached shore, they were alone, so the pair decided to wait for dawn before deciding what to do. Discovering a little sailboat when the sun came up, they set off again down the coast and three days later found themselves in Balayan Bay. Friendly Filipinos in Balayan made certain the two young Americans were safe and brought to the López hacienda, where all four now squatted in the shade. The younger Marines were impressed that Bill and Ed had survived the hellish fighting east of Malinta Hill, and both were relieved to have one of their own officers present again.

For the next few weeks, the four Americans rested, talked, and roamed around the five-thousand-acre plantation. There was hiking in the Mount Batulao foothills, quiet afternoons fishing along the Dacanlao River, or visiting with locals as they roasted corn over open fires. There was always food now, and starvation was just a bad memory. Bill filled out again, regaining his muscle tone and agility. He could

---

* Both were riflemen; Armstrong served in I Company, while Chamberlain was attached to M Company.

sleep again, and with his improved physical state once again felt like a clear-eyed, decisive Marine officer. Not that there were any overt military formalities on the hacienda; though Carlos and "Army" Armstrong were enlisted men, they were all in this together, and Bill had never been a martinet. There was no need; when he made a soft suggestion, it was inevitably carried out like an order.

On rainy days they stayed in the hut and chatted about the war and their plans, or read from the piles of old copies of *Reader's Digest* that Don López kindly provided. Though they laughingly agreed to a postwar meeting at the Coconut Grove in Los Angeles, each man knew the chances of surviving till then were slim. First, they had to decide what to do next, and this was hardly simple. China was still out due to the seasonal winds, so that left two choices. One was to head to the southern Philippines and join one of the guerilla groups said to be operating on Mindoro or Panay. This meant traveling through Japanese-held waters, but the trip was less than two hundred miles and would put them all back in action fast. Still, no one seemed to know exactly from where any such groups operated, nor any of the leaders. The second choice was Australia. Daunting as the two-thousand-mile, open-water trek was, they all favored this option. They were American fighting men, not guerillas; each man wanted to rejoin the regular military and take part in crushing Japan.

Through the Filipinos they heard rumors of two big sea battles, one near Australia and one way out in the Central Pacific, but no real details. Had Australia been invaded? Or Hawaii? After Bataan and Corregidor, Bill knew anything was possible, but he couldn't imagine Australia in enemy hands. Not this quickly, anyway. It was too big, and the Aussies he knew would never surrender. Hawaii made more sense. Much smaller, and if held by the Japanese it was 4,500 miles nearer to the U.S. West Coast. Harris wasn't worried about an invasion of North America; the Japanese would have to empty their Chinese garrisons to have anything close to a sizable enough force, and he knew from his time in Shanghai that Tokyo would never risk that. Besides, the entire Imperial Navy didn't have the logistical capability to move such an army across the Pacific.

For that matter, neither did the United States—yet. But Bill knew his own country and had an unshakable belief in its latent power, which was why he intended to make for Australia rather than becoming a guerilla fighter here. America would be gearing up for war, and would eventually be coming across the Pacific with a vengeance thirsty for Japanese blood. Bill wanted to be part of that: payback for their sneak attack and for all his dead Marine brothers. He wanted to see the sky dark with American warplanes and watch guns from hundreds of warships shatter eardrums and break Japanese bodies. Bill wanted to break a few himself for the beating he'd received on Corregidor. How satisfying that would be . . . to get his big hands around the enemy's throat and squeeze the life out of him. Squeeze until his skin purpled and his eyes bulged. Bill wanted to smile at the shocked look in his cruel eyes as he realized death had come for him. No, Harris had already decided. It was Australia, and back into the war as soon as possible. Glancing around, he admitted it was tempting to remain safe, fed, and warm right here.

Tempting maybe, but Bill couldn't do it.

"Do you suppose they really intend to get a boat for us, or are they just stalling?" Harris asked one day to the others as they lounged on the porch. Rain dripped on the thatch, and a cool breeze was flowing down the mountain, but after nearly five weeks of too much food and not enough action, he was a bit edgy. "I like this place okay, but I'll be damned if I'm not about ready to pull stakes," Armstrong agreed. "I'd sure like to get back to civilization and see what's happening." After some discussion, it was agreed that they would inform their host that they were leaving in three days, with or without a boat.

Miraculously, the craft was delivered seventy-two hours later to a private spot on Balayan Bay near López's sugar warehouses, and

Bill felt a bit sheepish for doubting. It was a "thirty-foot, relatively fat-bottomed *banca*, five feet wide at its greatest." There was a boom sail, and Don López had stocked it with "water, canned goods, tobacco, dried beef, coffee, matches, and quinine." There was some sugar, and two hundred pounds of rice, along with firewood and even a stove, a five-gallon gasoline can with sand in the bottom, an eight-inch vent cut through the side, and a wire grate for grilling. López had also thoughtfully provided a marine compass, a Philippine Census Bureau Atlas covering the entire archipelago, and an old school wall map detailing island passages, coves, and reefs.

Shoving off into the black waters of the bay, Bill took the tiller and Carlos, who had sailed often off Silver Strand beach near San Diego, worked the sheet. For thirty minutes it was idyllic; the sail filled well, the rigging groaned, and stars twinkled overhead. Phosphorescence sparkled along the rudder and in the wake as the boat skimmed southwest across the bay. Best of all, they were free, and Bill felt exuberant. Escaping from Corregidor had been a necessity—he was certain it meant death to remain. The trip up Mount Mariveles and over to Subic Bay was similarly dictated by fate—there had been no place else to go. Just like the voyage here to Balayan, with all the weeks of danger and starvation. Even here it was barely thirty-five miles from the Rock—but they were heading out to sea, and south to freedom. Now their fate was back in their hands, to succeed or fail, win or lose, live or die. It was a magnificent feeling.

And it should have been a warning.

Abeam San Pedrino Point, Bill felt the wind hit his cheek a heartbeat before it caught the sail and instantly threw his weight against the tiller—and it saved them. When the wall of wind struck, it didn't quite catch them broadside, which gave Carlos a moment to release the sheet and drop the sail. Curtains of cold driving rain slammed into them, and for a few wild moments all they could do was hang on. Suddenly, a powerful white beam arced up from the water not two miles away, and the men instinctively ducked, their stomachs knotted. Lancing through the blackness, the searchlight could only be from a Japanese patrol craft, and Bill was certain they'd be discovered.

Straining every muscle in his body, he put the tiller further over and kept the bow into the four-foot rollers by jamming his body against the gunwale. Soaked and cold, the men rode out the squall, and the searchlight eventually vanished. When it cleared, they changed into their one set of dry clothes and had just raised the sail again when a second storm hit. Thoroughly miserable now, they hunched together in sloshing water at the bottom of the boat until it passed. Peering through red, salt-stung eyes, Bill stared at the shore to try and get his bearings.

No . . . it couldn't be. He looked up and down the low green shore. But it was.

The smaller U-shaped bay on the western edge of Balayan Bay was behind them—almost due west. Straight ahead to the east, a dark cone rose above the haze that had to be Mount Maculot. *Son of a bitch . . .* the squalls had blown them back to the northeast corner of the bay. So, after an entire night, they were not five miles from the sugar warehouse where they'd started. *Son of a bitch,* he swore again, and the wind was now completely gone. There was nothing for it now but to paddle, which they did. With the sun, at least, came warmth, and the men put their backs into the chore of rowing the sluggish *banca.* Horribly exposed, they had to get off the bay before a Japanese patrol found them, and by alternating they kept a slow but steady pace toward the eastern shore. By noon, Bill's shoulders ached, and searing pain shot through his muscles each time he bent forward. The others felt the same, and the old shirt wrapped around the oar was streaked with blood. To make thing worse, they discovered the water drum hadn't been properly scrubbed, and there was oil in the drinking water. They drank anyway.

Finally pulling onto a "sandy border fronting a small valley cupped out of the low, rough hills," they staggered ashore and collapsed on the beach. Sleeping till dusk, they ate a soggy rice dinner then clambered back aboard. Against the southerly wind and constant rain, they took turns rowing around the peninsula, "like a passage up a river of hell, but not hot, not even warm." By early morning on Monday, July 27, they managed to get out of Balayan Bay by rounding the spike-like projection of Cazador Point. Raising the sail at last, Bill tacked the *banca* through the narrow passage above saddle-shaped Maracaban Island and by dawn put into a little cove on the northern shore. A fisherman invited them to his home and gave them dry clothes, a warm meal, and best of all, *tuba*, a "delicious, intoxicating . . . wonderful, fermented, cider-like palm sap." He also gave them some strong manila rope and a new anchor.

For three more backbreaking, mind-numbing nights, the four men rowed, tacked, and drifted east along the length of Maracaban, across Batangas Bay, and down the jagged shore "past mile after mile of the sparsely inhabited, almost roadless coast" under the shadow of Mount Pinamucan.

As dawn arose on July 31, six days after leaving Balayan, the *banca* grated onto a rocky beach near the mouth of the Lobo River, and the four exhausted Americans tumbled out onto the beach. They were bearded, red-eyed, and irritable, and their clothes were dank and wet. Bill smelled like seawater, salt, and woodsmoke from their little stove, but he couldn't have cared less. Since clearing Cazador Point, their voyage totaled less than twenty-five miles, and everyone was discouraged and fed up—at this rate it would take over a year to reach Australia. A Filipino farmer who saw them land appeared and invited them to his house for breakfast, and they gratefully accepted.

"The trouble," Carlos said after a welcome hot meal, "is that the winds blow fine in the daytime, but at night, when we are sailing, they die down. I think we ought to sail in the daytime, at least until we get away from Luzon."

Bill had been thinking the same thing. Though they could always be spotted by a Japanese patrol boat or aircraft, most of the enemy activity was to the north near Manila, and the farther south they went, the safer it appeared. Besides, they were all skinny again, long haired, and dressed nondescriptly. He thought it a good idea.

Ed Whitcomb did not. "Well, I'm sure not for it." He shook his head. "I think we ought to try it this way for a couple more nights; then we will be out of the danger zone. The only reason we left Balayan this time of the year was because we had the Japs on our trail. Well, we've shaken them now, and we're at a place where we can safely wait for the wind."

"I think we should sail on today," Armstrong spoke up, staring out to sea.

Ed shook his head again. "I say stay until November when the northeast monsoon's blowing strong again. Then we can get a new start. In the meantime, we can join the guerrillas and maybe pick up a better boat."

"Let's take a vote on it," Chamberlain suggested, looking them over, and the three Marines each raised a hand. Ed was unmoved, and crossed his arms over his chest. "You can count me out of your vote, because I'm not willing to sail in the daytime under any conditions. You can outvote me, but you can't force me to go."

Bill knew his friend well enough by now to recognize he could not be swayed. Ed's point was valid, but so was the case for pushing on ahead, so today looked like an unexpected farewell. After resting and taking another meal, they all walked down to the boat again to change into dry clothes. Pushing the *banca* out into knee-deep water, Chamberlain scrambled up forward and wrapped the sheet around his hand, while Armstrong held the boat steady. Bill turned to Ed, and both men stared into the other's face. The Marine lieutenant stuck out his hand, and as the army officer firmly grasped it, a flood of memories rushed back. The shock of capture and the baking heat on Malinta Hill; the endless buzzing and foul stench of the 92nd Garage; their eight-hour swim across the dark, dangerous waters of Manila Bay; and the spine-tingling exhilaration of freedom. Whitcomb remembered the Marine's strength, calm fortitude, and bravery, while Bill recalled Ed's cheerful optimism. They made a good team, and both knew they could not have done it alone.

Still, every man has his limits, and Ed Whitcomb had reached his own. Letting go, Bill nodded and turned, holding the boat while Armstrong jumped in. Scrambling into the stern, he took the tiller as the sail flapped and the *banca* bobbed in the surf. Glancing back, Bill raised his hand, and the thin, lonely figure returned the gesture with his arm up, palm out. Cresting a wave, a dash of salt water caught Bill in the face, but, spluttering and blinking, he manhandled the tiller and got the boat through the surf line. Now, heeling into the wind with a full sail, he twisted around for one final look at the beach . . . but Ed Whitcomb was gone.

✳

SIX

CURRENTS

FOR SEVEN DAYS THE TRIO TRAVELED EAST, INITIALLY ALONG BATANGAS, then out into the open waters of Tayabas Bay. They stayed offshore to catch the wind, but not so far as to attract Japanese attention. Several times they saw gunboats or aircraft, but none approached. There were other *bancas* and larger fishing vessels all around, and from a distance there was nothing "American" about the three men. From the faded maps, Bill decided to cut across the bay north of the island province of Marinduque rather than continue hugging the Quezon provincial coast, since this would save time and get them to the Bondoc Peninsula much faster.

Heading out from Locoloco Point early on August 3, they caught a near-gale-force wind that skimmed them fifty miles across Tayabas Bay to the coast north of Catanauan, where they ran aground on a reef just before midnight. It was a long night trying to get the *banca* off the coral, which they did with the rising tide. Three more exhausting days passed as the three men rowed and tried tacking against the strong southeast wind. "I expected trouble travelling during this monsoon," Bill later wrote, "but I never expected *this* trouble. I thought the southwest monsoon would blow from the southwest; but not in these parts because it has to blow from the southeast."

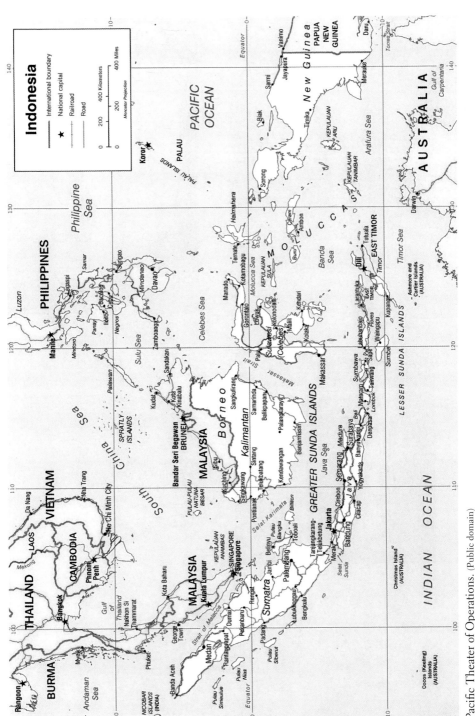

Pacific Theater of Operations. (Public domain)

Bill Harris, USNA Class of 1939,
with Field and Katie Harris.

Midshipman Bill Harris
with Lt. Earl Harris, 1937.

Captain Field Harris with
Katie and Bill. Cavite,
Philippines. ci 1920.

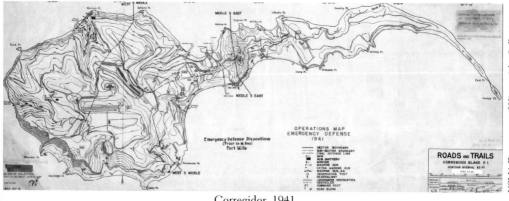

Corregidor, 1941.

Harris Family at Yellowstone, 1929.
Author collection, courtesy of Katey Harris Meares

Surrender at Malinta Hill.
National Archives, Philippine Collection

Betty's over Corregidor, May 1942.
U.S. Marine Corps History and Museums Division

Poster.

Women in the War.

Reid Carlos
Chamberlain.

Tramble Armstrong.

BGen Field Harris (right), Torokina
Airfield, Bougainville, 1943.

Omori camp,
Tokyo Bay.

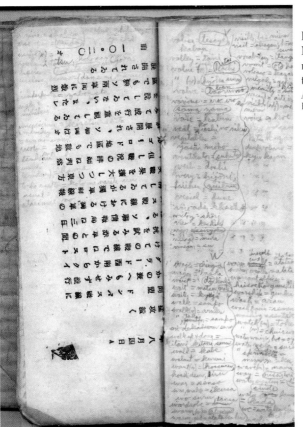

Bill Harris' POW diary. Note the stolen Japanese newspaper and his translation. 1944.
Author collection, courtesy of Katey Harris Meares

Omori Liberation, 1945.

National Archives

Navy Message, September 3, 1945.

Author collection, courtesy of Katey Harris Meares

Flyover of Tokyo Bay by U.S. aircraft. September 2, 1945.

Jeanne Glennon christens the USS Glennon (DD-620), 1942.

Ensign Jeanne Lejeune Glennon.

Major Bill Harris with Jeanne Glennon, 1946.

Bill Harris and Ed Whitcomb,
January 1946.

Bill and Katey, 1950. Jamestown, RI.

Bill and Jeanne with Katey.

Lt. Colonel Bill Harris, USMC.

Eight days after leaving Lobo, on the afternoon of August 7, 1942, the battered *banca* scraped over the rocks on an excellent little beach just north of a fair-sized village.* The Marines all agreed to avoid the barrio until they could get their bearings and the lay of the land, so they bedded down in the hills north of the town. Filipinos all along their trip had told them there were guerillas here, and more to the south, which Bill fervently hoped to be true since they needed help. By now, it was apparent to him that the thirty-foot *banca*, though fine for inter-island travel and fishing, could not possibly carry them two thousand miles to Australia. Harris knew the guerillas would be able to help, especially in return for military expertise, and they might also have some news about the war beyond the Philippines. If they could be located.

He needn't have worried.

A wet, cold, morning followed the wet, cold night, and with it a small band of locals materialized from the trees bordering the beach. The Marines were wary, and surprised to see them openly carrying long, curved bolo knives, several Springfield rifles, and a few home-made shotguns known as *baltiks*. Apparently, they'd seen the *banca* approach, and had decided not to kill the three men until they got a closer look. As always, Bill was cautious; most Filipinos remained loyal to the United States, and loathed the "Hapons," as they called the Japanese, but one never really knew. There were also criminal gangs who, like thugs everywhere, saw opportunity in any sort of chaos. Fortunately, these turned out to be the right sort. Identifying themselves as members of Vera's Tayabas guerillas, they offered each man a dark little hand-rolled cigarette.

One man, older than the rest, revealed he was a veteran of the Philippine Revolution, said that his name was Rosales and that he had recently been asked to join the "gurreelas." He had not done so, but would take the Americans to their leader after they rested at his

---

* The village is Mulanay, in Bondoc, Aurora.

nearby ranch. His daughter Patty recalled that the Marines looked "sick, tired, and hagard [*sic*]." She liked Armstrong, and later wrote his mother that Tramble always helped her gather coconuts, had a lovely singing voice, and spoke Tagalog. She also liked Bill Harris very much, "but the lieutenant was so refined in manners that I seldom talked to him. He was nice . . . but he was always reading."

After several days, Rosales took them inland along the narrow Mulanay River, then through a coconut plantation with tiny clearings farmed by nomadic gardeners called *kaingineros*. Even through the hills it was less than twenty miles across the peninsula, and they reached the heights above Gulf of Ragay a day later. The view was magnificent; the ridgeline on which they stood paralleled a little peninsula sheltering the village of San Narciso from the gulf, and fifteen miles beyond this to the east lay the green, flat coastal plains of Camarines Sur. South down the ridge, the blue-green smudge of a large island poked from the haze, and far out along the horizon Bill could see the spikes from distant mountains.*

Taken to the guerilla "captain," Harris was mildly surprised with Vera. "He had a chubby, smooth, clean-shaven face, chocolate skin, neatly trimmed, slicked down hair which was long on the top and sides and carefully combed back in a pompadour. And his clothes were loud and flashy, an intensely blue, silk shirt, open at the neck and short-sleeved, well pressed, tan-colored, palm beach pants with a stripe design, and beautifully shined shoes, and an expensive gold wristwatch, and a gold chain from his watch pocket."† His teeth were bad, and his voice was "extremely high-pitched."

Nevertheless, Vera was able to fill in a few blanks regarding the state of the war. Wainwright's May 6 surrender on Corregidor, a day

---

* Burias Island. The mountains are Isarog, Iriga, and Malinao in Camarines Sur.
† This was not Captain Epifano Vera, who had formed the Tayabas guerillas, but Sergeant Gaudencio Vera, a former cook for the Philippine Scouts. Captain Vera had been captured and executed during the summer, and somehow the sergeant assumed command and eventually promoted himself "general."

all three Marines would never forget, did not have the effect the Japanese and General Homma anticipated. True, many Americans and Filipinos obeyed Wainwright's order, but quite a few did not—the logic being that a commander who was now a prisoner of war had no legal authority over combatants. Many intended to fight on despite Wainwright's May 8 order for all United States Army Forces in the Far East to lay down their arms. There were also those Americans who simply gave up and used the war as a way to desert the military. Many would never surrender, regardless of the legalities, and officers like Don Blackburn, Claude Thorp, Russell Volkmann escaped at their first opportunity. Hundreds of Filipino officers of the Philippine Army, including Lieutenant Colonels Guillermo Nakar and Macario Peralta, similarly refused to capitulate and faded back into the hills with groups of their men.

From Vera, Bill Harris heard shocking details of what the Filipinos were calling the *Martsa ng Kamatayan sa Bataan*: the Bataan Death March. The day following King's April 9 surrender on Bataan, prisoners were marched northeast from Mariveles, while those captured in the western peninsula were sent northeast from Bagac. Converging on Balanga, the flow of wounded, starving, and emaciated men shuffled north for thirty-five miles to the San Fernando railhead. Anyone who collapsed was murdered by the Japanese guards, frequently with a bayonet or sword. At the Pantingan River, the Japanese 122nd Regiment executed nearly four hundred Allied soldiers from the 1st, 71st, and 91st divisions of the Philippine Army.

Along the march's route, food, and especially water, was scarce, which caused more deaths among the weakened prisoners. At San Fernando they were jammed, a hundred at a time, into boxcars built for thirty men, and shipped an hour north to Capas. From there, those who survived staggered another nine miles to the former 71st Division (PA) base: Camp O'Donnell. No one knew the exact casualty figures from the estimated seventy thousand men who were marched north, but Filipinos believed as many as twenty thousand of their fellow countrymen died, or were murdered. Of the dead Americans, Vera had no number, but word was passed that dozens of men died each day in the hell of Camp O'Donnell.[*] Bill wondered if Uncle Squire had managed his escape or if he'd been marched to the camp.

In the chaotic months after Corregidor, while Japan ran rampant in the Pacific, hundreds of armed groups sprang up throughout the islands. Many were simply bandits looking for power, enrichment, or the settling of old scores—or all of these. Others faded as rapidly as they formed, especially after the immediately anticipated American counteroffensive never occurred. Several groups, notably the Hukbalahap and several large, well-organized Filipino guerilla units, were created with an eye toward an independent postwar Philippines.[†] Whether this would be a democratic republic or communist-socialist nation remained to be seen, but to their credit, and to the credit of the United States, these disparate groups realized they had a better chance of realizing their nationalistic goals with the Americans than with Imperial Japan.

Many Filipinos, especially significant numbers of the ruling elites striving to protect their wealth and power, initially collaborated rather quickly with the Japanese, while those in the countryside largely did not. Nonetheless, Tokyo was already lacking resources and was anxious to begin its exploitation of the islands. Throughout the confusing summer of 1942, while the Japanese attempted to consolidate their gains in the Philippines, combat troops were rotated out and second-line occupation troops, accompanied by the dreaded Kempeitai, moved in.[‡] As it became clear that the islands, at least the interior provinces, were in no way truly conquered, the 32nd and 35th Independent Infantry Battalions were sent to Mindanao, and two additional regi-

---

[*] According to the Office of the U.S. Provost Marshal General's *Report on American Prisoners of War Interned by the Japanese in the Philippines* (November 19, 1945), nearly 1,600 Americans and 26,768 Filipinos perished at Camp O'Donnell.

[†] *Hukbong Bayan Laban sa Hapon* (People's Anti-Japanese Army), or simply "Huks" for short.

[‡] Military secret police.

ments into Bohol and Negros, respectively. The actions of occupying forces, coupled with rising numbers of Kempeitai atrocities, only increased popular support for the guerillas.* In an effort to mollify the populace, the Japanese granted amnesty to thousands of their Filipino "Asiatic brothers" captured during the fighting, and this also failed, as these men returned home angry and full of eyewitness accounts of Japanese brutality that revealed the Pan-Asian lie for what it was.

Torture, looting, and, most despicable of all, wanton rape hardened Filipinos of all classes, against the Japanese. Word was passed and disseminated along a "bamboo telegraph" of couriers and runners throughout the occupied territories, and the events were loathsome. Men were skinned alive, beheaded, crucified head-down over slow fires, or had their armpit hair burned away. Women and girls were rounded up and forced into service as "comfort women" for Japanese soldiers. One story about Loling, a seventeen-year-old girl from Mindanao, spread across the telegraph. Abducted at a village market, she and other schoolgirls were taken to the school where she'd studied as a little girl and gang-raped by a "long line of giggling soldiers."

She was dead the next morning.

"The Hapons are sick men," the telegraph reported. "For who but sick men could think of the things they do?"

Eventually, a series of north-south and east-west routes would be established, with substations every five hours or so, but in August 1942, this had not yet happened. Vera and other territorial leaders had only vague information regarding other such groups, and actions were not yet coordinated. They had enough to do battling the Moros or roaming bandit gangs, who were often worse than the Japanese, and maintaining their own secure areas. Guerillas had to have a base; they needed food, medical supplies, and things they could not obtain by

---

* Many occupation troops were Formosan, Korean, or from the dregs of the regular Imperial Army. However, their officers were Japanese, who understood perfectly that their actions were violations of the rules of war. They simply did not care, as they believed they would be victorious and there would be no consequences for their actions.

raiding the enemy. They needed support from the population, and this they received in return for providing some measure of safety. Filipino guerillas also needed military support. Though many had police or army experience, very few had been professional soldiers, and most were aware that they lacked tactical and logistical expertise—which is precisely why Vera asked Bill Harris and his fellow Marines to remain in Tayabas, at least until the weather shifted.

The prospect of long, wet days battling contrary winds convinced Bill to do exactly that. The Tayabas guerillas were a group of 120 men, all Filipinos and mostly farmers, and Vera was the only one with any military experience, though he was sufficiently vague about his background to make Harris suspicious. Vera seemed equally elusive about fighting the Japanese, and was more interested in controlling the nearby barrios, from which he exacted provisions and money. Bill was certain this particular group was one of the bandit gangs, but didn't want to end up with his throat cut so he played along for several weeks. In return for the promise of a boat, the Marines did what they could to improve sanitation, organize the guerillas, and teach them the basics of squad-level combat. Still, Harris slept lightly and kept his newly acquired Moro blade with him at all times.

Not overly surprised at the duplicity, Bill knew that when the existing American and Philippine Army structure collapsed, many units were left fractured and leaderless—at least at the upper levels. Many mid-grade officers followed their superior's orders and lay down their arms, but a surprising number did not. These men gathered survivors and stragglers and then took to the hills, which would remain largely beyond Japanese control for the duration of the war. The Japanese had committed sizable forces against population centers on the main islands, but they gave the countryside little thought. This made perfect sense by their logic, as the Americans would be cut off, and they expected the Filipinos to embrace their Asian "liberators." Tokyo, and General Homma, did not expect or plan for a guerilla war. Frontline combat troops were needed elsewhere, and Homma considered any residual resistance the responsibility of the Manila puppet government and the Philippine Constabulary.

It was a costly miscalculation.

Though the Japanese 48th Division occupied Manila on January 1, 1942, the stubborn resistance of Bataan and Corregidor shattered the thirty-four-day time line allotted for the conquest of Luzon. Bill was gratified to learn the delay in subduing the Rock had cost the Japanese dearly. Most of the big enemy units were in northern Luzon, where most of the resistance was rumored to be based. Vera knew of several Japanese regiments in the Camarines across the Ragay Gulf, but none here in Tayabas, though there was lots of action on the big island of Panay, about 150 miles south across the Sibuyan Sea. Rumors were that Philippine Army stragglers formed a provisional resistance unit there, and the Japanese had deployed an entire regiment to deal with them. It would be a good place to avoid, and Bill was told that there were Americans on Mindanao, farther south.

This made sense.

Harris recalled from the early days of the war that the Visayan-Mindanao Force under Brigadier General William Sharp consisted of five Philippine Army divisions commanded by American officers on Cebu. MacArthur took two of these divisions for Bataan and promoted Sharp and moved him to Mindanao to protect the Del Monte airfield. With the 61st, 101st, and 81st Divisions (PA), plus two regiments and the Philippine Constabulary, Sharp did just that. Army Air Force B-17s and B-25s used the field to harass the Japanese, and a second runway was constructed for fighters. Bill remembered that remnants of the 24th Pursuit Group were there in April, but the field was abandoned in early May. Sharp obeyed Wainwright's order and surrendered on May 10, but the 81st Division commander, former cavalryman Guy Fort, did not.

A longtime resident of the islands, Fort had been a Philippine Constabulary officer who, along with his unit, was absorbed into the Philippine Army in November 1941. Promoted to brigadier general, Fort fought on against the Japanese until the end of May, then reluctantly surrendered while Harris was hiding out on Mount Mariveles. Vera believed there were guerillas operating on Mindanao, but said they would likely be Moros, and recommended the closer island of Panay instead. There was, he had heard through the bamboo telegraph, a large guerilla force in the northern Iloilo Province. After a month on Tayabas, Bill was restless and decided to go the distance, so, with a Filipino guide named Joe, the three Marines set out for Mindanao, by way of Panay, on September 6, 1942.

Contrary winds and violent, cold squalls in the Sibuyan Sea forced them aground on Burias and Masbate Islands, so it wasn't until September 25 that they limped into the fishing hamlet of Carles on Panay's northeastern tip. "We've had the most God damned luck on this trip I've ever seen . . . all bad," Harris lamented. "It's too late now, but if I had to do over again, I'd be a lot more receptive to that idea of going over to Mindoro and waiting for the northeast monsoon."

As it was, the southwesterly gales that had plagued them were fizzling out as the season changed. Northeast monsoons would begin in earnest during October, and Bill thought this might be the right time to try for China—but first things first. It was easy enough to find the guerillas because, as on Tayabas, they found him almost immediately. Intrinsically linked to the civilian population for whom they provided security, the guerillas possessed an excellent intelligence network and very little occurred that did not make its way to their commander.

Informed through Joe by the fishermen that the nearest Japanese garrison was in Roxas City, some thirty-five miles distant, the Marines relaxed. Only occasional, infrequent enemy patrols ventured this far east, and there was always plenty of warning given so the locals could hide their food, valuables, and, most of all, their women. Harris and the others had never ventured this far south, and the lieutenant found the indigenous people, broadly known as Visayans, quite different from the Tagalogs of Luzon. They were quiet and reserved, and the few visible women, who did not speak at all, wore a long cloth wrapped around their waist and then folded over the shoulder to cover their chests.* Both sexes wore their hair longer, and were generally less clean than their northern neighbors. They were hospitable enough, but in a rather cold, obligatory manner compared to a Tagalog's unreserved openness.

Nevertheless, Joe was able to make the Visayans understand that they wished to be taken to the closest guerilla camp, and the next day several men appeared to do just that. They were from the "Town Unit" of Pilar, a village about ten miles west toward Capiz, and were part of the reorganization of locals into the Panay guerilla structure. Through them, Bill had his first inkling that the situation on Panay was vastly different than that in Batangas or on the Bondoc Peninsula. Favorable geography naturally divided the island into three separate areas quite conducive to guerilla operations, and, more important, Panay had been home to the 61st Division (Philippine Army) until May 1942.

Initially commanded by Colonel Bradford Chynoweth, a U.S. Army regular officer of long experience, the division was activated throughout the fall of 1941, and absorbed the existing Philippine Constabulary personnel on Panay and nearby Romblon Island. Nominally composed of four infantry regiments with accompanying support units, manpower was never an issue, but weapons and ammunition were. By the time the Japanese invaded Panay, the division was down to two regiments, having deployed the 61st and 62nd, plus the field artillery, to Mindanao. Chynoweth, now a brigadier general, had been ordered by MacArthur to assume command of the Visayan-Mindanao Force so the remnants of the 61st Division fell to Colonel Albert Christie in March 1942.

Bill Harris had heard of the shuffle while on Corregidor but thought little of it. Little did he know then how much such a move would affect him six months later. Christie, also a regular officer, had his own ideas about defending the island, and enjoyed the wholehearted

---

* Called a *patadion*, much like a Scottish great kilt.

support of his Filipino subordinates—particularly an energetic young lieutenant colonel named Macario Peralta. Trained as a lawyer, Peralta had taken a reserve commission in 1936 but moved to the regulars and graduated top of his class in the 1940 Philippine Army Infantry School. Peralta was also the divisional operations officer and thus had a complete grasp of the men, officers, logistics, and terrain on Panay.

In April word filtered down about the fall of Bataan, and when Wainwright surrendered Corregidor, the 61st Division on Panay moved back to prepared defensive positions deep in the island's rugged interior. Christie had no intention of trying to prevent a Japanese invasion, but rightly figured he could hold out indefinitely by conducting guerilla operations, which began with the destruction of locomotives, bridges, and thousands of gallons of fuel. Stockpiling fifteen thousand bags of rice and five hundred cattle, plus cases of canned goods, Christie figured his seven thousand remaining men could fight on at least the six months required under Plan Orange until the Americans returned in force to free the Philippines. When Major General Saburo Kawamura invaded Panay on April 16, 1942, his 4,160 men landed unopposed at all three provincial capitals, but every move was reported back to Christie on Mount Baloy. Moving along the north and south coasts, Japanese combat units secured the single-track railroad connecting Iloilo with Capiz, then waited to be replaced by garrison units.

Three days after Corregidor's capitulation, Colonel Jesse Traywick and a Japanese escort hand-delivered a letter from Lieutenant General Wainwright to Major General Sharp informing him that if Sharp did not surrender, then the Japanese would destroy the Corregidor garrison. The following day, May 10, while Bill lay unconscious in the 92nd Garage area on Corregidor, Sharp surrendered the Visayan-Mindanao Force and directed the same on Panay. Christie, now a brigadier general, had no intention of obeying and felt that without a direct order from MacArthur such a "surrender might be treason." He rightfully questioned the authority of a senior officer who had capitulated to issue lawful orders to an unsurrendered combatant like himself. A week passed, and on May 19 a Japanese plane landed at Tiring Field north of Iloilo carrying Lieutenant Colonel Allan Thayer with a letter from Sharp, which read, in part:

> You will understand from the letter addressed to me from General Wainwright, my commander, that in the name of humanity, there is but one course of action to take. Lest there be any misunderstanding, I shall explain that General Wainwright has not surrendered Corregidor and is not a prisoner—likewise I am not yet a prisoner. However, I have pledged the surrender of all forces in the Visayas and I likewise expect you to carry out my orders in this matter.

Believing he had now received a direct order from his own commander, Christie felt he had no alternative but to comply. Nevertheless, he sympathized with his Filipino soldiers and told Peralta as he made ready to leave that "if I were in your place, I would do the same." The general also relinquished the division's weapons, supplies, and one hundred thousand pesos to the Filipino officer and then added, "But you will realize that, as commander of this Division and as an American, I have the responsibility to comply with the order of surrender."* Peralta didn't think so and later wrote, "I considered Sharp's letter as one coming from a prisoner and of no binding effect, notwithstanding Sharp's statement to the contrary."

So, on May 22, Christie issued the official order for surrender and he, with all thirty of the division's American officers, "sadly trudged their way" to the provincial jail in Iloilo City, and then into Fort San Pedro. Peralta, and some 80 percent of the division's strength, immediately dispersed into the hills, eventually establishing his headquarters in the Mount Carabao foothills at Daan Norte. Laying low for the

---

* The letter was dated May 12, 1942, so when Sharp wrote it, Wainwright had been a prisoner for six days. Whether he knew it or not, word had certainly not reached Christie on Panay.

next sixty days so as not to give the Japanese cause to kill the prisoners
taken on Bataan and Corregidor, Peralta used the time to reorganize
his "Freedom Fighters of the 61st Division" into three provincial military commands. He established a workable chain of command, sup-
pressed banditry, and planned the initial round of attacks against the
Japanese, which began in earnest during August 1942. These started
small, but gained in scope and forced the enemy garrisons out of the
countryside. Peralta was successful enough to move his headquarters out of the mountains and begin his plan of reconstituting the
61st Division into a cohesive fighting force.

This, Bill Harris gathered from his escorts, was the general state of
affairs now in late September, which was why he was being taken to
Sara, less than ten miles from Concepcion Bay on Panay's east coast.
There was a decent road running down the island's west coast, and
the little party traveled quite openly through the flat plains around
Balason and Batad. Paralleling a mountain range off the west, they continued south, stopping at night for rice and corn or various fish dishes
seasoned with red peppers.* Chewing betel nuts and smoking, the
Visayans chatted among themselves in a dialect neither the Americans nor Joe could understand. Bill, always observant, noted more
Spanish-style architecture in the towns, which all seemed to have at
least one church.

Angling in from the coast and gradually climbing into the interior,
they eventually came to an enormous banana plantation near Sara,
and here in the hills the guerillas had an extensive, well-organized
camp. Peralta lived nearby in Maligayligay, but the headquarters group
was in Alibayog and it was here that Bill met the guerilla leader. Dark-
eyed and slender, Peralta, or Mac as he was sometimes called, retained
the upright bearing of a regular officer. Clean-shaven with full lips
and somewhat protruding ears, the colonel received the Marine officer graciously, and the two spoke at length about Bill's ordeal, other

---

* Mounts Bacod and Alapasco.

guerilla bands, and Japanese movements. He was particularly interested in Corregidor and the condition of Luzon because, though born
in Manila, he'd grown up in Tarlac.

Peralta was also much better informed than Vera, and passed
along some news from the outside world. Much of this was received
through Captain Guillermo Nakar of the 14th Infantry Regiment,
who possessed a SCR-177 command field radio that was left behind
when the Americans on Luzon surrendered. Trying since June to
contact MacArthur, on July 10 Nakar's message was intercepted by a
coast watcher on Java and relayed to Australia. "Detachment of Fil-
American forces—we have not surrendered and are actively raiding
northeast towns of Pangasinan, including Dagupan." This was vital as
the message was the first real communication from the Philippines
since Corregidor fell in May.

Nakar had gone off the air in August, but not before relating that
the Japanese *had* been given a short, sharp bloody nose in the Battle
of the Coral Sea.* However, the big news passed along the bamboo
telegraph came from the Central Pacific. On the morning of June 4,
as Bill was skirting the western edge of Bataan in his *banca*, attacking
aircraft from Nagumo's Mobile Striking Force slashed through the
Marine fighters over Midway and pummeled the atoll. Operation MI,
Admiral Isoroku Yamamoto's plan to crush the U.S. Pacific Fleet, was
under way.

The idea was to attack Midway, which, since it was less than
1,500 miles from Pearl Harbor, would force the Americans to respond,
and in order to ensure this, another force was to assault and invade the
Western Aleutian Islands—American territory. Nagumo's carrier-based
assault would neutralize the air threat from Midway, which would then
be invaded and conquered. The seizure of American territory and
the imminent threat to Hawaii and the West Coast must, Yamamoto

---

* Nakar was captured by the Japanese and would be executed in September at Fort
Santiago.

believed, compel Nimitz to commit his ships. Once they were lured into open water beyond land-based air cover, Yamamoto could then destroy the Pacific Fleet with the cornerstone of Japanese naval tactics: the "decisive victory" from a big-gun naval battle.

Despite, or perhaps because of, these lofty objectives, Operation MI began to go wrong almost immediately. Invading the Western Aleutians was an unnecessary diversion that weakened Yamamoto's main force by two smaller aircraft carriers that could have added another 963 additional aircraft to the Midway assault.* Also, the Japanese greatly overestimated the importance of those frozen islands and the imagined affront caused by their loss. Nimitz did not take the bait and, through the superb efforts of American code breakers, knew the real enemy objective was Midway. The admiral also had another asset: the USS *Yorktown*, which the Japanese thought was sunk in the Coral Sea, and which comprised another carrier task force with ninety combat aircraft. Unaware that their JN-25b code was compromised, the Japanese believed they retained the element of surprise and walked into Nimitz's trap.

By 0915 of June 5, all four of Nagumo's fleet carriers had been destroyed, 254 aircraft had been lost, and 3,057 Japanese were dead, including 110 of their top naval aviators.† Additionally, two battleships were badly damaged, with three cruisers and three destroyers sunk for good measure. The Americans lost approximately 150 aircraft and 307 men, and two ships sank: the destroyer *Hammann* and the *Yorktown*. At 0443 on the morning of June 7, while Bill Harris waited to dash across the mouth of Manila Bay, the tough, hard-fought carrier rolled to port and at 0501 she sank, stern first, with her American flag still flying defiantly.

Despite the *Yorktown*'s loss, the battle was an American victory, though not decisive in that it did not determine the outcome of the

---

* *Ryūjō* and *Jun'yo*.

† *Akagi, Kaga, Sōryū, and Hiryū*. All four were part of the December 7, 1941, attack on Pearl Harbor.

Pacific War. Bill Harris, and others like him, understood that what America needed in 1942 was time, time to manufacture, produce, train, and deploy. Midway did do that. Through it, the United States regained parity in naval airpower, and dealt the empire a material blow from which it could not recover. Losing four fleet carriers, with a shipbuilding industry that could not make good the loss, was critical. The human loss of 110 highly trained aviators, though bad enough, *could* have been made good if the Imperial Navy immediately altered its selection and training process—which it did not.

From Bill's perspective sitting on an island in the Philippines, he hoped the battle would severely curtail Japan's offensive capability, which it certainly did. Japanese momentum was interrupted at the Coral Sea, but was stopped cold at Midway, at least for large-scale strategic initiatives. This would eventually force the empire into defense reactions rather than offensive action, and from behind a defensive barrier that was incomplete. Japan's strategic priority until the Doolittle raid had been isolating Australia from the United States, and it intended to do this through Operation FS: the occupation of New Guinea and the Solomons and the cutting of supply lines by taking Fiji and the Samoan Islands. This July timetable would now have to be recalculated. It also further isolated Japan from her Axis partners and destroyed any feeble hopes of cooperation against the Allies. Essentially, World War II would be decided in Europe or on the steppes of the Soviet Union, and Japan was now truly alone against the United States.

Harris also learned that Germany had other priorities. Three weeks after Midway, while Bill was hiking across Batangas on the way to Balayan Bay, Rommel captured Tobruk and seemed poised to take all of North Africa. If this happened, Britain would lose the Suez Canal and be severed from her immense Indian resources. Rommel could then conceivably drive north into the Middle East, capture Iran's vast oil wealth, then cross the Caucasus Mountains to link up with Von Paulus in southern Russia. It seemed to him that only here in the

Pacific had the Axis been seriously bloodied in 1942, though he knew the Japanese well enough to understand that they would never stop as long as their emperor commanded them to fight.

Macario Peralta, Bill discovered, was a versatile, well-informed professional. He understood the implications of the larger war and was happy to discuss them with a man who had seen much of the world but his focus, rightfully so, was on the Philippines—specifically Panay. Just thirty years old during the summer of 1942, Peralta earned a law degree from the University of the Philippines and, until May, had served with Brigadier General Albert Christie's 61st Division (PA). Peralta, a regular army captain and the divisional operations officer, possessed excellent knowledge of Panay, his men, and the enemy that would be invaluable in the hard years to come.

Harris remembered that Iloilo City and the military airfield on Mandurriao were bombed during the weeks following Pearl Harbor, but it wasn't until Bataan fell in April that Panay was invaded. He learned from Peralta that two weeks before the surrender, Major General Saburo Kawamura's Reinforced 9th Infantry Brigade sailed from Singapore for the Philippines, escorted by several destroyers and the light cruiser *Kuma*. Departing Lingayen Gulf three days following King's capitulation, the 41st Regiment of the Kawamura Detachment anchored off Trapiche, some six miles west of Iloilo City. Splashing ashore unopposed at dawn, they found the air over the city heavy with the "sweet sour odor of burnt sugar," the bridges destroyed, and most of Iloilo in ashes. Fifty miles distant on the island's north shore, another force landed at Baybay on the outskirts of Capiz and was similarly uncontested. Two weeks after landing, Kawamura declared Panay secured, and on April 30 departed for Mindanao. The 33rd Independent Infantry Battalion took over occupation duties, and at this point the Japanese seemed largely content to occupy larger coastal towns, leaving the interior alone with the exception of several small, scattered garrisons.

Christie's 61st Division (PA) had wisely decided not to fight on

Japanese terms, and faded back toward Mount Baloy to begin guerilla operations. Vast amounts of ammunition, equipment, supplies, and weapons had been moved here following Bataan's defeat in anticipation of fighting on alone. This continued for the next month, until Traywick's order for Christie's surrender and the news that Corregidor had fallen. One Filipino captain tore up the surrender order and exclaimed, "I do not desire to be a prisoner in my own home and the Philippines is my home." Peralta also had no intention of capitulating and stated, "I would rather face court-martial after the war than surrender to the Japanese."

Christie understood, and granted permission for those who wished to disperse into the hills in return for a promise to delay guerilla operations for sixty days so the Japanese could not blame the Americans. Peralta and the others agreed. There were, Bill also learned, a group of American miners and missionaries who had escaped the Japanese and set up a small community they called Hopevale. About thirty miles east of Sara, it was near the Panay River in the valleys around Mount Panginraon. If the Marines wished, Peralta would provide guides to take them to their countrymen. Bill politely declined. He was a fighting man, and there was a war on, so his priority was getting back into it. The Filipino colonel quite understood that point of view and offered whatever assistance he could provide to get them on their way. Harris was grateful, but also grasped that Mac's ultimate goals differed from his own, as the reconstituted 61st Division officially contained no Americans, and the colonel seemed intent on keeping it that way.

Bill suspected the man had postwar ambitions centered on Philippine nationalism, which was fine, but the Japanese had to be defeated first, and that would not happen without America. Peralta knew this, and was positioning himself to fill the power vacuum, so that when the empire was beaten, Filipino leaders like himself would have significant influence over their country. He was certainly willing to assist any stragglers, especially a fellow officer like Bill Harris, who might be in a position to relay favorable information to the U.S. authorities.

There were other Americans in Peralta's camp, like Captain Henry Meider and Claude Fertig, but the combat unit commanders were all Filipino.

Meider flew Stinson Trimotors for Iloilos-Negros Air Express before the war, then General Chynoweth commissioned him as an Air Corps captain and made Meider his personal pilot. In December 1941, with war imminent, he created the Panay Airbase Squadron at Mandurrio, which was decimated by air attacks in late December. Meider helped build a new airfield at Tiring, north of Iloilo, but when the Japanese invaded in April 1942, they killed his two-year-old baby and sent Meider's wife to an internment camp. Betrayed to the Japanese by a Filipino, the pilot killed the peasant and then made his way inland to join the guerillas. "This was September 1942 and that is when I decided to join Peralta." Meider was outwardly calm, but Bill could sense his rage and did not blame him.

Claude Fertig was another war "orphan." A mining engineer from La Junta, Colorado, he left during the Great Depression and followed his brother Wendell to the Philippines in the 1930s gold rush boom. When Claude ended up at the Casbay Mine on Masbate, his officer's commission was activated and he joined the 61st Division on Panay. Like Peralta, Major Fertig had no intention of surrendering and slipped into the hills with the Filipinos, where his organizational skills and technical background proved invaluable.

It was now nearly October, and with the rainy season beginning, the monsoon winds would soon shift to the northeast. This now made a sea voyage to Australia impossible until late spring of 1943, so Bill had another choice to make: remain in the Philippines as a guerilla, or try again for China. Remembering the excitement of those exotic prewar days and his elegant house in Shanghai made him smile a bit. "It really is a swell set up," he'd written Katie in 1940 following his arrival there for his first duty station. "The house is large and has a large yard. To make things perfect, we pay no rent." The place had been taken over by the Japanese after their 1937 invasion, but U.S. Marines had chased them out since the house was close to the American cantonment, and the owner made it available for Marine officers of the 4th Regiment stationed in the city. His name was Tse-ven Soong, a Harvard and Columbia graduate who also happened to be Chiang Kai-shek's brother-in-law.

There was a sizable Chinese population in the Philippines, with some 3,500 on Panay alone, so Peralta had good intelligence regarding the situation across the sea, and it had not changed much since Harris left Shanghai in November 1941. Aside from Manchukuo, as the Manchurian puppet state was called, Japanese troops controlled most of the eastern seaboard down to French Indochina, which they also occupied. But, as in the Philippines, this was largely restricted to ports and substantial cities, so there were gaps—gaps big enough for a small group of men to slip through to the interior. Most of the million-man Imperial Army was in Manchukuo preparing to fight the Soviet Union and protecting the region's essential resources.

Gaps.

Bill knew the coastal area south of Shanghai, and if he aimed between Hong Kong and the thumb-shaped Leizhou Peninsula, there was an excellent chance of landing undetected. From here, with some anticipated local help, they could skirt the northern border of French Indochina and get up country to Yunnan Province. It was six hundred miles from the coast, but Bill recalled that the American Volunteer Group, or AVG, flew their P-40 fighters from Kunming on the shore of Lake Dian. He also remembered that Tse-ven Soong's sister Mei-ling, known now as Madame Chiang Kai-shek, directly financed these American mercenary pilots. Poised and articulate, Madame Chiang held a degree in literature from Wellesley College and spoke fluent English with a charming, educated southern accent.

Through his Chinese contacts, Peralta was informed there were still Americans and aircraft in Kunming and agreed that this was a workable plan. Such a connection suited his purposes quite well since the 61st Division's codebooks had been destroyed in April, and if Peralta was successful in acquiring a suitable radio, he would need new codebooks to establish secure communications with Australia. Such a code, Peralta felt, could be procured from U.S. forces in China, especially if his request was vouchsafed by a Marine officer like Bill Harris. As for Bill, he was certain that once in China, passage to Australia through British India could be arranged, or he might even return to the United States.

Both men agreed to delay a month while the weather settled, and in the meantime Peralta would welcome the assistance of three American combat veterans. He offered Harris a captured boat in return for his expertise, and if he would allow Lieutenant Sergio S. Estoiko, a Signal Corps officer, to accompany them to China to procure American radio codebooks. As for the boat, the enemy had dispatched motor launches from Semirara Island and Capiz City to make random landings along the coast hoping to catch guerillas. This didn't work, but it did succeed in keeping the locals off balance and disrupting Peralta's attempt to train and organize his men. One of these launches was captured on September 27, and Bill was taken to see it.

It was a "craft painted mahogany brown . . . its length approximately fifty feet, its greatest width perhaps twelve to thirteen, a boat mounting a small, seven-foot-high wheel house, about a quarter of the length from the bow; and abutting on the wheel house with the same width and about half the height was the above deck part of the engine room, a structure which extended back to a point about a third of the way from the stern." Taken during a raid on Semirara Island, the launch was moved to Culasi on Panay's west coast, then up and around to the mangrove swamps near Capiz City. With a British-built marine diesel engine, the boat seemed perfect for the thousand-mile trip across the South China Sea.

Peralta's plan was ambitious. There were small enemy garrisons scattered around the island, most within fifteen miles of the coast, and the guerilla leader wanted to force the Japanese out of the interior by wiping these out. Iloilo City boasted the main enemy strength, with a regimental-sized force deployed between Dumangas, Pototan, Santa Barbara, and Mandurriao. There were battalion-strength units on the west coast at San Jose and north at Capiz City. The Filipino guerilla leader correctly reasoned that if his Free Panay Guerilla Force controlled the countryside, then the Japanese would be very limited in what they could do on the island. This would allow Peralta to expand his own forces and, in time, perhaps link up with similar movements on nearby Negros and Mindanao.

If the garrison at Capiz was attacked, then the Japanese would have to weaken their defenses around Iloilo to reinforce it, and any such deployments across the countryside would be exposed to ambush. Peralta directed Lieutenant Colonel Chavez to assault the positions around the port and city with his provincial military forces on October 5, 1942. The enemy had about three hundred soldiers total, with light mortars and machine guns, but they were scattered about in various pro-Japanese barrios. Bill's expertise was invaluable in planning an attack on a 120-man enemy unit garrisoned outside the city on the main road. Forming a reinforced company, Harris had two shotgun platoons, a rifle platoon, and one platoon armed with native spears called *sibats*, which could be thrown or used in close combat. About four feet long, the *sibat* had a double-edged blade, and Harris carried one himself. Planning to assault in the darkness of early October's new moon, the guerillas infiltrated from the mangrove swamps through the Capricho District on the north bank of the Panay River and took the enemy completely by surprise. Huddled in the brush thirty yards from the nearest barracks, Harris watched the plan unfold.

"Two soldiers came into sight in the moonlight about seventy-five yards up the street," Bill recalled. "They were wearing the light cloth caps of the Japanese Army, and they were strolling along very lazily with their bayonetted rifles slouching slightly over their shoulders." Having surrounded the barrio, Filipino infiltrators were quietly killing the sentries patrolling the enemy compound. *It has finally begun*, Harris thought, staring at the sturdy compact soldiers walking and talking.

Both wore wrap leggings and had wide leather belts, and their hel-
mets were strapped behind their backs.

Dogs barked, but no one paid any attention; dogs always barked in
Filipino villages, and the Japanese appeared accustomed to the baying.
There was "nothing bad or evil about their faces," he wrote. "They may
be good men for all I know. In fact, they probably are, yet in a moment they're going to be killed at my orders. That's a hell of thing . . ."
Two dark shapes swiftly flitted from the shadows behind the soldiers
and ran noiselessly on bare feet. Heart pounding, Bill was certain the
Japanese would turn, but they did not and, leaping forward, the Filipinos struck simultaneously. Thin, muscular left arms "smoothly went
under the chins of the Japs and tightened up as almost concurrently
they delivered side wise kicks to the rears of the victim's right knees
and dragged them over backward."

Rifles clattered on the ground, and Bill realized he was holding
his breath as both Filipinos drove their long blades into the soldiers'
chests, withdrew, then "drove them in again and again." Gurgling and
sputtering, the Japanese quickly went limp, and their bodies dropped
in the bushes. Other Filipinos appeared and gave the throat slicing "all
clear" signal that the other sentries were dead. Bill signaled to the men
behind him, and they moved off through the trees into position. Fifteen minutes later, according to the plan, each group moved into the
five-building compound from a different side. Heart pounding, Harris
felt the tenseness and tingling, heightened awareness most men experienced before combat. *Just a few more seconds and we ought to catch
them in bed . . .*

Suddenly, a wild cry split the night air, and Bill jumped as a rifle
cracked close by. Tagalog curses rang out, and in an instant, there
were men everywhere. Rectangles of light spilled from open doorways
as the startled Japanese tumbled into the street. Shotguns boomed
as rifles barked, and as he watched, a spearman dashed around a
barracks and impaled a Japanese soldier. The Filipinos attacked all
the barracks except the largest one closest to Bill. "There three re-

doubtable Japanese champions were holding their own against ten assailants," he recollected, one with a bayonetted Arisaka rifle and a pair of officers with "two-handed swords they handled with great dexterity." Parrying and thrusting, the three soldiers were rhythmically killing the attacking guerillas, and as Bill watched, the largest brought his sword down in a savage, vertical slice that split a Filipino skull down to the neck. Roaring with triumph, the man jumped into the street and ran straight at the Marine.

Leaping forward with his spear, Bill met his enemy as the man skidded to a stop with his samurai sword held in both hands over his head. Feinting low, Bill then stabbed high at his opponent's eyes. "He wasn't fooled," Harris wrote. "The Jap was a master." Deflecting the spear, he stepped in with "savage, homicidal triumph" on his face. Off balance, Bill staggered back and fell to one knee. As the man hunched forward to bring the blade down, Harris knew instantly he was too late to save himself and flinched reflexively.

The man's black eyes suddenly widened and his booming roar became a shrill scream. Blinking and scrambling to his feet, Bill saw the soldier's tunic billow outward just below his chin, then split apart as a spear tore through the cloth. Dropping his sword, the enemy officer seemed puzzled as he stared down at the bloody point. Spear up now, the Marine drew back for a thrust, but it wasn't necessary. Blood and froth poured from the man's mouth as the blade vanished. When the Japanese soldier sagged to his knees, Bill saw a Filipino kick him then drive the spear into his back again. Screaming in agony, the officer flopped over, and the *sibat* flashed down again. Tearing the man's throat open as he yanked the blade free, the Filipino snarled in English, "The son of a bitch made one big mistake when he turned his back on me!"

Weak-kneed, Bill exhaled and thanked his savior. Abruptly, the shooting stopped, and moans from the wounded floated into the gunpowder-laced air. Guerillas stood panting, wide-eyed, with dawning comprehension that they had survived the battle. Dogs began barking again. A few Japanese soldiers jumped from windows and were instantly cut down by shotguns. One staggered to his feet, lurching toward the trees while stuffing his intestines back into a gaping belly wound, but, howling with rage, the Filipinos slashed him to pieces. Harris had the officers see to their own casualties, inventory captured equipment, and scrounge up hot meals. One hundred twenty-one Japanese corpses were unceremoniously dumped into a pit, and he noted they were generally clad only in the peculiar *fundoshi* loincloth used for underwear. All told, thirty-seven guerillas died, including the man who had saved Bill's life, but the enemy garrison was wiped out. A large stock of Japanese medicine was confiscated, along with 111 rifles, four light machine guns, six samurai swords, and an assortment of pistols and grenades.

A good night's work.

To celebrate, the locals and guerillas held an impromptu dance in the schoolhouse. Sitting with his back against a wall, Bill slowly relaxed as the strumming guitars played and memories came flooding back. "The last night at the Army-Navy Club in Manila," he recalled, and "those mad, last nights in Shanghai, [and] the gay, happy, carefree ones which had preceded them." Sometime before sunrise, he passed out from sheer exhaustion, sleeping till late in the morning, when a guerilla named Montero awakened him with disturbing news.

"A man came last night," the Filipino was grim. "Six Japanese soldiers stole a *banca* down there to the south like fifteen kilometer." So . . . a few had escaped by following the Pontevedra River to its mouth. When the corpses didn't match the rifles collected, he'd figured that. "They must have already reached Masbate," Montero continued. "Sometime today they will reach their own forces."

That made sense. The Japanese garrison at Iloilo was over a hundred miles by sea on the south side of Panay, but the tip of Masbate lay only thirty miles northeast of Capiz across the Sibuyan Sea. It was enough for Bill, and he gave orders for the guerillas to pack up. The locals would fade into the countryside with their extended families, and the guerillas would burn the village, then withdraw west toward the mangrove swamps around Pandan Island before vanishing into Panay's northern hills. His caution was justified the next morning as the guerillas, safely concealed beneath banana trees along the Aklan road, watched Japanese planes bomb and strafe.

Splitting up into small groups, they dispersed in all directions and Bill headed southeast along the shoreline past Pontevedra, and from there into the countryside of the Capiz province. The promised motor launch was concealed in a river flowing into Banga Bay, a swampy area in the Aklan province west of Capiz, which Peralta used for access to the sea. This was a comparatively easy three-mile hike from the guerilla stronghold and concealed within a high valley behind Mount Sinalay, just inland from Panay's northern coast. Rejoining Armstrong and Chamberlain there, Bill spent the next three weeks training the Filipinos on their captured weapons and making final preparations for the next leg of his trip. He also watched, but was careful to take no part in, the guerilla trial and hanging of several Japanese sympathizers from Capiz. Throughout his time with the locals, Harris deliberately avoided any such acts against the Filipinos. Most appeared justified, especially executing the Sakdalistas from Capiz, but as a serving officer on technically foreign soil he was aware of the gray area.* Such purges were also a convenient way to settle old scores, or consolidate control over an area, just as Vera was doing in Tayabas. With captured Japanese nautical charts, Bill plotted a course west along Panay's Aklan Panhandle, around southern Mindoro, then northwest to parallel the Philippine coast into the South China Sea. Clearing Luzon by at least fifty miles, Bill planned a landfall on the shoreline southwest of Hong Kong near the Leizhou Peninsula.

Nine hundred and twenty nautical miles.

Conducting sea trials off the Panay coast, Bill calculated a best

---

* Sakdalistas were a pro-independence group favoring land and wealth redistribution and believed the Japanese to be the saviors of the Philippines.

cruising speed of six knots, about seven miles per hour, which consistently burned a gallon of diesel fuel for every 3.1 nautical miles traveled. This meant 168 miles covered and fifty-four gallons of fuel consumed every twenty-four hours, which could, under good conditions, put them on Chinese soil by sunset on the fifth day after departing Panay. *That* was exciting. Nonetheless, Bill knew there was no such thing as perfect conditions—not really—so a week was more realistic. Still . . . a week. Then back with his own people, and on his way to Australia or the United States to rejoin the war.

It was more intoxicating than the *tuba,* or the local Sara rum. He'd come to the Philippines almost a year earlier with a fresh heart, faith in his leaders, and absolute belief in the cause for which they would fight. This had changed. Scarred from the men he'd lost and the hardships endured thus far, his heart was harder. Also, Bill admitted to himself, faith in his leaders had taken a beating equal to the one received by the Japanese guard on Corregidor. Anger shot through him, hot and quick, at that memory. He was the son of a general, a southern gentleman, an Annapolis graduate, and an American officer. There would be, Bill swore as he pushed the anger down to a cold place in his heart, a reckoning for *that.*

Escaping had been an excellent first phase of his planned revenge, and now getting all the way out to China, then back into fighting, would be a superb act of vengeance on the Japanese Empire. He could see himself leading a company of howling Marines onto a beach someplace, cutting the enemy to pieces with a bayonet, and grinding his boot into their upturned faces. No sadistic grins then—just broken teeth, smashed bodies, and blood. William Frederick Harris, Marine lieutenant, would repay them for the deaths they'd caused and the pain he'd suffered, but for now there was other work to do.

The thirty-foot *banca* they'd sailed to Carles from Aurora was brought to the little bay and tied up alongside the big motor launch. Everything of value was transferred over, including the mast and sail, which Bill fervently hoped he'd never need again. In addition to the charts, the Japanese had two big coils of rope, tools, and oil. Peralta had an excellent supply system for his fighters, and through this provided an enormous *kaban*, or chest, of rice; dried beef and fish; a cookie tin of sugar; coffee; matches; and several bags of local cigarettes. There was enough space along the afterdeck beneath the awning for ten fifty-five-gallon drums of diesel fuel, and these were securely lashed in place. A few jugs of *tuba* and fifteen bottles of precious quinine were also added—all that was lacking was a large, sturdy water drum, which Peralta promised to obtain.

While the boat was provisioned, each man stowed his meager belongings, and Bill and two of the Filipinos cleaned the fuel injector valves and reassembled the Vickers marine engine. With this done, they fired up the diesel and slowly edged from the mangroves into a tidal stream flowing into the Agbablili River. With an ebb tide, there was barely enough water to power the boat through the reeds and over the mud, so as soon as they reached the river mouth, Bill idled the engine in a cloud of blue exhaust as the Filipinos moored it fore and aft to a pair of trees. There were other fishing boats beyond the river in the bay, so the launch was inconspicuous, and the Japanese did not come here—not yet.

Leaving the boat, Bill and the others walked up over the low, coastal hills then through scattered little barrios toward the mountain two miles distant. Hiking up a spur on the north face, he stopped on the spine and took a deep breath marveling, as always, at the mix of heavy salt air and the lighter, fresher air atop the mountain. Not that Mount Sinalay, at eight hundred feet, was much of a climb, but it seemed larger here on the coast and provided a neat, natural pocket for the guerilla camp below him in the valley. Sinalay certainly didn't compare with Mariveles, though, and the memory of that mountain drew his gaze northward across the Sibuyan Sea. He couldn't see it, of course, but Bataan was up there past the misty blue ridgelines barely 250 miles away. It had taken six terrible months to get this far away from that hellhole yet tomorrow, incredibly, they would motor out of Banga Bay, cross the sandbar at Floripon Point, and head north again toward that reeking, deadly peninsula. Then, loosed from the physical and psychological currents working against him all these months, Bill would cross the sea beyond Luzon toward China's far horizon—and his freedom.

SEVEN

LOST SOULS

FISH.

The deck stank of fish, and old brown scales rotted in the crannies and corners. Heavy and unmistakable, the stench hovered just above the worn deck like an invisible, slightly foul cloud. Though not a fishing boat, the Japanese had plainly used the motor launch that way to supplement their diet, and who could blame them? Inside the wheelhouse, the smell wasn't much better. Fumes from the old diesel floated around the engine room until thick enough, then escaped into the wheelhouse, where they swirled around until sucked out by the breeze.

Bill Harris didn't mind one bit.

Once again free of land, this time he had an engine instead of a sail, plenty of food and water, and a crew. There were five Filipinos, including Lieutenant Sergio Estoiko along with Chamberlain and Armstrong. A surprise addition were two army soldiers, both claiming to be lieutenants, who appeared at the guerilla camp on November 13, the night before departure. Barefoot and skinny, they were thrilled to find the three Marines and immediately asked to accompany them to China. Errold Glew began the war in the 48th Material Squadron of the 24th Pursuit Group at Clark Field. After its mauling by the Japanese, the remaining aircraft deployed to Del Monte Field on Mindanao until Bataan surrendered. Glew and a few others, not wishing to be prisoners, made their way across the Bohol Sea to Cebu, where they joined up with Colonel Irvine Scudder's 2nd and 83rd Infantry (PA). Arriving just before the Japanese landings on Cebu, Glew retreated with Brigadier General Bradford Chynoweth's survivors into the hills, where, according to him, the general commissioned him a lieutenant.* Hiding in the hills, Glew finally made it across the Visayan Sea to join the guerillas he'd heard of on Panay.

Paul Cothran, from McClain County, Oklahoma, followed a different path to Panay. Enlisting in 1940, he'd served with the Coast Artillery at Charleston's Fort Moultrie before transferring to the 31st Infantry Regiment in Manila. A sergeant by the time war came, Cothran fought with the 31st under Lieutenant Colonel Jasper Brady all through the Bataan campaign and was awarded the Bronze Star with an officer's commission. After his regiment was wiped out at the Alangan River on April 8, 1942, Cothran joined those fleeing south and ended up on Panay, where he was captured during the summer. Escaping in August from the Japanese prison camp at Iloilo, he'd come north with Glew looking for Peralta's guerillas in August.†

They were all on deck now, except Bill, who remained at the wheel. A crowded mass of cheering Filipinos lined the bank, and Harris remembered shouting over the wind and chugging engine, "So long . . . I'll see you after the war!" Easing the launch away from the shore into Banga Bay, he turned around and glanced down the river mouth for a moment, then beyond to Mount Sinalay. With a final wave, Bill leaned from the wheelhouse and stared west over the bow at Tabon Island. It was early afternoon on the morning of November 14, 1942;

---

* Though field commissions were granted during the chaos of the Philippine defense, official American records do not support this particular claim. Errold Thomas Glew (number 11010492) of Maine is listed in the National Archives casualty roll as a private, 48th Material Squadron, 24th Pursuit Group.

† Paul L. Cothran is listed in the casualty rolls as a second lieutenant (O-890176).

the sun was shining, the tide was high, and Bill felt an optimism he'd lacked for several months.

Fighting with the guerillas had been necessary, and he'd recovered his physical strength, but hope was another matter. In war, surviving and killing the enemy was supposed to be enough to sustain a man, yet Bill knew that for himself, at least, this was not true. He could have remained here, relatively safe, and fulfilled his duty to kill Japanese, so why sail off into more danger? Why risk everything one more time just to get to someplace else to kill his enemies? There was, Harris knew on that bright Saturday, no real answer to that. Each man must call the shots as he sees them, and for him that meant rejoining the Marines—or die trying. That was what gave him hope.

Spinning the wheel to starboard, Bill felt the launch swing over the pewter-colored water as he headed up the channel around Tabon. Inhaling the heavy salt air, he smiled: rice paddies, fish, and woodsmoke. It smelled like the Philippines, and he wondered, not for the first time, if he would actually ever return here. In the meantime, there was a more immediate concern facing him as the launch rounded Tabon Island. There, just a mile ahead, was a narrow cut leading from Batan Bay into the Sibuyan Sea. It was barely five hundred yards wide at best, and the locals had been explicit about the treacherous currents. Now, during high tide, was the only time a deep-draft boat like this could clear the sandbar in the mouth of the cut and escape into the open waters beyond. Fifteen minutes later, with a man crouching on both sides of the bow, Bill charged through the entrance and opened the throttle as the current tried to suck them back into the bay. Panay didn't want to release them, he thought, as the boat bobbed, strained, then suddenly broke through. With water cascading over the deck, he smacked the wheel excitedly

They were free!

Every man aboard began cheering wildly, and as the launch cleared Floripon Point, Bill brought the throttle back a bit, then spun the wheel hard left. Paralleling the north coast, when breakers at the mouth of a big river on Aklan Point passed his port side, he angled away from the flat, green shoreline toward a line of dark bumps along the northern horizon. With the battered Philippine Census Bureau atlas on the console, Bill set a northwest heading toward a narrow strait between Carabao and Borocay Islands off the tip of Panay. Six hours later, with the western sky splashed red and orange, the launch rounded Borocay Island and headed into open water past Panay. There was a shorter route closer inshore to Mindoro, but Bill didn't want to chance it at night. Once clear, he turned the wheel over to Reid Chamberlain and went aft for dinner. They'd decided to stand four-hour watches, rotating between the wheelhouse, engine room, and sleep, so after a hot meal of rice mixed with pork, Harris turned in.

During the dark hour before dawn Bill took the wheel again. Cupping a chipped mug of steaming coffee—real coffee—in his hands, the Marine stood barefoot staring at a rugged line of mountains ten miles to the east. Mindoro. As the eastern sky lightened, he could see two smaller islands between the boat and the lights of a town on a small bay.* San Jose. He tapped the chart. It had to be San Jose. Satisfied with the position, Bill set a 330-degree heading up the Mindoro Strait and told Joe, one of the Filipinos, to continue paralleling the coast. At five knots it would take all day to run eighty miles up to Cape Calavite, but this way they would cross the Calavite Strait west of Lubong Island and be fifty miles out to sea from Manila Bay by sunrise.

Dawn's golden fingers spread over Mindoro's Mount Baco as the sun rose, warm and comforting. Smooth seas with a cloudless, powder-blue sky promised an idyllic day—or as close to one as possible under the circumstances. "A great school of long, speedy dolphins, two to four feet long, took to following their craft and frolicking around it," he wrote of that day. There were also flying fish, which fascinated the men who had never seen them, and slowly circling sharks. With the worn, wooden wheel in his hands, Bill felt the diesel's steady throb as he

---

* Ambulong and Ilin Islands, with Mangarin Bay just beyond.

balanced easily against the gentle rocking and thought about the day. Inhaling the fresh, salty air, he hoped these would be his final twenty-four hours in the Philippines, at least until he stormed ashore leading a company of vengeful Marines. Both of these were happy thoughts. "It [was] my job to get back in the big war," Bill later wrote, and aside from seeing his family again, this is what kept him going.

With the men lounging on the afterdeck behind the wheelhouse, chatting and pointing toward shore, the sun arced overhead as the launch chugged northwest of Dongon Point and Santa Cruz. Yet, despite the beauty of the day and the tremendous mental boost of getting to sea, Bill picked up an undercurrent of tension from the muttering behind him. Cothran was from some rural area in Texas or Oklahoma, and didn't care much for the Filipinos. "These God damned stupid gooks," he was saying. "They drive me nuts. Honest, they ain't much better than blacks."

Bill's gut tightened at those words, and his face flushed with anger. *Dirty ungrateful bastard,* he thought. *I can't imagine a finer, more loyal people than the Filipinos.* As for the blacks, well, he'd never understood the prejudice. The blacks he'd known in Kentucky, Virginia, and Maryland had been fine, decent folks. Andre, one of his best childhood friends in Haiti, had taught him French. Joe, Harris's companion from Batangas, made no response, but Lieutenant Estoiko was having none of it and returned some low-voiced reply Cothran didn't like. "I'd watch my manners if I was you," the army officer snarled. "Did I ever tell you about the first man I ever killed?"

"No."

"It was when I was fifteen. I was ridin' a freight and there was a big queer hobo on it too. He tried to get me. When he grabbed me, I punched him in the nuts. Then I picked up a piece of iron pipe and beat his God damned head to a jelly. Then I kicked his body off."

Errold Glew, who was from Van Buren, Maine, said nothing racist, but was quite vocal about his war experiences. Bill knew it was almost axiomatic that those who crowed the loudest had the least to crow about—men who had been there and done that didn't feel the need to tell the world about it. Both situations were irritating, but it was only the second day, and Harris hoped they'd both relax a bit. More concerned with the upcoming night crossing than personality conflicts, Bill took his break as afternoon passed into early evening and the great claw shape of Cape Calavite appeared off the bow. Sunset was about 1800, so with sunrise twelve hours later, they had to cross at least seventy miles to clear Manila Bay.

They could make it.

At six knots, nearly seven miles per hour, they could travel the distance in ten hours with good weather and be north of the bay by sunrise. This, everyone had agreed, was the riskiest leg of the trip, as the Japanese were using Manila as a primary staging area for their southern operations and there was likely to be traffic in and out of the bay. As dawn rose on November 16, Bill took over from Joe, who said they'd passed just west of Lubang Island about four hours ago. Checking the atlas, Harris figured them to be at least forty miles off the Bataan coast, directly opposite Mount Mariveles. That, Bill decided, was ironic, since once again he'd boomeranged back to the spot from which he'd fought his way out. Staring east, he thought the horizon was darker where land ought to be, but there was no way to know. The sky, however, should be brighter than it was, but that could just be the light.

By nightfall he knew it wasn't.

The waves had changed; long rollers coming off Luzon were still smooth, but deeper, and the air smelled heavy, like land, not the sea. Dawn arrived later on November 17, with dull, nickel-colored skies over "a rough sea and high winds." By noon the wind reached gale force with menacing gray waves breaking over the bow; salt caked the wheelhouse windows, and visibility fell to a few hundred yards. The launch was pitching so badly they'd extinguished the stove, and dinner was a cup of cold rice with nothing hot to drink. Legs spread against the yawing, Bill gripped the wheel and managed a grin. He wasn't riding out this storm in an open *banca*; at least there was some shelter here, a keel, and power from a diesel engine rather than a sail.

But that also changed for the worse during the night.

Jammed into a wet corner of what passed for the engine room, Harris came out of his half sleep when the noise stopped. Not the wind, which was truly howling now, nor the boat, which was creaking like bones being pulled apart. No, the chug of the diesel was gone. Staggering to his feet, Bill groped his way aft as the launch lifted alarmingly, dropped into a trough, and rolled sickeningly on its beam. Voices screamed topside as he clambered up the short ladder and stumbled into the wheelhouse. "The waves were mountainous in size as they charged down from the northeast," Bill recalled. "Their heads rose twenty to twenty-five feet above their troughs."

Without control, the launch would broach, or roll over, in the heavy seas, and the only way to maintain headway now was with a sail. Atop the wheelhouse was an eight-foot mast used for mounting a radio antenna or flags; in this dire case, it might support a sail. Quickly raising the mast they'd brought from the old thirty-footer on Panay, Joe and two others lashed it horizontally to the wheelhouse mast as a boom. As Bill muscled the rudder full starboard, Joe beat the flapping canvas into place with his fists and tied it off. Against the shrieking wind, he could only manage two feet of sail, but it was enough. There was no time to rig a tackle, so the boom had to be manually held in place in relays of two men. Somehow it lasted the night, and as the black skies faded to charcoal-gray, the men knew they'd survived—temporarily.

With dawn, the wind abated slightly and they were able to thread a line through eyebolts on the launch's transom, which created crude but workable tackle for controlling the boom. There was no question of blocks or pulleys, but at least one man could handle the sail. They also ran vertical lines, or shrouds, down from the wheelhouse mast to add support. The jury-rig certainly wasn't pretty, but it worked well enough for basic control under sail while they worked to fix the diesel.

Their hope evaporated after Cothran and Armstrong, who knew engines quite well, climbed on deck looking grim. Without a machine shop there was no way to fix the diesel, and without the engine it was impossible to make headway against the northeast monsoon. The hard truth was that China was now out. The wind was blowing them southwest, but with the sail they could control the vessel somewhat and at least head for the southern Philippines, or perhaps Borneo.

"Head for" . . . that produced a rare smile. They weren't heading for anything in a fifty-foot motor launch with no motor and a makeshift sail. Bill, by virtue of his years at Annapolis, was a sailor, and this was not sailing. The mast-boom rig permitted them to control the drift somewhat, and that was it, which meant that instead of being blown southwest, they were sliding nearly due south along the waves. Day and night the routine was the same: four-hour watches for a man at the wheel, and two men at the rigged sail. The others slept or lolled about in the sun. Tempers grew short, but several storms forced them all to work together for survival, and the backbreaking task of bailing the leaky boat never stopped.

Three weeks passed, and as the water and food ran out, even storms couldn't lessen the smoldering animosity between Cothran and the Filipinos. The American was tall and wiry and, Bill had noted, quick and decisive. Undoubtedly competent in the field, as a mustang officer he lacked the formal education and training to use tools other than fists for problem solving.* Growing up rough in Oklahoma and Texas also left him socially intolerant and woefully ill prepared to deal with foreign cultures. One day, as they sat down on the engine-room roof to eat their skimpy meal of salty rice, Cothran growled to the group, "We're eatin' so God damned little anyways that I think it'd do us more good just to go ahead and eat it two meals a day and not try to stretch it out."

---

* A "mustang" is one who worked his way up through the enlisted ranks and was commissioned as an officer.

"No," Bill recalled Joe's reply, "that would be foolish."

Cothran lashed out instantly. "Listen here, you black bastard," he snarled. "When I want your opinion, I'll ask for it. See?"

The others froze, obviously shocked, and the boat went silent. Joe blushed and very deliberately laid aside his plate. "Don't call me that." He said quite slowly, and glared at the other man from beneath dark, knitted brows.

"You black bastard, I'll call you what you are whenever I feel like it."

Joe came up off the roof with his legs spread and fists up as Cothran did the same. The others also got up to intervene, and Bill stepped between the two. "Let me handle this, Joe," he said calmly, though inwardly the Marine was furious. "He's too big for you."

"No. This is my fight. I defend myself."

Bill reluctantly stepped back and the others did too, as the two men faced off on the deck between the engine room and transom. Joe moved in quickly, but Cothran just smiled and waited. This situation was, Harris saw, nothing new for a man who'd been fighting since the age of ten. At six feet, he was nearly Bill's height and towered over the Filipino. Joe threw a fast left, which the soldier easily parried, then countered with a quick, hard left to the Filipino's face that sent him reeling back. Recovering, Joe darted in again with another left that Cothran merely sidestepped with a slight smile. But Joe instantly pivoted and slammed a fist into the American's kidney, which drove him against the stanchions.

"Damn you!" Cothran snarled. Clenching his teeth, he stepped in, blocked a punch, and sent a powerhouse left across Joe's jaw that knocked him around and across the deck into Bill's arms. Setting the Filipino down, Harris stepped over his limp body and faced off with the army officer. "You white son of a bitch . . . I'll fix you." The other lieutenant replied with a tight-lipped smile and gestured for the Marine to come on in.

"It became a slugfest," he remembered. "Toe-to-toe." Harris received some hard blows, but they didn't slow him down. Parry and punch; parry and punch—there was no room for two big men to move around so they just hit. Bill was keeping Cothran off balance, and giving better than he was getting when the other man landed a "terrific right" on his left eye that sent the Marine staggering backward. Seeing stars, he struggled to keep his feet on the gently rolling deck as Cothran, now confident of victory, came straight in. Watching with his good eye, Harris waited till the man drew back for a punch then jabbed a left into his Adam's apple. Cothran's jaw dropped and his eyes widened with shock. Gurgling, he lurched back and tried to gulp in air but could not. Leaping forward, Bill came up from a crouch with all his weight and strength behind a tremendous punch that caught Cothran under the breastbone. It was a powerful, heart-stopping blow that did just that; unconscious, the other officer toppled back against the engine-room roof, then sagged into a limp heap of arms and legs.

"You know," Harris heard someone behind him calmly say, "that was long overdue. There's a guy who had it coming."

Cothran still hadn't moved, and no one rushed to help him. Bill sat down on the transom, and as Armstrong examined his eye, it occurred to him how tired he was. The lack of food, not to mention the last tough eleven months, had taken their toll. While Tramble washed the cut, Joe walked over and carefully sat down. "Thank you," he was subdued. "He made me very ashamed."

Harris shook his head and grasped the other man's forearm. "Joe, I've never had a better friend in my life than you, and I've never had better collective friends than your people. When the chips were down, you all stood up to be counted. Here's one American anyhow who really appreciates it."

Over the next few days, the weather moderated and warm sunlight lifted everyone's spirits. Cothran kept to himself and said very little. When he did, it was with a hoarse whisper, courtesy of the Marine's throat strike. The fight, such as it was, had vented frustration, anger, and even some of the fear most of the men felt. It did not, however, solve two pressing issues: lack of food and water. They'd intended to spend only a week, or perhaps ten days, on the boat, so Bill wasn't surprised to discover only ten gallons of water remaining. This situation had to be alleviated, or all other points were moot. While the others fished, he dug through the cluttered storage lockers and engine room for parts to construct a freshwater still.

With Armstrong and Chamberlain, Harris removed the auxiliary fuel tank and about twenty feet of copper fuel lines. While the others went topside to flush out the gear, Bill found two old tubs and a bucket that he deposited on the afterdeck. There, over the worn, weathered planking, he built his still. The larger of the two tubs would be the furnace, and atop this he placed the auxiliary fuel tank, now relatively clean, which would serve as the boiler. A copper line was already running into one corner, so this was left in place but cut off a foot above the apparatus.

Armstrong bent another length of tubing ninety degrees, splayed the end, and then jammed it down over the vertical piece coming up from the boiler. Covering this with a slice of rubber, he lashed sacking over the joint, which, without a welding set, was now as tight as it could be. Twisting the long end of the copper line into a spiral, Bill carefully bent it down far enough to rest inside the bucket, which was placed atop an oil drum. Bending the line up over the bucket's lip, he ran the remaining copper into the smaller tub, which had been shoved into the now-empty water drum and would, he hoped, catch the distilled water.

They were ready to try.

Having the men extract cork from the Japanese lifejackets, he dumped a pile of the stuff in the furnace and doused it with oil while Joe filled the boiler with salt water. Heated up, the steam would pass through the copper tubing as it dipped into the bucket, also full of cold salt water, which transformed the steam to fresh water. "A puff of steam blew from the outlet end carrying with it several drops of water," Bill recalled. "A moment later the crackling was continuous. The drops were too."

Brackish and salty, the initial batch was tossed overboard, but the men clustered expectantly around the drum saw that Bill's contraption worked. Keeping the fire lower, no salt water boiled over into the fresh, and the second batch was better. Each cycle produced cleaner water, though it was labor intensive to keep the fire going, and the bucket slowly filled. As they added a work shift on the still, Cothran emerged from below carrying a harpoon he'd fashioned from "a four-foot length of three-eighths-inch copper tubing." Using a hammer and nail, he made a hole through one end large enough for a rope, which he stuck through and knotted. Carrying it aft, the army officer crouched on the transom and watched the water. A half hour later, a dolphin arced gracefully from the sea about ten yards behind the boat, and Cothran hurled the harpoon with all his strength.

It missed.

By late in the day, he'd caught nothing, but the water drum was nearly full and everyone seemed a bit more relaxed when a sudden shout split the air. "Land!" It was Joe, and he sounded overjoyed. "Land!" He screamed again and pointed over the port bow. There, against the horizon, was a low, dark smudge. Everyone stared to the left, and Bill figured if this was land, it must be Palawan—but which part? Just north of Borneo, this archipelago of 1,700 islands stretched hundreds of miles along the southwestern edge of the Philippines, and it had to be occupied by the enemy. Joe agreed, but believed the Japanese would stay on the eastern, sheltered side of Palawan in Puerto Princesa. Bill thought this was logical, given the enemy's tendency to avoid the interior, as he'd seen on Panay. Approaching as they were from the west ought to be safe enough unless a patrol boat happened by.

In any event, with a marginal sail and no engine, they had little choice but to go ashore. For the next six days, Bill kept the boat lurching eastward, and signs of land increased. Palm fronds, some with coconuts still attached, floated by, but even as hungry as they were, the men learned not to eat the meat. It was nearly rancid and tasted of vinegar. One day two birds appeared, the likes of which the Americans had never seen. They were "black-plumed, crested, long-necked . . .

With red spots on their throats, whose bodies were about the mallard size." Their wings were "something un-godly, they were so long," and Joe said they were called frigate birds.

Grabbing a Springfield rifle, Tramble Armstrong tried to shoot one, but missed. He did nail one of the fat, lazy sharks that always followed the boat, yet after thrashing a bit, the creature disappeared beneath the waves. Cothran was luckier; he harpooned a juvenile dolphin that got too close, and successfully hauled it in. Twenty pounds of fresh steak grilled over their little stove improved everyone's spirits, as did the stable supply of fresh, distilled water, though a few days of storms dampened the mood again. Tree branches became more frequent, always from the east, and one morning Bill noticed that the sea's color had changed from deep sapphire blue to jade green. The water was shallower, and from the Census Bureau map he saw a wide coral bank extended west from Palawan, so this, plus the growing haze along the horizon, had to mean real land ahead.

Yet this hope, like so many others, was dashed by another monster storm. Awakened one night by the howling wind and wildly pitching boat, Bill groped his way up to the wheelhouse and stared, appalled, through salt-streaked windows. "There were raging twenty-five-foot billows with violent, white crests," he vividly recalled. "They were filled with giant power . . . waves which tossed us about, which shivered the craft with blows . . ." With a crack like a pistol shot, the boom snapped, and the boat wallowed sickeningly in deep, rolling troughs. Several men jumped on the afterdeck, frantically splicing and splinting the wood so it would hold a scrap of sail. Bill strained against the wheel, jamming the rudder full to port in a desperate effort to keep the bow pointed into the massive waves, and feeling his stomach drop each time the boat pitched.

This might be it . . . this might just be the end of this trip. No. No . . . he felt bile rise, bitter and stinging, with his anger. Not like this. Not after escaping Corregidor and surviving that damnable swim across Manila Bay, and not after everything else since then. Cursing and growling, his bare feet slipping on the deck, half-blinded by salt spray, Bill Harris roared back at the storm and threw his entire weight against the wheel. *I . . . will . . . not . . . die . . . here! I will not.*

Slowly and sluggishly, the launch lurched and swung into the waves. This time when the bow lifted impossibly, they were almost perpendicular to the boiling seawater wall. Riding upward, Bill blinked and leaned forward, not daring to move at all. With spray feathering around the bow and blowing into the wheelhouse, the launch bobbed over the crest, and for a split second horrible lines of deep waves were visible on all sides. Dark gray and angry, they were rolling in as far as he could see, and Bill swallowed, afraid for once in his life. There was no way to fight nature, he thought as the bow dropped and the panoramic view vanished. From behind, a muted shout got his attention, and he saw a blurry figure on the afterdeck waving and pointing. The boom . . . they had repaired it well enough to take a bit of sail, and Harris waved gratefully. That was something, at least. A tiny measure of control.

By dawn the storm had mercifully blown itself out, and with the watery sunrise Bill felt numb relief as he stared east into the weak gray light. Hands . . . his hands were aching. Looking down, he realized they were tightly curled around the wheel and he really couldn't move them. Blinking just smeared more salt water over his eyes, and they burned. He shivered. Soaked to the skin, he'd been too afraid all night to feel the damp cold, but it hit now. Forcing himself to relax, Harris leaned forward, swallowed painfully, and was desperately thirsty. Pitching slowly on the deep, wide waves, the boat felt heavy, and he wondered how much water they'd taken on below. Squinting through the windows, Bill also realized the horizon was empty: no haze, or promise of land at all.

The others trudged up slowly like soggy wraiths, red-eyed, bearded, and bone-tired from bailing all night. "We were surely lost souls in the grip of a malicious fate," Bill wrote of that morning and of his companions. No one spoke; they simply slouched against the wheelhouse and tried to absorb any stray light or heat. For a long time, they remained that way: eight men suspended from reality and the outside world. There was just the undulating sea, the boat, and themselves. Joe took the wheel, and Bill feebly groped his way around the launch. The still had miraculously survived the storm, but the launch was full of salt water and needed to be flushed out. Happily, he discovered a few flying fish flopping on the afterdeck that would make a decent meal.

Grudgingly, the others began moving about and eventually got a fire going, which immediately improved the mood, along with the appearance of seaweed in the water. Distilling recommenced, portholes were opened, and wet clothes laid out to dry. There was much discussion about their position, and a few men, Cothran included, believed they'd missed Palawan altogether, but Harris didn't think so. The storms and wind were all from the northeast, so the launch had to be south of their last position, which was west of Palawan. He wanted to get the sail up and continue east, but the boom was beyond repair, and nothing else was suited to replace it. Then Bill recalled that ancient mariners, especially the Vikings, never used booms—they simply manhandled their sails with rope and muscle. Rope they had. Muscle was a different matter under the circumstances, but with no real choice, the others rigged the sail and began taking turns on the ropes, with Bill instructing them on the afterdeck.

"But that damned horizon," Cothran growled, "is as empty as ever. Not a rock in sight. I've damned near forgot what land looks like. You know what I think . . . I think we've blown way out in the center of the sea."

The army lieutenant had recovered from his beating, but was irascible and quarrelsome. Bearded and skinny like everyone else, Cothran had been grousing about being lost since the storm quit. Certain the man was wrong, Bill decided to just nod and say nothing. A few days earlier he figured they were close to the northern tip of Palawan, and the storm's fury had driven them southwest. However, the island was oriented in that direction, so with any luck they would be somewhere near the center of it. But out to sea, no. Thumbing through the atlas, he noted another archipelago due west of Palawan, and if they'd been blown in that direction, they would be in the middle of it. The Spratly Islands, a cluster of reefs and atolls scattered over 160,000 square miles. No, if they were west of Palawan by any great distance, they'd see something, and there was nothing in that direction but open water.

"What we ought to do is to sail west to Indo-China instead of south." Cothran wasn't letting it go. "We're way east of Palawan. We must be . . . or else we would have hit it by now."

"It would be foolish," Bill replied quietly, "for us to change course now. The only way to get out of this is to pick a logical direction and stick to it. We'll never get through if we keep changing direction. Besides I still think Palawan's ahead. We just haven't been making enough time."

"Don't call me foolish," Cothran snapped back. "What makes you think Palawan's just ahead? We're out in the center of this God damned sea, I tell you."

"Suppose we are past Palawan," Bill tried logic again rather than his fists. "Borneo will still be ahead. Another thing, the wind's been blowing us southwest, so if we were blown west of Palawan, maybe we were also blown south of Indo-China. How about that? If we let it upset us so much that we change course every day, we'll never have a chance."

Cothran spun around, instantly hot. "I ain't getting upset, Harris — get that straight! And I don't like your patronizin' manners either, so get that straight too." He took a step toward the Marine, jaw thrust out and eyes bright. "Who the hell do you think you are, giving orders to everybody? You think you're boss, huh? Well, you ain't no God damned boss of mine. I'm an officer too, as high as you, if you don't remember, and I got a score to settle with you anyhow. It might as well be now."

Bill shifted his weight slightly, convinced that the other lieutenant was going to strike again, and realizing now was as good a time as any. "We agreed back on Panay I was the captain of this boat, such as it is, because you don't know shit about sailing and *someone* has to be in charge." Some men, even in dire circumstances like this one, could not rise above their own insecurities, and Paul Cothran was plainly such a man. Bill flashed his best smug Annapolis smile, knowing it would thoroughly piss the man off. "Or didn't they teach you about chain of command at the Point? Oh yeah, you didn't go to the Point . . . or Officer Candidate School, either. I've always meant to ask . . . did you even finish high school? Never been sure, based on your bad grammar and poor manners."*

Roaring with fury, Cothran lunged and swung a wild left haymaker. The Marine ducked easily and punched him on the right cheekbone as he stumbled past. *I'm going to fight him slow,* Bill recalled thinking, knowing he was too weak to trade hard punches. Cothran was also weak but enraged, and if he used up his strength, Harris would have him. Sidestepping and blocking, he let the army officer swing and mostly miss. The blows that did connect were "lacking in strength."

Maybe a minute into the fight, Bill noticed Cothran could barely stand. Throwing a hard, straight left to the man's nose, as the other man toppled backward Harris followed up with a right to the jaw. Falling against the raised deck, Cothran couldn't lift his arms to ward off the Marine's series of "rights and lefts, one-two, one-two." Falling into a sitting position, the army lieutenant was bleeding badly and gasping for air. Standing over him threateningly, Bill took a deep breath and jabbed a finger at the other man.

"Cothran," he panted, "I'm satisfied. There's no point in beating you more. Let's knock it off now and have no more bullshit arguments."

Staring up at him wide-eyed, Cothran nodded weakly and held up one arm, palm out. It was enough. Nodding once himself, Bill turned and walked into the wheelhouse, where Joe was waiting. Giving his friend a small smile, the Filipino gestured toward the bench, and Harris

---

* The "Point" refers to the U.S. Military Academy at West Point, which commissions regular U.S. Army officers after four years of training, just as Annapolis does for the U.S. Navy.

slumped down immediately. Another thirty seconds would have finished him too, but it had to be done. Now, at least, he wouldn't have to worry about another attack. Joe left and returned with a plate of wet, salty rice and a cup of water, but it still took an hour before Bill felt reasonable. He could not show weakness, though, not here and not now. *This world belongs to the strong,* he repeated his prayer over and over. *This world belongs to the strong.*

The next day dawned clear and warm. Both boat and men aired out, dried off, and soaked up the sun. Distilling was in full swing, and by the end of the day fully six gallons of fresh water sloshed in the drum. They'd been at sea for twenty-four days now, and Bill realized, somewhat belatedly, that today was Tuesday, December 8, 1942: one year to the day of the attack on the Philippines. One year . . . and it was just three years ago he'd been a proud, newly commissioned second lieutenant attached to the Philadelphia Navy Yard enduring the extra schooling required of a Marine officer. If someone had told him then that now, today, he'd be floating off Palawan in a disabled launch evading the Japanese, what would he have done differently?

Nothing.

Nothing except escaping when Corregidor fell, rather than blindly following orders. That, he promised himself, was something he would never do again. Just because a man outranked you didn't make him right. Bill understood and appreciated the need for discipline and order—this boat trip had reinforced that—but he also fully realized that this really worked only if those in command had their heads out of their butts. Admittedly, this made him question the hidebound traditions beloved in the peacetime military, which were fine at Annapolis and West Point, or on parade grounds, but didn't transfer well to combat. *If I live through this,* he told himself, *I won't forget that lesson.*

"Look!" Someone atop the wheelhouse yelled. "Land! Land . . . there!"

There. Where was "there"? Bill craned his neck through the window and squinted to port, which was the most hopeful direction. And there it was . . . "exceedingly faint bluish outline like that of two peaks and the saddle between," he recorded. "To the right and left it faded away to nothing in the haze." A cloud, he thought. Tough to tell at sea level like this. A six-foot man standing on a wheelhouse could see about five or six miles on a good day, though if those "peaks" really were mountains, they'd show up much farther away. Tomorrow. They would know tomorrow.

December 9 began with a high overcast and haze, which made the horizon impossible to see. Cothran, sitting up forward with a Springfield shooting at birds, was convinced they were in the middle of the ocean. Joe was at the wheel, and Bill sat on the transom trying to spear another dolphin when the rifle cracked suddenly. As he turned, one of the black seabirds cartwheeled from the sky and splashed into the water thirty yards away.

"I got him!" Cothran shouted. "Someone else go in after him."

"I will," Bill yelled back. Ravenously hungry and forgetting the sharks, he dove cleanly from the stern and swam to the flopping bird. One wing was broken, and as he swam it occurred to him that his noise and the bird's thrashing was just the sort of racket sharks loved. A burst of cold adrenaline shot through him at the thought of one of them circling unseen in the dark water beneath him, so Harris grabbed the creature's neck and held it under while he breaststroked back to the boat. Clambering quickly up the rickety ladder, he exhaled with relief when his feet were out of the water and tossed the bird on deck. Joe had luffed the boat and came aft to help. As Bill sat against the transom gasping for breath, the Filipino pointed toward the water.

"Look there."

Everyone did. Just where Harris had retrieved the bird, two dorsal fins sliced through the water—and they weren't dolphins. Bill shrugged nonchalantly, but his stomach tightened at the sight. Another close shave. Examining the frigate bird, they discovered most of it was feathers and wings, so they decided to boil it into a soup. While distilling another six gallons of water, the rest of the afternoon passed quietly as the launch slowly bobbed east. Then, with the sun setting behind them, an amazing sight appeared "like a curtain lifting before a stage," Bill wrote. Haze and glare from the sun was gone, and just a few miles before them was a "misty, mountain-like outline. It was darker than before and much plainer."

Irritations and animosities were forgotten—temporarily—as everyone came on deck, pointing, shouting, and backslapping. Frustrations melted away, and Bill took a deep, relieved breath of air. He could smell the land now: a heavy, musky odor from the earth and trees. Slipping into the wheelhouse, Harris pulled out the torn, battered Philippine Census Bureau maps and stared at the coast. Joe and Tramble Armstrong joined him, and Bill carefully compared the contours of the coast with those on the China Sea coast of Palawan.

"That bay there," he announced after a few minutes, "can only be one of two places—either Buenavista Bay or this bay to the north by Caruray."* That meant they hadn't been pushed as far south as he'd believed. Land; perhaps the sea had at last let them go.

"You ain't proved nothing to me," Cothran loudly objected. "I bet this here's Borneo."

Still miles offshore, Bill set a 190-degree course to gently angle in toward shore during the night, then turned the wheel over to Armstrong. He knew the Philippines well enough to be cautious of its submerged reefs and rocky coastlines. No use taking any more chances this close to land, especially since feathers of spray were now visible from lines of shoals on both sides of the bow.† Joe would take the midwatch, and Bill would be up before dawn. Going below, he found it hard to sleep as all the future options whirled through his head. "One thing I was sure of was that I wanted to take a long time out to rest and

---

* Caramay and Ulugan Bays. In fact, the storm had blown them farther south by about a hundred miles.

† Brechtel and Merlin Shoals, about three miles offshore.

rehabilitate," Bill recollected, then would decide whether to sit out the war here or go on. The past few months, he admitted, had taken their toll, and he was uncertain that getting out of the Philippines was now the right choice. There was plenty of fighting to do here. Still, exhausted and hungry was not the state of mind for deep decisions, and it could wait a few days.

Of one thing he was certain, with neither regret nor doubt, that he would part company with most of the men on this boat. His fellow Marines had, as expected, pulled their weight, and he would certainly welcome Tramble Armstrong if he chose to come with him. Tough, quick, and competent, Reid Chamberlain had, on closer acquaintance, revealed a surly side for which Harris had no tolerance. The army lieutenant was a different matter altogether, and Bill had no intention of traveling further with him. In the hour before sunrise, Harris softly groped his way to the wheelhouse to take over with Joe, and they decided to make for the larger of the two bays, given that there would be a barrio and people to help them. If the island slowly emerging from the morning haze *was* Palawan, then, according to the Filipino, it had a sizable Tagalog population that would assist anyone escaping the Japanese. There were also Muslim Moros, called Molbogs on Palawan, whose presence made Joe extremely leery.* Joe believed that the Moros were unpredictable, and seemed relieved when Bill brought up the subject of splitting up, so they discussed this as well. "Whatever we do," Harris said quietly but firmly, "we're going to split into two parties."

Joe agreed, his teeth flashing white in the dark wheelhouse. "I'll admit that Cothran has some good qualities and that Chamberlain is less objectionable . . . but just the same, if I never see those two again, it'll be way, way too soon."

With the lightening sky, both men could see two peaks starkly

---

* Derived from "Mauru," a Spanish name for the old Roman province of Mauritania in northwest Africa. Philippine Moros were descended from fourteenth-century Muslim traders and corsairs from the Persian Gulf and Malay Peninsula.

outlined against the orange sunrise with a pronounced saddle between them.* A small point of land at the entrance to the bay was now visible off the bow, and they could see a serrated coastline angling southwest into the haze.† Hills rose inland, and beyond them a line of north-south mountains was silhouetted against the thinning orange sky. Aiming for the "notch in the skyline," Bill headed into the bay with Joe perched at the bow as others stepped into the wheelhouse to watch. The water changed dramatically from shades of blue to shades of green, and up ahead it looked like weak coffee. Shallows. Darkness rolled back suddenly, and Bill made out a small island a half mile off the starboard bow, so he altered course to pass between it and the point.‡

"This is a wild-looking coast," Glew remarked.

"Palawan is mostly all like this," Joe called back.

"So is Borneo." Cothran was obstinate. Bill wondered how much he believed and how much was just his desire to contradict a man who had beaten him twice in a stand-up fight. Harris permitted himself a small smile at that; he'd encountered much of the "proud poor" attitude in the military, especially among the army soldiers he'd known, but Marines were too well disciplined to let it show. Personally, he scorned many enlisted men's deeply held belief that "college boy" officers, especially West Point or Annapolis grads, were lightweights. Could the rank and file command warships or lead large numbers of men in combat? Who designed the weapons they used, the aircraft that protected them, and the logistics that supported them? It didn't matter here, though, since he'd proved several times that he knew more of hand-to-hand combat than a roughneck, mustang officer from Texas or Oklahoma, or wherever Cothran was from. Grinning openly now, Bill looked forward to parting ways.

His smile faded as the interior of the bay unfolded off the bow.

---

* The saddle lies between the Iwiig Range to the north and the Bulanjao Range to the south.
† Balintang Point with Bulaloc Bay beyond.
‡ Ditadika Island.

Frowning, Harris realized it didn't match the contours of either place on his map. He was still flipping pages in the atlas when Glew called from the starboard rail, "Damn! You ought to see the coral heads we're running over. I bet we don't go much farther."

Nor did they.

"A moment later the bow crunched in with a grinding, rasping noise," Bill recorded. "It slightly lifted, and the deck took on a definite list as all way ceased. The point and the island were now each about three hundred and fifty yards distant." Quickly lowering the sail, the men decided to wade ashore over the coral heads. After gathering his gear into a big, burlap sack Bill was first over the side, and the others followed. Toward the point, the water was chest deep, and he stepped carefully over each bit of rock or coral. But fifty yards from the boat, as the water reached his neck, Bill knew they could go no farther, at least while carrying a load. Angling back into the bay with his rifle over his head, Harris and the others staggered onto a sandy shelf about three feet deep and decided to try again for the point.

This time, farther into the bay, they made it, and collapsed on a narrow, white sand beach lined with coconut trees. Bill was dizzy, and his head was swimming. He gulped in the heavy air and realized his inner ear was not coping well with solid ground after twenty-eight days at sea. Everyone else seemed to be suffering, too, so they all sat for an hour enjoying the warm sand and *not* being on a boat. Other than the breeze, the only noise came from screaming monkeys deep inside the thick trees. Staring at the water, Bill had second thoughts about the bay and pulled his map from the bag. "I don't think we're on the Caruray Bay," he said to the others. Here's where we are, right here." He pointed at Bulaloc Bay on south Palawan while the others gathered around. It seemed exact, right down to a pair of small islands he could see.*

Joe agreed—and, surprisingly, so did Cothran. There was nothing on the Borneo coast similar to this, and he finally admitted to being

---

* Ditadika and Bucid Islands.

on Palawan. Joe discovered a native dugout, a footprint, and a path inland, so there were people nearby. Heading up the trail, Bill wobbled a bit as his balance slowly returned to normal. Monkeys still screamed, and large white parrots flapped away as they eventually came to a little clearing containing "a village of forty to fifty rude little stilted houses, with low, nipa thatched roofs, split bamboo floors, and no sides," Harris wrote. "In various places, fires could be seen burning. Here and there chickens squawked and clucked. A rooster crowed. Not another person was to be seen, however."

The locals had obviously seen or heard them and fled with the fires still burning. Bill and the others immediately ate everything in sight: hot rice, chunks of chicken, and strips of dried fish. Images of poisoned darts and long knives faded as he ate and ate . . . and ate. He knew they should set a watch, but at this particular time he didn't really care. Every man had a rifle, and if the locals *were* hostile, they'd be on the receiving end of a fast, lethal demonstration in modern technology. Cothran expertly checked his rifle, stirred the fire, and complained about the lack of cigarettes. The grating voice reminded Harris of his decision.

"Cothran," he wrote of the incident. "This party's going to break up tomorrow . . . and you aren't going with us."

. The man squatted on his haunches and stared blankly across the flames as the Marine lieutenant continued. "We're on a bay near the southwestern tip of Palawan." Bill pulled out his maps and spread them out. "The nearest settlement is the barrio of Culasian to the north about ten or twelve miles as the crow files. To the south the nearest place is the barrio of Canipan which is twenty to twenty-five miles the same way." He tapped each place as he spoke. "Now my proposition is that one group goes north and the other one goes south. What do you say?"

Unshaven and ragged, the army officer looked rough and mean. However, he was clearly reluctant for another fight and rubbed his bearded chin. "I don't know," he finally said, noncommittally. "How're you going to decide who goes which way?"

"I figure that the one which goes south will get the native dugout pulled up on the beach. If we both want to go the same direction, we'll match tomorrow morning for it."

"Okay." Cothran scratched his chin again. "It's a deal with me, and I'll tell you right now I want to go south. I ain't convinced you know where we are, and I want the boat just in case."

"All right," Bill agreed, pleased to have it done with so easily. "I'll tell you tomorrow which way we want to go."

Stretching out near the fire, each man, lost in his own thoughts and the jungle cacophony, eventually drifted off to sleep until after sunrise. Eating what scraps remained for breakfast, Harris spread the map out for Glew, Joe, and the Filipino lieutenant, Sergio Estoiko, to see. The latter seemed quietly relieved that they were still in the Philippines, and he hadn't needed to trek through China. Estoiko could, he said, make his way back to Panay from northern Palawan, and Errold Glew enthusiastically agreed. Rumors on Panay were that members of his old unit, the 48th Material Squadron, were somewhere up there, and he wanted to rejoin them. It would be north, then, Bill decided, and thought this was the best direction, given that it was farthest from Borneo's Japanese garrisons. They all agreed that it would be much easier to get up the coast by boat rather than hiking through the jungle.

"I'm half sorry you were so God damned fair in your offer," Glew remarked. "I practically feel like taking the boat and telling them to go to hell."

"Yes," Joe nodded. "That's good thinking."

"I don't like them either," Bill sighed, "but I'm still for being fair to them. We'll probably regret it afterwards if we're not—in our consciences, I mean, we will. Anyhow you've got to admit that although Cothran was troublesome on the trip, he did about as much as anyone to get us through. He collected more food than anyone else."

That said, Harris rose and stepped over to Cothran's fire. "We want the boat too." He kept steady eye contact with the other officer. "Are you ready to match for it?"

"Sure," Cothran yawned. "How're you going to work it? Another fight?"

"Don't think so," Bill drawled. "You all should have a chance."

Cothran stiffened, then saw the Marine's grin and managed a smile himself. Harris gestured to the ground, and both men sank to their knees. "Do you know how to shake rocks and scissors with your hands?" Winning the children's game of chance depended on which symbols one made with a fist.

"Sure do," the smile widened. "That'll be okay."

They raised their closed fists up, then brought them down and up once, twice, and then finally down to a stop, where Bill's fist remained clenched in the rock. Cothran's fingers were splayed as paper. Though a rock would defeat scissors, paper covered the rock.

"You win." Bill remembered being supremely disappointed, and for a long second, he thought of just taking the boat anyway. Cothran certainly couldn't stop him, but no, differences aside, they were Americans and had made a deal. Rising, he shook his head once, then turned back to the other fire, where the others were cooking everything they could find and gathering gear. Tramble Armstrong and Reid Chamberlain ambled over and squatted down next to Bill. They'd been talking and wanted to head out with Cothran, who, though not their type of officer, was going in a direction they favored. They preferred Bill, but going north was heading back into the Philippines, and both Marines were fed up with the islands. Given the circumstances, their relationship with Lieutenant Harris had been relatively informal over the past months, but they were still Marines, and he was their officer, so he could, if desired, keep them with him. Harris was taken aback by the request but understood and did not order them to remain.

Everyone gathered around then, and Bill offered his hand to the army lieutenant.

"So long, Cothran."

"So long."

The handshake was "stiff and formal," Harris recalled, but at least neutral. As Cothran's group headed south back down the trail to the bay and the boat, Tramble Armstrong suddenly stepped aside and turned. Lifting an arm, he held his lieutenant's gaze a long moment, smiled, then vanished into the trees.

It was last time Bill Harris ever saw them.

At this, his second parting with fellow Americans, Bill couldn't help thinking of Ed Whitcomb, and what might have happened to him. The eddies and currents of war, he mused, and no one knew where any of them would end. That day, December 14, 1942, Harris set off with Errold Glew, Joe, and Lieutenant Estoiko north through the mangrove swamp along the Panalingon River. Following a foot-path, they entered a barrio and traded several boxes of matches, which the locals had never seen, for a night's hospitality. Curly-headed with sharp, filed teeth, the Palawanos took them four miles up the coast by dugout around a wide point into Culasian.* They would not step foot on the beach, and Bill discovered why when two barefoot men approached "clad in black fezzes, full loose trousers of light material — resembling women's slacks of the western world, and full-sleeved, loose shirts." Both wore "great long, fat, sheathed knives," about twenty inches long, and the leader possessed a "strong, lined, middle-aged face . . . decorated by a flowing, black, downward curving mustache."†

Joe halted abruptly and reached for his gun. "Moros," he hissed under his breath. The older man sported "circular, gold rings in the lobes of his ears," and flowery, embroidered pants, a white silk shirt, and an ivory-handled knife. He looked, Bill thought, exactly like a Hollywood pirate. Joe had heard nothing good about Moros, and was not eager to get closer. Nevertheless, the gaudily dressed leader spoke Tagalog and through Joe made it clear they were invited to his barrio for dinner. "I have never known Moros," Bill recalled the Filipino's reluctant whisper. "I have heard many bad things of them. Maybe they

---

* Bacao Bacao Point.
† The knives were barongs, and were used as swords.

will poison our food or else maybe as we eat, they will strike us with these big barongs."

As it turned out, the Moro leader was a *datu*, a sort of noble lord, and was quite hospitable. Over dinner of "rice and an exceedingly fiery, peppery stew of chicken and vegetables," served on china plates, the men smoked strong, dark cigarettes and talked. The *datu* was well informed, as a local ruler should be, and was well aware of the war. The only Japanese on Palawan were on the east side of the island in Puerto Princesa, where they kept a prisoner-of-war camp, and there was a guerilla base at Brooke's Point, directly across the island from Culasian. He volunteered to have some men take them over if they wished. "There is a white man," Joe translated, "a Mr. Kerson, who leads it."[*] The Americans were not excited about that, and Bill remembered he was "going to be very careful about joining another guerrilla force" after his experiences with Vera and Peralta.

The *datu* offered to have them taken twenty miles north to Eran, where they could find Christian Filipinos and decide their next course of action. He didn't say so, but intimated that remaining in Moro lands could be dangerous since there were some Muslims who hated Christians more than the Japanese. The Americans agreed, though Sergio Estoiko asked for a guide to the east coast and Brooke's Point. He was certain that from there it would be possible to return to Panay. So, down to three now, Bill's little party set out the following evening in a large Moro boat called a *kohmpeet*. It was "thirty-five feet long and seven wide at its greatest width," Harris recorded. "In its center was a tent shaped shelter of thatched nipa leaves which covered a twelve-foot-long section."

Due to contrary winds, the normal forty-eight-hour trip up the coast to Eran took four days. Taken to Abdul, the *teniente del barrio*, or village chieftain, the *datu*'s men conveyed his order, and with hand-

---

[*] Vens Taivo Kierson.

shakes they departed. Abdul, dressed in a "white, Moro shirt above his blue Moro trousers, a white fez, with a barong in his belt," had traveled widely beyond Palawan and proved a gracious and interesting host. After a night of rest and plenty of food, he personally guided the three men north in "clear, refreshing morning air along the side of the glistening China Sea.

"To look at that sea now," Glew shook his head, "you'd never know how mean it is."

"It is like the Moros," declared Joe, and Bill remembered chuckling at that. They were all happy *not* to be on a boat at sea.

After an hour and several miles along a dry, wide trail, they came to a large hacienda perched on a rounded hilltop five hundred yards off the beach. The doors and windows of the main house were nailed shut, dark-green paint peeled from the wooden walls, and several steps were rotted out. Yet staring at a pair of antlers nailed over the door, Bill thought it looked like the Royal Hawaiian Hotel. They could stay, Abdul said, as long as they liked. The owner, a Christian missionary well-liked by the Moros, had been murdered by a Spanish overseer called Don Fernando, but, he assured them, the Spaniard had already been "taken care of" with Moro barongs. Though the interior had been looted, there was still furniture and beds in three of the rooms. Real beds. Abdul informed them that the local villagers would provide food for as long as the party wished to remain, and he wished them well, then left. So, a few days before Christmas, 1942, Bill Harris found himself dry, fed, and safe for the moment. He couldn't help recalling last December and redeploying to Mariveles from Subic Bay on Christmas Eve. What, he wondered, would next Christmas hold in store for him?

The next few weeks passed quite pleasantly. One day Bill shot a wild cow, and for the first time in months they had beef for dinner. This became a weekly event, and the Moros happily butchered whatever was shot in return for a share of the meat—except for wild pig, which they would not touch. Rice, coconuts, and coffee were frequently brought to the hacienda, and the three men supplemented their diet with fresh vegetables, sea turtle eggs, and roasted peacock stuffed with local spices. Palawanos came in from the countryside and introduced them to *pangasi*, a fermented rice drink every bit as potent as the *tuba* they'd enjoyed farther north. Life, for first time in a year, passed quite pleasantly and with no worries. The Japanese apparently never strayed from Puerto Princesa, and with the *datu's* protection Bill's little group had nothing to fear from the Moros.

Swimming every day, eating, and sleeping soundly every night was almost enough to make Bill forget the war. "I like this living so much," he wrote, "I'm almost getting ready to sit the whole thing out right here. Uncle Sam put me out in this rat-trap and cheered like mad while I fought; but he sure didn't do much else. He decided to sacrifice us. In a way, that pays my obligation. I did my duty and did it well, and was left to fight it out alone as a sacrifice. Besides I paid off more on Panay, and I've done near my damnedest to get back in the show and nearly killed [myself] doing it."

A few days later, a *banca* tacked into the cove below the hacienda, and Bill went to meet the new arrivals. The first man off spoke good English and said he owned a coconut plantation on the other side of Eran but was originally from the island of Cuyo just north of Palawan. Juan Dako, he was called, had been told by the Moros that other Christians had arrived and decided to come greet them. Full of news, the man told them that the guerilla camp at Brooke's Point was growing larger and that two new men, one American and one a Filipino officer, had recently joined.* He also heard through the jungle telegraph that two other Americans sailed over three thousand miles in a twenty-two-foot sailboat from Mindoro, through the Makassar Straits past Java, and into the Joseph Bonaparte Gulf. They docked at Wynd-

---

* This was Reid Carlos Chamberlain, who had split from the others to make his way north to Mindanao, and Lieutenant Estoiko, who was trying to return to Panay. In late January 1943, Paul Cothran and Tramble Armstrong would set out south for Borneo.

ham, Western Australia, on October 11, 1942, after a harrowing, fifty-two-day journey.*

This changed everything for Bill Harris.

If those two could make it, then so could he, and his attitude toward the war shifted. "Even if I did get sold down the river by Washington," Harris recorded, "I can't actually say my obligation has been paid, because you know you can't exactly pay off your country. A war is something you're all in together and you've all got to do your best to win. If you don't, you'll lose." Continuing, he wrote, "If everyone just pays what they consider their obligation and then quits, why you'll lose. Then where are you? You'd wish then you'd paid off a little more but it'd be too late. I feel I owe more duty especially since I'm a regular officer." The Marine officer in Bill had recovered from the disappointments, brutality, and privations of the past year, and was ready to resume the fight. "It may sound Victorian, but I really feel that way, and Victorian or not, it's right."

A major problem, at least in Eran, was a suitable boat—there just weren't any for a lengthy deepwater voyage, and after his previous attempts Bill knew what would work and what definitely would not. After some discussion, the men decided to visit Dako's coconut plantation and ask for suggestions. Packing to leave, Bill had profound second thoughts; this place was warm, dry, and safe. They were as well off as could be expected under the circumstances. "I've thought that out thoroughly," Harris wrote later. "You can't really be well off when you don't feel well off inside." Bill knew he would have no peace sitting out the war on the sidelines, eating peacock and drinking *pangasi*. He had to go. He had to keep trying. This world, the marine reminded himself yet again, is for the strong.

Juan Dako was glad to see them and helpful. He confirmed that no suitable boats were available nearby and suggested leaving from

---

* Captain William L. Osborne, the army, and Lieutenant Damon "Rocky" Gause, the air force.

Balabac Island off Palawan's southern tip, as the people there were great fishermen and possessed boats capable of venturing into either the South China or Sulu Seas. They were Molbogs, like the *datu*, and if he would send along a guide, then Bill's party would be assured of assistance. The problem was getting there. Cutting across seventy-five miles of jungle was not appealing, and, in fact, the wind was wrong to sail around Palawan from the west, so they'd cross over to the east coast and then take a boat south. For this, Dako recommended a relative in Caramay and would, if Bill wished, make arrangements accordingly.

This was how, by late January 1943, Lieutenant Bill Harris found himself on a dirt road near the gentle slope of a small mountain in northeastern Palawan. On the far bank of a river up ahead, he could see the usual collection of huts, with an occasional larger house surrounded by farms. The most substantial structure was a squat, ocher-colored building that had to be a parish church. Looking east, he was high enough up to see where the river widened to a delta, then spilled out into a broad, curving gulf of green water pocked with white spray from dozens of reefs. Mottled greens and browns flowed down to a strip of tan sand, and several roofs poked up from tree houses built near the beach. A large, white three-masted boat was pulled up on the sand and tilted over on one dark blue outrigger. This interested Bill. These were fishermen and seafarers, quite familiar with the Palawan coast and Sulu Sea, and anything was possible. This, he considered as they continued down the slope, was vital since only three months remained before the monsoon winds shifted again. Ninety short days to finally cross the South China Sea, or be forced to run the gauntlet of Japanese-occupied islands south to Australia.

Time was running out.

PART III

JANUARY 1943–SEPTEMBER 1945

Out of the night that covers me,
Black as the pit from pole to pole,
I thank whatever gods may be
For my unconquerable soul.

— "Invictus"

EIGHT

✷

ODYSSEY

GLEAMING COLDLY AGAINST THE BLACK VELVET NIGHT SKY, STARS glistened like shards of wet, broken glass. Pale and frothy, the creamy Milky Way splashed across the dome from horizon to horizon. It was breathtaking, and Bill knew it was a sight unseen except on the open ocean or deep within a desert—both places devoid of the clutter of civilization. Not that he wouldn't trade it all right now for a bit of friendly civilization. A real steak dinner and shaker of martinis. Closing his eyes as the boat gently rocked, the Marine enjoyed the memory. He was trying to conjure the taste of rare beef when a long blowing sound, like air escaping from an enormous tire, filled the darkness. Swallowing hard and sitting up, as he squinted out over the black water salt spray suddenly crashed down into the boat. Ducking under the *kajong*, a native tent woven from nipa fronds, he crouched as a second batch of water cascaded over the craft. The boat's other occupant, a bearded, bedraggled man sleeping on the narrow deck, bolted upright.

Bill's first thought was a submarine, which would either be incredibly bad or good luck depending on whose flag it flew. Again, the massive blowing sound floated over the waves, and this time Bill peered into the darkness, then slowly smiled. Clambering forward, he pointed out over the bow, and his companion joined him. It was a whale, maybe fifty yards away, and as they watched, another stream of white spray shot up against the sky when the massive creature breathed. His companion chuckled, and Harris laughed outright. It was a welcome, lighthearted moment in a trip otherwise plagued with adversity. At one point, the Marine recalled, "I'm beginning to think it's just not meant for us to leave the Philippines . . . we run into a stone wall every time we try."

It was now May 12, 1943, as near as Bill could figure the date, and the lieutenant felt as if he was finally going to make it to Australia. Errold Glew had parted ways with them and headed for Cuyo, a little island a hundred miles northeast of Palawan, looking for survivors from his old unit. So, with Joe, a local guide named Johnny, and an outrigger canoe, Harris had left Caramay on February 28, bound for Balabac Island at Palawan's southern end. Arriving on March 4, Bill learned Cothran, Chamberlain, and Armstrong had been there but departed for Borneo at the end of January. Two days later with a pair of Filipinos, including his faithful Joe, the Marine also headed out for Borneo planning to follow Gause and Osborne's route through the Makassar Strait, past Java, and into the Timor Sea north of Australia. About 1,500 miles, it was the shortest route, but also the most dangerous since the Japanese controlled the entire area.

However, "very bad, squally rainy weather" forced Bill to put in on Banguey Island, British North Borneo, where the Filipinos, even Joe, insisted on returning to Balabac. While on Banguey, Harris discovered Cothran's boat had been wrecked but repaired there, and they had apparently sailed on for the Sulu archipelago a month earlier. Back on Balabac, Bill delayed for six weeks due to the early storms, but met Robert William Kellam, a new arrival and navy seaman from the submarine tender *Canopus*, which was scuttled in Mariveles Bay after Bataan fell. Kellam and 221 of his shipmates were sent to Corregidor to form the Provisional 4th Battalion under Major Francis Williams, which was badly mauled attempting to recapture Battery Denver. The hundred or so who survived that attack had joined Bill's battered A Company at the road junction east of Malinta Hill. Kellam had been just another grimy, bloody face at the time, but Harris was glad to have an American with him now.

Procuring a seaworthy, thirty-foot Moro *kumpit* from a Philippine Constabulary sergeant named Anzay, the two Americans set out for Australia from Balabac during the third week in April. This time they decided to take the longer, safer route to Tawi-Tawi in the Sulu Archipelago, then through the Celebes Sea and past the Moluccas to Australia. Three days out from Balabac, they spotted a small mountain atop an equally small island, and put in for fresh water. According to the faded Census Bureau map book this was Cagayan Sulu, about a third of the distance to Tawi-Tawi. Bill had been warned about stopping there by the Balabac islanders, who believed the island was home to "evil ones" they called Berbalangs, ghouls without eyes who ate human flesh. Bill laughed it off, but calculated he had enough trouble without adding supernatural enemies to his list. Besides, the farther south they ventured toward New Guinea, the more likely they could encounter actual cannibals and headhunters, so why chance it?

From Cagayan, Bill set a course for Hog Point on northeastern Borneo, just over a hundred miles away across the Sulu Sea. Just past midnight on May 1, they spotted a weak light shining from a great, southward-curving coastline and tossed out a sea anchor for the night. Certain it was Hog Point, Bill had no wish to cross the narrow, reef-strewn Sibutu Passage between Borneo and Tawi-Tawi in darkness. Daylight found them a half mile off a mangrove beach with Harris noting "that little lighthouse back there is in almost exactly the same position as when we stopped." He was surprised the Japanese still used it, but this was, he reminded himself, deep within enemy territory. Shading his eyes eastward, Bill could plainly see "a set of high steep mountains rising up from the sea."

Tawi-Tawi.

A steady, northeasterly breeze carried them forty miles across the passage, which was dotted with local fishing boats and even a tattered Chinese junk. A cargo ship flying the Japanese flag steamed up the channel but took no notice of them, and by late afternoon the Americans passed a few miles west of an island with a strange hill facing the sea, like a "grotesque foot with big, stone toes," Bill recalled. Less than ten miles ahead was another green smudge, this one nearly flat, and if the directions given on Balabac were accurate, then their destination was just beyond.* It took an hour to round a wide, reef-edged point, but the pair found themselves in a narrow strait, barely two miles wide, facing another small island.

Manuk Manka.

A "flat topped mountain" loomed from the haze, and a barrio of "nipa houses built for the most part on stilts out over shallow water" sprawled along the north shore exactly as described. Lowering the sail, Harris and Kellam paddled through the coral heads and brightly colored fish up onto a beach, where a collection of locals stood staring. One man, taller and thinner than the others, wore khaki trousers, a white button-down shirt, and a black Moro fez. With near perfect English, he introduced himself as Ahmed Karim, the school superintendent for Tawi-Tawi before the war.

Karim was well-traveled, cosmopolitan, and married to a charming Christian girl he'd met while they were both students at the University of the Philippines. Inviting them to stay in his home, he cautioned against trying for Australia and related another piece of startling news. "There were three other Americans who passed by here a couple of months ago," the young Muslim gravely stated, "and they were captured by the Japanese at Tarakhan in Borneo." Their names, Karim remembered clearly, were Cothran, Armstrong, and Chamberlain. They also had gone across to see Suarez, then departed soon after, and Karim advised Bill to stay in Tawi-Tawi. "You know after you leave the Philippines, you will not find the people against the Japanese—not

---

* Bongao, with Simunul Island beyond it to the south.

much anyhow. They seem to like the Japanese as well as the Dutch and English."

"It is our duty we feel," Harris replied politely, "to go back and help General MacArthur reconquer the Philippines."

They understood this, and in the end it was decided that Bob Kellam would stay behind to help repair the boat while Bill traveled the fifteen miles across the Manuk Manka Channel and Tawi-Tawi Bay to meet Colonel Suarez in Batu-Batu. Like many others, the Filipino leader was a Constabulary officer when war broke out, but he'd escaped to Tawi-Tawi aboard a *kumpit* and was reorganizing the 125th Infantry Regiment. Unlike Peralta on Panay, Colonel Suarez seemed to have no postwar political ambitions, and had no hesitation in offering Harris a commission if the American would remain to fight the Japanese on Zamboanga and Jolo.

Again, Bill smoothly refused, emphasizing his desire to get back into the war with his own military. Suarez understood, and suggested the boat be brought across to Batu-Batu since there were more resources available and they could then leave from here when ready. He also informed Bill that one of the three Americans—Chamberlain—did not go to Borneo with Cothran and Armstrong. Chamberlain remained on Tawi-Tawi "for approximately a month . . . and had left to go to Mindanao in the early part of April." He confirmed Karim's statement that Cothran and Armstrong had been captured on Borneo, then passed on the latest war news.

Before leaving Panay, Bill heard of Operation Torch, the November 8, 1942, Allied invasion of North Africa with three task forces landing in Morocco, Tunisia, and Algiers. Aside from gaining a foothold in the Mediterranean, the American presence in force convinced Admiral François Darlan, the extremely French commander of Vichy North Africa, to once again change sides. Though the French were of little tactical use, their switch deprived the Germans of strategic control in North Africa, and, like many others, Harris believed the victory meant America was now fighting back on a large scale. This could mean big things for the Pacific, including a speedy reconquest of the Philippines. Unfortunately, Suarez had different news. On February 19, 1943, the U.S. II Corps was routed at the Kasserine Pass, and even now, in May, no word of victory had reached Suarez on Tawi-Tawi.

Yet there was some good news as well, at least here in the Pacific. While Bill was in Caramay, the last eleven thousand Japanese on Guadalcanal had been forced back to a tiny pocket northwest of Mount Gallego and trapped. Desperate to save what remained of the 14th Army, for several nights Imperial Navy destroyers ran down New Georgia Sound from Bougainville to evacuate the diseased, emaciated survivors. February 7, 1943, six months to the day from the American landings, saw the last 1,796 tottering Japanese wraiths hauled aboard, and the destroyers dash northwest toward safety. Only 10,652 Imperial troops made it off Guadalcanal from the 36,000 committed, and it signaled the end of Japanese offensive capability in the Pacific.

Suarez also related that during early February, three hundred thousand men of the German Sixth Army had been cut off and surrounded in the Soviet Union, an unmitigated disaster for the Axis and a welcome ray of light for the Allies.* Nevertheless, the Germans were in no way defeated, and no one was speculating when, or if, an invasion of Europe would occur. Likewise, though the Japanese had been badly bloodied, their withdrawal into a fortified, defensive posture was more alarming than their initial string of battlefield successes. They would, Harris knew, die for every square foot of conquered territory now under the banner of the Rising Sun. As for invading Japan itself, he was aware that the fanatical devotion to their god, the emperor, and the inbred cultural mysticism surrounding the Home Islands made that necessity a vicious, bloody prospect. Between the Imperial troops in China and those scattered throughout Malaysia, the Philippines, and the Dutch East Indies, there were also upward of a million

---

* Only ninety-one thousand Germans survived to surrender on February 2, and fewer than five thousand of them would eventually return home in the early 1950s.

idle Japanese soldiers who could, and certainly would, be committed to fight.

After seventeen months of fighting, escaping, and evading, Bill burned to be part of the battles that would seal Japan's fate, so on May 7, 1943, he bade farewell to Alejandro Suarez. That Friday, Harris and Kellam set out from Tawi-Tawi Bay across the Tijitiji Reef, and with contrary winds but light hearts, they paralleled the Sulu Archipelago eastward. The euphoria was short-lived; five days of bad weather only allowed some forty agonizing miles of progress up the island chain until, on that brilliant night of May 12, the wind changed and they headed southeast under a three-quarter moon. With whales cutting across the bow, Bill found the Great Bear upside down just above the horizon and traced a line across the sky with his finger to Polaris. The North Star was so low on the horizon that he figured they were only a few degrees above the equator; any farther south, and the constellation wouldn't be visible.

"We're in a new sea now," Harris wrote optimistically, "the Celebes Sea, bound for the northeastern tip of Celebes." Full of hope at finally breaking out of the Philippines, his happy state of mind matched the clear skies and fresh breeze that was sending them south to freedom.

It wouldn't last.

Five hundred miles southeast of Bill's *kumpit* lay the Moluccas, the fabled Spice Islands of antiquity and, until the eighteenth century, home to the only supply of cloves and nutmeg in the world. Ternate, Tidore, Halmahera, Ambon, and dozens of others — evocative locations largely responsible for triggering the European Age of Discovery, the consequences of which, some five hundred years later, led to Bill Harris's current predicament. Emerging victorious from a series of conflicts over the Portuguese and British, Dutch ascendancy in the Moluccas was brutal, ruthless, and, when deemed necessary, genocidal. Headquartered in Batavia, the Dutch East India Company ruled supreme until its holdings were nationalized by the Dutch government in 1800, yet its mark remained indelibly stamped on the island people of Indonesia.

Initially, this deep-seated, anticolonial, anti-white sentiment aided the Japanese, who presented the war as a fight to liberate their fellow Asians, and many bought into this lie, realizing too late that Japanese overlords were far worse than the Europeans. Hoping for preferential treatment or eventual independence, there were natives who sided with the Japanese throughout the war. These villagers, some with European blood and the benefit of good colonial school educations, were highly sought after by the Japanese—in particularly the Kempeitai; the vicious and barbaric military police. Recruited from regular army personnel, the field officers usually possessed a better education and higher physical fitness levels than their counterparts. Interestingly, their uniform was the standard *kihei rentai*, or dark-green cavalry tunic, riding breeches, and black leather boots. Officers wore regulation cavalry sabers, generally carried a Nambu 8mm pistol, and were easily identified by a white armband around the left biceps.

A branch of the Imperial Army, they had broad, nearly unrestrained wartime powers, especially in occupied territories, and could apprehend, arrest, and interrogate any person suspected of undermining the concept of *hakko ichiu*, the dearly held belief in Japan's divine right to world domination.* Kempeitai wartime duties included the maintenance of order for civilians and military personnel, intelligence gathering, surveillance, espionage, and propaganda. Special units conducted combat operations and biological and chemical warfare. Loathsome, depraved human experimentation was performed on conquered peoples and prisoners of war, over whom they also had absolute governance. One Kempeitai officer's diary entry recorded the following: "Two prisoners escaped last night in the jungle. The two prisoners were later dissected while still alive [by] Medical Officer Yamaji and their livers taken out . . .

---

* Literally, "Whole World Under One Rule."

for the first time I saw the internal organs of a human being. It was very informative."

Japanese doctors, supervised and controlled by the Kempeitai, conducted a wide range of experiments on prisoners, rivaling, and often exceeding, the better-known atrocities perpetrated by their Nazi allies. Under the guidance of Lieutenant General Shiro Ishii, a medical doctor, thousands were injected with plague, cholera, anthrax, and other lethal strains to ascertain which could be developed into weapons of mass destruction. Women were raped by doctors or Kempeitai soldiers to make them pregnant, so their fetuses could be removed alive and dissected. Freezing experiments were conducted to study gangrene, and experimental amputations and reattachment surgeries were performed. Organs were removed from living humans, including terrified, screaming infants, so they could be studied. Takeo Wano, a former medic, testified that he saw a "six-foot high glass jar in which a Western man was pickled in formaldehyde. The man had been cut in two pieces, vertically."

Cannibalism was also practiced on multiple occasions, and Army Major Matoba later admitted, "The battalion wants to eat the flesh of the American aviator, Lieutenant (j.g.) Hall." A dinner was planned for which there was insufficient "eats," so it was decided to dine on the American. Similarly, General Yoshio Tachibana, commander of the 109th Division, ordered the systematic butchering of captured American pilots so their organs could be cooked and served to his officers, as did Rear Admiral Kunizo Mori, a fervent believer in the medicinal value of human liver. Official 18th Army policy was that "while troops were permitted to eat the flesh of Allied dead, they must not eat their own." Lord Russell of Liverpool would later recount that "cannibalism was frequently practiced when there was other food available, that is to say, from choice and not of necessity." In all of this, the Kempeitai were willing suppliers and executioners.

As the administrators of Japanese military law, Kempeitai officers could arrest anyone up to three ranks higher, and were accomplished and enthusiastic torturers. Any technique that extracted information was permissible, and these included floggings; electric shocks, particularly to the genitals; knee spreads; cigarettes to the nipples; and especially variations of the water treatment. For this, a pipe or tube was forced down a prisoner's throat and water poured in until the victim's abdomen swelled and he passed out. The interrogator would then jump on the swollen belly, which induced vomiting and caused internal injuries. Training manuals encouraged something be "pounded into his nostrils to break the bones so he had to breathe through his mouth."

In the occupied territories, Kempeitai units created and subsidized drug networks to weaken the indigenous population through addiction. They organized forced labor camps and brothels, or "comfort stations." Eurasian, Australian, Asian, and particularly European women, were valued as sex objects for Japanese officers. Captured women, with a few rare exceptions, were meant for only one purpose: sexual entertainment. Mass rape was widely documented in China, the Philippines, and throughout the occupied territories, with upward of two hundred thousand women assaulted during the course of the war. Facilitating this was a Kempeitai specialty, and considered quite normal for Japanese soldiers raised in a society with no stigma attached to prostitution. Captured women, like any other war prize, belonged to the conqueror to be disposed of how he pleased.

Less valued than women were prisoners of war. Within the Japanese social structure, the lowest order of life was the *burakumin*, or "untouchables": criminals, destitute beggars, and certain tradesmen, like tanners or animal trainers. Beneath this lowest level were prisoners of war; they were foreigners, or *gaijin*, subhumans with no value. They could be worked to death, tortured, or used for any purpose whatsoever since they were not human and had no rights as such. Japan was a signatory to the 1907 Hague Convention that provided for humane treatment of prisoners, and also to the 1929 Geneva Convention. The latter was never ratified, yet in 1942 Tokyo tacitly agreed to abide by its precepts. Though the Imperial Army physically administered prison camps, ultimate authority over captured enemies unfortunately belonged to the Kempeitai.

In 1943 the area bordering the Celebes Sea and south to Australia was controlled by the Japanese Army, which held sway over land installations and had overall responsibility for dozens of prisoner of war camps scattered throughout the islands. Headquartered on Ambon, Lieutenant General Nobumasa Tominaga's 19th Army presided over the most infamous camp in the area: Tan Tui on Ambon Bay. Prisoners of war confined within Indonesia technically belonged to the army and the Yasen Kempeitai, which were numbered field units. Eventually any captured man, even a naval prisoner, would fall into their hands. Several such units were attached to each area army and were further divided into Sections, Detachments, and Sub-sections. This last group included a Special-Duties unit; field officers who were often sent to remote locations for reconnaissance and the recruitment of natives into spy networks or, more often, as informers. However, the Imperial 2nd South Seas Fleet was headquartered in Makassar, and Allied naval personnel, especially high-value prisoners and officers, were interrogated by the Tokketai, the less well-known, but equally vicious, naval police. Often sent to remote locations under naval control, their responsibilities and duties were identical to those of their Kempeitai competitors.

In the Moluccas, the northernmost Japanese outpost was a tiny village called Wajaboela. Perched on Morotai's Raoe Strait, this forsaken backwater was home to the sole representative of Japan's empire; a naval ensign who hated Morotai, and desperately wished for an opportunity to be transferred back to Makassar, or at least Ambon. Posted with two Malay soldiers, he was responsible for setting up informant networks on surrounding islands and keeping an eye on the locals. A linguist who understood Dutch, Portuguese, and several native dialects, the young man knew the islanders and, surprisingly, had established good relations with most of them.

He also happened to be a Tokketai field officer.

Sunrise, three mornings after clearing Tawi-Tawi, Bill was rubbing sleep from his eyes and yawning toward a brightening eastern horizon. Damp and itchy from salt spray, he was thinking about rice for breakfast and a bed, a real bed with sheets and pillows, when he stopped, mid-yawn, and stared through the haze at a "long string of blue mountains paralleling their course on the south side." Excitedly, because every landfall was exciting, he thumbed through the battered maps. Running a grimy fingertip along the Celebes Sea, he found a mountain similar to the one off his bow.* Nothing else was long enough, and as the haze lifted, Bill saw land stretched across the southern horizon as far as he could see. Waking Kellam, both men decided they were approaching the horn-shaped, northernmost tip of Celebes,† one of the greater Sunda Islands, which included Java, Sumatra, and Borneo. There were certainly Japanese there, so Harris altered course nearly due east to keep clear of the mainland.

Running all day under a steady southwesterly breeze, Bill spotted several smaller islands north of the Bangka Strait, and decided to put into the near one for water. From fifteen miles out, the cone-shaped volcano of another island was plainly visible, but with the *kumpit* pitching wildly in a rising south wind, Bill made for a string of coves along the northern lee shore.‡ "The wind had shifted somewhat east of south, and by now was blowing very fiercely up through the Molucca passage," Harris recalled. "The waves became white-capped and the boat began to shiver, rock, and dip roughly."

Lowering the sail, both men paddled the final "fifty yards through

---

* Mount Klabat.
† Modern-day Sulawesi.
‡ The Ruang volcano on Thulandang Island.

a narrow channel with massive coral formations" in toward a little bar-rio "located on a sandy beach immediately behind a small cove." An-choring twenty yards off the beach, they waded ashore toward a crowd of villagers, and were relieved to see only friendly, questioning faces. Bill's Tagalog greeting was understood well enough to garner a few cheerful Malay replies as the locals gathered round. He was trying to make them understand he wanted to trade for water and food when a curly-headed young man stepped forward and said something in Dutch.

"I'm sorry I don't understand."

The man's face brightened. "Oh, I speak little English."

"I'll be damned. Where on earth did you learn?"

"I went to the school in Manado."

Bill stretched out his hand, and the two shook firmly. The Malay looked him up and down, then asked, "Where come you from?"

"From the Philippines. Where are the Japanese around here?"

"At Manado and Gorontalo." Harris visibly relaxed. Both places were on Celebes and not close. "You want to trade rice?"

"Yes." Bill smiled. "We also want some fruit."

"That is good. We have little rice here."

"And where is here?"

The Malay looked puzzled, and the American chuckled, then pointed at the ground. "I mean, what is this place called?"

"Ah. Biaro."

Biaro. Bill remembered this as the third island north of Celebes, so the Molucca Sea was just to the east, and he now had to choose a route. His Philippine Census Bureau maps ended at Celebes, and he only had a very general map of the East Indies, but was able to trade a bag of rice for an old Dutch regional map. The shortest distance to Australia, some eight to ten days, was down the Molucca passage, past Taliabu and the Banda Arc. From there, they could weave through the Lesser Sunda Islands and cross the Timor Sea to Darwin. This was about a thousand miles altogether, through waters heavily used by the

Imperial Navy, and quite dangerous. The other way was due east to the Spice Islands, south past Papua into the Ceram Sea, then down to Darwin. Longer by some two hundred miles, it was more sheltered, less utilized by warships, and full of islands they could duck into if needed. Of course, the islands were also home to headhunters or cannibals who hated the Dutch and thought anyone with white skin *was* Dutch.

Japs or cannibals . . . which was worse?

Japs, he decided. Primitive islanders knew nothing different, but the Japanese did, and claimed to be civilized, so there was no excuse for their sadistic barbarism. Both routes gave Maluku a wide berth, as the enemy maintained a large naval base at Ambon, and Bill had had enough Japanese hospitality to last a lifetime. *I'll never be captured again if I can help it,* he vowed. *Never.* Still, the closer route would get them to Australia four or five days sooner. *I can almost taste the scotch and feel the sheets,* he thought. In the end, he knew, it would come down to the weather.

So it did.

The next day dawned gray and wet, with the wind coming straight up past Celebes from the south, which eliminated the short route to Darwin. So . . . it was to be headhunters and cannibals instead of warships. Stowing a good supply of pork, bananas, and water, the Americans bade farewell, raised the anchor, and paddled out into the channel. Raising the sail, Harris leaned out over the gunwale, straining on the sheet as the *kumpit* caught the strong southerly breeze. Racing across the bay, he tacked round the easternmost edge of Biaro, and the two young Americans headed out into the Molucca Sea on the morning of May 16, 1943.*

On Palawan a few months earlier, Bob Kellam was bitten by a mosquito and contracted malaria. Sunshine, fresh food, and sea breezes eventually abated the symptoms, but once the nasty *Plasmodium vivax*

---

* Cape Baloemeo.

organism is in a human's system, it can remain indefinitely, especially without treatment. Physical weakness and the constant dampness brought it back, and the second day out from Biaro, he collapsed in a shivering, sweaty huddle. If that wasn't bad enough, Bill discovered that he too was hosting the dormant disease. Aching and feverish, he found that just handling the boat was nearly impossible. He tied the sheet to a cleat whenever possible and tried to rest, but contrary winds made this dangerous; if the boat capsized, in their present condition there was no way they could right it again.

Eating was a nightmare. Bill's stomach clenched painfully, then his bowels filled with fluid, and he spent many minutes hanging from the gunwale passing diarrhea into the sea. This attracted sharks, which made defecation a life-threatening event. Kellam was often too weak to move, and there was no way Bill could hold him, so the narrow wooden deck ran with feces and vomit, which spoiled most of the rice and pork. Four foul-smelling, gut-wrenching, miserable days passed as the wind howled and hard, driving rain pelted down. The boat became saturated, and no dry space remained, which exacerbated both men's malaria and ruined what remained of the rice. With no visible stars, Bill had no way to check their position, and could only keep a rough easterly heading with his old compass. If they missed the Moluccas, there was nothing beyond but a thousand miles of open ocean until the Bismarck Sea, and that, he knew, would kill them.

Four days out of Biaro, the weather finally broke. Creaking and leaking, the *kumpit* rocked about on the flattening waves, and warm sun flowed down through widening breaks in the clouds. The circling sharks were gone, or at least far below them, so both bedraggled and filthy men managed to bathe in the sea. Stripping naked, Bill hung his ragged clothes from the mast, then dumped buckets of seawater over the stained deck until the stench was gone. Food was a problem; aside from bananas, there was nothing else, and though he'd collected water during the rains, it was tainted with salt and barely potable. Of course, now that the malaria had abated and the sun shone, there was no wind.

Aside from being weak, hungry, and thirsty, by the third day following the storm Bill was thoroughly disgusted. There was an island ahead, but no way to get to it without wind. Doubts plagued him; should he have stayed in the Philippines, on Panay, Palawan, or Tawi-Tawi? Fighting and maybe dying in the jungle was certainly better than drifting east on the current with no control over his destiny whatsoever. Maybe he should have stayed on Corregidor . . . at least he'd be in a camp someplace. No. Bill shook his head angrily and stared at the distant, fuzzy horizon. No. Nothing could be as bad as that. At least out here he was free — just as Ed Whitcomb had said on that long-ago morning as they staggered ashore on Bataan. Leaning back carefully to avoid the splinters, Harris frowned and realized today was May 23, 1943. Or at least he thought so.

One year to the day since he swam off Corregidor.

As Bill squeezed his eyes shut, images of the 92nd Garage flooded back: the suffocating heat and thirst, flies, dysentery . . . and the beating. He'd never forget those eight hours in the black, shark-filled bay, or evading the Japanese through Bataan. Guerilla fighting, storms at sea, and those awful twenty-eight days adrift in the South China Sea. He thought of the men he'd known: Ed Whitcomb, Chamberlain, Cothran, and Armstrong . . . and Joe, of course. Kites in the wind, each one dancing through the Pacific war clouds to end up . . . where? Slowly opening his eyes, Bill knew he was lucky to be here, to have lived this long. Squinting at the island's dark outline in the haze ahead, he knew they could make Australia with a bit of luck. They *had* to make it.

But not yet. Three more agonizing days passed as the two Americans bobbed in the waves four to five miles offshore. The sporadic, feeble breeze came from the southwest, but any headway gained was canceled by the current, which flowed around the island from the east. Finally, on the morning of May 27, they'd drifted far enough north to

catch a breeze that carried the *kumpit* around a spade-shaped northern point bordered by a wide, pale beach.* Drifting into a little cove,
Bill wearily dropped anchor between two sandbars at the mouth of a
sluggish brown river. It looked like most of the other islands he'd seen:
reptilian hills coated with a dozen shades of green. The beach here
was a curiously dark gray, almost black, and he was relieved to see a
native village sprawling along the shoreline.

Natives were standing along the beach staring at the boat. That's
good, Bill thought. It means they don't see many strangers, which hopefully included the Japanese. A few clambered into outrigger canoes
and paddled toward the anchored *kumpit*. A "grinning, good-looking
Malaysian boy," about fourteen, with light-brown skin and European-
style clothes, was first aboard. Through pantomime, and mixing a bit
of English, Dutch, and a language Harris guessed to be Galela, he understood that they were invited to the teenager's home for food and
to rest. Gratefully agreeing, they were rowed to the beach, but as Bill
climbed out, the horizon spun and his knees gave way. Clutching the
canoe, he cursed his weakness, and the islanders seemed concerned.
Nodding toward the village, he carefully stood and slowly walked
up a path as his feet crunched over the hard gray sand. Volcanic, he
thought absently, gazing at the coconut trees and nipa huts. Startled
to see a pig trot across the trail, he pointed questioningly, and the boy's
smile widened.

"Pig? Oh. Yes. Yes. We are Christians. There are many Christians
here. But also Mohammed," he waved toward another group of houses
back down the beach. "There is our church." He pointed proudly at a
small white wooden structure with a galvanized iron roof.

"We're Christians too."

"Rome or Protestants?"

"Protestants," Bill replied.

The boy patted his chest. "Henrik da Costa . . . Portuguese."

---

* Cape Sopi, Morotai Island, Northern Moluccas.

Religion, it seemed, did not cause much of a problem here. Maybe they had other things to worry about, though as he looked about at the bamboo and nipa huts, he couldn't see any. The village was peaceful and relatively clean, with no evidence of war—and no Japanese. Stopping before a large, well-built house back from the others, Henrik smiled and gestured toward a walkway made of small logs. The house was set directly on the ground, like the ones in Biaro, and the walls were nipa thatching woven between bamboo poles. Wood steps led up to a small patio, where a well-dressed man with Caucasian features was patiently waiting. A small woman next to him was definitely Malaysian, with darker skin and long black hair. "In America," Bill recalled, "she could have passed for an Indian squaw." Smiling and gesturing, they invited the Americans for tasty chicken stew, cold water, and a long nap.

Villagers crowded in, grinning and chattering loudly. "I can remember," Bill recalled Kellam muttering, "how when I was a kid I used to like to go to the zoo and watch the animals eat. I sort of understand now how they must have felt." Using pantomime and "Nippon" a great deal, the Americans deciphered that there was only a single Japanese soldier on the other side of the island, and this was at least a three-day trip.

Relaxing then for the first time since leaving Tawi-Tawi, Harris felt safe. After the meal, satisfied and comfortable, Bill remembered to ask the island's name. Henrik nodded, waved an arm around at the huts, and smiled broadly.

"Morotai."

The following day dawned bright and clear beneath a brilliant sapphire sky. Kellam suffered another malaria attack, so Bill strolled alone through the village down to the beach and stood there breathing in great lungfuls of clean sea air. Whitecaps dotted the little bay as palm trees bowed in the steady breeze. Passing a few children, the Marine was amused to see them growing turtles in a hollowed-out log. Like everyone else, they smiled and pointed at him, gabbling excitedly in Galela before scampering away. The small Muslim village was identical to its Christian counterpart, and so were the people, except for an occasional fez or ragged turban. Religion, it seemed, was the only difference.

Tiring easily, Harris returned to his borrowed hut and found a newcomer waiting for him with Henrik da Costa. Sitting at the table smoking with Kellam, he was "a very dark-skinned, straight-haired, middle-aged man with Hindu, rather than Malayan, features and wonderfully piercing black eyes." Taking a seat, Bill was surprised to see "a look of extreme dislike" pass between the dark man and Henrik. What, he wondered, was that all about? Then another surprise.

"Hello," the dark man said in slow, careful English. "I been Moses Troekarno. I Java. I know English. School Java. Welcome Pan-gee-oo. Welcome Morotai." Harris reached across the table, shook his hand, and introduced them both.

"You come Manila?" Moses asked.

"Not exactly, but we come from the Philippines."

"You go Australia?"

Bill looked at him warily and hesitated. As Henrik didn't like him either, Harris wondered if the newcomer was pro-Japanese.

"We go to the Solomon Islands," he finally answered, deciding to be cautious. Neither he nor Kellam was strong enough for much of a fight, and if they had to run again, a red herring or two might help.

"Why? Long way. Many Jap."

Kellam, who seemed confused by the subterfuge, pointed at Harris. "His father is a general there . . . a Marine general. He wants to join him."

Blank looks.

"Jen-er-raal," Bill patted his chest. "Father . . . papa."

Henrik's eyes cleared. "Oo vader? Gene raal," he said in Dutch, smiling, then blurted in Portuguese. "Vocês pai." Your father.

Moses understood as well. He pursed his lips and nodded. "Best you go now. Japanese on this island."

"Yeah? Only one, isn't it?" Bill held up a finger. "One."

"One? Yes. At Wayabula." He pointed west and held up three fingers.

Henrik frowned, unable to follow the English, but watching their faces closely. Moses slowly rose to go, then turned and pointed directly at Henrik.

"Da Costa," he said clearly and low. "Da Costa *all* snake."

Later, walking down to the boat, Harris decided to tell their hosts they would depart in two days, but they'd actually sail tomorrow. Bob Kellam agreed. High tide was midmorning, so Bill figured to eat breakfast, then stroll to the boat as they were doing now and just leave with no warning. It wasn't that he didn't trust the da Costas, but in truth he didn't trust any islanders too much. They were not Filipinos, and Bill recalled that Cothran's group had been betrayed by Indonesian locals. Moses might have a grudge against Henrik's family, or another reason entirely for wanting the Americans gone. On the other hand, Harris remembered his initial impression of da Costa and the faintly sly look on his face. This could be nothing, and was probably no more than some local rivalry, yet . . . well, why take a chance? The *kumpit* was shipshape enough to get them across the Halmahera Sea to Papua, about a four-day sail, and from there other plans could be made.

Kellam agreed, and brought the Springfield '03 rifle from the boat, just in case. As they returned to the village, Bill felt a cold twinge of fever stir deep inside and "a familiar hateful ache in his legs and knees." From beneath his ribs, the chills fanned out through his forearms up toward his neck. Stopping, he swallowed hard and squeezed his eyes shut. Flashing spots danced across the lids, and he shook his head to clear them. No. No . . . *not now*. Breathing hard, he continued slowly toward the hut, then wrapped up in a blanket and collapsed on the bed. Muscles clenched and shivering, Bill stared painfully at the rough walls, wondering, not for the first time, how in the hell he'd arrived in this awful position. He'd done everything right: good family, good grades, athlete, Annapolis . . . and now he was in a sweaty native bed on Morotai. At some point, still trying to make sense of it all, Harris mercifully passed out.

Tuesday, June 1, 1943, dawned clear and warm. When Bill opened his eyes, it was already steaming hot, but from his window he could see the palm fronds steadily waving. A good day for sailing. Lying still a moment, he inventoried his body and was relieved to feel no fever — some aches, of course, and he was weak, but he had an appetite and was desperately thirsty. Throwing off the damp, stale blanket, Bill stretched, pulled on his extra shirt — torn but clean — then stepped out of the hut. Blinking in the sun, he watched the children play a moment then walked across to the da Costa house.

A group of villagers were there, as always, and Kellam was sitting at the table eating a juicy papaya. Bill noted that rifle leaning against the wall behind him, but everyone seemed as relaxed and friendly as they had been for the past four days. Deciding fever had gotten the best of his imagination, Harris pulled up a chair and sat while Henrik brought out heaping plates of rice, followed by his father and a big bowl of steaming chicken stew.

"I wonder why Mr. da Costa decided to help serve us this morning." Bill looked around but didn't see Henrik's mother. Maybe she was sick.

"Beats me," Kellam replied, shoveling more stew in his mouth. Harris shrugged, then glanced around as he tucked into breakfast. There were a lot of villagers in today, he noted, even more than normal. Spicy and hot, the stew tasted wonderful to a hungry man, as did the pitcher of cold water, which he drained. Wiping his mouth, Bill realized more villagers were lining the walls and standing in the door. What would they do for entertainment, he mused, when he and Kellam left? With that in mind, and with Henrik's help, Bill conveyed their departure plan to Mr. da Costa, who smiled and nodded. Food and water would be taken to the *kumpit* now, Harris gathered, so as to be ready for sailing tomorrow. Chewing the stew, Harris was pleased.

There would be nothing to stop them from suddenly leaving here in a few hours on today's tide. Sighing deeply, he leaned back. All, it seemed, was going well.

Suddenly, he "felt a muscular arm around his throat under his chin and felt hands grasping at his arms." Reacting instantly, Bill twisted sideways and stomped on the nearest foot as "he was pulled over backwards in his chair." Rather than resisting, he kicked the table with both feet and toppled over backwards with the chair. Totally unexpected, this move caught the villagers by surprise, and they all tumbled against the wall in a thrashing heap that shook the house. Catching a glimpse of Kellam fighting a half-dozen men, Bill hooked his hand under the strong forearm across his throat, found the man's hand, and snapped his little finger. Bellowing with pain, the villager's grip slipped away, and the Marine shoulder-rolled to his feet. Spinning around, he drove a fist into the nearest man's face and saw "the nose transformed to a blob of red" as the man crashed back into the wall.

Malaysians were everywhere, shouting and jumping, but the fighting man in Bill took over and he reacted by instinct for the next minute. Another set of arms grabbed him from behind, so he viciously kicked backward and had the satisfaction of feeling a knee shatter. Shrieking in agony, the islander let go, and Bill pivoted, trying to get his back against the wall. Two more villagers lunged, and Harris jabbed stiffened fingers into an eye, then caught the other with a palm strike under the nose. As they fell back, four more leapt in from the sides and Bill crashed through the thin wall onto the ground outside. Landing on a villager, he felt the Malaysian go limp as ribs broke and his lungs deflated. Rolling sideways with a head under each arm, Bill twisted their necks as he staggered upright. One abruptly stopped screaming as his neck snapped, and the Marine dropped them both.

Surrounded now by enraged villagers, Harris was spinning around to face the closest when his "head felt like it had been struck by a bolt of lightning." Lights exploded in his skull; everything went red, then black, and he felt his legs give way. Bill didn't recall hitting the ground, but when he came to, he was lying faceup staring into a ring of angry faces. Several Malaysians had long, wicked knives, and they seemed to be arguing about the best way to cut him up. Men were standing on his arms and squatting on his legs, but Bill roared and thrashed. Even in his weakened state, he knocked a few off, then arched his back for a final thrust when the flat edge of a sword smacked his chest. Surprised, Harris followed the blade sideways . . . and saw the boots. Black riding boots, faded now like a weathered charcoal briquette and cracking apart down close to the sole. The blade moved up and deliberately rotated so the sharp edge lay against his throat. Squinting upward, he saw the riding pants on a man who was definitely not Malaysian.

He was, in fact, a Japanese officer.

"The Jap was a good-looking young man in khaki green with an anchor on the front of his cap," Bill recalled. As the villagers hauled the bleeding Marine to his feet, he noticed the "insignia of an ensign on his collar." A naval officer. Obviously the one from Wajaboela. Blinking blood and dust from his eyes, Harris glared around at the crowd, then saw the da Costas. Henrik looked faintly shocked and was standing very close to his father. *As if that would save you if I could get loose*, Bill fumed, hot rage running up from his gut and making his face burn. The elder da Costa wore the same smug, slightly foxy look he'd had when the Americans first arrived. No mystery as to how the Jap got here, Harris realized. The hospitality and concern were all bullshit. They must've sent a runner across the island that first night for the enemy to arrive so quickly.

"If I ever get free again, I'll come back here and cut your fucking throat," he snarled, and both da Costas stepped back, eyes widening. They couldn't understand his words, but they understood him perfectly. The officer looked up into Bill's eyes and said something in Japanese, quite softly, but menacing, then he lowered the sword and barked a few sentences in Galela. Another dozen villagers closed in, pinning Harris's arms behind him as they marched him down the main path through Pangeo. The Marine was gratified to see nearly a dozen villagers were down, bleeding and moaning. Several weren't moving at all. The Jap also noticed, said something to Bill, then nodded appreciatively.

In front of the house another crowd surrounded Bob Kellam, and Harris noted a half-dozen villagers nursing broken bones and bloodied faces. *Too bad I couldn't have gotten to the Springfield.* Then he observed "two Malayans in gray uniforms with beak visor caps. One carried a rifle and the other a pistol." No chance. There was no chance at all against three armed men and at least thirty enraged locals.

Shoving Bill to the ground, the villagers backed up, and one drew a knife. Spitting angrily, he pointed toward the nearest dead Malaysian, then waved the blade back and forth. *They're going to kill me anyway*, Harris realized, *but this time I'll go down fighting.* He knew several ways to take a blade away, and was considering the best choice when shouts echoed down the little street. Everyone looked up as two boys came sprinting up the path from the beach.

"I only wish," Kellam muttered low enough for Bill to hear, "that I had shot that da Costa . . . and his brat Henrik too."

"Moses sure had the dope on them when he said all da Costas were snakes." Bill watched the boys gasp for breath before breaking into excited jabbering. "I'd like to see that guy again and apologize for the things I thought about him. He's the only real man on Morotai."

"I'd like to come back here one day," Kellam hawked, spat a bloody gob in the dirt, and wiped carefully around his broken nose, "and exterminate every one of these dirty shitheads that go around disguised as humans."

Harris nodded grimly. "An honest enemy is one thing . . . but a traitor deserves a slow death."

The crowd parted as the Japanese officer waved at the Americans, then pointed toward the beach. Roughly, with a few sucker punches and kicks, the villagers hauled both men to their feet and pushed them down the road. Chickens clucked, dogs barked, and pigs scattered as the mob veered right and cut through the trees to the black beach. Kellam staggered and dropped to his knees on the coarse sand. Their *kumpit* was still bobbing at anchor between the sandbars, and Bill figured he'd never see it again. So close. Just two weeks to Australia after 391 days on the run. He straightened and glanced around. If the Jap drew his sword, Bill intended to twist sideways, hip-roll the Malaysians, and at least stomp a neck or two before he was cut down. If his hands were free, he'd try to swim for it. How to do that, he wondered, and was thinking it through when the Japanese officer suddenly shouted, then pointed.

Then Bill saw it.

A small gray warship flying a white ensign was coming around the point about a half mile away. Feathered spray blew up from its bow, and he could make out dark figures darting along her deck. Some type of corvette, Harris thought, or maybe a minesweeper. Staring at the ship, he realized how well planned this snatch had been. All the food and rest . . . right from the beginning it was a trap to keep them here until the Japanese arrived. Son of a bitch . . . we should've left yesterday. One more day—the anger rose and Bill's breathing quickened. One more fucking day and we'd have been gone.

Entering the bay, the ship swung around, idled into the wind, and lowered a motor launch. Why send a ship? With the help of forty nearby villagers, the Jap officer could have simply snicked their heads off in Pangeo, so why bother? Why? Bill's stomach flipped as he thought of one possibility and suddenly wished he hadn't mentioned his father to da Costa. Swallowing, he stared out over the whitecap-scarred bay wondering if that bit of news had survived interpretation and got passed to the Japanese.

Maybe this was because of *where* they were captured. If an enemy base was nearby, they might believe the Americans were spies; the Japanese were obsessed with spies. Hopefully, that was it. Besides, as long as he was alive, there was still hope . . . and another chance for escape. Then, as the launch headed in toward the beach, the Japanese officer turned and looked straight at Bill. His dark eyes were expressionless. A small smile flitted across the man's face. A smug little glance, and not at all encouraging. A now-familiar knot of fear settled in Bill's gut, but he fought it back and thought of all the effort that went into this capture. Surely it wasn't to simply torture or execute them.

Not yet, at least.

NINE

✳

ABYSS

IRONICALLY, ON JUNE 1, 1943, AS HIS SON WAS RECAPTURED, FIELD
Harris was less than 1,800 miles to the southeast in the Solomon
Islands, the same distance from Bill's home in Lexington, Kentucky,
to California, where he'd shipped out for the Philippines. It was as
close as they'd be to each other throughout the entire war, though
their situations were entirely different. With Guadalcanal secured
in February and the Japanese advance blunted, America was up off
the dark ground of 1942 and flexing her considerable military muscles.
Half a world away, Rommel's Afrika Korps was driven back into Tunisia, where its tattered remnants would eventually surrender, and the
Germans were fighting for their lives on the Russian steppes.

Closer to home, the Japanese suffered a strategic defeat in the Bismarck Sea that solidified the Allied hold on New Guinea and took
another beating off the Komandorski Islands, which would permit the
reconquest of the Aleutians. Faced with fading offensive fortunes, Admiral Isoroku Yamamoto conceived Operation I-Go, a counteroffensive designed to slow the Americans' advance in New Guinea and the
Solomons. Stripping his increasingly vulnerable carriers of aircraft,
the admiral planned a series of massive, ground-launched air assaults
against Guadalcanal, the Russell Islands, and New Guinea. Allied

losses, Yamamoto hoped, would be severe enough to force a pause while preserving his great base at Rabaul. During the lull, he also planned to finish constructing impregnable island defenses between the enemy and the Home Islands.

Like Yamamoto, I-Go was bold, audacious . . . and flawed. Also, as with most Japanese plans, its success depended on the Americans doing precisely what was expected of them—something that rarely happened. Commencing on April 7, 1943, while Bill Harris was on Balabac, the initial air assaults were a resounding success, according to the pilots, and each mission returned with tales of ships sunk and planes shot down. All told, the Allies lost twenty-eight warships and 175 aircraft of all types; Yamamoto was thrilled, and decided to tour the front himself to boost morale and spur his men on to even greater efforts. There were two problems with this. First, the Japanese pilots wildly exaggerated their "victories." In fact, the Allies lost only five ships and twenty-five planes against a cost of fifty-five Japanese aircraft. Yamamoto's time to "run wild" in the Pacific had expired, and his personal time was also up. This occurred due to the magnificent efforts of Allied code breakers, who were able to decipher the great admiral's upcoming itinerary at the front. His precise time of arrival and exact destination were passed up the chain, and this information led to a decision to intercept and kill Japan's top military officer.

At 0710 on the morning of April 18, 1943, the first of eighteen U.S. Army P-38s roared down Guadalcanal's Fighter Two runway. Minutes later, sixteen of them let down into the haze over the Solomon Sea and commenced Operation Vengeance. Led by Major John Mitchell, who flew a flawless, radio-silent route over 416 miles of open water, two of these fighters ambushed Yamamoto's Betty bomber over southern Bougainville. At 0940 local time, Lieutenant Rex Barber, an Oregon farm boy turned fighter pilot, fired four bursts into the bomber and sent it burning into the jungle. Isoroku Yamamoto, commander of the Combined Fleet and architect of the Pearl Harbor attack, was dead. Given the tremendous psychological blow it would cause, his death was kept secret until May 7, when Imperial Headquarters acknowledged that the beloved admiral had "met a gallant death" while directing frontline operations. As the battleship *Musashi* stood out from Truk lagoon bound for Tokyo Bay with Yamamoto's ashes, Bill Harris and Bob Kellam sailed from Tawi-Tawi some 1,900 miles to the west.

In June 1943, Field Harris was now planning Marine aviation's role in Operation Cartwheel, the Allied offensive designed to isolate Rabaul by taking New Guinea and the Solomons. His old friend and fellow Guadalcanal veteran Colonel Harry Liversedge commanded the First Marine Raider Regiment and would be in the thick of it. Field rarely thought of the many friends he'd lost in the past nine months; like all men who find a way to cope with combat, he could not dwell on the deaths—that would come later. He tried the same coping techniques regarding his son, but the general could not do it. Images of the gentle, serious child he'd been always flooded back: playing with his baby boy on Virginia Beach, eight-year-old Bill in knickerbockers with a jaunty car cap or wearing the Indian costume Field made for his son's sixth Halloween.

His son haunted him. Was he in a filthy camp someplace in the Philippines, or had he died in agony on Corregidor? The thought of his boy being tortured or of his torn body tossed carelessly into an unmarked grave was too heartbreaking to consider, and his chest tightened at the thought. He *had* to be alive, and that for now must be good enough. Slapping a mosquito and cursing the humidity, Field had work to do if Cartwheel was to succeed, but somehow, the general knew, he would find out about his son.

Seven thousand miles northeast of the Solomons in her lonely Washington apartment, Katie Harris desperately hoped for the same. Kalorama Park's pale-pink cherry blossoms had faded by June, but it remained an oasis of color amid the grim grays of a wartime capital. Orange Icelandic poppies, purple foxgloves, red lilies, and an occasional royal blue Siberian iris splashed across the little green triangle near Rock Creek. She'd had no letter from Bill in fifteen months, and even her husband could discover no official news. Her son had been on Corregidor and was not listed among the 4th Marine casualties, but Katie knew this meant very little in the chaos of the Philippines. They had eventually received notification that Field's little brother, Lieutenant Commander Earl "Squire" Harris, had survived Corregidor but was then taken to a prisoner of war camp. Nothing else was known.

Like most of America, by June 1943 Washington was booming, and despite the war it was hard not to be caught up in the capital's raw energy. Blackouts were still a rule, but no one took them too seriously any longer. Nightclubs and restaurants were packed, and uniforms were in vogue everywhere. President Roosevelt's optimistic 1940 goal to turn the nation into the "great arsenal of democracy" had been met. Unemployment, and the dreary pessimism of the 1930s, vanished as shipyards, factories, and defense plants now churned out an astonishing 120,000 aircraft and tanks per year, with fully half of the entire world's wartime production now centered in the United States. By itself, Ford Motor Company outproduced the entire economy of Italy and could roll out a B-24 bomber every sixty-three minutes. Chrysler's Detroit Arsenal constructed more tanks than the entire Third Reich, yet even these companies were dwarfed by General Motors, which produced 119 million artillery shells, 206,000 aircraft engines, and over five million rifles and machine guns—among other things.

Using the very real Axis threat, the War Production Board melded with the capability and flexibility of a free market to transform 70 percent of American manufacturing capacity toward war materiel. Frigidaire now made .30-caliber machine guns, Lionel Trains constructed compasses, and Underwood Typewriters turned out M1 carbines. Liberty ships, the seagoing workhorse of the war, were sliding into the water every forty-two days, and by now 160 of these absolutely essential yet ugly little ships were being launched each month from shipyards all over the country. However, newspapers and radio tended to carefully publicize the more glamorous warships that physically took the fight to the enemy. With her son and husband at risk, Katie was proud to know that by May 1943, three new *Essex*-class carriers had been launched, two were due out by year's end, and eleven more would be commissioned during the next twenty-four months.* The navy was also building smaller *Casablanca*-class escort carriers for antisubmarine warfare, convoy duties, and amphibious operations. By now, shipyards were constructing these "jeep" carriers at the astonishing rate of about one per week. All the *South Dakota*–class battleships were now at sea, and by June a pair of the massive *Iowa*-class ships had been commissioned.† Mounting nine sixteen-inch guns, these 887-foot warships could charge through the ocean at thirty-three knots and carried the latest radar, communications, and fire-control systems.

It was all good news and showed the country was finally united in conducting the war. The paper announced next year's military program would exceed 106 *billion* dollars—an astronomical, nearly inconceivable sum. According to *The New York Times*, this month's aircraft output would pass 7,200, which exceeded the previous month's production by a thousand planes, and she could only pray these would be used to pound Japan and perhaps keep her men safe. Still, Germany was lashing back hard, and Japan just adopted a new plan to crush the Allies, declaring the "Atrocious and Cruel America and Britain must be quickly defeated."

Katie didn't think so.

Yet proud as she was, Katie was equally dismayed that while fighting men risked their lives overseas, draft-deferred workers backed by labor unions petulantly walked off their Stateside jobs demanding a raise of two dollars per day. Correctly despised by service-member families and speared by the press, these people only returned to work after President Roosevelt threatened to rescind their exemptions, put them in a uniform, and send them into action. Such baffling attitudes

---

* USS *Essex* (CV-9), *Yorktown* (CV-10), and *Intrepid* (CV-11). Thirty-two were ordered, of which fourteen would see combat during World War II.
† USS *Iowa* (BB-61) and *New Jersey* (BB-62).

angered Katie and the millions of other Americans who had men in combat. To be sure, there were valid critiques of America's social and racial issues, but now, in the middle of a world war, was not the time for dissent, Katie felt; but dissent there was. She'd read about the "zoot suiters" in Los Angeles—gangs of Hispanics, along with some blacks, called pachucos, who chose to protest government mandates in June 1943 by purposely tailoring full-cut jackets with baggy trousers (called zoot suits), which defied wartime regulations against using excessive fabric. Worn with wide-brimmed hats and pointed shoes, it was a distinctly colorful and wasteful outfit intended as a racial statement—and in the worst possible place.

The Port of Los Angeles, Camp Ross, Camp Anza, and nearby facilities were major hubs for hundreds of thousands of embarking and returning troops, many of whom were southerners with racist attitudes, especially toward those who lived in safety at the military's expense. On June 3, eleven sailors were accosted by a group of zoot suiters, so the following day over two hundred naval personnel went hunting in East Los Angeles to settle the score. This escalated and was fanned on by the local press, who viewed the pachucos as street thugs. In the end, the military men were temporarily confined to their barracks and over five hundred Hispanics were arrested. "NO MORE ZOOT SUITS!" and "NAVY BANS LOS ANGELES" ran the headlines, as the entire city became "temporarily restricted." Nonetheless, Katie had more important things on her mind than social injustice, actual or perceived. America was leading the fight against global injustice—the real thing—and against world domination by militaristic ideologies intending to enslave the world. For her, everything else could wait until her men returned.

Jeanne Glennon, now twenty-one years old and a junior at George Washington University, had another view. She wanted to be part of the struggle; her father and brother both were in it, and her boyfriend had died at Pearl Harbor. She wanted to fight. That was impossible, at least physically, but the Lejeune in her refused to give in. Jeanne left Sweet Briar for George Washington in 1942 to complete her degree in history and enter the WAVES as an officer. With a year remaining, she was becoming restive—but there was no alternative, since her father, Captain James Blair Glennon, was still close by at the Naval Ordnance Laboratory and would not let her enter the military in any other capacity. Thinking of him turned her thoughts to Father's Day, just a week away now. He wouldn't wear civilian clothes during the war, though it was interesting to see that many stores now advertised British shirts and suits. Maybe a watch. She'd seen an Orloff Valjoux that he would wear, or perhaps a Longines—they were both available in Washington on New York Avenue or in Georgetown.

With the throng of young officers in D.C., Jeanne hadn't paid for dinner in two years, so she could afford to buy her father an expensive gift and nice clothes for herself. Despite the leather shortage, a girl could buy a nice pair of pumps for $9.95 or a gown for $3.98. Surely it was a sign that things were better now that stockings were now being openly sold again. Rayon, to be sure, but still stockings, which meant several of her friends could cease drawing lines on their calves with mascara pencils to keep up appearances. It seemed silly, she knew, to be concerned about trivial things at a time like this, but it also struck her as patriotic. If America could live in some semblance of normalcy despite the array of enemies against her, wasn't this defiance of the tyrannies across the sea? She'd heard Japanese civilians were wearing paper underwear and only eating rice, yet here, for $1.45, she could be taken out for a prime rib dinner.

That produced a stab of guilt, and she wished her brother Jimmy could have a good meal, wherever he was. Daddy believed him to be in the Aleutians, but exact postings were nearly impossible to discover for security reasons, and her heart quickened at the thought. In the first invasion of the continental United States since 1812, the Japanese occupied the Aleutians in June 1942.* This shocked and alarmed Washington, as the West Coast was now truly vulnerable to attack, and if the decisive Battle of Midway had ended differently, such an invasion might have occurred. In any event, reclaiming American territory became a top priority, and with Japanese offensives blunted after Guadalcanal, this became a reality. Just weeks ago, on May 30, a headline read "FINAL VICTORY BELIEVED NEAR," as the entire Japanese garrison in Attu's Chichagof Valley was annihilated during a banzai charge.

No dreaded Western Union telegram had arrived, so she and her mother believed Jimmy had survived. Still, being safe and warm in D.C., listening to Glenn Miller's "In the Mood" or "You'll Never Know" from that skinny Sinatra kid made her long to do more. If, in some small way, Jeanne could avenge Marshall Darby, or help her brother, she wanted to do it. Staring out over the kaleidoscope of uniforms, slender girls, and busy streets, she suddenly thought of her brother's classmate from the Naval Academy she'd met so many years ago. Bill . . . Bill Harris. Where, she wondered, had he ended up during this crazy war? Jimmy hadn't mentioned him during the few letters she'd received, which he certainly would have if his friend had been killed, so she assumed he was still alive. He'd been nice, in a serious sort of way, and she hoped, wherever he was, that Bill was alive and well.

At that moment, 8,076 miles away in the Pacific, Bill Harris wasn't sure himself. He was alive, but "well" would certainly be a stretch. From Morotai, he and Bob Kellam were taken to Ternate, a volcanic pyramid of an island just west of Halmahera. Held in an old Dutch fort near the town center, Bill had been surprised by their treatment. They treated his cuts from Morotai, and he was given cigarettes, food, and

---

* Refusing to be evacuated by the U.S. Navy, native Aleuts did little to resist the invasion, believing, as many did, that the Japanese came as liberators. Sent to internment camps in Hokkaido, the locals from Kiska and Attu belatedly realized the Americans were definitely preferable to the Japanese.

quinine.* Watchful, but polite, the Japanese had not abused them, but Bill noticed a great deal of latent hostility from the permanent guards at the fort. From the gold stars on their caps, he noted that these men belonged to the Imperial Army, whereas his captor was a naval officer, who, incidentally, was never far away. Though he never gave his name, the ensign spoke passable English, and related that Bill was quite a prize given his father's rank. The Japanese also seemed to respect him because he hadn't surrendered—he'd been subdued while fighting and then captured—this made a difference. The other possibility for his continued existence was Corregidor, though there was no record of him there that he knew of, and as a junior officer, why would anyone be looking for him?

The Philippine guerillas.

That thought, and a cold stab of fear, hit him hard. The Japanese hated defiance and despised guerillas, so this dull dread stayed with him the entire ten days at Ternate. Every time a door opened or someone shouted, his gut clenched. But nothing had happened, and on 13 June both Americans were marched onto a small cargo ship bound for Ambon in the south, the ensign informed him. Allowed on deck, Bill relished the salt air, staring at the passing coastline and picturing the map in his head. Steaming west of a line of small islands, he could see a very large, long shore that had to be Halmahera. *Maybe*, he thought, *I could slip overboard at night and swim ashore. This time I'll stay put.* No more adventures. But what would be the point? Everything around here was occupied, and he'd seen more shark fins than before. The point, he reminded himself, was freedom.

But at every sunset, he was herded belowdecks and chained to a water pipe, so it was a moot point. Besides, Kellam was too weak from malaria for a swim, and Bill knew he'd be executed in retaliation for an escape. So, thirty hours after departing Ternate, both men were still aboard as the little ship nosed around a hilly green cape

---

* Fort Oranje.

and slowly chugged into a long, triangular bay. Bordered by a peninsula to the east, about six miles in, Bill could see aircraft landing on the western coast.* As the bay narrowed, the boat angled east and eventually dropped anchor below a town he assumed to be Ambon. Conquered by the Japanese in February 1942, its European influence plainly showed in wide streets lined with trees and, surprisingly, stone buildings with red roofs. From here, under army guards but still led by the naval officer, the Americans were driven east along the shore in a battered green Dodge truck with wide fenders and a rotting wooden bed. After passing another Dutch colonial fort, they continued about a mile to an ugly, irregular enclosure surrounded by a "12-foot high, double barbed wire fence."

A wood jetty stuck out into the bay, and a hundred yards inland a pair of wooden sentry boxes topped with corrugated tin flanked the road. Army guards wearing wrapped leggings snapped to attention, their rifles made longer by fifteen-inch-long, Type 30 bayonets, as the vehicle turned toward the compound's western edge. The truck lurched to a stop before a substantial prewar building with a Japanese flag drooping from a pole, and the Americans were commanded to stand at attention in the hot sun. Another fence separated this area from the main camp, and Bill could see sorry groups of emaciated, pale-skinned ghosts wandering aimlessly inside the wire.

Captain Ando Noburo, the short, vicious commandant who spoke fairly good English, arrived with an evil-looking interpreter named Ikeuchi Masakiyo and a navy lieutenant named Miyasaki Yoshio. Looking them over, they began an argument that Bill interpreted as a turf battle, but the naval officers stood firm and the Americans were eventually taken to "individual small, well-guarded cells" within a smaller building near the entrance. "Tan Toey," the young ensign said, waving an arm around. "You here for now." The officer stood a moment and looked up at Bill, his dark eyes unreadable; then he did an odd

---

* Cape Lia, Ambon Bay, the Laitimor Peninsula, and Laha Airfield.

thing. He bowed slightly at the waist, smiled a tight little smile, and then turned and left. Harris never saw him again.

Bill was surprised by the concrete floors, which were decidedly better than dirt. The building also had solid wood walls and tin roofs that kept the cells dry. For over a month he remained isolated, even from Bob Kellam, who was imprisoned on the opposite side of the building. Given quinine but very little food, Bill was questioned only sporadically and was able to feign ignorance about American plans. He had escaped from the Philippines by boat and had never fought with guerillas or killed any Japanese. They seemed to believe it, so he was largely left alone. There was reveille every morning before dawn, which Bill heard through his small window, and under guard he was permitted to walk around the perimeter between the main camp and the Japanese barracks. As the weeks wore on, he sometimes managed to swap short conversations with the few prisoners on the other side of the wire.

Desperate for news of the war, the other prisoners were extremely interested in the growing American campaigns in New Guinea and the Solomons. He also filled them in on the "other" war in Europe, with what he'd heard about Russia and North Africa. Bill learned that most of these men were the remnants of the Gull Force, an eleven-hundred-man Australian detachment that arrived at Ambon on December 17, 1941, to shore up the local Dutch East Indies contingent. Cut off, abandoned, and overwhelmed, they surrendered to elements of the Japanese 228th Infantry Regiment and 1st Kure Special Naval Landing Force on February 3, 1942.

Harris was further surprised to learn that this site at Tan Tui was the Gull Force's former barracks and that the non-Dutch prisoners were segregated from the former Netherlands East Indies troops. Apparently, the Aussies weren't happy about being sacrificed for the Dutch, and the Dutch thought the Australians gave up too easily—then there were English prisoners recently arrived from Java who believed no one had fought hard enough for the empire. Remaining at Tan Tui for seven weeks, Bill remained isolated but, as a special prisoner, was not mistreated. The others were not so fortunate, and beatings increased as Allied air attacks against nearby Laha Airfield intensified. "The main fault here," Harris later wrote, "was the strictly limited nature of the confinement and the scanty food." He was already thirty pounds lighter than normal, and a bowl of rice and cassava three times a day did nothing to put weight back on the rangy Marine. Malaria still plagued him, though the quinine helped, and so far he had avoided beriberi.*

On the morning of August 1, with no warning, Miyasaki Yoshio appeared with a pair of guards and took Bill from the camp in a pug-nosed little Ford truck. Winding up Ambon Bay's eastern shore, the Marine stared across the sun-flecked water at the green mountains and wondered if this was his last morning. Nothing had been said, but he'd heard from the other prisoners that summary executions occurred at Tan Tui and that the Japanese preferred sunrise beheadings. *By God, I'll go down fighting if that's what they have in mind.* Weak or not, he planned on killing at least one of them and surreptitiously flexed his muscles. Strange, he mused, how the little things are overlooked. The breeze on his face, or the earthy smell of land mingling with fish and salt from the water. Looking east at the sun, he was amazed, as always, by the colors: shades of orange and yellow that leaked out onto the blues. Filling his lungs with air, Bill was gathering as much strength as possible when the truck rounded a curve and slowed.

Looking around the cab, he saw a half-moon-shaped inlet of shallow brown water, where several large four-engined flying boats bobbed gently at their moorings. Roughly shoved from the truck, Harris was considering the possibilities when Yoshio approached, barked at the guards, who promptly moved back, and informed Bill they were flying to Yokohama on the Home Island of Honshu. Relief washed through him initially, then despair. There was no chance of escape from one of the Home Islands, but at a regular POW camp at least his family

---

* Caused by a thiamine deficiency and exacerbated by the white rice diet common among prisoners of war.

would learn he was alive. So, on August 1, 1943, a Type 97 Kawani-
shi flying boat called a Mavis roared northwest across Ambon Bay,
bounced into the air, then banked north through a valley. Climbing
out over the Piku Sea, the big aircraft leveled off at 10,000 feet, then
flew northeast for six hours to Palau. Taking on a few officers returning home, the Mavis departed at dawn the following morning, heading northwest for eleven hours across the vast Pacific. Visualizing it
all in his head, Bill figured they passed within a few hundred miles of
the Philippines.

How ironic.

Twenty months of fighting, evading, and hardship, and he was back
where he started. Well, nearly. Yoshio told him they would spend the
night in Formosa and go on to Yokohama the next day, which they
did. On August 4, 1943, eight hours after leaving Taipei, the flying boat
let down in Tokyo Bay, and Lieutenant Bill Harris stepped onto Japanese soil. Taken from Yokohama in an older-model Chevy Cabriolet,
he was driven a dozen miles southwest through the countryside to a
remote valley on the Kashio River. Led to a wooden stockade, he was
roughly shoved through a gate into a U-shaped compound, whose east
and west sides were formed by a pair of 150-foot-long pine barracks.
The compound's base consisted of a shorter barracks, with a cluster of
smaller buildings scattered about. The guards he could see all wore
naval uniforms.

Inside the short barracks, Harris was stripped and doused with dis-
infectant; then, as he wiped the stuff from his eyes, his head and beard
were completely shaved. A "green cotton two-piece Jap work fatigue
uniform" was dumped on the wood floor along with a pair of very
thin cotton blankets and pair of old tennis shoes that were much too
small. Taken down the hall, he was pushed into a small bare room
and made to dress, then stand at attention. Swaying with weariness,
he wiped his face and was promptly punched in the gut by the guard,
who screamed at him in Japanese. This brought in another guard, who
barely reached the tall Marine's chin, but who slapped him hard with

an open palm and also yelled. Bill was blinking away the sweat when the door opened, and both guards snapped rigidly to attention as an officer stepped into the room. Barking sharply, he sent them scurrying outside, then shut the door. In perfect English, the man introduced himself as Captain Yuzuru Sanematsu of the Imperial Navy, gave Bill a cigarette, and gestured for him to sit.

Disarming and polite, Sanematsu related that he'd lived in Washington, D.C., during his time as assistant naval attaché and asked a few questions about favorite spots. Bill was aware this was an oblique attempt to gather information about wartime Washington, but as he hadn't been there since 1941, he saw no harm in creating a few illusions rather than stonewalling the man. It worked. The captain relaxed enough for Harris to ask where, exactly, he was, and Sanematsu told him through a cloud of cigarette smoke that this place was the To-45 Naval Interrogation Center at Ofuna, and he was the commander, though the day-to-day affairs were managed by another officer.

After an hour or so, he smiled courteously, stood, and left. For a few minutes Bill thought things might not be so bad here—then the door flew open. A big Jap strode in, nearly six feet tall, stocky, and seemingly furious. Hauled to his feet, Bill was slapped hard several times, his head violently snapping sideways. Red and yellow lights sparked beneath his lids, and his ears were ringing when a powerful punch landed just under his rib cage. Eyes bulging, the Marine collapsed and gasped agonizingly for air, but nothing came in. Other blows struck his neck and shoulders, then a kick knocked him against the knotty pine wall. Yanked upright, he gulped in a few breaths before being dragged into the bright sunlight. Struggling to his feet, Bill blinked and inhaled painfully. A hard blow between his shoulders sent him stumbling forward, and as his vision cleared, he made out shapes of men shuffling around an open space between the barracks. Shoved around a corner to a very small barracks against the west fence, Harris was physically tossed into a small cell and left panting on the floor.

Through watery eyes, he saw the little room was about six by nine feet, with a small electric light and a straw sleeping mat.

Over the next few days, he learned the routine. A bell clanged promptly at 0700, and prisoners had thirty minutes to wash and assemble for *tenko*, or roll call. In the main barracks, called "Sanku," they stood in parade formation until directed to bow to the emperor. Any hesitation resulted in a beating, so the prisoners complied, adding a fart and a muttered "fuck you" when possible. During what passed for breakfast, their cells were searched by the guards, and any excuse was enough for a beating; contraband, misfolded blankets, or just a guard's bad mood would result in slapping, punching, or beating with a bat. Prisoners were forced to clean the barracks with a knotted length of rope, all the while being harassed, until "physical training" just before noon. This could be laps around the compound, variations of physical torture, or nothing at all. For several hours in the afternoon, they might be let alone, and during this time the prisoners chatted, helped each other as needed, and generally dreamed of home.

Bill, like all new prisoners, was kept in "Ikku," the isolation barracks, up against the western perimeter fence. The fence itself was ridiculous—only six feet tall, so most of the prisoners could see over it into the surrounding rice fields. The horizontal braces were on the inside, which would make climbing over the fence a snap. But where would one go? Honshu was the largest and most populous of Japan's islands, and there was no chance of disappearing among the locals. Even if he could, the closest land was Korea, at least two hundred miles across the Tsushima Strait. But Bill Harris would never give up. He alternately considered stealing a boat from Yokohama, or a plane if he could find a pilot to escape with him. Living off the land didn't bother Harris a bit after Bataan, but he still had to get out of Japan. There was always a way—he just had to think of it, and until then he would survive.

After moving to Sanku, Bill was able to mix with the other prisoners, and this was a tremendous relief. Commander Arthur Lawrence Maher was the ranking American officer and was, like Bill, a Naval Academy graduate. From the class of 1923, the navy commander was calm, with large, thoughtful eyes and a quiet confidence Harris found reassuring. Maher was the surviving senior officer from the USS *Houston*, a heavy cruiser sunk during March 1942 in the Sunda Strait. Raised in a coal-mining town in Pennsylvania, at age forty-two, Maher was older than the other prisoners, but a very tough, capable man. The second-ranking officer was Lieutenant Commander John Allison Fitzgerald, a feisty, hard-faced little Irishman from Modesto, California, who'd left his mark at the academy as a boxer. Dark-eyed and intense, Fitzgerald had commanded the USS *Grenadier*, a very successful *Tambor*-class submarine sunk by Japanese aircraft in the Malacca Strait on April 22, 1943.

Both men laid out the camp for Bill, and it wasn't good.

Called Ofuna, it was a former elementary school that reopened as a detention center on April 8, 1942. This was an unusual facility because all prisoners of war nominally came under army control, and the Imperial Navy could only temporarily detain enemy personnel until their transfer to an appropriate facility. Bill had been fortunate in that he'd remained in navy hands since Pangeo, and even at Ambon the army guards left him alone. Rivalries between the two services rarely allowed shared intelligence, so whenever the navy captured a high-value prisoner, they would "temporarily detain" the man to extract whatever useful information possible. This applied particularly to captured Allied naval personnel, including American Marines, along with pilots and especially submariners. Ofuna, under the auspices of the 3rd Department (Intelligence) of the Naval General Staff, existed to obtain valuable intelligence without sharing it with the Imperial Army.

The center was physically run by the Yokosuka Naval Defense Corps. The guards were all navy enlisted men, while the interrogators, collectively called the Quiz Kids, were 5th Section (North and South America) intelligence officers who commuted to the camp from Tokyo several times weekly. These men had all lived in the United States, spoke English perfectly, and understood how Westerners, particularly Americans, thought. Along with Sanematsu, the other frequent interrogator was Kunichi Sasaki, nicknamed Handsome Harry because of his preference for "snazzy suits and saddle Oxfords."

Ofuna was not a regular POW camp; therefore, no notifications had ever been sent to the Red Cross or U.S. authorities, and no one on the outside knew they were here. This was done purposely, so information could be extracted without consequences, and the prisoners here were completely at the mercy of the guards. They were considered not prisoners of war by the Japanese but "unarmed enemies," and most were officers, though there were a few enlisted aircrew and submariners. This latter group was particularly hated by the Japanese since the Home Islands depended on merchant shipping for raw materials, food, and vital resources. The largely American campaign to destroy Japan's transport capacity had resulted in the destruction of hundreds of irreplaceable merchantmen, and submarines were effectively strangling the empire.*

Bill learned the big guard who beat him the first day was the worst in camp; Kangocho (Hospital Sergeant) Sueharu Kitamura, invariably nicknamed the Quack due to his official duties. A sadist, he enjoyed causing pain and took a clinical interest in suffering and mutilation. Though Captain Sanematsu was the overall commander, day-to-day operations were supervised by the *taichō*, Warrant Officer Kakuzo Iida, called the Mummy because of his wizened, drawn appearance and bad teeth. Not good enough for combat, "Crummy," "Metal Mouth," "Swivel Neck," and most of the other guards were the dregs of the

---

* According to the Naval History and Heritage Command, U.S. submarines alone accounted for 1,113 Japanese merchantmen and over 4.7 million tons of lost materiel.

Imperial Navy. Embarrassed by their position as jailers while Japan was fighting for its life, they vented their anger, shame, and frustration through torturing their helpless prisoners.

One signature method was known as the Crouch, which was "standing on the ball of your foot, knees half bent and arms extended over the head," as John Fitzgerald described. Beatings were also normal, and Kitamura favored a club, much like a baseball bat, just as the Jap sergeant had used with Bill on Corregidor. There were variations of water torture, exhaustive calisthenics, and burning with cigarettes or candles, which was widely practiced. The "knee spread" involved kneeling with hands bound behind the back with a pole inserted between the knees and a man's bent legs. Guards would the jump on the man's back and the resulting pressure around the pole separated the knee joints. Flogging, slapping, and punching were so commonplace that many prisoners didn't consider them torture given the brutality of the other treatments.

"From now on," one Japanese officer stated, "you have no property. You gave up everything when you surrendered. You do not even own the air that is in your bodies. From now on, you will work for the building of Greater Asia. You are the slaves of the Japanese."

Bill fell into the routine, initially attempting to keep a low profile, though his height made this difficult. Finding that superficial politeness forestalled some beatings, he would bow and greet the guards with a measured "*Ohio, Heitai-san*," (Good morning, Mister Guard) and always received a "*Ohio, Horio-san*" (Good morning, Mister Prisoner) in reply. He also always managed to pass gas when forced to bow to the emperor. Possessed of a photographic memory, Bill kept his mind sharp by recalling favorite books and essentially putting himself back through Naval Academy academics. Lieutenant Frank Tinker, a Juilliard graduate turned army pilot, often found Bill "reading" a textbook in his empty hands, recalling every word he'd seen six years earlier. Keeping one's spirits up and mind occupied were full-time occupations in Ofuna, and since many of the prisoners were officers, they could teach each other their college-degree fields and languages and debate various subjects. Having acquired Latin and French during his school days, Harris had a natural gift for languages, and also picked up Spanish and Tagalog in the Philippines. Here, with little else to do, he set about learning Norwegian, and also Japanese with Art Maher's assistance. This led him to begin a project that, if discovered, likely meant death—or at least a near-death beating.

Starting as a log, or journal, he collected every scrap of paper available in the camp, including trash and packing fragments. Newspapers, discarded by the guards, were highly prized.

Tying these together with bits of dirty string into a letter-sized rectangle, Bill cut down the flaps of an old cardboard box for the covers, and the Canadian Red Cross label, with its fading maple leaf stamp, was still quite legible. Onto these pages he inscribed Norwegian recipes for "pickled pig's ears," "fried squash," and dozens of others. He also wrote Spanish phrases, numbers, months, and common expressions in several languages. Hoarded newsprint was used for Japanese grammar practice, and he constantly added useful phrases to his dictionary. Bill also carefully recorded dozens of names and addresses from his fellow prisoners: Brits, New Zealanders, Irish, Canadians, as well as Americans from New York to Oregon. These included Frank Tinker from Cedar Street in Lapeer, Michigan, and Louis Zamperini of Torrance, California.

Through the winter of 1943 and into 1944, Bill Harris kept the faith and survived—that is, as much as 300–500 calories per day from barley and soybean-paste soup would allow.* Meat—it became an obsession, and the others felt the same. Men are starving when they talk food instead of women, but that was the case here now. Recounting past feasts, arguing about the best way to fricassee a chicken or

---

* At this time, civilians in America were consuming 3,360 calories each day and averaging 146 pounds of meat per year.

roast a leg of lamb replaced sports and girls. Except *the* girl, the one he seemed to dream of when things got really bad. Bill had recalled her face, or at least thought he had—she was Jim Glennon's little sister, Jeanne. This was curious, as he'd never said more than a dozen words to her, and couldn't understand why he thought of her now. But he did, and right now it was enough to have someone to think of. She'd been a pretty kid when last he saw her, and Bill wondered how she looked now as a woman.

However, food still occupied most of his thoughts, and Bill figured the last meat he'd eaten was in Pangeo, just before he was ambushed; like everyone else in Ofuna, the constant gnawing in his gut never went away. Dropping weight fast, by Christmas Day 1943, he was already down fifty pounds. At least here they were spared heavy labor, and aside from interpreting, Harris had no other significant duties—other than formulating escape plans and avoiding beatings, though by this time they were a normal part of the day and generally correlated to Japan's combat defeats.

Through the fall of 1943 Operation Cartwheel, the multipronged Allied campaign to eliminate the main Japanese South Pacific base at Rabaul, had made drastic strategic and tactical gains. West through the Central Pacific, Admiral Spruance's Fifth Fleet was charging toward the Marshalls, while another prong moved up the Solomons and took Bougainville, with Brigadier General Field Harris among those who came ashore at Empress Augusta Bay. From eastern New Guinea through Lae, the battle-hardened 1st Marine Division crossed the Dampier Strait on December 26, 1943, to land on the tip of New Britain at Cape Gloucester, and both pincers prepared to snap shut on Rabaul. Battered by carrier air strikes, it was determined that the base could now be bypassed, which isolated and cut off the Imperial Eighth Area Army. Some 1,200 miles northeast, the 2nd Marine Division conquered Makin and Tarawa, which would be used as a springboard into the Marianas, a location that, when taken, would put the Japanese Home Islands within range of the new B-29 bomber.

Languishing in Ofuna, Bill Harris and the others were generally unaware of the larger war beyond the stockade. Though he could now read scraps of Japanese newspapers, Bill distrusted them, since stories of glorious Japanese victories seemed too fantastic to be true. Radio, if he could have heard it, was even worse. "America has lost the war," Radio Tokyo announced. "Japanese forces have now complete air and sea superiority . . . all the Japanese have to do in future operations is to project their indomitable spirits at the enemy. The Occidental mind, of course, will not understand the great Oriental power."

Only through the arrival of new prisoners could any type of accurate information be acquired, and to Bill's delight, another Marine arrived on March 7, 1944. Major Greg Boyington was the commanding officer of VMF-214, the famous "Blacksheep," and with twenty-six kills to his credit, he was tied with Captain Joe Foss as America's leading Marine ace. Shot down off Rabaul on January 3, Boyington lost his clothes and floated naked for eight hours in the Saint Georges Channel until picked up by I-181, a Japanese submarine. Taken from Rabaul to Truk, Boyington, like Harris, was eventually flown to Yokohama. A decade older than most of his pilots, "Pappy" had been a Flying Tiger in China, a member of Guadalcanal's Cactus Air Force, and commander of two other line-fighter squadrons. Hard drinking and irreverent, he was beloved by his men and distrusted by most of his superior officers—but this was war, and Boyington killed the enemy.

Once released from Ikku, Pappy passed on that the Axis was reeling; Italy had been invaded, and with Mussolini arrested on July 24, King Vittorio Emanuele III assumed control. Rome was declared an open city on 14 August, and the Italians changed sides to declare war on Germany in October 1943. On the Eastern Front, the great battle for Kursk had finally blunted Germany's offensive capability, and ten armies deployed from the Baltic to the Black Sea were now falling back west toward the Polish and Lithuanian borders. West of Germany, some three hundred thousand men were dug in along the Atlantic Wall: 1,700 miles of beach obstacles, concrete fortresses, and six million mines. Less than seventy-five miles from Cherbourg across the English Channel, hundreds of thousands of Allied soldiers waited in hundreds of camps for the invasion of France to commence. Collectively, the Allies took a deep breath with the realization that they could not now be defeated by the Axis. However, not suffering defeat was a long way from unconditional surrender, and most fighting men knew the worst was yet to come.

Pappy also outlined the Cartwheel plan, noting that both Rabaul and Truk were to be bypassed. It made sense to Bill, because without seaborne resupply, those great bases would simply wither and weaken. The Marine in him was proud of the improvements in amphibious tactics, and he was particularly keen on the new equipment. Boyington related the reorganization of the Corps following the hard combat lessons learned during the Solomon campaign that included M1 rifles and carbines, twelve-man squads, and a much beefier weapons platoon with new 60mm mortars. His description of the new *Essex*-class carriers, *Iowa*-class battleships, planes, and submarines gave everyone heart. Contrary to Japanese propaganda, the United States was in no way finished. In fact, the Japanese were getting their lights punched out by an angry, vengeful American juggernaut inexorably tightening its stranglehold on the empire.

Boyington described, firsthand, what Operation Hailstone had done to Rabaul; while imprisoned there, he had a ringside seat, courtesy of the Imperial Navy's 81st Guards. Escorted by seven battleships, nine American carriers attacked the base with five hundred aircraft, and sunk at least eleven warships while destroying 275 Japanese aircraft. Most damaging was the loss of the twenty-six oilers, freighters, and scarce cargo ships that now rested on the bottom of Simpson Harbor. Rabaul was a shell, and Truk, the empire's Pearl Harbor, was soon to follow. The dates, Harris noted, roughly corresponded to increased beatings from the guards and further slashes in the prisoners' meager rations.

Summer 1944 proved favorably decisive for the Allies, disastrous for the Axis, and increasingly dangerous for Bill Harris and all prisoners held captive in Japan. By May, the U.S. 8th Air Force raided Berlin with over 1,500 heavy bombers, and the German 17th Army surrendered in the Crimea. June saw the first B-29 combat deployment from India to Bangkok in preparation for raiding Japan. On June 6, 1944, 6,900 ships from eight navies supported 150,000 Allied troops storming ashore in Normandy; Overlord, the invasion of Hitler's Fortress Europa, had begun. A week later, the first V-1 rockets were launched from France at targets around London, while on the other side of the world that same day, Vice Admiral Ray Spruance's Task Force 58 commenced Forager, the conquest of Palau and the Marianas.

Fifteen American carriers, including seven big fleet carriers containing nine hundred aircraft, stalked into the Philippine Sea and engaged the newly reorganized 1st Mobile Fleet. Adhering to their cherished doctrine of the "single decisive battle," the Japanese hoped that inflicting enough casualties would force Washington to consider peace. Having spent a year training replacement pilots, the Imperial Navy believed they could win such a fight, but in what became known as the Great Marianas Turkey Shoot, the aerial battle over the Philippine Sea cost the Japanese 90 percent, some 445, of their remaining naval aviators, in less than two days. Combined with the loss of three fleet carriers, the Imperial Navy's offensive striking power was eliminated.*

Following this defeat, and the loss of the Mariana Islands, including Saipan, Imperial leadership knew the Home Islands were now vulnerable to aerial attack and eventually an invasion. Prime Minister Hideki Tojo resigned the next month, and Tokyo's inflated wartime propaganda effectively ceased as the prospect of invasion loomed large. Admiral Paul Wenneker, longtime German naval attaché in Tokyo, later wrote: "Saipan was really understood to be a matter of life and death. About that time, they began telling the people the truth

---

* American losses were 130 aircraft and 76 aviators, with several ships damaged. The Japanese lost the fleet carriers *Hiyo*, *Shokaku*, and the newly commissioned *Taiho*.

about the war. They began preparing them for whatever must happen. Before that they had been doing nothing but fooling the people."

The Japanese people were shocked, and it was now glaringly obvious why their sons and husbands and fathers had never come home. Once the truth was revealed, the mood of the guards at Ofuna shifted perceptibly. With America closing in on their homeland, they lashed out at the only enemy they could hurt—the prisoners. According to Louis Zamperini, later the subject of the bestselling book *Unbroken*, one day Kitamura discovered Bill's cache of sketches, maps, and part of his dictionary. After punching and kicking him, the Quack grabbed a thick wooden crutch and pummeled the Marine until he sagged to the ground. Retreating deep within himself, Bill focused on memories: the enormous tree his family had driven through at Yellowstone when he was ten, the bright garden of his childhood home in Manila, standing with his father on Pikes Peak, and the girl who haunted him . . . the girl from his dream . . . Jeanne. He felt the blows in a detached, distant state, and as waves of nausea bubbled up from his gut, Bill sank into a gray abyss of dull pain and dim light. Beating Harris unconscious while the prisoners watched helplessly, Kitamura finally stopped as rain began to fall. Dragging the limp body through the mud, the other guards propped Bill up in his cell and left.

Eyes open, but empty and devoid of expression, Bill didn't move for hours. Zamperini, who thought of Bill as "a giant" and greatly admired the Marine, stayed with him, dressed his wounds as best he could, and tried to feed him. Though battered and bleeding, the worst injury was to his head. Severely concussed, Harris was in a near vegetative state for days, unable to speak or feed himself, and he was badly confused. Zamperini later related "when he finally emerged from his cell, he wandered through camp, his face grotesquely disfigured, his eyes glassy. When his friends greeted him, he didn't know who they were."

The beating on Corregidor and now this one would have killed most men, and nearly did kill Bill Harris, but something inside him refused to quit. Maybe survival itself was an act of defiance—perhaps the last one he could make—and so he intended to go on doing it. By the time Bill recovered sufficiently, there had been changes in Ofuna. His friend Louis was gone, and so was Frank Tinker; they'd been taken to Omori, a regular POW camp run by the Imperial Army forty miles north of Ofuna. Also, the Marianas had been captured, and on October 12, 1944, the first B-29 landed on Saipan's Isley Field.*

The bomber was a game changer: a long-range, pressurized, heavily armed aircraft capable of surviving without escort because it could fly above most enemy fighters and anti-aircraft artillery fire. Delivering the specifications in 1939, the U.S. Army Air Corps accepted Boeing's proposal and delivered an initial production order in May 1941. With a wingspan of 141 feet, a max gross weight of seventy tons, and capable of dropping five thousand pounds of bombs from 30,000 feet against a target 1,600 miles away, the Superfortress was a flying behemoth. Eleven men flew in pressurized and heated comfort, protected by ten .50-caliber Browning machine guns and one 20mm cannon. However, it had been hurried into production and deployed to war too fast to correct literally thousands of defects and make necessary modifications, which left it more vulnerable to itself than to the enemy.

Nevertheless, General Hansell himself led the October 27 attack with fourteen B-29s of the 73rd Bomb Wing against Truk's Dublon submarine pens. On November 1, Captain Ralph Steakley's 3rd PRS (Photoreconnaissance Squadron) B-29 became the first American aircraft since Jimmy Doolittle's 1942 raid to penetrate Tokyo's airspace. Japanese Army Ki-44 fighters from the 47th Sentai couldn't gain enough altitude to engage, and Steakley took some seven thousand photos of the capital and surrounding suburbs, including suspected prisoner of war camps. The bombers flew four missions over the next few weeks against Truk and Iwo Jima while photo analysis and identification pinpointed targets in the Tokyo area.

---

* *Joltin Josie* was piloted by Brigadier General Haywood "Possum" Hansell, leading the 21st Bomber Command.

Late in the fall, another officer arrived at Ofuna who was able to shed more light on the war. Lieutenant Commander Dick O'Kane had served as executive officer under Dudley "Mush" Morton on the legendary submarine *Wahoo* (SS-238) before assuming command of his own boat in November 1943. A brilliant tactician, by the time O'Kane and his *Tang* (SS-306) stood out from Pearl Harbor on their fifth war patrol, he was credited with 72,052 tons of destroyed enemy shipping. At the end of O'Kane's most successful patrol, *Tang* was struck by its last faulty Mk 18 torpedo early in the morning of October 25, 1944, in the Formosa Strait. Sinking in seconds, thirteen of her eighty-seven-man crew managed to escape, with nine, including O'Kane, picked up by the Japanese Type C escort ship P-34, then taken to Formosa.

Though beaten by the ship's crew and Japanese survivors from *Tang's* last kill, O'Kane was surprised when one of the guards brought him an ice pop, stating quietly, "I am a Christian." The American commander was further shocked the following day when he was piped aboard a destroyer, side boys and all, headed for Japan. "The captain," he wrote after the war, "a lieutenant commander of my age, escorted me to his cabin," where O'Kane waited with warm clothes and a meal until the officer returned. Throughout the short trip to Japan, they discussed literature, specifically *Gone with the Wind*, and naval tactics. The enemy captain was perplexed that O'Kane knew no Japanese and stated, "How could we expect to understand each other's problems when you made no attempt to learn even a word of our language? Our nations might have found a solution to the problems and avoided this war."

From Kobe, *Tang's* survivors were taken by train to Yokohama, then by bus to Ofuna, where they were confined in Ikku like all new arrivals. Once released into the main camp, O'Kane and his two officers, Frank Flanigan and Larry Savadkin, were able to confirm the news about the Marianas and the recapture of Guam. He'd also heard of a huge airborne assault in Holland called Market Garden, which was supposed to pave the way into Germany over the Rhine. A few days before his capture, O'Kane received word that Allied soldiers had crossed the Meuse River and captured a German city named Aachen. It was all good news, but Bill was especially gratified to learn that Morotai was taken in September and that MacArthur, even now, was invading the Philippines. The tides of war, it seemed, had turned fully against the Japanese, and though now in mortal peril, Harris couldn't help but rejoice.

Even if he did not survive the war, neither would the empire.

✳

TEN

THE LONG ROAD HOME

JUST AFTER DAWN ON THANKSGIVING DAY, MAJOR ROBERT KNIGHT Morgan released his brakes and *Dauntless Dotty* (42–24592) rumbled down Saipan's runway, lifted off to the east, then climbed out north toward Japan to make history—again. Morgan, originally a B-17 pilot, departed the European theater in May 1943 with his *Memphis Belle* after completing twenty-five combat missions, and he now commanded the 869th Bomb Squadron.* Beside him was the thirty-eight-year-old commander of the 73rd Bombardment Wing, and though he'd been a major when the war began, Emmett "Rosie" O'Donnell of Brooklyn was now a brigadier general leading 111 B-29s in their first strike against Tokyo. Plagued by their temperamental Wright Duplex-Cyclone engines, only ninety-four of the big bombers made it to Japan that day. Encountering the jet stream for the first time, the bombardiers were unprepared for 200-mile-per-hour winds at altitude over the primary target, so only twenty-four planes dropped on the Nakajima Aircraft Factory in Tokyo's Mushashino suburb. The rest dropped their AN-M66 two-thousand-pound bombs on the Tokyo docks quite close to Omori.

---

* *Memphis Belle* was named for Margaret Polk, Morgan's sweetheart in 1943, and *Dauntless Dotty* for his third wife, Dorothy Johnson Morgan.

Twenty-five miles south, Bill Harris heard the sirens scream and loudspeakers blare out through the neighborhoods surrounding Ofuna. Anti-aircraft fire arced upward from all over Tokyo, and eventually a few contrails showed through the broken clouds as Japanese fighters tried to claw their way to the B-29s at 32,000 feet. Privately elated, Harris knew better than to show any emotion around the guards, who were plainly agitated by the event. Seven additional bombing missions hit Tokyo during late 1944, and the guards became increasingly brutal as waves of silver Superfortresses passed overhead. For Christmas 1944, his second in Ofuna, Bill noted the arrival of a few Red Cross packages, though they'd been picked clean of cigarettes and chocolate. Shivering in his tiny, unheated cell wrapped in a threadbare cotton blanket, the Marine wasn't wishing for peace on earth, or even a good Christmas meal; he wished for heat, since Tokyo was blanketed by a foot of snow and suffering from the coldest winter in nearly fifty years.

Back home, Americans were buying cardboard Bild-a-Sets or wooden toys for their children and chopping down trees to decorate with candles and popcorn. Christmas lights were still generally non-existent, and Bing Crosby's heart-wrenching "White Christmas" had given way to Judy Garland's "Have Yourself a Merry Little Christmas." Yet, for the first time since 1940, there truly was some good cheer and hope—until 0530 on December 16, when the 1st SS Panzer Army crashed into U.S. forces on the Elsenborn Ridge in the Ardennes to commence Operation Watch-on-the-Rhine, soon known to the Allies as the Battle of the Bulge.

Nor were the Japanese finished.

As the American noose closed in around the Home Islands, fortifications were completed in several crucial spots, including an ugly, eight-square-mile chunk of rock whose sole value lay in its location, just 650 miles south of Tokyo: Iwo Jima. Lieutenant General Tadamichi Kuribayashi, arguably one of Japan's finest generals, constructed a honeycomb defense-in-depth for his 109th Division that promised no easy victory, nor did he expect one. Like Yamamoto, the general had lived in America, studied at Harvard, and believed there was no way for Japan to win this war. "America's productive powers are beyond our imagination," he once confided to a subordinate. "Japan has started a war with a formidable enemy and we must brace ourselves accordingly." Yet he was a career officer from a samurai family and considered it a duty to cause the greatest number of casualties to his enemy as possible. It was, he believed, a preview for America should Japan be invaded, and in so doing might make Washington consider a negotiated peace. Seven hundred forty miles east, another extremely capable general, Mitsuru Ushijima, was preparing a similar defense on Okinawa, the southernmost of Japan's Home Islands.*

New Year's Day 1945 saw Bill transferred to Omori, where he was happily reunited with Art Maher. "Conditions were much better," he would report. "Food was quite good, considering the conditions in Japan." Officially Base Camp 1, Omori was the headquarters for all such facilities in the Tokyo area and was used as a receptacle for "problem" prisoners, which obviously included Bill Harris. Built on a man-made island seventy-five yards into Tokyo Bay, the compound comprised a rectangle measuring sixty by fifty yards surrounded by an eight-foot wooden palisade connected to shore by a ramshackle wooden bridge. Inside the gate, past a sentry box, was a long administration building backed by a smaller barracks for POW officers. The rectangle's main area had five substantial barracks inside its eastern fence, each measuring one hundred by twenty-five feet, with three more across the courtyard to the west. Large latrines, two per wall, stood between the barracks and palisade, while a large kitchen and bathhouse occupied the north wall. Unlike Ofuna, Omori was also a regular POW camp administered by the army that contained about five hundred Americans, Brits, Aussies, New Zealanders, and other Allied prisoners. This, Bill discovered, was a good thing, since the place was too large for the

---

* Both Japanese generals opposed war with the United States, and there is reason to suspect they were given their final field commands as a way to prevent any negotiation attempts.

"personal attention" so common at Ofuna, and the camp was regis-
tered with the Red Cross. Work was comparatively light, and usually
consisted of stacking debris from B-29 raids just across the bridge.

He also had another surprise reunion of a much different sort. A
few weeks after arriving, a truck stopped by the gate, and several prisoners were escorted into the camp. Walking with Maher and a few
others, Bill was beating his arms to keep warm when he saw the men
and abruptly stopped. He'd never forget that pinched, sly face with its
slit of a mouth and shifty, beady eyes. The man was bony and thin,
like everyone else, but his arrogance was palpable, as if he shouldn't
be here with the prisoners. Maher followed Bill's gaze, saw the man,
and snorted disgustedly.

"Provoo is his name," the commander said, "John David Provoo.
Got here a year ago from a camp on Formosa with another sergeant
named Newton Light. The second guy wanted nothing to do with Provoo, and told us all about him. Said he was known as the Traitor of
Corregidor."

"No shit. I was there . . . and that's exactly what the bastard is." It
was the same loathsome, kimono-wearing sergeant from the Rock.

Maher looked at him and nodded. After the surrender, Provoo had
offered his services to the Japanese and used his new position to make
life more miserable for his countrymen, especially officers, whose education and commissioned authority he bitterly resented. Shaving his
head, the sergeant had taken to wearing khakis with a white shirt and
sandals rather than his uniform, and carried a Japanese fan. To further curry favor, Provoo had approached Colonel Theodore Teague,
MacArthur's deputy signal officer, and advised him to reveal classified
U.S. codes to the Japanese. Teague, known as Tiger, snapped: "You
son of a bitch. I didn't ask your advice. The war is not yet over, and, if
I survive it, I will try my best to have you brought to justice for this."

Another officer, Captain Burton Thomson, had been placed in
charge of Malinta's food distribution after the surrender and repri-
manded Provoo several times. The sergeant puffed up and told the

captain, "I take orders from nobody; I am working for the Japanese."
To which Burton replied, "Go to hell." Infuriated, the sergeant used
his new status with a Lieutenant Yanase of the Kempeitai to have Captain Thomson executed. When Maher discovered all this, he'd told
Provoo off and spit in his face. The Japanese, also contemptuous of
the traitor but willing to use him for propaganda broadcasts, kept him
at another facility called Bunker Hill near the Imperial Palace, where
he conducted a radio program called *Circle of the Sun*. Provoo periodically returned to Omori for medical treatment and was carefully
watched for his own safety. Harris didn't see how he could kill the man,
but silently vowed to do so if an opportunity arose.

Meanwhile, life went on. Work details continued, as did minor
beatings, though the guards appeared increasingly nervous. Captured
B-29 crews became more frequent, and through these men the prisoners kept up to date on the war. In Europe, the Nazis were being inexorably crushed in a massive East-West vise between the Soviets, who had
taken most of Poland, and Patton's Third Army, which was charging
toward the Rhine. On February 16, an enormous raid composed of
hundreds of B-29s darkened the sky over Tokyo, protected, for the first
time, by a thousand carrier-based fighters. Bill and the others believed
this meant the Philippines had been reconquered, but, in fact, the
navy strike launched from the *seventeen* aircraft carriers of Task Force
58, just 125 miles southwest of Omori.

Down to 120 pounds now, Harris fought his own battles against
beriberi, dysentery, and starvation. Camphor shots didn't help, and rations had been cut again, though sometimes Japanese civilians left
small piles of roasted soybeans for the prisoners near the work sites.
Prisoners also learned how to catch and skin the mangy cats that
prowled everywhere, much to the disgust of the Japanese. Three days
after the big Tokyo raid, though Bill didn't know it, the 4th Marines
stormed ashore on Iwo Jima. "I don't know who he is," Marine general
Holland "Howlin' Mad" Smith exclaimed, "but the Japanese General

running this show is one smart bastard." True to his word, Kuribayashi fought intelligently and ferociously, bitterly contesting every foot of ground, though the outcome was inevitable. Mount Suribachi fell on February 23, and by the end of March virtually the entire 22,000-man Japanese garrison had been annihilated. Allied casualties surpassed 24,000, with 6,140 dead—more than twice those killed in Normandy on D-Day. Yet even before the island was secure, B-29s began making emergency landings. Heavily damaged, *Dinah Might* limped in on March 4 low on fuel and landed under fire on the South Field.* For the next five months, 2,251 bombers would land safely there rather than ditch at sea, a living testimony to the sacrifices made on Iwo Jima.

Unfortunately, Bill never got the chance to break the traitor's neck—in fact, he never saw the coward again. On March 1, Harris and a few others were moved thirteen miles north to a railroad yard nestled in a bend of Tokyo's Sumida River. Sumidagawa, also known as Tokyo-10B, held half as many prisoners as Omori, and most were British. The senior American was U.S. Navy Lieutenant James Willoughby Condit, whom Bill had known at Ofuna. A torpedo pilot from Illinois, he'd been a POW since mid-1942 and was a friend of Greg Boyington. Altogether, there were six American officers in camp, including an army captain and two lieutenants also from Ofuna, while the senior Allied officer was Major Edward J. Curran of the British Royal Army Medical Corps.

Though there was still never enough food, it was better here than any other camp Bill had experienced, and they were able to obtain occasional black-market pork or shark from the Japanese civilians encountered during outside work details, though there were no cats. Work was comparatively light, with the ten officers, British and American, supervising prisoner work parties used by the Nippon Transport Company to service railcars at the Sumidagawa hub. Over half the

---

* B-29 42–65286.

prisoners were Dutch captured at Java or Canadian survivors of the Hong Kong garrison; neither group had officers of their own.*

Just after midnight, nine days after Bill's arrival at Sumidagawa, the first of 279 Superfortresses roared over Tokyo and "almost instantly it seemed as if the entire city burst into flames."† In a major doctrinal shift, the B-29s were at low (for bombers) altitudes of 4,900 to 9,200 feet dropping incendiaries and napalm, versus high explosives, on a city largely made of wood. Postflight analysis during the past four months showed less than 10 percent bombing accuracy from releases above 30,000 feet, so the decision was made to go in low for greater concentration. This seemed a logical gamble since the Japanese possessed no credible night air defense and very limited radar, and a majority of structures were vulnerable to fire. Fifty percent of Japan's remaining small industry was located in residential districts, and this, plus the skilled workforce that made up these companies, made the densely populated areas of Tokyo a legitimate target.

Each bomber could carry forty cluster bombs filled with 1,520 M-69 napalm bomblets or M-47 incendiaries, which were just thin canisters filled with jelled gasoline and white phosphorus. The results were catastrophic, and 16.8 square miles of Tokyo were decimated during the first such raid. Pathfinder B-29s laid out an immense burning X over the Chūō and Koto Wards, and subsequent waves simply bombed the spot. Harris, at ground zero on the Sumida River, felt they were aiming directly for him. Searing heat created massive updrafts that sent flames thousands of feet into the air and created a "complete circle of fire" around Sumidagawa. Bill considered escaping in the confusion, but there was literally no place to go unless he could get into the river, which was also burning with residual napalm. Over the next ten days 1,595 B-29 sorties were flown against large Japanese cities, resulting in the destruction of 50 percent of residentially

---

* The Canadians came from the Winnipeg Grenadiers and Royal Rifles.
† 73rd, 313th, and 314th Bombardment Groups.

located industries, 470,000 barrels of crucial oil, 83 percent of refineries, and 75 percent of aircraft engine plants. Bombing accuracy at low altitude, now during daylight as well, put 40 percent of all bombs within one thousand feet of their intended impact point.

War had unmistakably come to the Home Islands, and American wrath was now as clear to the people as it had been to their military for the past three years. Eight million city dwellers left for the countryside, and by the late summer of 1945, nearly 70 percent of the civilian population did not believe victory was possible. They could not, with American bombers and fighters flying uncontested over their country, so disaffection spread rapidly as full realization of their situation hit home. Bill Harris was both elated with the awesome destructive power of his own military and wary of Japan's reaction to an inevitable defeat. Most ordinary Japanese he observed alternated between shocked politeness or fear, and he hoped they might rise up and end the war. It was, he knew, a pipe dream, though the firebombing did bring the war shockingly home to the emperor. Even those who did not believe Hirohito was a god yielded to the ingrained culture of veneration, and whatever he ordered would have to be obeyed, whether this meant fighting to the death, surrender, or carrying out orders to kill all Allied prisoners. No one knew, but men like Bill Harris were certain that every Japanese defeat brought each prisoner that much closer to death.

Losing Okinawa did not help.

The 466-square-mile island was part of the Ryukyu chain, just 350 miles south of Kyushu, the proposed landing site for the invasion of Japan. At dawn on April 1, 1945, 150,000 men from the hybrid U.S. Tenth Army were committed to battle under the protection of the Fifth Fleet.* Lieutenant General Mitsuru Ushijima, like Kuribayashi on Iwo Jima, did not oppose the landings since there was no way to keep the Americans from coming ashore. His clever defensive strategies and

---

* The Tenth included the 1st, 2nd, and 6th Marine Divisions plus the Army 7th, 27th, 77th, and 96th Infantry Divisions.

refusal to permit wasteful banzai charges resulted in the bloodiest single battle of the Pacific War. By July 2, when Okinawa was declared secure, 12,520 Americans were dead, and at least 49,000 were wounded.* The navy was especially hard hit by kamikaze attacks, suffering five thousand casualties, 386 ships damaged, and thirty-six ships sunk, including twelve destroyers. Nearly eighty thousand Japanese soldiers, including Ushijima, were dead, along with some thirty thousand conscripts, many of whom were Okinawan children pressed into service. Fourteen hundred aircraft were lost, and sixteen ships sunk, including the super battleship *Yamato*, which was detected by American submarines in the Bungo Strait and sent to the bottom on April 7 by carrier aircraft.

The combination of firebombing Japanese cities and the loss of Okinawa brought down the prime minster, Kuniaki Koiso, who had succeeded Tojo following the loss of Saipan. Replaced by seventy-seven-year-old Admiral Kantaro Suzuki, the fate of Japan, and the prisoners, was now precarious as the Allies closed in. B-29 raids continued through April, with P-51 fighters regularly strafing targets around the city and bombers dropping mines in Tokyo Bay. Then news filtered through the POW grapevine that Franklin Roosevelt was dead; on April 12, at his cottage in Warm Springs, Georgia, the president suffered a massive cerebral hemorrhage and died.

He'd been in office for twelve years, nearly half of Bill's life, and was the only president he really remembered. Harris had never heard of the vice president, someone called Truman, and he wondered what affect his accession would have on the war. May was another big month for raids on Japan, which seemed preparatory to an invasion, so Bill continuously updated his escape options and waited for opportunities. Word again reached them that Hitler shot himself on April 30, as the Soviet 8th Guards Army prepared to assault Berlin. German

---

* Twenty-four Medals of Honor were earned during the three-month, six-day battle.

units began surrendering, and May 8, 1945, was declared Victory in Europe Day.

America now turned its entire might against the empire, and this was not lost on the Japanese. Bill noted the food was worse and there was much less of it, yet to keep up his strength he ate the moldy bread and occasional rotten vegetables. Curiously, some of the guards had become a bit easier on the prisoners, at least in Sumidagawa, perhaps recognizing that the end was near. Red Cross packages appeared, and one guard even passed out Skoki cigarettes. The locals were still unpredictable; one day he'd catch baleful, hate-filled stares, and another nothing but polite kindness.

Harris wasn't fooled. He completely believed the rumor that a "Kill All" order was in effect to eliminate all prisoners of war when the Americans invaded mainland Japan. As this looked increasingly likely, Bill once again thought of escape, and this led him to wonder again what had happened to his first escape buddy, Ed Whitcomb. Had he remained in the Philippines, or was he dead? Harris would've been inspired to know that at that moment, three days after Germany's surrender, Ed was in a B-25 attacking a Japanese base near Chiayi, Formosa—less than 1,300 miles from Sumidagawa.

Running through his own escape possibilities, Bill still didn't have great choices. Getting into a sewer system seemed a good way to disappear, but he couldn't find one, since most sewage was deposited directly into the rivers, and from there into Tokyo Bay. Floating down the Sumida to the bay was another possibility, but this entailed passing through twelve miles of heavily populated areas, and the chances of discovery were excellent. A disused canal ran across the camp's north edge and emptied into the larger Arakawa River, barely two hundred yards east, and this was a more direct, seven-mile route to the bay. However, he figured the best plan was to stow away on a southbound railcar until clear of the city, then hide himself in the hills until the invasion. Estimating his weight at 120 pounds, Bill believed this was the quickest way out of Tokyo, and one that would preserve his waning strength. The thought of watching American Marines charge ashore was a happy one, and he played it over and over in his head, never doubting they would come.

But they did not; there was, thankfully, no need.

At 0245 on Monday, August 6, 1945, a B-29 call-signed Dimples 82, lifted off from Tinian's North Field. Four minutes later, two other Superfortresses were airborne and joined up with the leader as it made a wide, slow turn northwest, then headed for Japan. Aside from a very few who knew the mission, no one else gave it much thought, including the Japanese, who believed the planes to be just another reconnaissance flight. Thirty-two-year-old Colonel Paul Tibbets, commander of the 509th Composite Group, was carrying a single ten-foot-long, 150-kiloton atomic bomb called Little Boy in the belly of his bomber, which he'd named *Enola Gay* after his mother. *Great Artiste*, flown by Major Charles W. Sweeney, was carrying an instrumentation package to record data, while the third B-29, known only as Plane 91, carried photographers.* Released over Hiroshima, Little Boy detonated at 1,968 feet and in seconds largely obliterated the city.

A Sumidagawa guard who had always been decent to the prisoners had family in Hiroshima and could not speak with them, so he asked Bill if one bomb could destroy a city. Harris didn't think so—if such a weapon existed, he didn't know of it, and thought the whole incident was a misinterpretation of a B-29 raid. However, on Tuesday, August 7, while supervising a work detail at the rail depot, Bill spoke with a civilian railroad engineer who told him that Hiroshima was gone—leveled, and the people burned to cinders. No one in Japan immediately understood the weapon, nor grasped the consequences, and though quite aware of the possibility of atomic weapons, Imperial General Staff Headquarters refused to believe the Americans had developed this before their own scientists. Nonetheless, Japan's preem-

---

* Plane 91 would later be appropriately named *Necessary Evil*.

inent physicist Yoshio Nishina was directed to Hiroshima on August 7, where he was able to verify that the Americans had not only developed a workable atomic bomb in complete secrecy, but got it across the world and dropped it on Japan. This was verified by a public statement from President Harry Truman:

> Sixteen hours ago, an American airplane dropped one bomb on Hiroshima, an important Japanese Army base. The Japanese began the war from the air at Pearl Harbor. They have been repaid many fold. And the end is not yet. It is an atomic bomb . . . the force from which the sun draws its power has been loosed against those who brought war to the Far East. We are now prepared to obliterate more rapidly and completely every productive enterprise the Japanese have above ground in any city. We shall destroy their docks, their factories, and their communications. Let there be no mistake; we shall completely destroy Japan's power to make war.
>
> It was to spare the Japanese people from utter destruction that the ultimatum of July 26 was issued at Potsdam. Their leaders promptly rejected that ultimatum. If they do not now accept our terms they may expect a rain of ruin from the air, the like of which has never been seen on this earth.

Many Americans, mainly those safely away from the fighting, hoped the Japanese would hold out and give an excuse for more such bombs to be dropped. "Let the dirty rats squeal," a congressman stated. "Let the Japs know unqualifiedly what unconditional surrender means." Bloody stories filtering back from Iwo Jima and Okinawa hardened a public that had lost fathers, brothers, and sons to the empire. Even President Truman, who would always maintain he held no doubts or regrets about the decision, wrote, "When you deal with a beast you have to treat him as a beast."

Staggered, Japanese military leaders dithered; it was an American gamble, they decided, to pressure a surrender rather than invade. Surely there could not be another such bomb.

They were wrong.

Bockscar, flown by Major Sweeny with Captain Fred Bock, departed Tinian with *Great Artiste* on August 9 and dropped a second bomb on the port of Nagasaki, which vanished beneath another supersonic shock wave of searing fire, and a dark, boiling six-mile-high cloud. As the Japanese digested this, word also reached Tokyo that 1,577,725 Soviet soldiers had crashed across Manchuria's borders and were set to crush Japan's Kwantung Army in three massive pincers.

It was enough.

What most terrified the Japanese was being conquered by the Russians. The Americans, though determined, ruthless, and uncompromising, were not brutes, and though Tokyo expected retribution from the United States, whatever the Americans had in mind was preferable in all respects to the Soviet Union. Indeed, keeping the Soviets under control was another quite plausible explanation for using the atomic bomb, which only the United States possessed in 1945, and was an unmistakable warning against Russian opportunism. Incredibly, there were those Japanese leaders who still believed they could impose conditions on the Americans, including no occupation of the Home Islands, and the emperor himself had to finally be consulted to break the impasse. Historian Ian Toll eloquently phrased Hirohito's epiphany that "a mortifying loss of face must be endured for the sake of national survival," which led the emperor to accept the Potsdam Declaration, ending the war and halting any Soviet pretexts for further aggression. The Japanese asked for only one condition: that the emperor and his family remain rulers of Japan.

Sweating it out in Sumidagawa, Bill Harris knew none of this. His perspective was truly from ground zero, and it wasn't promising. The same friendly guard warned the American about a "Kill All" order that each camp commander had received:

Whether they are destroyed individually or in groups, or however it is done . . . dispose of them as the situation dictates. In any case it is the aim not to allow the escape of a single one, to annihilate them all, and not to leave any traces.

This would take effect in a week, and the prisoners discussed the problem at length. Some were for fleeing now and taking their chances, while others insisted on waiting. Harris and the other American officers took a middle path; they would wait, for the time being, to see how the game played out, but rather than be murdered like sheep, each man vowed to go down fighting if escape became impossible. For a few unsettling days, neither the Japanese guards nor the Allied prisoners knew how to act or what to expect; for their part, those at Sumidagawa went through the motions with work details, eating, and sleeping—but the mood was tense.

On August 15, exactly at 1200 (Tokyo Standard Time) the "Kimigayo," Japan's national anthem, began to play from loudspeakers all over Tokyo. Bill was well accustomed to it, but during the past few days, it seemed less powerful, less frightening, than before. Perhaps the winds of fate were finally blowing his way—or perhaps the new wonder weapon had created those winds. Either way, he had a sense that his life, as he'd known it in Japan, was about to change. "May your reign continue for a thousand, eight thousand years . . ." As the anthem played out, Harris chuckled quietly. Such a reign seemed highly unlikely under the circumstances, but immediately after the music stopped, something occurred that, in the last 2,400 years of Japanese history, had never happened: the emperor directly addressed his people. Speaking *kobun*, a classical, literary form of Japanese unfamiliar to many commoners, Hirohito's prerecorded, "jeweled" voice was broadcast over every available public address system and radio station. All over Japan, people clustered, awestruck, to hear their god speak, and Bill, listening to the rail-yard PA system, translated for the other prisoners.

"We have ordered our government to communicate to the governments of the United States, Great Britain, China and the Soviet Union that our empire accepts the provisions of their joint declaration." The emperor's high-pitched voice was scratchy but clear. "We declared war on America and Britain out of our sincere desire to ensure Japan's self-preservation and the stabilization of East Asia . . . the war situation has developed not necessarily to Japan's advantage, while the general trends of the world have all turned against her interest." That, Bill knew, was an understatement. Clearly, America was closing in, and he grinned savagely as Hirohito continued. "Moreover, the enemy has begun to employ a new and most cruel bomb, the power of which to do damage is, indeed, incalculable, taking the toll of many innocent lives. Should we continue to fight, not only would it result in an ultimate collapse and obliteration of the Japanese nation." Another understatement. Apparently, the new wonder bomb had shocked them to their core. Saburo Sakai, a leading naval ace, recalled, "We were rooted to the floor, unbelieving. We had known that the end would come, but we had not anticipated this." But Sakai grasped the efficacy of the new weapon and later remarked, "Had I been ordered to bomb Seattle or Los Angeles in order to end the war, I wouldn't have hesitated. So, I perfectly understand why the Americans bombed Nagasaki and Hiroshima."

Afterward, those Japanese Bill could observe seemed confused until a live voice came over and carefully explained that the emperor had, indeed, just surrendered. The guards were shocked. "*Senso a wari,*" they muttered in disbelief. "*Senso a wari.*" The war is over. Railway men got off the train and simply walked away into the crowd. *This is my chance!* Harris looked around and wondered if he could make it to the river—but it was broad daylight, and he had no idea what the reaction might be to Hirohito's speech. At Sumidagawa, as in other camps, some of the guards just left, and those that remained were unpredictable. Waving swords and drunk on sake, one group at Omori tried to break into a barracks but were stopped by a Japanese officer.

Others weren't so fortunate. A captured American flier was tied to a truck and then dragged through the streets until dead.

"Those two weeks were the longest in my life," Bill Harris later confided in a letter. The weather was generally bad, and the uncertainty of his situation unnerving. Would there be an invasion after all? Would the guards abandon the camps and let the civilians kill the prisoners? On a brighter note, storage areas in many camps were raided by ravenous prisoners, and often huge caches of Red Cross packages were found. In some places, prisoners' uniforms had been stored, and these were quickly reclaimed, though nothing fit. All over Japan, ex-prisoners used anything possible to paint "P.W." in huge letters on any rooftop they could use. If there was no paint, then toothpaste, talcum powder, or even bird droppings were smeared in plain sight of the P-51 fighters that continuously buzzed overhead. Relief drops began on August 27, from B-29s now filled with fifty-five-gallon drums containing clothes, candy bars, and coffee.

That same day also saw the arrival of the U.S. Third Fleet's Task Force 31 off Tokyo Bay. Through prior arrangement, a battered, dirty Japanese destroyer with her guns depressed and breeches open timidly approached the Allied warships just after dawn. Aside from escort duties, *Hatsuzakura* carried two Imperial Navy captains, Otani and Takasaki, with an English-speaking ensign, who were all brought aboard the USS *Nicholas*. Taken below, their sidearms were removed, and they were given a bath and a medical exam before transfer to the *Missouri*. When Captain Otani requested his pistol, a nearby American admiral remembered, "I made it quite plain to him that we were prescribing his uniform from now on, and it must be remembered that these are the same Japanese whose treachery, cruelty, and subtlety brought about this war; we must be continually vigilant for overt treachery, and equally vigilant that we not become blinded by outward subservience and docility. They are always dangerous . . ."

The Americans were taking no chances.

Too many had died by taking the Japanese at face value, so when

the vast armada of ten battleships, fifteen cruisers, fifty-seven destroyers, and twelve submarines steamed slowly to Sagami Wan, just outside Tokyo Bay, it was at general quarters and ready for anything.*
Fast Carrier Task Force 38 remained offshore, wary of a trap and ready
to pounce if Japan so much as blinked.† At 0900 on Tuesday, August
29, 1945, the light cruiser *San Diego* entered Tokyo Bay; from Guadalcanal to Okinawa, she'd been in the thick of the fighting, and her
eighteen battle stars proudly symbolized American tenacity. Sliding
silently along behind was *Missouri*, battle-gray and ominous, with
an enormous American flag streaming from her masthead. Wartime
paint had been holystoned from her decks, and the warm glow of teak
was reflected in her newly polished brass. Followed by HMS *Duke of
York*, the rest of the mixed Allied fleet entered Tokyo Bay and eventually dropped anchor. Their first objectives were to occupy Yokosuka
Naval Base and Atsugi Airfield, then demilitarize all Japanese units.

Once the army was ready, as ordered by MacArthur, Operation
Swift Mercy was to be initiated to locate and free all former prisoners
of war. But the first night at anchor in Sagami Wan, a picket boat recovered two Brits who'd swum out to meet the fleet, so the navy acted
immediately. "Those are our boys!" Admiral Halsey bluntly stated. "Go
get them!" Commodore Rodger Whitten Simpson, a fighting sailor
who'd commanded destroyers and the light cruiser *Atlanta*, now had
the task of locating and rescuing all Allied personnel in the Tokyo area.
Accompanied by Commander Harold Stassen, Admiral Halsey's flag
secretary, they approached the shore near Omori and "the appearance of the landing craft in the channel off the prisoner of war camp
caused an indescribable scene of jubilation and emotion on the part
of hundreds of prisoners of war who streamed out of the camp and
climbed up over the piling. Some began to swim out to meet the landing craft."

---

* The USS *West Virginia* and USS *Detroit* were veterans of Pearl Harbor.
† USS *Lexington, Hancock, Bennington, Belleau Wood,* and *San Jacinto.*

COME AFTER US! and COOEE AUSSIE were painted on nearby buildings and waterfront pilings. All through the city, aided by spotting aircraft, teams fanned out to release and safeguard those who'd survived hell on earth at the hands of the Japanese military. When Simpson and Stassen, both unarmed and unafraid, stepped into Omori, the only remaining Japanese officer demanded their credentials. Simpson merely turned, looked over his shoulder at the harbor full of warships, then stared back at the nervous officer. The soldier stammered and stated, "I have no authority to release these men."

"You have no authority, period!" Stassen snarled, and without a word both Americans brushed past into the camp.

On August 30, 1945, a group of big, healthy American sailors liberated Lieutenant Bill Harris and 255 other men from Sumidagawa. When his fellow countrymen strode into camp, cheers rose in Dutch and English, and Bill choked back tears. As he shook hands and clapped backs, the Marine was very conscious of his own emaciated frame and relative weakness. Always proud of his physical strength, Bill was embarrassed at his own feebleness, but Simpson's team, like all those who would deal with the former prisoners, was kind, gracious, and gentle. Initially taken to the Shinjuku rail station, Bill and hundreds of prisoners from all over Tokyo were recorded, briefly fed, then transported to the bay via Omori.*

That same morning, the USS *San Diego* tied up at Yokosuka Naval Base at the mouth of Tokyo Bay. Teams of men quickly spread out, including sailors from Underwater Demolition Team 18. Led by Commander Thomas J. Flynn of the *Iowa*, they boarded the battleship *Nagato* and demanded the Japanese flag be lowered. It was from

---

* Provoo, the "Traitor of Corregidor," was arrested at Bunker Hill by the senior American officer there, Major Williston Cox, and turned over to Commander Art Maher, who had him transported to the *Benevolence* and thrown in the brig. He was eventually found guilty of aiding the Japanese and causing the death of Captain Burton Thomson. The conviction of this deplorable individual was eventually overturned on a legal technicality, and after his release he lived out his life on Hawaii as a Buddhist teacher.

this very ship that Admiral Isoroku Yamamoto had sent the coded phrase "Climb Mount Niitaka" in December 1941, which launched the attack on Pearl Harbor. A veteran of Midway, the Philippine Sea, and Leyte Gulf, *Nagato* remained the symbol of the Imperial Japanese Navy. When Rear Admiral Masamichi Ikeguchi stiffly ordered a subordinate to lower the old battleship's flags, Commander Flynn raised a hand and said, "No. Haul them down yourself!" Also that morning, as Bill Harris had so often dreamed, the U.S. Marines arrived on Japanese soil. The operation's spearhead was composed of the 4th Marines, his old regiment from China and Corregidor, which had been reconstituted as part of the 6th Marine Division to see combat on Guam and Okinawa. Better still, Bill's own 1st Battalion led the way ashore on the beach southeast of Yokosuka Air Field.

It was surreal. Despite the past two weeks, he still couldn't completely come to grips with the situation. Was the war that had governed his life for nearly four years really over? At first, doubt raged. It was a huge Japanese trick—one final, awful attempt to completely break everyone's spirit. But there was no way to hide the dozens of obviously American fighters buzzing overhead or the low-flying B-29s dropping drumfuls of Mounds bars. Then there was the fear of execution—and it was the worst. To have survived all this and to be so close to going home and then killed was an unbearable thought—so he didn't think it. He kept quiet, as always, and watched for any signs of rampaging Japanese.

There were none.

Keeping Hirohito installed as a mouthpiece worked. Very few were prepared to question the will of god, it seemed, and those who did were quickly silenced by the others. Without the emperor, Bill was certain Tokyo would have been a bloodbath, and he was grateful that it wasn't. He still didn't trust any of them, but the guards seemed resigned to their imagined fate, while the civilians were positively meek. In any event, his doubts vanished when he got his first look at Tokyo Bay in nearly six months. Bill was astonished. Warships were everywhere, and he recognized none of them. Huge battleships bristling with guns, powerful cruisers, and sleek destroyers. "It looked like you could walk across the bay just by jumping from ship-to-ship," he recalled. Motor launches darted about like beetles, and landing craft ran continuously from the beach area out to the fleet.

It was the most beautiful sight he'd ever seen. Lieutenant Bill Harris, combat veteran and Marine officer, could not fight back the pride, relief, and gratitude welling up in his chest, or the salty tears running down his gaunt face. Standing on the pier beside Lieutenant Jim Condit, he swallowed hard. Through blurred eyes Bill saw a seaman who'd accompanied them from Shinjuku watching him and also crying. The next half hour was euphoric; just stepping off Japanese earth onto an American landing craft was enough to make him dance, but he just sat, dazed, inhaling the sea air and reveling in the chatter of friendly voices all around.

With the wind in his hair and sun on his face, Bill smiled all the way out to an enormous ship, gleaming in the sun with huge red crosses stark against its bright white paint. Passing under the stern, Bill read U.S. NAVY HOSPITAL SHIP BENEVOLENCE stenciled in huge black letters. Groups of men on the fantail waved, and Harris waved back. She was beautiful. Over five hundred feet long, she boasted 802 beds with a full complement of doctors and nurses. Still mildly shocked, the lieutenant politely declined any help and slowly walked up a sturdily rigged gangway to the wide, clean deck. Blinking in the sunlight, this time Bill couldn't suppress a toothy smile. He was safe aboard an American ship and free of Japan. Safe. He hadn't really been safe since December 8, 1941—nearly four long years ago. His legs felt weak as relief washed through his body and gratitude through his mind.

After a quick deck diagnosis, each man was given an escort to guide him through processing and the maze of the ship's three interior decks. His full name, rank, last unit, date and place of capture, and next of kin were added to another docket. Next of kin . . . warmth spread up from his gut at the thought of seeing his mother and sister— and his father. Maybe someone here could find out about his father and his friends: Bill Hogaboom from the Philippines and Jim Glennon from Annapolis. Thinking of Jim always brought his little sister to mind, and Bill briefly wondered how she'd fared during the war. Probably married, he thought. *I hope to a Marine.*

So it went. Cycling through a decontamination ward, he was deloused and disinfected before taking a truly hot, soapy shower—and not a "navy" shower either, but one with no time limit. It was pure heaven. Finally drying off with a thick, soft towel, Bill was given loose-fitting pajamas and then taken for a medical and dental exam. Next was a shave with a razor—a real razor—and a haircut. Shown to his berth, he was given underwear, new summer cotton khakis, socks, and black shoes, which could be worn now if he wished. Feeling better by the minute, from a row of boxes he took a Marine globe and anchor, then a pair of shiny silver first lieutenant's bars. There'd been a rumor that all POWs were to automatically advance at least one rank, which would make him a captain, but at that moment Bill couldn't care less.

Scraped, combed, and clean, he felt like a new man.

For the next forty-eight hours he enjoyed the navy's "refeeding" regimen: bacon, eggs, toast, hot coffee, fresh orange juice—nearly anything he wanted. The whole arrangement was astounding, and Bill grasped just how far the military had come in four years for him to be stuffing himself on hash browns and biscuits while sitting in Tokyo Bay. Planes flew overhead all day, and boats plied back and forth to the waterfront. From the wide afterdeck, he leaned on the railing and stared across the water at the Japanese capital. From here it didn't look so bad, though there were wide, flat gaps in the skyline from the bombing, and the whole place seemed gray. He tried to begin and end each day by gazing at the city and reminding himself how lucky he was. Of course, this came after a moment every morning when he relished the clean sheets, heard the hum of activity on the big ship, and was desperately afraid it was all a dream, that he would awake nearly naked, cold, and hungry under his own cloud of desperation and fear.

But it was real.

On his second morning aboard ship, Bill was contemplating all of this while loitering on deck as a big motor launch weaved through the clusters of anchored warships. To his surprise, when it approached *Benevolence*, eight gongs rang out over the deck, and a deep, southern-accented voice announced, "Commander, Third Amphibious Corps . . . arriving." As the startled lieutenant and everyone else on deck watched, eight scrambling, white-clad sailors lined up in two rows before the accommodation ladder leading down to the water. A few minutes later, as a man's head came level with the deck, a bosun's mate piped, "Over the Side." Ruffles and flourishes scratchily played from the speakers three times to honor the three stars gleaming on a Marine Corps officer's garrison cap. A stocky bulldog of a man stepped aboard, saluted the American flag aft, and returned the salute of a very flustered young officer of the deck. Bill's eye's narrowed as he stared at the man, and he walked toward him to get a better look. Close-cropped gray hair and steady eyes; he'd seen this man before . . . but where?

Benevolence's skipper, Captain Clyde Laws, and Captain McDaniel, chief medical officer, greeted the man and the two Marine brigadier generals who followed. The side party was dismissed, and the officers talked a moment. Then, to the lieutenant's confusion, McDaniel looked around the deck and pointed at Bill. They all moved toward him, and he blinked, swallowed, and straightened to attention, worried that he was in trouble. Disobeying the surrender order on Corregidor? No . . . it couldn't be that. But something he'd done brought three generals here, and that couldn't be good.

He was dead wrong.

Harris tried to salute, but the three-star was having none of it. His pugnacious face broke into horizontal smile lines, and the hard eyes glittered merrily as he grabbed the utterly astonished lieutenant's shoulders and squeezed hard. The other two generals slapped his arms, grinning broadly and all speaking at once. Bill tried to keep his jaw from dropping, but was too wide-eyed and shocked, which amused the three generals even more. As it turned out, he *did* know the man. Lieutenant General Roy Geiger was one of his dad's oldest friends. The one-stars, Joe Fellows and Bill Clement, had also served with Field Harris during the course of the war. Later, in *Benevolence's* wardroom, Geiger related that he'd served with Bill's father on Guadalcanal in the Cactus Air Force and later during the Bougainville campaign; Field had survived the war and was on Guam. Pulling a thin standard naval message form from his breast pocket, Geiger handed it to Bill. It was addressed to Admiral Bull Halsey, commander of the 3rd Fleet, and read:

REFER BOYINGTON STORY TREATMENT PRISONERS MENTIONING LT HARRIS SON OF MAJGEN HARRIS.

Bill was shocked. Then not shocked. Marines were a close-knit group, and apparently Pappy Boyington also survived and mentioned his fellow officer to someone. Someone — he peered at the sender's block and felt his mouth go dry. This came from the chief of naval operations and commander in chief of the U.S. Fleet. Swallowing hard, he continued reading:

REQUEST ANY INFORMATION ON PRESENT LOCATION OR CONDITION OF LT HARRIS. IF RELEASED AND PHYS-ICAL CONDITION PERMITS REQUEST HE BE ALLOWED JOIN MAJGEN HARRIS AT GUAM ABOUT 7 SEPTEMBER.

"You're going home, son." Geiger smiled warmly. "The fast way." Bill's heart raced, and he tried to stammer out his thanks, but the general just brushed it off. It was the least he could do for Field, who'd been desperately worried about his son. "Over three years with no word." Geiger shook his head slowly. "He never gave up on you. One more thing" — he looked Bill up and down, then nodded — "I want you to come over to the *Missouri* tomorrow. As my guest, to represent our Marines who were prisoners of war."

"I'd . . . I'd be honored sir." Harris recalled trying to keep his voice steady. "But . . . represent the Corps . . . for what?"

All three Marine generals cracked smiles at that, and Geiger chuckled. "The unconditional surrender of the Empire of Japan."

And so, at 0700 on September 2, 1945, Lieutenant William Frederick Harris, USMC, found himself on the starboard veranda deck of the battleship *Missouri*, directly under the massive sixteen-inch guns of her Number 2 Turret. He'd never seen a ship so big, and marveled at the latent firepower. Former prisoner Lieutenant Jim Condit from Sumidagawa was with him, as were Commander Arthur Maher from Omori and Machinist's Mate L. C. Shaw, a survivor from the submarine *Grenadier*. Within a half hour, there were more generals and admirals than Bill had ever seen milling about on the deck. Short, brightly uniformed foreign officers were a stark contrast to the big, serious Americans clad in uniformly plain khaki. The Soviet general wore a dark brown tunic topped by enormous shoulder boards, with dark pants and red stripes. Another officer, obviously French, sported a ludicrous kepi trimmed with gold. How, Bill wondered, had France or Russia contributed to this moment?* Maybe he'd missed hearing about the Pacific battles they'd bled for and won—he'd have to ask someone.

Behind a simple mess table covered with green cloth, the major-power signatories were aligned, ready to sign for their respective nations. When Fleet Admiral Chester Nimitz was piped aboard, the ship's band crisply played the American national anthem as his five-star flag unfurled at the masthead. General Doug MacArthur came aboard next, and his own five-star flag appeared on the same masthead. Bill hung back against the barbette beneath the turret, trying to be inconspicuous while watching the crowd. It was a cool, overcast gray day, and he shivered in his summer khakis. Wrapped in a borrowed olive-drab navy deck jacket, the soft garrison cap he wore did nothing to keep his head warm. Though he'd gained back ten pounds in two days,

---

* Lieutenant General Kuzma Derevyanko and General Philippe Leclerc.

Bill was terribly self-conscious of his thin frame and tried to avoid the seventy-five-odd photographers scattered about. To his right, mounted on a door, was another American flag, though it contained only thirty-one stars. He was told by a nearby navy commander that this was the same flag flown in 1853 by the USS *Susquehanna*, Commodore Perry's side-wheel frigate flagship, when he anchored near this very spot and threatened the Japanese shogun with a modern navy.* Bill appreciated the irony, though he knew the Japanese would not.

Precisely at 0900, those on deck were called to attention and General MacArthur stepped up to a bronze microphone pole mounted on a polished wood base. At 0902 he began to speak, and by craning his neck Bill could just see the army general. How, he wondered, could the man who lost the Philippines, fled Corregidor, and, by all accounts, treated the war as his own publicity machine now be speaking for the Allies during this supreme moment? Why not Nimitz, who Bill understood had done so much to win the Pacific war, or Wainwright, whom Bill had not seen since Corregidor but who was standing, wraithlike, behind MacArthur? Yet Doug MacArthur continued, and Harris had to admit the man was a natural showman as he said, "We are gathered here, representatives of the major warring powers, to conclude a solemn agreement whereby peace may be restored." His diction was perfect, with a measured cadence and weighty words, as if he knew the world would never forget what was said—nor should they, Bill reminded himself.

MacArthur continued: "The issues involving divergent ideals and ideologies have been determined on the battlefields of the world, and hence are not for our discussion or debate. Nor is it for us here to meet, representing as we do a majority of the peoples of the earth, in a spirit of distrust, malice, or hatred."

Bill glanced around. Everyone was mesmerized. Sailors and pho-

---

* Flown out from the U.S. Naval Academy for the occasion, the flag was mounted on the captain of the *Missouri's* door.

tographers were hanging everywhere off the superstructure, watching and listening. The Japanese delegation was thoroughly cowed, and in the center of them the tiny minister with a shiny top hat was staring, unseeing, at some point on the table. What, Bill shook his head slightly, what were you thinking in 1941? Those of you who knew better should have convinced the others that this day was inevitable. Maybe they tried, he thought. Well, they should have tried harder and spared America her hundreds of thousands of men.*

"It is my earnest hope," MacArthur's grave voice continued, "and indeed the hope of all mankind, that from this solemn occasion a better world shall emerge out of the blood and carnage of the past—a world founded upon faith and understanding, a world dedicated to the dignity of man and the fulfillment of his most cherished wish for freedom, tolerance, and justice."

Looking very small and thoroughly ill at ease, the eleven-man Japanese delegation was arranged in three rows facing the table. Bill could see several civilians, all dressed in dark trousers and frock coats over white shirts with silk top hats. The man in the center, obviously the delegation's leader, leaned on a cane with a white-gloved hand. Beside him was an army general, his ribbons and gold aiguillette bright against a dark olive tunic. The riding boots and spurs were incongruous aboard a warship, but Bill decided it didn't matter now. Watching them board, he noticed no one returned their salutes. His fellow Americans weren't arrogant, but they were decidedly cold and formal. Anyway, this was much better than the Japanese behavior he'd witnessed. At 0904, MacArthur paused, looked up from his notes, then waved toward the table.

"I now invite the representatives of the Emperor of Japan and the Japanese government and the Japanese Imperial General Headquarters to sign the Instrument of Surrender at the places indicated."

---

* According to the Naval History and Heritage Command, America suffered 279,867 worldwide dead. Of these, 111,606 were combat deaths in the Pacific.

And so they did.

Mamoru Shigemitsu, Japan's foreign minister, awkwardly limped to the table and, after some fidgeting that irritated several American officers, signed his name in kanji at the top of the second page. Bill watched Yoshihiro Umezu, chief of the army general staff, step forward briskly and also sign. He stepped back, eyes lowered, and stood expressionless as MacArthur, at 0908, began scrawling his name at the top of the Allied signatories. He abruptly stopped writing, turned, and handed the first pen to General Wainwright. After finishing, MacArthur handed the second pen to General Arthur Percival, who surrendered Singapore in 1942. MacArthur rose then and stood back while Admiral Chester Nimitz signed on behalf of the United States. Bill saw the general put his arm around Bull Halsey's shoulder and whisper something.* Halsey nodded, and gestured to his flag secretary while the other representatives signed. There was no sound other than clicking cameras and the odd cough.

After Air Vice Marshall Leonard Monk Isitt, representing the Dominion of New Zealand, signed and stepped back, MacArthur stood before the microphone once again:

"Let us pray that peace be now restored to the world, and that God will preserve it always.

"These proceedings are closed."

The Second World War was over.

Twenty-three minutes.

According to Bill's new watch, that was the extent of the entire ceremony. By his calculation, the world had been at war for six years and two days, beginning in Poland and ending here, now, in Tokyo Bay. He remembered the beginning very well, as a proud young Marine lieutenant fresh from Annapolis. *I'm still a lieutenant*, Bill thought,

---

* MacArthur said, "Start 'em now!" referencing the orbiting carrier planes waiting to fly by.

uncertain whether to laugh about that or not. He was considering the irony when a low, rolling thunder swelled up over the harbor. Watching the Japanese trudge rather forlornly back to the starboard gangway, he noticed those around him were pointing skyward. Lifting his eyes, Harris squinted into the rising sun, and his mouth dropped open slightly. The eastern horizon over Chiba was black with airplanes—American carrier planes from the USS *Lexington, Hancock, Bennington, Belleau Wood,* and *San Jacinto*—over 450 Helldivers, Corsairs, and Hellcats sweeping in over the fleet's mastheads in an awesome display of America's unmistakable power.

Passing east to west, the deep-throated roar drowned out all conversations, and thousands of faces turned upward to watch. Higher up, the enormous silver crosses of the Twentieth Air Force's B-29s now crossed south to north over the bay. It was incredible and inspiring, and his throat tightened at another very graphic illustration of why the Allies had won the war. Guts and courage were not enough; the Japanese had learned that, and Bill would never forget the lesson. This was more than a display of military might and total victory; the flyby was intended as a warning, and he wished he could see the faces of the Russians . . . or the Chinese. To his surprise, General MacArthur's closing benediction ran through his mind. *Let us pray that peace be now restored to the world, and that God will preserve it always.*

I certainly hope so, he thought. He was surprised how fervently he believed that.

Standing on the great battleship's deck, Lieutenant Bill Harris stared slowly around Tokyo Bay and breathed in the bracing sea air. North, south, east, and west—he took in hundreds of ships with thousands of his countrymen. It was still disorienting to be here, and it seemed impossible that only forty-eight hours ago he'd been half naked and mostly dead, clad in filthy rags, emaciated, and bruised. And these were just the visible scars from his thirty-nine months of fighting, evading, and captivity. The other wounds . . . well, Bill wasn't thinking much about it, but he suspected these would take much longer to heal.

Maybe some never would.

What, he mused, must the Japanese ashore think of this vast, invincible armada at anchor within their sacred bay, just a dozen miles from the god-emperor himself? Harris didn't know and, in fact, did not care. This was the price they paid for their hubris, and though the average Japanese had no choice in the matter, it would have made no difference if they had.

Yet Bill knew how *he* felt.

Proud. Shrugging his gaunt shoulders back beneath the oversized khakis, Bill stood straighter as pride welled up from his heart, and a new strength flowed into his tired, aching muscles. Pride. In his country, in the unconquerable valor of those who fought and died to bring this day about, and in himself. Fighting when he could, he'd taken enough enemy lives during his 7,404-mile odyssey to justify the faith his nation and family had placed in him; he'd never given up or betrayed his fellow men, and he'd never ceased to struggle for freedom. Tugging the carefully folded naval message from his shirt pocket, he read again how his father was awaiting him on Guam. Taking a deep, slow breath, the lieutenant let the clean salt air fill his lungs. Smiling now, Bill Harris lifted his chin, and once again felt like an officer, a man, a victorious United States Marine.

And he was going home.

EPILOGUE

Show me a Hero and I will write you a tragedy.

—F. Scott Fitzgerald

Twining her arms around her tall father's strong neck, the beautiful little brown-haired girl laughed merrily as he spun them both around before collapsing on the soft green grass. Salt air blew gently in off the nearby Mystic River, the sky was clear, and the sun shone on the happy, giggling child. It was late spring 1950, and lying on the warm grass of his in-laws' backyard in Jamestown, Rhode Island, Lieutenant Colonel Bill Harris was deeply content. His daughter Katherine came into the world at Camp Lejeune, North Carolina, in 1947, and Jeanne had given birth to Ellie in 1949, in Boston. The Glennons had planted trees for each granddaughter among the raspberry bushes lining the yard, and it was a wonderful place to play with a child. Running his fingers through Katey's hair, he felt the little head on his chest and closed his eyes. It was easier now to forget the war, and he often did, until glorious days like this occurred; then the fear of losing it all bubbled up from some hollow place deep inside, and he'd fight it back down again. Bill discovered over the years that recalling the remarkable ending to his war cleared away the lingering gray memories—most of them, anyway.

True to his word, General Roy Geiger arranged immediate air transportation for his friend's son, and Bill flew out of Japan from Atsugi Naval Air Base on September 4, 1945. As the Army C-47 lifted off from Japan, Harris felt the last four years fall away like leaves in a breeze as they climbed out and headed south for Guam. Landing before his father, Bill wrote "My dear Mama and Nancy and all" while awaiting Field's arrival. "I am just dropping you a line to let you know that I am all right and will be seeing you soon." Field Harris, now a major general, flew in later that day, and Bill was there to greet the plane. The elder Harris tried an outstretched hand that, despite his reserve, instantly changed into a bear hug. He hadn't actually known his son was alive until hearing a September 2 radio broadcast covering the surrender on board *Missouri* that mentioned a lieutenant named William Frederick Harris representing Marine prisoners of war at the ceremony.

Both Marines stood together on the tarmac at Guam's Harmon Field for a long, long minute, completely ignoring the gawking onlookers, and squeezed hard. Pulling back, Bill had been shocked, and deeply moved, to see tears in his father's eyes. In the following days, from Guam to Wake to Midway and into Hickam Field, Hawaii, the men caught up on the past four years. Bill recounted his experiences on Bataan and Corregidor, with Field particularly interested in his subsequent guerilla activities and the year of evading the Japanese. His son did not go into details regarding his captivity, nor did Field press the matter. For his part, Bill wanted to hear about Guadalcanal and the amphibious operations in the Pacific. Listening to his father talk about the Solomons, the Green Islands, and Bougainville made him wish he'd been part of it, and he said so to Field, who, surprisingly, shook his head. The casualties had been enormous, and if Bill had been *there*, then he very likely would not be *here* right now.

At Honolulu the pair was driven across the island, where, befitting

Field's status, they were given VIP quarters at Naval Air Station Kaneohe Bay, where Bill also had a chance to get a proper uniform, complete with his new captain's bars and ribbons. During three days in Hawaii, he continued to rest and eat—and eat some more. By the time the pair left for the West Coast, Bill had gained back nearly fifteen pounds and felt much more like his former self. Landing at Hamilton Field outside San Francisco, his father's rank got them aboard a C-87 Liberator Express bound for Washington, and on September 12, 1945, less than two weeks after his liberation from Sumidagawa, Bill Harris stepped off the plane onto Andrews Field, across the Anacostia River from Washington, D.C.

He had come home at last.

In Washington, Katharine Harris and her daughter Nancy anxiously awaited each telegram the elder Harris dispatched with mounting excitement. When her two men finally stepped down the ladder, Katie, also not prone to emotion, began to cry despite her best efforts to remain calm. Nancy didn't even try. Clasping together in a tight huddle, the Harris family held each other close, the ladies sobbing while the smiling ground crew looked on. Obviously the two Marine officers had been gone a long, long time, but they were now a family again. Bill Harris would never forget that homecoming, and how grateful he was to be home when so many sons, brothers, and husbands would never return.

Piling into Katie's 1941 Pontiac Streamliner, a gift from Field before he left, the family crossed the Anacostia River to enter Washington from the Maryland side. Bill and his father wanted to drive through the capital, so they headed up Virginia Avenue and turned left on Independence to parallel the Mall. Both men were shocked at the temporary buildings, and Katie explained the housing issue during the war and how packed the city remained. Never a fan of crowds, Bill was surprised to find he didn't seem to mind them now; they were all his countrymen, and after twenty-seven months with the Japanese, he was happy to see them. As his parents sat in the front, holding hands and talking, Bill sat in the back with Nancy, content to listen and look. People were everywhere—and on a Wednesday afternoon, too. Curving around the Lincoln Memorial, Katie took the Pontiac across the Arlington Memorial Bridge over the Potomac and across to the Virginia shore.

Gazing at the National Cemetery's gently rolling hills, memories came flooding back for Bill: trips home from Annapolis for the holidays, dinners at the Army-Navy Club with his father, then his last visit here before leaving from Union Station for the West Coast and Shanghai in May 1940. Remembering Nancy's tears, he glanced sideways and slowly shook his head; a graduate of George Washington University, she was a little girl no longer, and five years had transformed her into a stunning young lady. That made him think of *the* girl, and as the Pontiac wound north along Arlington Ridge Road, he asked Nancy if she'd ever seen Jeanne Glennon.

She had not.

Katie, who overheard the question, did have some related news. She'd read an August 1942 clipping of Jeanne christening the USS *Glennon* (DD-620), a destroyer named for her grandfather. Bill stared from the window. What had he been doing three years ago? Sailing across Tayabas Bay for Aurora and trying to escape the Philippines. The *Glennon*, Katie continued, covered the Normandy invasion in June 1944 but hit a mine and sank. A second destroyer of the same name had been launched this very summer, but Jeanne hadn't been there, and the last Katie heard she'd joined the WAVES. However, Bill's old friend Jim Glennon had survived the war and returned home, though she knew no other details.

Driving through Radner Heights and Colonial Village, Bill took it all in. His parents' voices, his sister's hand on his arm, and the peaceful, tree-lined streets of Arlington. He was still trying to mentally and emotionally catch up when Katie stopped at the intersection of North Harvard and 19th Street. Bill and Field just sat for a long moment, staring at the carefully trimmed yard and the steps leading up to the pretty stone house. It was just as he remembered: white columns supporting the portico, an American flag drooping from its staff; large windows with white sashes bright against the tan rock; and big chimneys at both ends of the house. As they got out, Field met his son's eyes across the car, and Bill understood perfectly.

This was, they both knew, a long, long way from Guadalcanal and Corregidor.

Five days later, Bill was granted rehabilitation leave by a paternal government, and he promptly set about recovering himself. Thoroughly enjoying his bed, clean sheets, and eating whenever he liked, Bill caught up with his family and slept. And slept. Yet he discovered that nighttime was the worst. Once the bustle of day faded and the big house fell silent, there was nowhere to hide when the shadows thickened. Faces of men who died on Corregidor or in the prison camps, and faces of men he'd killed in the Philippines or on Morotai. Bill was alone with his thoughts and memories—and nightmares. Bolting awake, panting and sweaty, he'd stare wide-eyed into the darkness of his room and try to remember where he was. There were no sadistic guards, bloating corpses stinking in the sun, or shocked, dead faces staring up at him. Slowly, his heart would slow to a dull thump, and Bill often sat at the window, gazing at the trees and houses splashed with silver moonlight until some peace, ever elusive, gradually returned. Thinking of kindness rather than cruelty helped, and he often recalled the Lopez family or the Moro villagers on Palawan, and always little Joe, his loyal Filipino friend, who'd seemingly vanished without a trace. Sometimes it worked . . . and sometimes not.

And, as always, he thought of the girl.

Had she been just a figment of his imagination, or was she real? If she was Jeanne, what could he do about it? Tell a girl he'd barely known he'd dreamed of her for several years? Bill was certain that would work with most girls, but certainly not with a Glennon or a Lejeune.

He was still thinking of what to do about it when fate intervened. Reading through the *Post* late in September, he was surprised by a paragraph titled "Glennon-Wyatte Marriage Solemnized at Indian Head." Anxiety gave way to profound relief as he discovered it was his friend Jim Glennon who married on September 15, not his little sister.

Working it out in his head for a few days, Bill finally telephoned Captain and Mrs. Glennon, ostensibly to congratulate them on the wedding, but also to find out about Jeanne. He learned Jim was now Lieutenant Colonel James Glennon, that he'd been wounded during a kamikaze attack aboard the battleship *New Mexico* in Lingayen Gulf and was now stationed, ironically, at Camp Lejeune in North Carolina. Overjoyed to receive his call, Mrs. Glennon eventually asked if he remembered Jeanne, and Bill managed a weak "yes, of course." Her daughter, she said, ran into the kitchen the other day waving the *Star* and cried out, "Oh Mom, that Bill Harris is still alive!" Now an ensign in the WAVES, she'd seen an article featuring Bill and his father and was quite excited.

It seemed too good to believe, but Bill decided he had nothing to lose and asked for her telephone number. To his surprise, Jeanne Glennon not only remembered him but appeared quite interested. They promptly arranged a date for the last Friday of September 1945, at the magnificent Shoreham Hotel near Rock Creek, about a mile from her Dupont Circle apartment and George Washington University. Meeting for cocktails in the Marquee Lounge, Bill and Jeanne sat in burgundy leather club chairs surrounded by mahogany paneling and swirling cigarette smoke, discovering they were not strangers after all. Bound together by family connections, a shared history, and individual tragedies, they were instantly and irrevocably drawn together; sometime that evening, while dancing in each other's arms on the Blue Room's fabled terrace, they fell in love.

The suddenness of it shocked Bill, but he came to realize that the girl he'd held in his mind through those dark, dangerous years had, in fact, been Jeanne Glennon. Whatever the reason, he was certain of his feelings, and so was she. "They were engaged in eight days after they met," Bill's daughter Katey recalled with a wistful smile. "Amazing, considering the time, place, and who these two people were." Fall of 1945 was a pleasant haze for both of them. Jeanne, on terminal leave from the WAVES, spent her days riding horses, attending football games at the Naval Academy, and planning her wedding. Happy evenings were spent with Bill's parents at dinner or at concerts and cocktail parties with her friends. The lights were on again in Washington, literally and figuratively, and everyone seemed to bask in the exciting postwar glow.

Assigned to Quantico, Bill was happy to be alive and in love. Befitting his new rank, Captain Harris bought a sporty red Dodge, made plans for married life, and wrote Jeanne constantly. "I am always catching my mind wandering over to you," he penned in January 1946. "Sweetheart, I'd give about anything just to be with you," Bill added as he counted down the days. Finally, on March 30, 1946, they were married in the shadow of the National Cathedral at Saint Alban's Episcopal Church in northern D.C., not far from the Glennons' new house on Foxhall Road. Passing through bright red doors set in gray stone, the twenty-seven-year-old major stood on the steps with the woman he loved, surrounded by family and a handful of surviving Annapolis classmates. Bill Harris was a whole man again—or at least as close as he could come to it.

Life was good.

Honeymooning in Hot Springs, a magnificent resort southwest of Washington near the West Virginia border, the young Marine was filled with hope for the first time in years. Yet, despite his happiness and newfound contentment, Bill, like most men who survive combat, was haunted by those who did not, and he struggled to answer the question all combat veterans ask: *Why me? Why did I live and they did not?* It came during the night, sometimes with the diminishing evil dreams, but most often when he watched his beloved Jeanne and felt, for the only time so far in his life, true contentment. *Why am I here and so many are not?* Bill had yet to discover an answer, but over time came to believe he had lived to give some measure of happiness to Jeanne, and perhaps to father his own children. Perhaps he had survived to train other Marines so they would not endure what he had. These were good reasons and might even be correct.

In the end, he had no concrete answers and could only believe they would eventually come—or that he would learn to live in the world as it was and that hopefully the pain would fade. Yet this worried him too. Bill Harris had learned to regard every day he lived as a gift—and he tried very hard to do this—but felt, deep within himself, that he was on borrowed time. What if, he sometimes wondered, fate had missed me during World War II and was hunting me even now to settle the score? Fate, they said, was a hunter, and from it there is no escape. A man has only so much time allotted to him, and when the last grain passed through the hourglass, the bill must be paid.

Despite his deeply personal thoughts and occasional misgivings, he gradually slipped back into the world of a Marine officer and free American. The Marine in him had doubts, which he expressed to his father, and for a brief time Bill considered leaving the Corps. There was, he knew, a big world in which he could surely find a place doing something else, and in which he never need fight again. Not in favor of this, especially in the light of his son's young family, Field persuaded his son to remain, which he did. The free American, at times, wanted to leave it all behind and find peace back in the mountains of West Virginia or Kentucky, but he knew this was not his path—at least, not now.

The Marine Corps seemed to agree. After his rapid promotion to major, Bill was at Quantico, Virginia, in May 1946, when he received a letter from Mrs. Ida Armstrong of Alabama. Did he know what happened to her boy, Tramble? Could he tell her anything that might help find him? Replying immediately, Bill outlined their meeting on the Lopez plantation in Batangas and their subsequent adventures in Panay, the China Sea, and their final parting on Palawan during

December 1942. He related that Colonel Suarez on Tawi-Tawi had said Tramble and Paul Cothran were captured on Borneo after being betrayed by natives. Beyond this, Bill had no facts, and neither did the military, though the military dispatched many teams of men throughout the Pacific looking for missing men or their remains.

After the war, several witnesses were interviewed on Borneo who confirmed the deaths of Lieutenant Paul Cothran and Private Tramble Armstrong. A Mr. Fatasini, an imprisoned oil company employee, stated that a Japanese Kempeitai told him he'd "witnessed the execution of the Americans" at Tarakan, Borneo. A Dutch prisoner in the same camp, H. A. van Seijl, swore before a postwar Tarakan magistrate that "one of them [the Americans] died of dysentery and that the other was beheaded by the Japs." The American Graves Registration Service would eventually conclude that "the remains of Lieutenant Cothran and Pfc. Armstrong are permanently lost."

Bill never personally liked Paul Cothran, but he respected his abilities and knew the United States had lost a valuable fighting man. Tramble Armstrong, like millions of American boys, was strong and honest, a man you could trust your back to in combat. Neither one lost faith in their nation or the cause for which they fought, and both lie now in unmarked graves somewhere on Borneo. In closing to Ida Armstrong, Bill wrote, "I want to tell you that your son was one of the most courageous, enterprising, and resolute men whom I have ever known. He was a credit to both you and to the nation."

Reid Chamberlain had been more fortunate. He made it to Mindanao by way of Basilan Island, where he'd contracted malaria, and there managed to fall in love with a beautiful Filipina nurse named Evangelista. Vowing to return for her, Chamberlain fought with Wendell Fertig's guerillas for six months, was commissioned a second lieutenant in the army, then left for Australia by submarine in the fall of 1943. Awarded the Distinguished Service Cross by MacArthur himself, Reid resigned his army commission and reentered the Marine Corps as an officer candidate at Quantico. He lasted three days.

Stateside duty wasn't for him, nor was the responsibility of being an officer. Now a sergeant, Chamberlain pled for a transfer to a combat unit and went ashore on Iwo Jima with Company A, 21st Marines, in February 1945. Eight days later, as he was climbing from a foxhole, a Japanese sniper shot him behind the ear, and Reid Carlos Chamberlain fell dead with the other 6,821 Americans who lost their lives on that black island.

Bob Kellam, who survived the USS *Canopus*, Corregidor, and twenty days in the Celebes before being recaptured on Morotai with Bill Harris, also lived to be liberated. Freed from the Osaka POW Camp (Chikko Osaka 34–135), he was repatriated to the United States on September 28, 1945. Though he tried, Bill was never able to ascertain Joe's fate, and continued to hope the faithful Filipino made it back north to his family, where he could live in peace.

Ed Whitcomb also lived to tell the tale of his Philippine adventures. Parting from the three Marines on July 31, 1942, he joined up with two mining engineers from the Lepanto Mine who had a boat and were trying to get to Australia. As they only planned to sail at night, Ed joined them, but all three were captured again by pro-Japanese Filipinos and turned over to the military. Ever resourceful, Ed passed himself off as a civilian engineer and was placed in an internment camp with the others. Spending time in Santiago and Santo Tomas, Roberto Johnson, as he called himself, was eventually sent to Shanghai, from Manila, through the very North Channel he and Bill crossed ten months earlier. Repatriated through a civilian exchange, Whitcomb sailed from the port of Goa on the Swedish liner *Gripsholm*, chartered by the United States, and then from South Africa through Rio de Janeiro to the Port of New York. Walking down the wet gangway, Ed Whitcomb stepped back on American soil on a gray December 9, 1943.

After spending Christmas at home in Hayden, Indiana, he made a special trip to Washington, D.C., to visit Bill's family and relate what he knew of their son. Field was fighting in the Pacific, but Ed met Nancy, then a college student, and Katie Harris, who flatly asked, "Why didn't you just beat him over the head and bring him with you?" They'd had no word of him, but Whitcomb was certain his friend was "still alive and still trying to get home."

Retrained and flying, Ed was back in action by mid-1944. Wrangling a reassignment to the 5th Bomber Command in the Pacific, by a remarkable twist of fate he found himself based at San Marcelino Field—just seventeen miles north of Mabayo, the little cove off Subic Bay where he and Bill set out in the *banca* during June 1942. Flying with the 345th "Air Apaches," Whitcomb was part of the strike against Formosa on May 11, 1945, and was on Okinawa by war's end.

"Honestly, the trouble which you took to find my folks to tell them what you knew about me was one of the nicest things that anyone has ever done for me," Bill wrote four days after arriving home, to Ed, who was now in Japan. Whitcomb would return soon, and he visited his friend in Washington during January 1946. Meeting Jeanne and Bill at the Army-Navy Country Club in Arlington, the reunion was joyfully emotional for two men who'd come so far from that lonely Philippine beach where they'd parted in 1942. Though he left active duty, Ed would remain in the reserves and eventually retire as a colonel. Finishing law school, he married Patricia Dollfuss, fathered five children, and entered politics: first as a state senator and later as the forty-third governor of Indiana.

Bill Harris took a much different path. After Quantico, he was assigned to Camp Lejeune, North Carolina, and then to the Boston Navy Yard in Charlestown, Massachusetts, where he awaited command of a Marine battalion. It almost hadn't happened. Some scars fade but never heal, and Bill had never quite recovered the complete trust he'd once possessed for his leaders, both military and civilian. On Palawan in 1943, he'd almost decided to sit out the war because of Washington's abandonment and willingness to put so many lives in the hands of generals like Doug MacArthur.

Now, with a young wife and two daughters, Bill had thought of other options. With his gift for languages, he could teach anywhere, and certainly Annapolis would hire him as a civilian instructor. Or he could go to law school, as Field had done. There were choices and options—the world was a big place. He came from a long line of military officers, true, but no one could argue that he hadn't done his duty for family and country. Maybe he'd done enough. Field Harris, now commanding the 1st Marine Aircraft Wing, disagreed. Father and son argued about it, but when Bill was told he was in line for a battalion command, he opted to stay in the Marine Corps—for the time being.

Now, on this sunny afternoon in the warm grass of home, it seemed like the thing to do. One assignment as a commander would fulfill his professional ambition—such opportunities were rare—then he could resign his commission with no regrets and do something else close to home. Bill didn't want his children growing up as he did, not knowing a father who visited occasionally and was largely a picture on the piano. Playing, fishing, swimming at the beach with Katey, as she was called, gave Bill a joy he'd never known and moments of true peace he never expected. Fate, it seemed, had decided to give him more time.

But he was wrong.

Just before dawn on June 25, 1950, ten divisions of the communist Korean People's Army (KPA) crossed the Thirty-eighth Parallel heading south. In four coordinated spearheads, largely composed of veterans who'd fought for Mao Tse-tung throughout the Chinese Civil War, they blitzed into U.S.-backed South Korea. Supported by Soviet-built T-34 heavy tanks, nearly ninety thousand North Koreans shattered the southern Republic of Korea (ROK) defensive lines and charged toward Seoul, which was captured three days later. Caught by surprise and unprepared to fight with an army that had been allowed to deteriorate since 1945, Washington ordered the 24th Infantry Division from Japan into Korea. Was this attack the first step in a communist offensive in Asia, or was the Soviet Union simply permitting its surrogate to fight? No one was certain, but the situation was complicated by two main factors. First, the Russians had detonated their own atomic bomb in August 1949, and for the first time the world faced a potential nuclear war. Second, Mao's Communists had defeated Chiang Kai-shek's Nationalists, and China was now "red" China. How would Beijing react to a war involving Korean Communists against United Nations troops on its southern border? No one knew the answer to that either. UN troops, overwhelmingly American, were committed piecemeal to slow the enemy advance, but were inexorably forced back into a defensive pocket centered on the port of Pusan in southeast Korea.

On August 2, the 1st Provisional Marine Brigade landed there, and throughout the month participated in holding the defensive line along the Naktong River. UN air superiority, combined with ferocious ground fighting, broke the back of the KPA advance, but not enough to force a retreat. Then, in the misty dawn of September 15, 1950, the 5th Marines came ashore at Inchon over one hundred miles *behind* the North Korean lines. Shattered, and very nearly cut off, surviving KPA units fled northward while the Americans recaptured Seoul. The biggest fear in Washington now was escalation, and the Chinese wild card was a real threat, so no move north of the Thirty-eighth Parallel was immediately contemplated—until October 5, when MacArthur ordered the 1st Cavalry Division out of Seoul and across the Thirty-eighth Parallel into North Korea. Three days later, the Seventh Marines embarked at Inchon and were taken around to the peninsula's eastern coast to land at the North Korean port of Wonsan. As the 3rd Battalion, Seventh Marines, moved up to their assembly area at Hamhung, their new commanding officer received his orders to Korea. Lieutenant Colonel Bill Harris, now thirty-two years old, departed Boston for Tokyo via the fastest method possible.

"Good-bye, Daddy!," three-year-old Katey, streaming tears, shrieked from her mother's arms. Bill turned, waved slowly and smiled sadly, then boarded his flight to New York. Arriving in San Francisco, he wrote, "You tell Katey that she really gave me a wonderful send-off. It was all I could do not to break away and run over for one last hug."

He hadn't been to San Francisco since embarking for Shanghai in 1940 and Bill spent his single day there eating at Fisherman's Wharf, then strolling through the Presidio to the Golden Gate Bridge. There had been no bridge, he remembered, when Field and Katie left here in 1919 for Manila, but the thought of being in the same place his folks had been was pleasing. With UN forces now chasing the battered North Koreans toward the Chinese border, there was now talk of the war being over by Christmas. Bill didn't really believe that, but kept a thin glimmer of hope in the back of his mind that he could see his family then.

Catching a commercial flight with Northwest Orient, Bill Harris arrived in Tokyo on November 4, 1950, landing at Haneda Air Base—a mere mile south of Omori. Face pressed against the window as the DC-4 circled to land, Bill had his first look at the bay and the former POW camp from the air. He hadn't looked back in 1945, but now he saw it all. Though there was a hollow pang in his gut, Bill somehow knew another circle had been closed, and maybe he could close a few more during the week he was supposed to be in Tokyo.

"I went out to Ofuna," he wrote Jeanne. "Only the hills are the same." Likewise, Sumidagawa had vanished in the reconstruction blitz Tokyo had undergone, thanks to the Americans, since the war. There was also more war news. While he'd been traveling, four Chinese communist (PVA) divisions had crossed the Yalu heading south, and U.S. forces in the area were falling back to Pyongyang, the North Korean capital. "I miss you and my little girls so much that it literally hurts," Bill scrawled out one final letter before leaving Tokyo the following day. "I love you. Kiss my girls for me . . . and don't let them forget me."

Whether a premonition or the natural fear of heading into a combat zone, Bill Harris undoubtedly felt a clenching deep in his gut when the Marine R4D lifted off from Itami Air Base bound for the

Korean Peninsula. Landing at Hamhung, Bill saw his father briefly
at the forward headquarters of the 1st Marine Air Wing, which Field
now commanded. The elder Harris briefed his son, and the situation
wasn't good; Chinese divisions were massing again, and despite the
warnings, General MacArthur was certain UN forces could still drive
north to the border. MacArthur, who never spent one night in Korea,
was running this war as he tried to run the last one—safe behind the
lines and isolated from reality. Field knew his son was heading up to
the 1st Marine Division's positions near the Chosin Reservoir—and
straight into the dragon's mouth: Hagaru-ri, an ugly hamlet on the reservoir's south end, less than sixty miles by air from China.

Taking command of the 3rd Battalion, 7th Marine Regiment, Bill
moved up with his men to positions west of Yudam-ni. The idea, according to MacArthur, was to have the Marines go up the west side
while the army's 31st Regimental Combat Team moved up along the
east shore. The temperature was freezing and the terrain awful. Major
General Oliver Prince Smith, the Marine commander, said, "This
kind of real estate was never intended for military operations. Even
Genghis Khan wouldn't tackle it." A tough, no-nonsense fighting man,
Smith was a veteran of Cape Gloucester, Peleliu, Okinawa, and Inchon; he distrusted MacArthur and refused to spread his division out
across the jagged hills and narrow valleys. Great friends with Field
Harris, he asked the aviator to survey the area around Chosin for an
airstrip, and Field did so, seeing his son again on November 17 at the
Marine camp in Hagaru-ri.

On November 24, MacArthur's grand offensive to destroy the remnants of the North Korean Army and drive north to the Yalu began: it
barely lasted one day. In the west, UN forces crossed the Chongchon
River and ran into eighteen divisions of the Chinese Thirteenth Army
Group. Shattered and demoralized, the Allies reeled back toward
Pyongyang in what one historian called "the most thorough defeat
of a previously victorious army in modern history." To the northeast,
the 1st Marine Division moved into the Taebeck Mountains west of

the Chosin Reservoir. The plan detailed that the Marines would fork west while the army's 31st Regimental Combat Team would head up the reservoir's east side. They would link up north of Chosin, join with the ROK II Corps, then push north to the Yalu.

Bill Harris's 3rd Battalion, in company with Lieutenant Colonel Randy Lockwood's 2nd Battalion, would lead out from Yudam-ni, and at 0500 on the morning of November 27, Marine artillery opened up as Field Harris's F4U Corsairs roared in with the sunrise. Bill led his battalion down a wide river valley west of the reservoir and collided head-on with elements of the PVA 20th Army. General Smith was aware the Chinese were massing, but Army General Ned Almond, a singularly incompetent MacArthur sycophant who commanded X Corps, did not believe it. The offensive was to commence as planned, Almond stated from his headquarters, fifty miles behind the lines at Hamhung, so Bill Harris and his nine hundred men found themselves facing four full-strength PVA divisions west of Chosin. Hit hard, he established the typical Marine horseshoe-shaped perimeter on high ground and dug in.

With sunset, tracers arced across the sky, machine guns stuttered, and the confusion of nighttime fighting deep in hostile territory ensued. Chinese bugles sounded everywhere, but the Marines fought back ferociously from frozen foxholes in the bitter cold. East of Chosin, RCT-31 was spread out over ten miles and cut up badly. By dawn, both Marine regimental commanders knew the offensive was over and they switched to defense. Late in the morning on November 28, Harris and Lockwood were ordered to withdraw toward Hagaru-ri at the south end of the reservoir. The Chinese, who had not expected two full Marine regiments, did not attack, but did filter through the mountain passes on both sides of Chosin to flank the only road open to the south, which would cut off the Marines' route to safety. Determined to never again be a prisoner, Bill destroyed his personal effects, then filled a pack with ammunition, medical supplies, and C-rations.

Withdrawing southeast through the Toktong Pass, which had been heroically held open by a single Marine company, Bill and the 3rd Battalion were last into Hagaru-ri on December 4, 1950.* The four-day breakout from Yudam-ni cost 1,500 American casualties, yet the 5th and 7th Regiments were still effective fighting units, while the three attacking PVA divisions were now decimated and out of the fight.† Bearded and filthy, the exhausted Americans wolfed down hot pancakes and coffee, then collapsed to sleep. Bill cared for his men, arranged to evacuate the seriously wounded, and then was summoned to work out details for the next breakout: south to Koto-ri.‡ Orange, green, blue, and red parachutes filled the sky all day as the air force continued round-the-clock airdrops of supplies, ammunition, and food. Opening the containers after one massive delivery, the Marines found tens of thousands of Tootsie Rolls; the "Tootsie Roll" code name was misunderstood by a rear-echelon supply unit, which loaded up genuine candy rather than 60mm mortar shells. The men ate them, of course, but also discovered they could start fires and plug bullet holes in vehicles. Morale was still high among the 1st Division, who had faith in their immediate commanders if no one else. Legendary Marine Colonel Lewis "Chesty" Puller barked, "So the Chinese are to our east. They're to our west. They're to our north. And to our south. Well, that simplifies things. They can't get away from us now!" A British reporter in Hagaru-ri referred to the impending south breakout as a "retreat," which was corrected immediately by General O. P. Smith, who pointed out that "when surrounded there was no retreat: just an attack in another direction."

At 0630 on December 6, the Seventh Marines led the column south out of Hagaru-ri, except for Bill's 3rd Battalion, which once again would be the vulnerable rear guard against the swarming Chinese. A half hour later, Corsairs roared in to bomb and strafe the enemy

---

* Fox Company, 2nd Battalion, 7th Marines.
† The PVA Ninth Army Group suffered some forty thousand casualties.
‡ USAF C-47s were flying the wounded out every fifteen minutes. By December 6, over four thousand were evacuated.

positions as trucks bearing the wounded and dead slowly lurched forward. The main supply route (MSR) heading south was an eleven-mile gauntlet of snipers, machine guns, and mortars. The hills on both sides were crawling with Chinese; the 76th and 77th PVA divisions were scattered among the rocks and in the ravines, while two more divisions had emerged from the mountains around Koto-ri. By sunset, the column had only traveled three miles but kept inching forward into Hellfire Valley, an exposed mile-long stretch of frozen ground halfway to Koto-ri. Its western side was mountainous and steep, but to the east, past a railroad embankment, was open ground offering clear fields of fire for concealed enemy positions.

Fighting continued during the night as the Chinese closed in around the Marines. When dawn broke on December 7, 1950, nine years to the hour from the Japanese launch against Pearl Harbor, Bill's borrowed time finally ran out. Dropping into a ditch on the west side of the road, he found one of his rifle platoons taking cover from an enemy machine-gun position.* Ordering the men east across the road, he told the lieutenant to wait for him in the shelter of the railroad embankment. Grabbing two rifles, Bill headed into a ravine below the Chinese guns to reconnoiter.

He was never seen again by his Marines.

A hasty and dangerous search was made for their commanding officer by Sergeant Robert Gault's Graves Registration Team and Major Maurice Roach, the regimental logistics officer. Marines never leave anyone behind if it can be avoided, but Bill's body was never found and no answers ever came. Given his resolve to never again be taken prisoner, it is likely that he was ambushed and badly wounded. If killed outright, the Chinese would have left him as he lay, and his body would have been found. Alive and incapacitated—or unconscious—he would have been taken prisoner, and given the lack of Chinese medical aid, Bill Harris very likely died somewhere in the

---

* 2nd Platoon, Item Company, commanded by Lieutenant Thomas M. Sullivan.

rocky, bitter hills east of Hellfire Valley. The citation of his Navy Cross, the second highest award for valor America can give, reads, in part:

> Directing his Battalion in affording flank protection for the regimental vehicle train and the first echelon of the division trains proceeding from Hagaru-ri to Koto-ri, Lieutenant Colonel Harris, despite numerous casualties suffered in the bitterly fought advance, promptly went into action when a vastly outnumbering, deeply entrenched hostile force suddenly attacked at point-blank range from commanding ground during the hours of darkness. With his column disposed on open, frozen terrain and in danger of being cut off from the convoy as the enemy laid down enfilade fire from a strong roadblock, he organized a group of men and personally led them in a bold attack to neutralize the position with heavy losses to the enemy, thereby enabling the convoy to move through the blockade. Consistently exposing himself to devastating hostile grenade, rifle and automatic weapons fire throughout repeated determined attempts by the enemy to break through, Lieutenant Colonel Harris fought gallantly with his men, offering words of encouragement and directing their heroic efforts in driving off the fanatic attackers.

Ed Whitcomb would later write of the Marines and his friend Bill, "What could be said about men like them—men who wouldn't quit or admit defeat—men who survived one battle after another and came back for more until they found their peace in a bloody grave? There must be some special place in heaven for men like William Harris, who would give their lives so that we on earth might live in peace."

However Bill met his end on that freezing December dawn in 1950, it is a stark, clear reminder that the American spirit cannot be vanquished and that there are men who will go down fighting rather than willingly submit. For some, truly there is no road home. Perhaps this is what he saw that piercing morning with blood on the snow and the Chinese pouring in through the hills. Maybe Bill saw his destiny and, being the man he was, simply turned to face it. And that he did; somewhere in that valley of stone and death beneath the cold, pale stars, Lieutenant Colonel William Frederick Harris valiantly met fate head-on, with his hard blue eyes staring fearlessly into eternity.

AFTERWORD

Katey Harris loved her grandparents' yard because she and her father spent so many happy hours there. She only came in on the afternoon of December 22, 1950, because she was cold. Now three and a half years old, Katey figured out about Christmas and knew it was coming soon. Maybe Father would be back by then—that would be the best present ever, she thought, rushing inside to tell Mother her Christmas wish. Finding Jeanne sitting near a window, Katey scrambled up onto her lap, gazed into her mother's face, and asked why she was crying.

"Your daddy," Jeanne finally whispered. "Your daddy is dead."

Katey knew what that meant. "But then he's in heaven," she answered, not really sure why this was a sad thing.

Jeanne cried harder.

Field Harris found out that his son was missing on the morning of December 11, 1950, after the 3rd Battalion arrived at Hungnam without its commanding officer. Colonel Homer Litzenberg, the 7th Marine regimental commander, came to the 1st Marine Air Wing headquarters to personally inform the general. "We have lost our boy," Field managed to write Katie that evening. "Colonel Litzenberg told me what a wonderful job that he had done with his battalion." Quietly grieving in his own way, the elder Harris clung to the hope, as he had during the last war, that Bill was still alive, though this dimmed with each passing day. "I feel sure he is not a prisoner," he wrote. "You will have to work out something for Jeanne and the children." It seemed MacArthur, who couldn't get Bill killed during the last war, had succeeded in this one.

Jeanne LeJeune Glennon Harris had three lonely years ahead of her, but in 1953, while playing tennis at the Army-Navy Country Club, she met a man who stirred her carefully shielded feelings and she found love again. Brigadier General Harris Hull was a decorated pilot who'd served in the 8th Air Force during World War II, and though thirteen years older than his bride, he married Jeanne in 1954 and raised Bill's daughters as his own. The youngest became a college professor, and little Katey grew up, married, and had three children of her own, who have since given Bill two great-grandchildren.

In the spring of 1955, remains believed to be those of Lieutenant Colonel William Harris were returned to the United States from North Korea and laid to rest with full military honors in Pisgah, Kentucky. Beneath a quiet dogwood grove beside the little stone church is far indeed from the frozen valley where Bill died, but very close to his parents, who rest nearby, and to his beloved daughter, who visits often. Here, in such a serene place, I fervently hope that this man who gave so much for his country has finally found peace.

NOTES

Prologue

1   **Sister Miriam Louise, an impish young woman:** *Corregidor*, Morris, 81–82.

2   **Two miles overhead, Captain Ryosuke Motomura:** *December 8, 1941: MacArthur's Pearl Harbor*, Bartsch, 272.

2   **It was really the only thing out here:** *Corregidor*, Morris, 168.

4   **Stimson immediately dispatched:** Bartsch, 259.

5   **Across the Cordillera Central:** Ibid., 287–88.

5   **Zero pilot Matasake Okumiya:** *ZERO!*, Caidin, Okumiya, and Horikoshi, 85.

6   **As she turned into the wind:** Bartsch, 275.

7   **"The General says no":** Ibid., 281.

8   **"the decision on offensive action":** Ibid., 296.

8   **Private Tom Lloyd:** Ibid., 298.

8   **This was duly reported:** Ibid., 299–300.

9   **"Instead of encountering a swarm":** *Samurai!*, Sakai, 64.

9   **One army sergeant:** *The Fall of the Philippines*, Young, 8.

9   **"Long strings of bombs":** Sakai, 65–66.

10   **"Clear the dock!":** *Harris Papers*, Harris, 194–95.

10   **Based on the number of bombers:** Young, 13.

10   **Bill Harris and the other officers:** *Harris Papers*, Harris, 181.

10   **"My poor country!":** Ibid., 190.

10   **"I can hardly believe it":** Ibid., 181–82.

11   "A most distressing incident": *Surrender on Cebu: A POW's Diary*, Miner, 64–65.

11   "We have just had word from Baguio": Ibid., 66.

11   it seemed ironic that here he was: *Over the Seawall: U.S. Marines at Inchon*, Simmons, 9.

12   Yet in less than an hour: *They Fought With What They Had: The Story of the Army Air Forces in the Southwest Pacific, 1941–1942*, Edmonds, 133–78.

ONE: Determination

17   "My dear Mama": Letters of Bill Harris, January 23, 1942.

17   A picture flashed in her mind: Katey Harris-Meares interview, May 11, 2020.

20   "The Japanese have attacked Pearl Harbor": *The Darkest Year*, Klingaman, 42.

23   "Good evening, ladies and gentlemen": *Eleanor Roosevelt's Weekly Radio Address*, George Washington University papers.

24   "Yesterday, December 7, 1941": *"Day of Infamy" Speech*. Franklin Delano Roosevelt, December 8, 1941. National Archives.

27   On the southern shores of Lake Michigan: Klingaman, 76.

28   According to *The New York Times*: *New York Times*, December 18, 1941.

28   Helpful advice was plentiful: *Life*, December 22, 1941, 36.

28   Armored doors and reinforced concrete: *SUN*, December 14, 1941.

29   "When the Little Yellow Bellies": *Songs That Fought the War*, Jones, 125.

30   In the Maryknoll convent: *Corregidor*, Morris, 169.

31   Low's plan surfaced: *I Could Never Be So Lucky Again*, Glines and Doolittle, 10.

31   "My outfit has been bombed": Bill Harris letter, January 1942.

TWO: A Little Piece of Hell

33   Red and green flares sliced: *Escape from Corregidor*, Whitcomb, 75.

33   "God, how many of 'em": *Undefeated*, Sloan, 213.

34   "shattering roar": Harris, Book III, 531.

34   Wide-eyed and heart pounding: Ibid., 532–33.

35   *How in hell did I ever make it*: Ibid., 533.

36   "Damn it, you guys!": Ibid., 535.

37   Even without beach-defense searchlights: *Corregidor: The Saga of a Fortress*, Belote, 146–47.

38 Gunnery Sergeant "Tex" Haynes: Young, 161–62.

39 "I truly believe we killed": Sloan, 213.

39 two thousand Japanese assault troops: *The Fall of the Philippines,* Young, 165.

40 Any soldiers who could speak English: Belote, 156.

40 "a group of 500 sailors with 500 rifles": "The Operations of the 4th Battalion (Provisional) 4th Marine Regiment in the Final Counterattack in the Defense of Corregidor 5-6 May 1942," Dalness, 20.

41 "The muzzle flash": Harris, Book III, 556.

41 Bill twisted his wrist: Ibid., 557.

42 In desperation, the lieutenant: Ibid., 561.

43 "When I recall all this": Statement of Yoshida, Feb. 9, 1950, ATIS Doc 62644, Statements of Japanese Officials on World War II, GHQ FEC, Mil Intel Sec, IV, 554.

44 "Now get the dope": Harris, Book III, 597.

44 "All I could do is die": Ibid., 599.

45 "But it was the terror": *General Wainwright's Story,* Wainwright, 219.

46 "We can't hold out very much longer": Belote, 167.

46 "Major Williams just got word": Harris, Book III, 600.

46 "Shame that the forces of the United States": Ibid., 601.

46 "My God . . . I had to be": Young, 181.

47 "Say, where's the water in here?": Harris, Book III, 605.

48 "Hey you!": Ibid., p. 607.

49 "I'm certainly glad to see you!": Ibid., 609.

50 "My name is Irving Strobing": Robert Thomas Jr., *New York Times,* July 24, 1997.

50 "The flag was slowly lowered": *The Lowering of the Flag,* Gavito.

51 "Going off the air now": *Ten Escape from Tojo,* McCoy and Mellnik.

51 "the Nips are coming": Harris, Book III, 612.

52 *That son of a bitch:* Ibid., 614.

53 *For two cents:* Ibid., 616.

55 "The last hope vanished": Sloan, 227.

56 "He's a miserable bastard": Harris, Book III, 628.

56 "It was purplish black in hue": Ibid., 630.

57 "I was so thirsty": Ibid., 634.

58 "swept through the camp like prairie fires": Ibid., 648.

58 "It would be a long haul": *Escape from Corregidor,* Whitcomb, 85.

58 "little pus-filled blisters": Harris, Book III, 648.

58   "Every individual at defecation": Ibid., 647.

60   *I'll do no work for you*: Ibid., 650.

60   "a senior non-commissioned officer": Ibid., 651.

THREE: Twilight Passing

63   "I'm sure glad to see you come to": Harris, Book III, 654.

65   he swallowed and slowly asked: Ibid., 654–55.

66   "MacArthur went and lost all our planes": Ibid., 641.

66   As with much of MacArthur's "heroism": *The Medal of Honor: The Evolution of America's Highest Military Decoration*, Mears, 144–45.

67   Walking to the beach: Harris, Book III, 655–56.

68   "I've got a proposition for you guys": Ibid., 656–57.

69   They were marched out: Ibid., 661–63.

69   "walking in a ghost-land": Ibid., 659.

69   a hand was severed: Belote, 179.

70   "I found several bottles": Whitcomb, 90.

70   "A guy has to be sensible": Harris, Book III, 659.

71   "at that time": Whitcomb, 90.

71   "We both tore our trouser legs off": Ibid.

72   "Let's get going": Harris, Book III, 671.

73   "a hard, driving downpour": Ibid., 673.

73   "As I swam along, I cupped my hand": Whitcomb, 92.

73   "Hey Bill! Where are you?!": Ibid., 93.

74   "It's a ship": Ibid., 94.

74   "That's Middleside . . . and Topside up there": Harris, Book III, 674.

75   "Nothing": Whitcomb, 95, and Harris, Book III, 674–75.

76   "What do you think": Harris, Book III, 677–78.

76   "Ed! Look!": Ibid., 678.

77   "Like two sea monsters": Whitcomb, 96.

77   "Our muscles evidently still thought": Harris, III, 679.

78   I don't think you can ever appreciate: Ibid., 681.

78   "Come on." Bill jerked his head: Ibid., 682.

78   "I haven't the slightest idea": Whitcomb, 97.

80   Cabcaben was just a field: Ibid., 38.

80   Called the New Mexico Brigade: *Battle of Bataan*, Young, 220–27.

81   "We were able to find shoes": Whitcomb, 97.

82   At its height, before the surrender: *Medical Service in the War Against Japan*, Condon-Rall and Cowdrey, 23–35.

82 One such atrocity occurred right here: Young, 250.

86 "legs, arms, heads, and bodies": *The Fall of the Philippines*, Young, 111–12.

88 "The way they're staring at you": Harris, Book III, 694.

88 "drank water as constantly": Ibid., 698.

89 "The water was delightfully cold": Ibid., 696.

89 "covered with huge boulders": Whitcomb, 101.

89 "For a long time": Ibid.

90 "half-submerged, westward-swimming sea monster": Harris, Book III, 697.

FOUR: Red Summer

98 "Don't let anyone tell you": *Chicago Tribune*, January 31, 1942.

98 In Washington, D.C., Katie Harris: *Washington Post*, February 21, 1942.

99 During 1941 the average American: *The Darkest Year*, Klingaman, 128.

99 At least 25 percent: *Let the Good Times Roll*, Casdorph.

100 H. L. Mencken happily decreed: Klingaman, 183.

100 during their first three weeks: *The Battle of the Atlantic*, Costello and Hughes, 168–203.

100 "to form a tower of paper": Klingaman, 190.

101 that a congressman sitting at a desk: Military Pay Charts 1942–1946 (navy.cs.com).

101 "Unless it is erased": *Richmond Times-Dispatch*, February 13, 1942.

101 It was, according to one: *Detroit Free Press*, February 5, 1942.

102 "This war is a new kind of war": *On Progress of the War*, FDR Fireside Chat, February 23, 1942.

103 Over 500,000 women: Klingaman, 264.

103 At the Douglas Aircraft plant: Cecilia Rasmussen, *Los Angeles Times*, August 4, 2002.

104 "Japanese warplanes set fire": (San Bernadino) *Sun Telegram*, December 7, 1941.

105 held a crew of 1,353 men: Action Report USS *Oklahoma*, December 18, 1941.

106 As of December 14: www.nps.gov/valr/uss-oklahoma-casualties.

106 President Roosevelt was "urging construction: *Nashville Banner*, March 13, 1942.

106 Nightclubs were jammed: *Santa Cruz Sentinel*, May 27, 1942.

107 "I wouldn't dare send a tablecloth": *Pittsburgh Sun-Telegraph*, April 3, 1942, 19.

107   "Japs live like rats": *Wisconsin State Journal*, July 26, 1981, 11.

107   "perhaps we are libeling": *Pittsburgh Sun-Telegraph*, April 3, 1942, 19.

108   **Accepted for the fall semester:** Acceptance letter, October 7, 1942. Harris-Meares collection.

111   "My situation out here": Harris letters, March 30, 1942.

112   "I have seen Uncle Squire": Ibid.

112   "When it comes to women": *Lucky Bag* USNA, 1925. 222.

112   "blown up in Olongapo": Harris letters, March 30, 1942.

112   "sighted strange ship": Deck Log, USS *Hornet*, April 18, 1942, 985.

115   **Station HYPO, officially:** *Combined Fleet Decoded*, Prados, 174–77.

115   **pell-mell pursuit of Doolittle:** *And I Was There*, Layton, Pineau, and Costello, 421–22.

117   **by early afternoon:** *Shattered Sword*, Parshall and Tully, 63–64.

120   **At 0600:** Parshall and Tully, 17–18.

121   **On May 27, a Japanese captain:** Frank, 31–33.

122   QUEZON ARRIVES AT SAN FRANCISCO: *New York Times*, May 9, 1942.

FIVE: Boomerang

124   **A Japanese patrol was combing the area:** *Escape from Corregidor*, Whitcomb, 106.

124   "About the size of a piece of chalk": Ibid., 102.

125   *We're going to do it:* Harris, Book III, 712.

125   "a lightly-framed Japanese soldier": Ibid., 725.

126   "Hey," Bill softly called: Ibid., 713.

126   "I've got a confession to make": Whitcomb, 106–07.

126   "battle scarred, spooky country": Ibid.

127   "We spoke never a word": Harris, Book III, 729.

127   "strewn with innumerable, wrecked, American-type": Ibid., 737.

127   "who rested his back against the cab": Ibid., 735.

128   "The whole village had been burned": Whitcomb, 108.

128   "Wake up," he hissed: Harris, Book III, 742.

128   "white-haired, wrinkled couple": Ibid., 745.

129   "They are very bad people": Ibid., 747.

129   "What a beautiful, beautiful day": Harris, Book IV, 751.

130   "We were literally in paradise": Ibid., 758.

130   **Harris also had a surprise reunion:** Ibid., 761.

130   "the base of a deep, horseshoe-shaped cove": Ibid., 765.

131   "an early December morning": Ibid., 766.

131 "keen, intelligent eyes": Ibid.

131 "The kindness and generosity of the people": Whitcomb, 112.

131 "rice, dried fish, bananas, coffee, sugar": Harris, Book IV, 779.

132 Both men got out several times: Whitcomb, 113.

132 The aircrews were up by 0245: *Shattered Sword.* Parshall and Tully, 117–29.

133 It just seems too wonderful: Harris, Book IV, 780.

134 "Just before dark on June 8, 1942": Whitcomb, 114.

134 "the Great Bear and the Southern Cross": Harris, Book IV, 781.

135 "The shore appeared to be a solid rock wall": Whitcomb, 115.

135 "It was miserable waiting": Ibid., 116.

135 "we stayed here among the natives": *Report of Period of Captivity.* Harris.

136 "delicious breakfast of rice": Whitcomb, 117.

136 "we could see the shore to the west": Ibid.

137 "We did nothing but eat and visit": Ibid., 118.

137 "We've been away from Corregidor": Ibid., 119.

138 seven miles northeast of Balayan: USMC 293 File: Tramble O. Armstrong, 23.

139 "You do not need to worry": Whitcomb, 120.

140 "get into a small cabin launch": Harry W. Pinto sworn statement, August 5, 1943.

140 According to Chamberlain: *Leatherneck.* August 1945, 28.

140 Both were riflemen: marines.togetherweserved.com. 3rd Battalion, 4th Marines.

142 "Do you suppose they really intend": Whitcomb, 124.

143 "thirty-foot, relatively fat-bottomed *banca*": Harris, Book IV, 841–42.

144 "sandy border fronting a small valley": Ibid., 844.

145 "like a passage up a river of hell": Ibid., 898.

145 "delicious, intoxicating . . . wonderful, fermented": Ibid., 869.

145 "past mile after mile of the sparsely inhabited": Ibid., 70.

145 "The trouble": Whitcomb, 126.

146 "I think we ought to try it this way": Ibid.

146 "You can count me out of your vote": Ibid., 127.

SIX: Currents

148 they caught a near-gale-force wind: Harris, Book IV, 870.

148 "I expected trouble travelling": Ibid., 868.

149 Eight days after leaving Lobo: *Report of Captivity*, May 13, 1946. Harris.

149 One man, older than the rest: Patty Rosales letter. December 27, 1945.

150 "but the lieutenant was so refined in manners": Ibid., 3.

150 nomadic gardeners called *kaingineros*: *They Fought Alone*. Keats, 21.

150 "chubby, smooth, clean-shaven face": Harris, Book IV, 895.

151 At the Pantingan River: *Tears in the Darkness*. Norman and Norman, 206–09.

152 Many Filipinos, especially significant numbers: *Philippine Collaboration in World War II*. Steinberg, 13.

153 Abducted at a village market: Keats, 80.

153 "The Hapons are sick men": Ibid., 81.

155 MacArthur took two of these divisions: Taruc, 21.

156 it wasn't until September 25: *Report of Captivity*, May 13, 1946. Harris.

156 "the most God damned luck on this trip": Harris, Book IV, 868.

156 They were quiet and reserved: "The Semi-Civilized Tribes of the Philippine Islands." Miller, 56–60.

158 Stockpiling fifteen thousand bags of rice: *Triumph in the Philippines*. Smith, 507.

158 "surrender might be treason": *Guerilla Warfare on Panay*. Manikan, 38.

159 "You will understand from the letter": Ibid.

159 "if I were in your place": Ibid., 41–42.

160 an enormous banana plantation: *They Never Surrendered*. Villamor, 111.

160 Peralta lived nearby in Maligayligay: *Guerilla Warfare on Panay*. Manikan, 44.

161 "Detachment of Fil-American forces": *MacArthur's Undercover War: Spies, Saboteurs, Guerillas, and Secret Missions*. Breuer, 46.

162 By 0915 of June 5: Parshall and Tully, 359, 524.

162 carrier rolled to port: Ibid., 383.

164 heavy with the "sweet sour odor of burnt sugar": *The Blood and Mud in the Philippines: Anti-Guerrilla Warfare on Panay Island*. Kumai, 1–18.

165 There were, Bill also learned: *The Edge of Terror*. Walker, 105–25.

165 "I do not desire to be a prisoner": Manikan, 40.

165 "I would rather face court-martial": Ibid., 41.

166 Meider flew Stinson Trimotors: Villamor, 110–11.

166 A mining engineer from La Junta: Walker, 70–74.

166 "It really is a swell set up": Harris letter. July 30, 1940.

168 He offered Harris a captured boat: Manikan, 134.

168 The enemy had dispatched motor launches: Ibid., 111.

168 "craft painted mahogany brown": Harris, Book V, 1147–48.

168 Taken during a raid on Semirara Island: Manikan, 111.

169 Peralta directed Lieutenant Colonel Chavez: Ibid., 105.

169 the guerillas infiltrated from the mangrove swamps: Ibid., 106.

169 "Two soldiers came into sight": Harris, Book V, 1128–29.

169 *It has finally begun*: Ibid.

170 "nothing bad or evil about their faces": Ibid.

170 "smoothly went under the chins of the Japs": Ibid.

170 *Just a few more seconds*: Ibid., 1133.

171 "two-handed swords they handled": Ibid., 1134.

171 "He wasn't fooled": Ibid., 1136.

171 "The son of a bitch": Ibid.

172 clad only in the peculiar *fundoshi* loincloth: Ibid., 1144–45.

172 "The last night at the Army-Navy Club": Ibid., 1151.

172 "A man came last night": Ibid., 1152.

173 Nine hundred and twenty nautical miles: Ibid., 1165.

173 Conducting sea trials off the Panay coast: Ibid., 1163–64.

175 an enormous *kaban*: Ibid., 1173–74.

SEVEN: Lost Souls

177 There were five Filipinos: *Report of Captivity*, May 13, 1946. Harris, 2.

178 "I'll see you after the war!": Harris, Book V, 1187.

180 It had to be San Jose: Ibid., 1198.

180 a cloudless, powder-blue sky: Ibid., 1199–1200.

181 "my job to get back in the big war": Ibid., 1201.

181 "These God damned stupid gooks": Ibid., 1204.

181 *Dirty ungrateful bastard*: Ibid.

181 "I'd watch my manners": Ibid., 1205.

182 "a rough sea and high winds": Ibid., 1209.

183 "The waves were mountainous": Ibid., 1211.

184 "We're eatin' so God damned little": Ibid., 1217–19.

185 "You black bastard, I'll call you what you are": Ibid.

186 "I've never had a better friend": Ibid.

187 Harris removed the auxiliary fuel tank: Ibid., 1249–51.

187 "A puff of steam blew from the outlet end": Ibid.

188 Cothran emerged from below: Ibid., 1231–32.

188 "black-plumed, crested, long-necked": Ibid., 1223.

189 deep sapphire blue to jade green: Ibid., 1242.

189 "raging twenty-five-foot billows": Ibid., 1265.

190 "We were surely lost souls": Ibid.

191 "But that damned horizon": Ibid., 1268–72.

193 *I'm going to fight him slow*: Ibid.

194 *This world belongs to the strong*: Ibid.

195 "exceedingly faint bluish outline": Ibid., 1275.

196 "like a curtain lifting before a stage": Ibid., 1278.

196 "That bay there": Harris, Book VI, 1356.

197 "Whatever we do": Ibid.

198 "notch in the skyline": Ibid., 1357–59.

199 "You ought to see the coral heads": Ibid.

199 "A moment later the bow crunched": Ibid.

200 "forty to fifty rude little stilted houses": Ibid., 1366.

200 "Cothran," he wrote of the incident: Ibid., 1370–72.

201 "I'm half sorry you were so God damned fair": Ibid.

201 "We want the boat too": Ibid.

203 "clad in black fezzes": Ibid., 1396.

203 "I have never known Moros": Ibid.

204 "an exceedingly fiery, peppery stew": Ibid., 1402.

204 "going to be very careful about joining": Ibid.

205 "white, Moro shirt above his blue Moro trousers": Ibid., 1420.

206 Rice, coconuts, and coffee: Ibid., 1426.

206 "I like this living so much": Ibid., 1429.

206 two other Americans had sailed over three thousand miles: *The War Journal of Major Damon "Rocky" Gause*. Gause, 84–171.

206 They docked at Wyndham: *Voyage into the Wind*. Osborne, 153–92.

207 "Even if I did get sold down the river": Harris, Book XI, 1428.

207 "I've thought that out thoroughly": Ibid., 1433.

208 This was how, by late January 1943: as before *Report of Captivity*. Harris, 3.

PART III

EIGHT: Odyssey

212 "I'm beginning to think": Harris, Book VI, 1492.

212 "very bad, squally rainy weather": *Report of Captivity*. Harris, 3.

212 While on Banguey, Harris discovered Cothran's boat: *Case History Report for Search Teams for Missing and Unidentified Dead*. March 4, 1946.

212 Back on Balabac, Bill delayed: *Report of Captivity*. Harris, 3.

213 Procuring a seaworthy, thirty-foot Moro *kumpit*: Harris, Book VI, 1455.

213   "that little lighthouse back there": Ibid., 1480.

214   "flat topped mountain": Ibid., 1483.

214   "There were three other Americans": Ibid., 1486.

215   Chamberlain remained on Tawi-Tawi: *Case History Report.* March 4, 1946, 1.

216   February 7, 1943, six months to the day: *Operation Vengeance.* Hampton, 269–72.

216   Only ninety-one thousand Germans survived: Ibid., 270–73.

217   May 7, 1943, he bade farewell: *Report of Captivity.* Harris, 3.

217   "We're in a new sea now": Harris, Book VI, 1491.

218   Officers wore regulation cavalry sabers: *Japan's Gestapo.* Felton, 135.

218   concept of *hakko ichiu*: *The Knights of Bushido.* Russell, 10–13.

218   "Two prisoners escaped last night": Ibid., 234–35.

219   Under the guidance of Lieutenant General Dr. Shiro Ishii: Felton, 121–24.

219   Cannibalism was also practiced: Russell, 233–39.

219   As Lord Russell of Liverpool would later recount: Ibid., 240.

220   "pounded into his nostrils to break the bones": Ibid., 30.

220   "comfort stations": Felton, 100–110.

220   Eurasian, Australian, Asian, and particularly European women: *Kempeitai.* Lamont-Brown, 42–45.

222   "long string of blue mountains": Harris, Book VI, 1502.

225   Four days out of Biaro: *Report of Captivity.* Harris, 3.

226   Three more agonizing days: Ibid.

227   Bill wearily dropped anchor: Harris, Book VII, 1508–10.

227   "Pig? Oh. Yes. Yes. We are Christians": Ibid., 1511.

228   "I can remember": Ibid., 1519.

229   "Hello," the dark man said: Ibid., 1528.

231   "I wonder why Mr. da Costa": Ibid., 1538.

234   "I only wish": Ibid., 1544.

235   A small gray warship flying a white ensign: *Report of Captivity.* Harris, 4.

NINE: Abyss

238   All told, the Allies lost: *Breaking the Bismarcks Barrier.* Morison, 126–28.

238   eighteen U.S. Army P-38s: *Operation Vengeance.* Hampton, 311–43.

240   an astonishing 120,000 aircraft and tanks: history.com.

240   Frigidaire now made .30-caliber machine guns: *Operation Vengeance.* Hampton, 274–77.

241 draft-deferred workers backed by labor unions: Ibid.

241 this month's aircraft output: *New York Times.* June 18, 1943.

241 "Atrocious and Cruel America and Britain": Ibid.

242 "NO MORE ZOOT SUITS!": Ibid. June 13, 1943.

244 "Final Victory Believed Near": Ibid. May 31, 1943.

244 given cigarettes, food, and quinine: *Report of Captivity*, May 1946, 4.

246 "12-foot high, double barbed wire fence": *Ambon.* Maynard, 98.

246 A wood jetty stuck out: Netherlands Intelligence Service Map 13. March 13, 1943.

246 Captain Ando Noburo: *Ambon.* Maynard, 103, 239.

246 "individual small, well-guarded cells": *Report of Captivity*, 4.

247 concrete floors . . . solid wood walls: Netherlands Intelligence Service Map 13. March 13, 1943.

248 "The main fault here": *Report of Captivity*, 4.

249 On August 4, 1943: Ibid.

249 Led to a wooden stockade: *Black Sheep One.* Gamble, 347.

249 "green cotton two-piece Jap work fatigue uniform": Ibid., 351.

251 the main barracks, called "Sanku": Ibid., 354.

252 calm, with large, thoughtful eyes: USNA *Lucky Bag*, Class of 1923, 43.

252 feisty, hard-faced little Irishman: USNA *Lucky Bag*, Class of 1931, 76.

252 on April 8, 1942: "POW Camp Ōfuna." Koichi, 1–3.

253 "snazzy suits and saddle Oxfords": Gamble, 353.

254 "standing on the ball of your foot": Bravin, *Wall Street Journal.* April 7, 2005.

254 Finding that superficial politeness: Gamble, 351.

255 Tying these together with bits of dirty string: Harris POW book, 1943–1945. Meares, 1–76.

255 These included Frank Tinker . . . and Louis Zamperini. Ibid., 38.

255 At this time, civilians in America: "From Plowshares to Swords: The American Economy in World War II." Rockoff, 82–93.

257 "America has lost the war": Radio Tokyo Broadcast. Tolischus, *Through Japanese Eyes*, 157.

260 "when he finally emerged from his cell": *Unbroken.* Hillenbrand, 235.

261 Nevertheless, General Hansell himself: 20th Air Force Association Mission Summaries.

261 The bombers flew four missions: Ibid.

262 A brilliant tactician: *Clear the Bridge!* O'Kane, 471.

262 Though beaten by the ship's crew: Ibid., 460.

262 "The captain," he wrote after the war: Ibid., 460–61.

TEN: The Long Road Home

266 "America's productive powers": *Picture Letters from Commander in Chief.* Kuribayashi and Yoshida.

266 "Conditions were much better": *Report of Captivity.* Harris, 4.

266 Officially Base Camp 1, Omori: *Foo: The Secret Prison Diary of Frank Fujita.* Fujita, 187–90.

266 This, Bill discovered, was a good thing: Ibid., 187.

266 too large for the "personal attention": O'Kane, 465.

267 "Provoo is his name": Harris, Book VI, 1411.

267 Shaving his head: *A Case of Treason.* Thomson, 193–204.

267 "You son of a bitch": Thomson, 197.

268 just 125 miles southwest of Omori: *Twilight of the Gods.* Toll, 482.

268 left small piles of roasted soybeans: O'Kane, 465.

269 *Dinah Might*: pacificwrecks.com/aircraft/b-29/42-65280.

269 2,251 bombers would land safely: Toll, 516.

269 there were six American officers: NARA, Philippine Archives. RG 407, Box 115.

270 "almost instantly it seemed": Fujita, 264.

270 In a major doctrinal shift: USSBS, 45–95.

270 16.8 square miles of Tokyo: 20th Air Force Association Mission Summaries. Mission Number 40.

270 Over the next ten days: USSBS, 45–95.

271 Eight million city dwellers: Ibid.

273 Ed was in a B-25 attacking: *Undefeated.* Sloan, 342.

273 Harris wasn't fooled: Harris, Book VI, 1450–58.

274 At 0245 on Monday, August 6: *Operation Vengeance.* Hampton, 385.

275 "Sixteen hours ago": Presidential Speeches, National Archives.

275 "Let the dirty rats squeal": *Eagle Against the Sun.* Spector, 556.

275 "When you deal with a beast": Ibid., 555.

276 Ian Toll eloquently phrased: Toll, 723.

277 "Whether they are destroyed individually": NARA, War Crimes, Japan, RG 24, Box 2011, Exhibits "J" and "O."

278 "We have ordered our government": "Text of Hirohito's Radio Rescript." *New York Times*, August 15, 1945.

278 "We were rooted to the floor": *Samurai!* Sakai, 348.

279 A captured American flier: *We Shall Suffer There.* Banham, 214.

280 "Those are our boys!": *Admiral Halsey's Story*: Halsey, 279.

280 "the appearance of the landing craft": CTG 30, 6 AR, dtd 22Sep45, Subj: Covering Evacuation of POW during period 29Aug–19Sep45 (OAB, NHD).

282 "Haul them down yourself": Halsey, 280.

286 **REFER BOYINGTON STORY TREATMENT**: Naval Message 312107. Author's collection, provided by Katherine Harris Meares.

286 "You're going home, son": Harris, Book VII, 1406.

BIBLIOGRAPHY

Adams, Michael C. C. *The Best War Ever: America and World War II*. Baltimore, MD: Johns Hopkins University Press, 1994.

Allen, Frederick Lewis. *Only Yesterday: An Informal History of the 1920s*. New York: Harper and Row, 1931.

Andres, Matthew Cenon. *Pinoys at War: Relative Deprivation, Motivation, and the Filipino Guerillas of World War Two*. Matthew Andres, 2013.

Argyle, Christopher. *Chronology of World War II*. London, UK: Marshall-Cavendish, 1980.

Arnold, Robert H. *A Rock and a Fortress*. Sarasota, FL: Blue Horizons Press, 1979.

Astor, Gerald. *Wings of Gold: The U.S. Naval Air Campaign in World War II*. New York: Random House, 2005.

Aviation History Online Museum. n.d. www.aviation-history.com. February–July 2013.

Baime, A. J. *The Arsenal of Democracy*. New York: Houghton Mifflin Harcourt, 2015.

Banham, Tony. *We Shall Suffer There*. Hong Kong: Hong Kong University Press, 2009.

Baritz, Loren. *The Culture of the Twenties*. Indianapolis, IN: Bobbs-Merrill, 1970.

Barker, Ted. *LTC Bill Harris in Korea*. May 8, 2021. Email.

Bartsch, William H. *December 8, 1941: MacArthur's Pearl Harbor*. College Station: Texas A&M University Press, 2003.

———. *Doomed at the Start*. College Station: Texas A&M University Press, 1992.

Belote, John H., and William M. Belote. *Corregidor: The Saga of a Fortress*. New York: Harper & Row, 1967.

Berger, Carl. *B-29: The Superfortress*. London, UK: Purnell, 1970.

Brand, Max. *Fighter Squadron at Guadalcanal*. Annapolis, MD: Naval Institute Press, 1996.

Breuer, William B. *MacArthur's Undercover War*. Edison, NJ: Castle Books, 2005.

Bridman, Leonard, ed. *Jane's Fighting Aircraft of World War II*. London, UK: Studio, 1946.

Bryson, Bill. *One Summer: America, 1927*. New York: Anchor Books, 2014.

Burkman, Thomas W. *Japan and the League of Nations: Empire and World Order, 1914–1938*. Honolulu: University of Hawaii Press, 2007.

Burns, Eric. *1920: The Year That Made the Decade Roar*. New York: Pegasus Books, 2015.

Butow, Robert J. C. *Tojo and the Coming of War*. Princeton, NJ: Princeton University Press, 1961.

Caceres, Michael Vincent P. "Rising Sun in the Southern Land: Destruction and Resistance in Sulu and Tawi-Tawi Archipelago (1941–1945)." 2018.

"Carriers: Airpower at Sea." n.d. www.sandcastlevi.com/sea/carriers. Accessed May 15, 2013.

Casdorph, Paul D. *Let the Good Times Roll*. St. Paul, MN: Paragon House, 1989.

Celedonia, A. Ancheta, ed. *The Wainwright Papers*. Vol. 2. Quezon City, Philippines: New Day, 1980.

Clavin, Bob, and Tom Drury. *The Last Stand of Fox Company*. New York: Grove Press, 2009.

Cleaver, Thomas McKelvey. *The Frozen Chosen*. New York: Osprey, 2016.

Commander, Air Solomons. "Pop Goes the Weasel." *Message No. 180229*. U.S. Navy, April 18, 1943.

Condon-Rall, Mary Ellen, and Albert Cowdry. *The Medical Department: Medical Service in the War Against Japan*. Washington, D.C.: U.S. Army Center of Military History, 1998.

Conn, Stetson. *Highlights of Mobilization: World War II, 1938–1942*. Washington, D.C.: Department of the Army, 1959.

Connaughton, Richard. *MacArthur and Defeat in the Philippines*. New York: Overlook Press, 2001.

Costello, John. *The Pacific War, 1941–1945*. New York: HarperCollins, 1981.

Craven, W. F., and J. L. Cate. *The Army Air Forces in World War II*. Vol. 6, *Men and Planes*. Washington, D.C.: Office of Air Force History, 1983.

Cureton, Thomas Kirk. *Physical Fitness Workbook: Fit for Democracy—Fit to Fight*. Champaign, IL: Stipes Publishing, 1942.

Dalness, H. E. "The Operations of the 4th Battalion (Provisional) 4th Marine Regiment in the Final Counterattack in the Defense of Corregidor 5-6 May 1942." Official Report. USAFFE-USFIP.

Doolittle, James with Carroll V. Glines. *I Could Never Be So Lucky Again*. New York: Bantam Books, 1991.

Dunn, Susan. *A Blueprint for War: FDR and the Hundred Days That Mobilized America*. New Haven, CT: Yale University Press, 2018.

Edmonds, Walter D. *They Fought with What They Had*. Boston: Little, Brown, 1951.

Farago, Ladislas. *The Broken Seal*. New York: Random House, 1967.

Felton, Mark. *Japan's Gestapo*. Barnsley, UK: Pen and Sword, 2009.

Finder, Henry, ed. *The 40s: The Story of a Decade*. New York: Random House, 2014.

Frank, Richard B. *Guadalcanal: The Definitive Account of the Landmark Battle*. New York: Random House, 1990.

Fujita, Frank. *Foo: A Japanese-American Prisoner of the Rising Sun*. Denton, TX: Univerity of North Texas Press, 1993.

Gamble, Bruce. *Black Sheep One: The Life of Gregory "Pappy" Boyington*. New York: Presidio Press, 2000.

Gause, Damon. *The War Journal of Major Damon "Rocky" Gause*. New York: Hyperion, 1999.

Gavito, Val. "The Lowering of the Flag." www.corregidor.org.

Gibney, Frank. *Senso: The Japanese Remember the Pacific War*. Armonk, NY: M. E. Sharpe, 1995.

Gordon, John Steele. *An Empire of Wealth*. New York: HarperCollins, 2004.

Groom, Winston. *1942: The Year That Tried Men's Souls*. New York: Grove Press, 2005.

Halberstam, David. *The Coldest Winter: America and the Korean War*. New York: Hyperion, 2007.

Halsey, William Frederick, and J. Bryan. *Admiral Halsey's Story*. New York: McGraw-Hill, 1947.

Hamilton, James M. *Rainbow over the Philippines*. Chicago: Adams Press, 1974.

Hampton, Dan. *Lords of the Sky*. New York: HarperCollins, 2014.

———. *Operation Vengeance*. New York: HarperCollins, 2020.

Harris, Bill. "Letter to Mrs. Armstrong." Quantico, MD, May 18, 1946.

Harris, William Frederick. "Harris Manuscript." 1948.

Harrison, Mark, ed. *The Economics of World War II*. Cambridge: Cambridge University Press, 1998.

——. "Resource Mobilization for World War II: The USA, UK, USSR, and Germany, 1938–1945." *Economic History Review* 41, no. 2 (1988).

Hartendorp, A. V. H. *The Japanese Occupation of the Philippines.* Manila, Philippines: Bookmark, 1967.

Hastings, Max. *The Korean War.* New York: Simon & Schuster, 1987.

Hata, Ikuhiko, and Izawa Yasuho. *Japanese Naval Aces and Fighter Units in World War II.* Annapolis, MD: Naval Institute Press, 1975.

Hattori, Takushiro. *The Complete History of the Greater East Asia War.* Tokyo: Masu Shobo, 1953.

Hayashi, Saburo. *Kogun: The Japanese Army in the Pacific War.* Quantico, MD: Marine Corps Association, 1959.

Herman, Arthur. *Freedom's Forge.* New York: Random House, 2013.

Hillenbrand, Laura. *Unbroken: A World War II Story of Survival, Resilience, and Redemption.* New York: Random House, 2014.

Hiroyuki, Ogawa. *The Reluctant Admiral: Yamamoto and the Imperial Navy.* Tokyo: Kodansha International, 1979.

Holland, James. *The Allies Strike Back, 1941–1943.* Vol. 2 of *The War in the West.* New York: Grove Atlantic, 2017.

——. *The Rise of Germany 1939–1941.* London: Bantam, 2015.

Hota, Eri. *Japan, 1941.* New York: Knopf, 2013.

Hoyt, Edwin P. *Japan's War: The Great Pacific Conflict.* New York: McGraw-Hill, 1986.

Hughes, Terry and John Costello. *Battle of the Atlantic.* New York: Dial Press, 1977.

Ienaga, Saburo. *The Pacific War, 1931–1945: A Critical Perspective on Japan's Role in World War II.* New York: Random House, 1978.

Jones, John Bush. *Songs That Fought the War: Popular Music and the Home Front, 1939–1945.* Lebanon, NH: Brandeis University Press, 2006.

Jose, Ricardo T. *The Philippine Army, 1935–1942.* Manila, Philippines: Ateneo Manila Press, 1992.

Keats, John. *They Fought Alone.* Nashville, TN: Turner, 1963.

Keegan, John. *The Second World War.* New York: Penguin, 1989.

Kelley, Robin D. G. *The Riddle of Zoot: Malcolm Little and Black Cultural Politics During World War II.* New York: New York University Press, 1998.

Kennedy, David M. *World War II Companion.* New York: Simon & Schuster, 2007.

Kimura, Matsato, and Tosh Minohara. *Tumultuous Decade: Empire, Society, and Diplomacy in 1930s Japan.* Toronto: University of Toronto Press, 2013.

Kiyosaki, Wayne S. *A Spy in Their Midst.* New York: Madison Books, 1995.

Klingaman, William K. *The Darkest Year.* New York: St. Martin's Press, 2019.

Kovner, Sarah. *Prisoners of the Empire*. Cambridge: Harvard University Press, 2020.

Kumai, Toshimi. *The Blood and Mud in the Philippines*. Iloilo City, Philippines: Malones Printing Press and Publishing House, 2009.

Kyvig, David E. *Daily Life in the United States, 1920–1940*. Chicago: Ivan R. Dee, 2004.

Lamont-Brown, Raymond. *Kempeitai: Japan's Dreaded Military Police*. Phoenix Mill, UK: Sutton, 1998.

Layton, Edwin T., Roger Pineau, and John Costello. *And I Was There: Pearl Harbor and Midway: Breaking the Secrets*. New York: William Morrow, 1985.

Leckie, Robert. *Challenge for the Pacific*. New York: Bantam Books, 1965.

——. *Helmet for My Pillow*. New York: Random House, 1957.

Liverpool, Lord Russell of. *The Knights of Bushido*. New York: Skyhorse Publishing, 2008.

Manchester, William. *American Caesar*. New York: Little, Brown, 1978.

Manikan, G. L. *Guerilla Warfare on Panay Island in the Philippines*. Quezon City, Philippines: Bustamante Press, 1977.

Maurer, M. *Air Force Combat Units of World War II*. Washington, D.C.: Office of Air Force History, 1983.

Maynard, Roger. *Ambon*. Sydney: Hachette, 2014.

McCoy, Melvin H. and S. M. Mellnik. *Ten Escape from Tojo*. New York: Farrar and Rinehart, 1944.

Meares, Katey Harris. *Bill and Jeanne marriage and honeymoon details*. May 2, 2021. Email.

——. *Bill Harris early life*. March 11, 2020. Telephonic.

——. *Bill Harris Personal Letters*. February 4, 2020. Email.

——. *Bill Harris Personal Letters and Photos*. August 18, 2020. Email.

——. *Bill Harris Photos*. January 24, 2020. Email.

——. *Bill Harris POW Recollections*. August 17, 2020. Telephonic.

——. *Family and Background*. February 26, 2020. Telephonic.

——. *Family History and Background*. May 15, 2020. Telephonic.

——. *Field and Katie Harris*. May 11, 2020. Telephonic.

——. *Harris Family in Manila*. June 6, 2020. Telephonic.

——. *Harris Family Photos*. February 2, 2020. Email.

——. *Harris Memorabilia*. April 8, 2020. Email.

——. *Harris Photographs*. November 13, 2020. Email.

——. *Jeanne Glennon Harris Letters and Photos*. July 7, 2020. Email.

——. *Korea Letters*. April 15, 2020. Email.

——. *Memories of Bill*. January 1, 2021. Telephonic.

———. *Post World War II Life, Marriage, and Korea*. March 15, 2021. Telephonic.

Mears, Dwight S. *The Medal of Honor*. Lawrence: University Press of Kansas, 2018.

Merrilat, Herbert Christian. *Guadalcanal Remembered*. New York: Dodd, Mead, 1982.

———. *The Island: A History of the First Marine Division on Guadalcanal, August 7–December 9, 1942*. Boston: Houghton Mifflin, 1944.

Miller, Oliver C. "The Semi-Civilized Tribes of the Philippine Islands." In *The Annals of the American Academy of Political and Social Science*, vol. 18 [Sage Publications, Inc., American Academy of Political and Social Science], 1901, pp. 43–63, www.jstor.org/stable/1009882.

Mills, John A. *Stranded in the Philippines*. Annapolis: Naval Institute Press, 2009.

Miner, William D. *Surrender on Cebu: A POW's Diary—WWII*. Nashville, TN: Turner Publishing, 2002.

Morison, Samuel Eliot. *Breaking the Bismarcks Barrier*. Vol. 6 of *History of United States Naval Operations in World War II*. Edison, NJ: Castle Books, 1958.

———. *Coral Sea, Midway and Submarine Action*. Vol. 4 of *History of United States Naval Operations in World War II*. Boston: Little, Brown, 1960.

———. *The Rising Sun in the Pacific*. Vol. 3 of *History of United States Naval Operations in World War II*. Boston: Little, Brown, 1959.

———. *The Struggle for Guadalcanal*. Vol. 5 of *History of United States Naval Operations in World War II*. Boston: Little, Brown, 1959.

Morningstar, James Kelly. "War and Resistance: The Philippines, 1942–1944." Ph.D. dissertation, University of Maryland, College Park, 2018.

Morrill, John. *South from Corregidor: The Remarkable Story of a Terrifying Escape*. New York: Simon & Schuster, 1943.

Morris, Eric. *Corregidor: The American Alamo of World War II*. New York: Cooper Square Press, 2000.

Morton, Louis. *The Fall of the Philippines*. Washington, D.C.: OCMH, U.S. Army, 1953.

Ness, Leland. *Rikugun: Guide to Japanese Ground Forces, 1937–1945*. Solihul, UK: Helion, 2014.

New York Times Archives. n.d. January–May 2016. http://query.nytimes.com.

Norman, Michael and Elizabeth Norman. *Tears in the Darkness*. New York: Picador, 2010.

Nimitz, Chester, and E. B. Potter. *Sea Power*. New York: Prentice-Hall, 1960.

O'Donnell, Patrick K. *Give Me Tomorrow*. Cambridge, MA: Da Capo Press, 2010.

O'Kane, Richard H. *Clear the Bridge!* New York: Presidio Press, 1977.

Okumiya, Masatake, Jiro Horikoshi, and Martin Caidin. *Zero: The Story of Japan's Air War in the Pacific: As Seen by the Enemy.* New York: J. Boylston, 1956.

O'Neill, Robert, ed. *The Pacific War: From Pearl Harbor to Okinawa.* Oxford: Osprey, 2015.

Osborne, William L. *Voyage into the Wind.* Osborne, 2013.

Owen, Joseph R. *Colder Than Hell: A Marine Rifle Company at Chosin Reservoir.* New York: Random House, 1996.

Parshall, J., and A. Tully. *Shattered Sword: The Untold Story of the Battle of Midway.* Dulles: Potomac Books, 2005.

Peattie, Mark R., and David C. Evans. *Strategy, Tactics, and Technology in the Imperial Japanese Navy, 1887–1941.* Annapolis, MD: Naval Academy Press, 1997.

Peattie, Mark R., and Ramon H. Myers, eds. *The Japanese Colonial Empire.* Princeton, NJ: Princeton University Press, 1984.

Phillips, Cabell. *The 1940s: Decade of Triumph and Turmoil.* New York: Macmillan, 1975.

Prados, John. *Combined Fleet Decoded.* New York: Random House, 1995.

Radio Transmitter No. 13C and 13CB Supplement. Warren, NJ: Western Electric Corporation, 1936.

Reischauer, Edwin O. *Japan: Past and Present.* New York: Knopf, 1964.

Rockoff, Hugh. "From Plowshares to Swords: The American Economy in World War II." National Bureau of Economic Research Historical Working Paper Series, No. 77. New Brunswick, NJ: Rutgers University, 1996.

Rosales, Patty. "Letter to Mrs. Armstrong." Manila, December 27, 1945.

Rottman, G. L. *US Marine Corps Pacific Theater of Operations.* London: Osprey Publishing, 2004.

Russ, Martin. *Breakout: The Chosin Reservoir Campaign.* New York: Penguin, 1999.

Sakai, Saburo. *Samurai!* New York: E. P. Dutton, 1957.

Sakaida, H. *Aces of the Rising Sun, 1937–1945.* London: Osprey Publishing, 2002.

Santelli, James S. *A Brief History of the 4th Marines.* Washington, D.C.: Historical Division, Headquarters, U.S. Marine Corps, 1970.

———. "4th Marine Regiment Order of Battle." n.d.

Schlesinger, Arthur M. *The Coming of the New Deal, 1933–1935.* New York: Houghton Mifflin, 1958.

Sherrod, Robert. *History of Marine Corps Aviation in World War II.* Washington, D.C.: Combat Forces Press, 1952.

Sherwood, Robert E. *Roosevelt and Hopkins: An Intimate History.* New York: Grosset and Dunlap, 1950.

Sickels, Robert. *The 1940s*. Westport, CT: Greenwood Press, 2004.

Sides, Hampton. *On Desperate Ground*. New York: Anchor Books, 2018.

Simpson, Carter Berkeley. "Diary of Carter Berkeley Simpson." 1944.

Simmons, Edwin Howard. *Over the Seawall: U.S. Marines at Inchon*. Delaplane, VA: St. John's Press, 2018.

Sloan, Bill. *Undefeated: America's Heroic Fight for Bataan and Corregidor*. New York: Simon & Schuster, 2012.

Smith, Robert Ross. *Triumph in the Philippines*. Washington, D.C.: U.S. Army Center for Military History, 1963.

Spector, Ronald H. *Eagle Against the Sun: The American War with Japan*. New York: Vintage Books, 1985.

Steinberg, David Joel. *Philippine Collaboration in World War II*. Ann Arbor: University of Michigan Press, 1967.

Stille, Mark. *USN Carriers vs IJN Carriers: The Pacific 1942*. New York: Osprey Publishing, 2007.

Stillwell, Paul, ed. *Air Raid, Pearl Harbor! Recollections of a Day of Infamy*. Annapolis, MD: Naval Institute Press, 1981.

Swanborough, Gordon, and Peter, M. Bowers. *United States Navy Aircraft Since 1911*. Annapolis, MD: Naval Institute Press, 1990.

Tassava, Christopher J. "The American Economy during World War II." http://eh.net/encyclopedia/the-american-economy-during-world-war-ii. 2010.

Thomson, Kenneth Burton. *A Case of Treason: The Traitor of Corregidor*. Altamonte Springs, FL: Thomson Publishing, n.d.

Tillman, Barrett. *Whirlwind: The Air War Against Japan, 1942–1945*. New York: Simon & Schuster, 2010.

Toland, John. *But Not in Shame*. New York: Random House, 1961.

———. *The Rising Sun: The Decline and Fall of the Japanese Empire, 1936–1945*. New York: Random House, 1970.

Tolischus, Otto D. *Through Japanese Eyes* (1945). Quoted in *Japan's Prospect*, edited by Douglas G. Haring. Cambridge, MA: Harvard University Press, 1946.

Toll, Ian W. *The Conquering Tide: War in the Pacific Islands, 1942–1945*. New York: W. W. Norton, 2015.

———. *Pacific Crucible: War at Sea in the Pacific, 1941–1942*. New York: W. W. Norton, 2012.

———. *Twilight of the Gods: War in the Western Pacific, 1944–1945*. New York: W. W. Norton, 2020.

United States, Department of the Army. *USAAF Casualties in European, North African and Mediterranean Theaters of Operations, 1942–1946*. Army Battle

Casualties in World War II: Final Report. Washington D.C.: Department of the Army, GPO, 1953.

———. *U.S. Army Air Forces Statistical Digest*. Washington, D.C.: Office of Statistical Control, 1945.

———. Department of the Navy, Naval History and Heritage Command. "Logistics and Support Activities, 1950–53." n.d. www.history.navy.mil. Accessed August 2013.

———. Military Analysis Division. *Air Campaigns of the Pacific War*. United States Strategic Bombing Survey. Washington, D.C.: U.S. Government Printing Office, 1947.

———. Naval Analysis Division. *The Campaigns of the Pacific War*. United States Strategic Bombing Survey (Pacific). Washington D.C.: U.S. Government Printing Office, 1946."USS Hornet Deck Log." 1942.

Vandegrift, Alexander A. and Robert B. Asprey. *Once a Marine: The Memoirs of General A. A. Vandegrift*. New York: W. W. Norton, 1964.

Verity, George L. *From Bataan to Victory*. New York: Carlton Press, 1992.

Villamor, Jesus A. *They Never Surrendered: A True Story of Resistance in World War II*. Quezon City, Philippines: Vera-Reyes, 1982.

Volckmann, R. W. *We Remained*. New York: W. W. Norton, 1954.

Wainwright, Jonathan M. *General Wainwright's Story*. New York: Doubleday, 1946.

Walker, Scott. *The Edge of Terror*. New York: Thomas Dunne, 2009.

Walton, Francis. *The Miracle of World War II: How American Industry Made Victory Possible*. New York: Macmillan, 1956.

Watkins, T. H. *The Great Depression: America in the 1930s*. New York: Back Bay Books, 1993.

Wheelan, Joseph. *Midnight in the Pacific*. Boston: Da Capo Press, 2017.

Whitcomb, Edgar D. *Escape from Corregidor*. Charlotte, NC: Ship to Shore Books, 2019.

Wolf, William. *13th Fighter Command in World War II: Air Combat over Guadalcanal and the Solomons*. Atglen, PA: Schiffer Military History, 2006.

Wolfert, Ira. *American Guerilla in the Philippines*. New York : Simon & Schuster, 1945.

"World Carrier Lists." n.d. www.hazegray.org/navhist/carriers/. June 5, 2013.

Young, Donald. *The Battle of Bataan: A Complete History*. Jefferson, NC: McFarland and Company, 2009.

———. *The Fall of the Philippines*. Jefferson, NC: McFarland, 2015.

Zimmerman, Major John L. *The Guadalcanal Campaign*. Washington, D.C.: Historical Branch, U.S. Marine Corps, 1949.

U.S.S. Texas
At Sea
7 August, 1938

Dear Mama, Dad, and Nancy,

It is really high time that I write you folks something, and I'll try to make up for the lost time here.

To begin with, I'll take my trip to Scotland. It was truly one of the most delightful trips imaginable. At first, I was a trifle doubtful in regard to the degree to which I could enjoy it in going alone; but now I am very glad that I took it that way. Had I gone with another midshipman, I would probably have seen no one else. As it was, I met innumerable nice people who are native to the country. This fact, I think, added considerably to the value of the trip.

On the railway trip up, I went through the length of England. My route was from Portsmouth to London where

---

Philippine Islands,
January 23, 1942.

My dear Mama,

We are so cut off from the States that it seems useless to write, but I think I shall anyhow just in case something turns up to take a letter back. I received the radio that you sent me last month and certainly appreciated it a lot. Unfortunately the radio I tried to send to you didn't get through. My outfit was out in the country at the time, and so we had to send our message in to regimental headquarters for forwarding. Somebody up there messed things up; and as a result no message from my battalion got through before the Japanese cut our radio communication by taking Manila. Incidently I have also written you some letters previous to this one, but I am afraid that they got lost.

Up to the present time, I have not been in action but have remained in rear areas. However, my outfit has been bombed a good bit. In fact, we ran one period of about ten days with a bombing raid or so every day. Lately, however, they have left us alone. I guess they are bombing someone else. These air raids are terrifying at first; but after ... them,

---

Guam
Sept. 4, 1945

My dear Mama and Nancy and all,

I am just dropping you a line to let you know that I am all right and will be seeing you soon.

Although I may be wrong, I don't believe that you knew before the end of the war that I was all right. The Japanese held me as an unofficial prisoner when they recaptured me on May 30, 1943 until last January 15. Then although I was eligible for registration and although they let me write letters every month, they were uniformly so poor on such matters that I shall be surprised if either they told you, or transmitted the letters.

I won't try to tell you all that has happened to me these past few years because it is just too much to write. Briefly, however, I escaped from Corregidor on May 22, 1942 and ran loose until May 30, 1943 when I was recaptured on Morotai island in the East Indies where I had arrived in

---

WFH:vn

15 May, 1946.

From: Lieutenant Colonel William F. Harris, (05917), USMC.

To: Commandant of the Marine Corps.

Via: 1. Director, Command and Staff School.
     2. Commandant, Marine Corps Schools.

Subject: Period of Captivity, Report on.

Reference: (a) Letter from the Commandant of the Marine Corps dated 6 May, 1946, File No. 2135-70.

1. On 6 May, 1942, on the surrender of FORT HILLS, CORREGIDOR, I was taken prisoner by the Japanese. I was at this time imprisoned in a camp set up on CORREGIDOR ISLAND to the southeast of MALINTA HILL. The senior officer of the U. S. Naval Service in this camp was Colonel Donald Curtis, U.S.M.C. I performed here no duties of any sort.

2. On the afternoon of 22 May, 1942, I, together with 2nd Lieutenant (now Major) E. D. Whitcomb, U. S. Army Air Forces, left this camp on a working detail. We stole away from the detail and hid in a dug-out until nightfall. Then we swam to BATAAN, arriving there just before dawn. We then walked northward, generally through the center and then near the west coast of BATAAN, until after six days we ran into Filipinos north of BAGAC, BATAAN who gave us our first food of consequence after our escape. We then walked up to MORON, BATAAN and thence to the south shore of SUBIC BAY.

Here a native gave us a small boat. Accordingly, in view of native reports on the unpropitious character of the north, we decided to go south. We started south and got across the mouth of MANILA BAY when our boat was wrecked by a squall on the coast of northern BATANGAS on about 8 June, 1942.

We stayed here among the natives for about two weeks, and then we walked generally southward across the province until we arrived in the vicinity of BALAYAN, BATANGAS. There, a wealthy Filipino family (Senator Sixto Lopez and his sister and

-1-